Christmas Cooking For Dummies®

Ten Steps to a Joyful Christmas Gathering

1. Decide what type of event you want to have. Will it be one large sit-down meal? A cocktail party before the big day or a brunch the morning of? Figure out your strategy and stick to it. Whatever you decide, make up your mind as early as possible — mid-November is not too soon.
2. Decide whom to invite. Plan carefully — if you invite Cousin Fred, don't you have to invite Cousin Wilma? As the guest list extends beyond immediate family, imagine you can hear your guests talking. Be sure to invite talkers — lively conversation is the secret ingredient of many successful gatherings.
3. Invite your guests. The week after Thanksgiving, extend invitations in person, by phone, via e-mail, or the old fashioned but still charming way by mail. Match the method of invitation to the event — if you're planning a casual get-together, you can extend a casual invitation. However you do it, have an RSVP date that allows you plenty of time to order foods and organize your cooking. A reply date that gives you two weeks of prep time should be enough.
4. Create the menu. By December 1, you should know what you're cooking and when each item will be prepared. To-do lists are a must. Take advantage of dishes you can make ahead of time.
5. Take stock of what you have on hand in terms of dishes, glassware, silverware, linens, and chairs and tables. Don't forget serving platters and utensils. Anything that you do not have can probably be borrowed or rented, but figure all this out in early December.
6. If guests have not RSVP'd (that is, told you whether they're coming or not), give them a call and find out! Following up a day or so after the RSVP date is perfectly okay.
7. Order the turkey, roast beef, or any other important item of food or drink at least two weeks ahead of the party date. If you wait too long and supplies of some crucial ingredient run out, not even Santa's Workshop can bail you out!
8. Accept the gift of help. If guests ask if they can bring something — appetizers, salad, dessert — by all means say yes! Not only will doing so relieve some pressure on you, it also will give your friends and family the gift of sharing.
9. Be prepared for surprises and take them in stride. Even with all of your planning, there will be glitches. But you know what? That's okay. The holiday is not about having everything go off perfectly.
10. Breathe. Breathe in, breathe out. Repeat. When we breathe, life flows, and we can accept help, accept presents, and take in the full spirit of the Christmas holiday.

See Chapters 1 and 2 for more planning details.

BESTSELLING BOOK SERIES

Christmas Cooking For Dummies®

Tips for Saving Time When You Cook at Christmas

- Order dishes and glassware from a local rental company. You can rent linens, too.
- Prepare recipes that can be made ahead.
- Use my menu planning strategies. Doing so prevents last minute, time-wasting tasks from popping up. See Chapter 3.
- Make extra food gifts such as marmalade or caramel sauce for last minute host gifts. See Chapter 15.
- Buy any wine and alcohol you need as far ahead as possible. They keep indefinitely.
- While you're at it, buy ice too. No need to make your own.
- Set the table for the big meal the day before.
- Use your microwave to heat made-ahead dishes.
- Make double batches of pie dough ahead of time and freeze for up to a month

Easy Christmas Decorating Ideas from the Kitchen

- Pile a bunch of cranberries in a glass bowl and nestle pillar candles inside.
- Make a gingerbread house as a stunning centerpiece. It's not that hard! (The construction plans are in Chapter 14.)
- Create the smells of Christmas by simmering fragrant spices and citrus peels on the stove.
- Let the kids string wrapped candies together to make decorative garlands to drape on the tree.
- Polish those apples! Vigorously rub bright red apples with a clean kitchen cloth until they take on a high shine. Pile in a decorative bowl and use as a beautiful and edible table decoration.
- Use your wonderfully colored and textured food as the star attraction. Especially if you do a buffet, create visual interest with levels — place varied sizes of broad, flat boxes underneath the tablecloth and set platters on top for decorative interest.
- Spotlight the traditional American symbol of hospitality — the pineapple. You can build a centerpiece by arranging other fruits and greenery around a handsome pineapple.
- Grace a side table with dessert. Practically any dessert will do.

Item 5407-7.
For more information about Wiley Publishing, call 1-800-762-2974.

For Dummies: Bestselling Book Series for Beginners

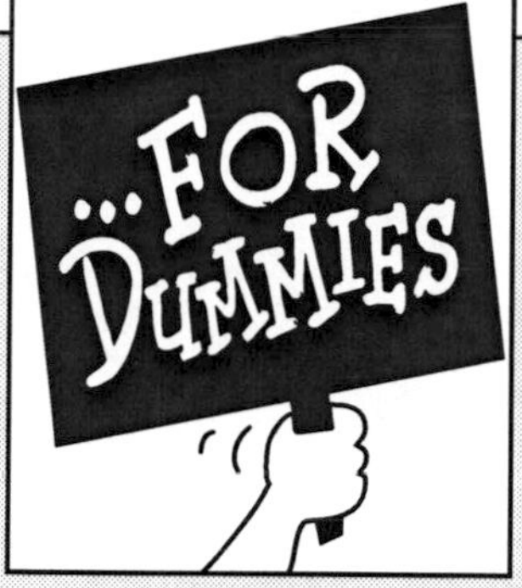

TM

References for the Rest of Us!®

BESTSELLING BOOK SERIES

Do you find that traditional reference books are overloaded with technical details and advice you'll never use? Do you postpone important life decisions because you just don't want to deal with them? Then our *For Dummies*® business and general reference book series is for you.

For Dummies business and general reference books are written for those frustrated and hard-working souls who know they aren't dumb, but find that the myriad of personal and business issues and the accompanying horror stories make them feel helpless. *For Dummies* books use a lighthearted approach, a down-to-earth style, and even cartoons and humorous icons to dispel fears and build confidence. Lighthearted but not lightweight, these books are perfect survival guides to solve your everyday personal and business problems.

"More than a publishing phenomenon, 'Dummies' is a sign of the times."

— The New York Times

"A world of detailed and authoritative information is packed into them..."

— U.S. News and World Report

"...you won't go wrong buying them."

— Walter Mossberg, Wall Street Journal, on For Dummies books

Already, millions of satisfied readers agree. They have made For Dummies the #1 introductory level computer book series and a best-selling business book series. They have written asking for more. So, if you're looking for the best and easiest way to learn about business and other general reference topics, look to For Dummies to give you a helping hand.

5/09

by Dede Wilson

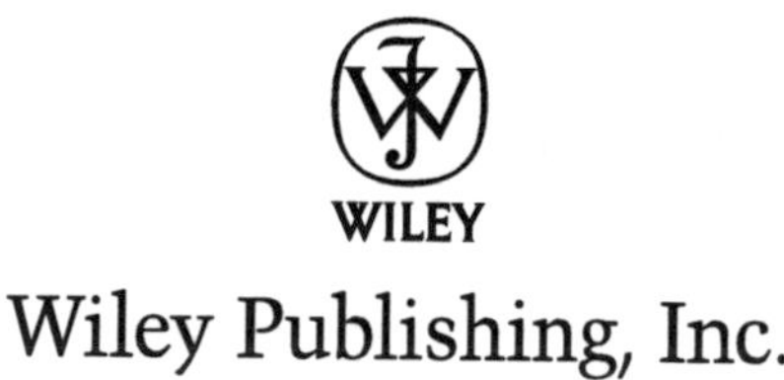

Wiley Publishing, Inc.

Christmas Cooking For Dummies®

Published by
Wiley Publishing, Inc.
111 River Street
Hoboken, NJ 07030
www.wiley.com

Published by Wiley Publishing, Inc., Indianapolis, Indiana

Published simultaneously in Canada

For general information on our other products and services or to obtain technical support, please contact our Customer Care Department within the U.S. at 800-762-2974, outside the U.S. at 317-572-3993, or fax 317-572-4002.

Wiley also publishes its books in a variety of electronic formats. Some content that appears in print may not be available in electronic books.

Library of Congress Cataloging-in-Publication Data:

Library of Congress Control Number: 2001092740

ISBN: 0-7645-5407-7

10 9 8 7 6 5 4 3 2 1

1B/QU/QZ/QR/IN

About the Author

Dede Wilson has planned parties — yes, including Christmas parties — for thousands of people since 1985 in her work as a party planner. In that time she has also worked as a restaurant chef, bakery owner, recipe developer, and radio talk-show host.

Dede writes periodically for *Bon Appétit* and is a contributing editor to *Pastry Art and Design* magazine and is the food and entertaining expert for CanDoWoman.com. Her first book, *The Wedding Cake Book* (Macmillan, 1997), was nominated for an IACP Julia Child Cookbook Award, and she now has three books to her credit. Dede is a Certified Culinary Professional (CCP).

Dede is a repeat guest on NBC's *Today Show* and appears frequently on major networks representing corporate sponsors.

Dedication

To my father, Moses Acosta, who taught me how to cook and more importantly, to appreciate food as more than mere sustenance. And believe me, he can carve a turkey like nobody's business!

Author's Acknowledgments

Thank you to Linda Ingroia, my editor, for bringing this project to me and, as always, to Maureen and Eric Lasher, my agents, for guiding my career.

A large support system brings any book *For Dummies* to fruition, and they have made the job smooth and easy. In part, thanks to Norm Crampton, project editor; Ben Nussbaum, copy editor; Pam Mourouzis, editorial team manager; Emily Nolan, recipe tester; David Bishop, photographer; Brett Kurzweil, food stylist; Donna Larsen, prop stylist; and to the marketing and sales staff.

Thanks to Carole Bloom for providing professional advice and to Juanita Plimpton and Judy Pozar for always being there when I needed to talk out an idea or work out a concept. Thanks to Amy Wasserman for my author photo. Huge thanks to Gabe Hmieleski and Evan Coppola for personal website support.

Thanks to David Kilroy and to my kids, Ravenna, Forrester, and Freeman, for tasting and critiquing Christmas food well into the spring.

And, as always, thanks to Mary McNamara for helping me during the recipe testing and writing phases of the book. Mary, you are my best brainstorming friend and I could not fathom writing a book without you.

Publisher's Acknowledgments

We're proud of this book; please send us your comments through our Online Registration Form located at www.hungryminds.com

Some of the people who helped bring this book to market include the following:

Acquisitions, Editorial, and Media Development

Project Editor: Norm Crampton

Senior Acquisitions Editor: Linda Ingroia

Assistant Acquisitions Editor: Erin Connell

Copy Editor: Ben Nussbaum

Technical Editor: Deborah Mintcheff

Recipe Tester: Emily Nolan

Illustrator: Elizabeth Kurtzman

Photographer: David Bishop

Food Stylist: Brett Kurzweil

Prop Stylist: Donna Larsen

Photography Art Director: Michele Laseau

Editorial Manager: Pamela Mourouzis

Editorial Assistant: Carol Strickland

Cover Photos: David Bishop

Production

Project Coordinator: Dale White

Layout and Graphics: Amy Adrian, Barry Offringa, Jacque Schneider, Betty Schulte, Brent Savage

Special Art: Elizabeth Kurtzman

Proofreaders: Marianne Santy, TECHBOOKS Production Services

Indexer: TECHBOOKS Production Services

General and Administrative

Hungry Minds, Inc.: John Kilcullen, CEO; Bill Barry, President and COO; John Ball, Executive VP, Operations & Administration; John Harris, CFO

Hungry Minds Consumer Reference Group

Business: Kathleen Nebenhaus, Vice President and Publisher; Kevin Thornton, Acquisitions Manager

Cooking/Gardening: Jennifer Feldman, Associate Vice President and Publisher; Anne Ficklen, Executive Editor

Education/Reference: Diane Graves Steele, Vice President and Publisher;

Lifestyles: Kathleen Nebenhaus, Vice President and Publisher; Tracy Boggier, Managing Editor

Pets: Tracy Boggier, Publishing Director

Travel: Michael Spring, Vice President and Publisher; Brice Gosnell, Publishing Director; Suzanne Jannetta, Editorial Director

Hungry Minds Consumer Editorial Services: Kathleen Nebenhaus, Vice President and Publisher; Kristin A. Cocks, Editorial Director; Cindy Kitchel, Editorial Director

Hungry Minds Consumer Production: Debbie Stailey, Production Director

◆

The publisher would like to give special thanks to Patrick J. McGovern, without whom this book would not have been possible.

◆

Contents at a Glance

Recipes at a Glance

Appetizers

Beverages

Breads, Scones, and Muffins

Breakfast Foods

Cakes, Pies, Puddings, Tarts, and Trifle

Cookies, Candies, and Ice Cream

Food Gifts

Main Dishes

Salads

Sauces, Relishes, and Spreads

Side Dishes

Soups

Table of Contents

Introduction

Whether you're a Type-A Christmas manager who starts planning menus in August or someone who feels pressed for time and ideas every day of November and December, *Christmas Cooking For Dummies* will help you have the Christmas you want.

I don't need to tell you that December is a great time for family meals, parties large and small, gift giving, and decorating the house or the apartment. After all, most of us have some vacation time at Christmas; the kids may be home from school or coming to visit; and days are getting shorter, and in some places colder — all of which means that we naturally gravitate towards hearth and home.

Parties are a great way to connect with friends and family, and there's nothing that kindles the party spirit faster and better than good food and drink, presented in a beautiful setting. Yes, I recognize there's more to Christmas than what you put on the table: Besides plenty of recipes and meal plans, this book includes chapters on edible gifts and food-based decorations.

So, however you celebrate Christmas, dive right into *Christmas Cooking For Dummies*. Prepare a classic Christmas dinner for the family, or make your first gingerbread house. You can find it all right here.

How to Use This Book

If you want to pick up some general ideas for designing your Christmas holiday, skim the book from cover to cover in either direction and see what strikes your fancy. You'll find many holiday recipes, from appetizers through main dishes, to desserts and beverages, each topic in a chapter by itself, as well as some tasty menus for parties ranging from two people to the whole tribe. Ideas for gift giving are here, too, and for decorating the house, inside and out.

If you have a specific Christmas cooking need, you can scan the table of contents and probably find just what you're looking for. I've written this book to suit the lifestyles of busy people who like to do very nice things for other people at Christmastime (and other times, probably). Someone like you.

How This Book is Organized

Start with the Introduction (you're here already!), in which all the chapters are briefly described, to orient you and set you on your way. There are six major parts, each of which contains chapters on related topics. Read on for the rundown.

Part I: Gearing Up for Christmas Cooking

This part opens with a chapter on reducing the stress of Christmas cooking and entertaining. I dispel the myth that you and I are just too busy for all of this. I write about what brings us joy, like making dinner for loved ones or giving a homemade gift. I talk about prioritizing, getting organized, and having fun! Chapter 2 gives you information about ingredients, tools, and techniques to help you sail through the Christmas season as effortlessly as possible.

Chapter 3 is all about menus. A lot of us like to begin our holiday meal planning with a menu in mind. This chapter offers delicious menu suggestions that you can feel free to use, as described or in part: Some of us want a total menu planned out, others want to pick and choose; either way is fine. All of the menus include shopping lists, step-by-step instructions for food preparation, and information on how to scale the recipes up or down to match the number of guests.

Part II: Holiday Meals: Opening Acts

This part contains everything you need to get started — to open the show, so to speak. Chapters on drinks, appetizers, and salads and soups reside in this part. You will find the chapters jam-packed with information about, for example, buying champagne, making instant appetizers, buying oysters. I even added my thoughts about purchasing salad greens.

Part III: Holiday Meals: The Main Event and Sideshows

In this part, I include breakfast main events like easy Overnight French Toast, dinner star attractions like Maple Glazed Turkey, Roast Prime Rib, Baked Fresh Ham with Herbs, and Low-Fat Seafood Stew. The sideshows of Part III are side dishes and relishes and sauces. All of the chapters contain my special tips and personal preferences, like why it's worth buying real maple syrup, how to defrost a frozen turkey, the difference between yams and sweet potatoes, and how to tell if a cranberry is fresh.

Part IV: Holiday Meals: Finishing Touches

What is Christmas without desserts and sweets? This large section has recipes for cakes, pies, tarts, cookies, candies, confections, frozen desserts, and puddings. Look for the recipe for an elegant Bûche de Noël, Classic Sugar Cookies, a Pumpkin Pie, Bittersweet Chocolate Truffles, and Eggnog Ice Cream. For those of us who love dessert but run out of time, I include some instant desserts and tips and tricks for shortcuts, such as using purchased piecrusts.

Part V: It's Beginning to Look Like Christmas: Decorations, Gifts

Chapters 14 and 15 cover kitchen projects: decorations and edible gifts, respectively. Making gifts from the kitchen — the heart of the home — can be quite fulfilling, as well as fun. Also, part of giving to your friends and family is surrounding yourself with things of beauty, so you will find several decoration projects for both inside the house and out.

Part VI: The Part of Tens

Every *For Dummies* book has a Part of Tens. In *Christmas Cooking For Dummies*, I give you my ten best tips on holiday cooking and entertaining, plus a reference list of ten reliable mail-order sources for ingredients and kitchen tools.

Icons and Symbols Used in This Book

An assortment of icons are sprinkled throughout the book along the left-hand margins. An icon calls your attention to a fact that helps you make the most of a recipe or of your Christmas entertaining plans.

When I want to emphasize something that helps you make the most of a recipe, I use this icon to bring your attention to it.

The caution icon is just that — a warning. I also typically include a brief explanation of why caution is advised; it's usually a matter of health or safety.

Some techniques or ideas bear repeating. This icon marks materials of this sort.

This symbol points out a gift, decoration, or recipe that is particularly suited to making with young children. After all, Christmas is a family holiday. Look for the smiley in the recipe title.

A Few Guidelines Before You Begin

There is absolutely no reason why you should go through the trials and errors that I have over the years. When you cook, you learn through experience — and boy, have I learned from experience! Here are a few pointers to make your recipes and projects come out the best they can be:

- Always read a recipe or project through, beginning to end, to make sure you have all the ingredients or items and understand the directions.
- Use kosher salt for seasoning recipes, except for desserts, where the measurements are for table salt.
- Always use freshly ground black pepper where pepper is called for, unless another type of pepper is suggested.
- All herbs and spices are dried unless specified otherwise.
- Temperatures are Fahrenheit.

And keep these general tips in mind:

- Plan ahead.
- Relax and enjoy the process of cooking and creating.
- Keep the Christmas spirit all year round!

Part I

Gearing Up for Christmas Cooking

"It was a tree trimming party! You should have kept the buffet separate from the ornaments! Now we've got a tree decorated with Brussels sprouts, cheese balls and chicken strips."

In this part . . .

No doubt about it, there's a lot to do at this time of year — so it's time to do some cooking! This part shows you how to make the most out of preparing foods for the holiday with a minimum of stress and maximum of fun and results. Part I also contains a chapter on ingredients, tools, and techniques that come in handy during Christmas-season cooking. Then it's on to some suggested menus and how to pull them together, from planning the shopping list to making sure all the food arrives on the table at the same time.

Chapter 1

Making Christmas Special and Stress Free

In This Chapter

- Listing the benefits of cooking at the Christmas season
- Getting prepared for Christmas cooking
- Giving to others

Christmas gives you the opportunity to prepare special food during a whole season, not just on one special day. Businesses hold holiday parties, most adults and kids get vacation time, and windows and streets from the biggest city to the smallest town are festive with bright lights. The whole month of December feels like a party — so I've included cooking suggestions not only for Christmas Day, but for the entire season of celebration.

The days get shorter, the temperatures dip, and those hazy days of summer when you casually invited the neighbors over for a barbecue have faded from view. Now is the time to savor the fact that Christmastime is family time. If your extended family gets together every year, consider hosting the party. Or, if it's just you and one other loved one, make the season as special as it was when you were a child — or as special as you wished it had been. If you're not near family, find friends who are also free and create a family for an evening.

Not only can you spread good cheer throughout the season, but you can also spread the responsibilities. Family members can take on tasks, such as watering the poinsettias, or they can help with food duties. Even young children can chip in. And someone has to take out all that garbage — it doesn't have to be you!

But Christmas Is Always at Grandma's House

Maybe you've never hosted a Christmastime meal because you think your mom would never give up the honor. Well, for all you know it has become a duty that she would be more than willing to pass on to someone else. You'll never know until you ask.

Or perhaps you've never offered to host a big holiday meal because you don't think you'll be able to live up to family expectations. Well, hey — maybe it's time to shake things up a little. Maybe it's time that you start your own tradition.

Take advantage of landmarks. Have you started a family this year? What a great time to start the tradition of Christmas dinner in your home. Or maybe your mother-in-law has hosted it for the past ten years. Time for a change!

Reasons you should make the big meal

There is more to Christmas than just the big meal on the big day, but, for a lot of us, that meal is still the focal point of the season. With that in mind, and just in case you need some further support, here are all the reasons why you should take on the responsibility of preparing the feast:

- When you're the host, you get to make whatever you like.
- Making the meal is less expensive than eating out.
- You get to choose whom to invite.
- You get to pick at the food in the kitchen (those calories don't count).
- You did the cooking, so someone else can clean up.
- No traveling!
- Making the meal is a way to give back to your family.
- Now all your guests have to return the favor.
- Guests bring gifts.
- Making hearty, delicious food is immensely satisfying.
- You have leftovers for the following week.

Can't I just take the whole gang to a restaurant?

You may be thinking that making a holiday meal is just too much trouble. You may even be tempted to let your fingers do the walking and make a restaurant reservation. There's nothing wrong with that. In fact, many restaurants have special menus for the season. But many other restaurants are closed on Christmas, and with good reason. The chefs and other employees want to be with their families.

Really, making the main meal isn't that big a deal. Set your priorities, and remember to breathe! You will be pleasantly surprised with the results. *Christmas Cooking For Dummies* helps you plan and make meals that are enjoyable to make, as well as delicious and beautiful to behold.

Prioritizing and Getting Organized to Beat the Time Crunch

Time, time, who has the time? Christmas can be the fastest-paced time of year. You may be thinking that you barely have time to shop for presents, let alone spend time in the kitchen. But even in these busy and stressful times, sharing the holidays with friends and family by preparing meals, decorations, and gifts can be fun and easy.

Prioritize. What is most important to you this year? Is it inviting over relatives who you have fallen out of touch with? Maybe it's making heartfelt gifts to give to cherished friends. Or perhaps you have a new home and want to show it off in style with a big party. We all have different motivations, but we can all benefit from being organized.

Okay, I'm Going to Throw a Party

You've made the decision to host a holiday party. You've made some prioritized lists. What next? Creating ambience.

Designing a party involves more than just choosing the food. In fact, so many different components make up a successful party that some people make a living as party planners. Mostly, be aware early in your planning that the food is only part of the equation.

What not to do

I have had my share of screw-ups. One Christmas in particular, I thought I had my priorities straight, but they got lost in the sauce. What I wanted to do was make wonderful food to share with family and friends and spend time with my guests.

Well, I had way too much food on the menu. I figured the more I made, the more impressive it would be; or more to the point, the more impressive I would be. I spent days in the kitchen chopping, stirring, baking, and roasting. I don't even want to think about the amount of money that I spent on ingredients.

The result? The food was great, although there were enough leftovers to feed a family of six for a week. My guests seemed to have a good time. But I can't say for sure if they had a good time, because I was in a stupor. I was in a fog of exhaustion. I couldn't enjoy the food myself because I was so sick and tired of cooking and just being around all of it.

Moral: Do not overextend yourself. If your priority is spending time with guests, then do not choose menu items that keep you in the kitchen.

What you are doing is creating an environment. Choose some music and buy some poinsettias. Hang a welcome wreath on the door so that the first thing your guests see says "holidays."

Knowing how much to cook

How much is too much and how much is too little is a big concern for a lot of folks. Most people try to do too much. They think they have to make every Christmas dish known to humanity in order to make the holiday special. I cannot stress enough that this isn't true. For parties ranging from 4 to 12 guests, which is a very common range, follow this advice for the main Christmas day dinner:

- Offer two or three appetizers.
- Have one main dish.
- Make one green, one starch, and one other vegetable side dish.
- Have at least one condiment, such as a cranberry relish.
- Have a couple of desserts; maybe one fruit-based pie and one chocolate.

Of course you can make more, add another appetizer, another side dish, another dessert, and so on, but don't feel that you have to. If you're comfortable in the kitchen, go ahead and add more. But do not tackle more than you can handle.

Making lists

If you're not a list maker, become one now — just for the holidays. Lists keep all your tasks front and center. Make the lists when you are calm and clear headed, so that when you're rushing through the supermarket with your food list you won't forget anything.

But don't stop with the grocery list. List any items you may need to get the job done. Make lists of tasks and put the tasks in the order that they need to be completed. If something can be made a month ahead and frozen, do it! Here is a list to help your list making:

- Pick a date for your Christmas party or parties.
- Prioritize tasks.
- Plan ahead by making lists of ingredients.
- Break down the recipes as much as possible to spread out preparation.
- Take advantage of recipes and projects that can be made ahead and refrigerated, frozen, or stored at room temperature.
- Take time to enjoy the process of creating.

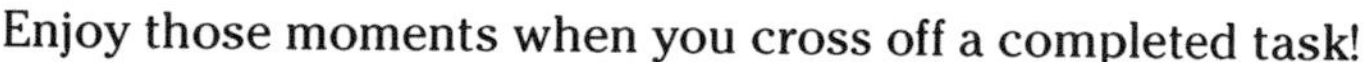

Enjoy those moments when you cross off a completed task!

Finding room for everyone

The very first Christmas dinner I hosted after I got married was in a one-room apartment. Our queen-sized bed was in one corner and the dining table in another. We had eight people crammed in there for drinks, appetizers, the whole meal, after-meal conversation, and so on. (I made a goose and there wasn't enough meat, but more about that later.)

The point is that the lack of space didn't matter. The fact that my husband and I wanted to please our guests was all that mattered. Our intentions were good, the food was good, and the party was good. If you want to make your guests feel at home, you can do it no matter where you are.

Decking the halls

Some folks have it all figured out. They have red velvet pillow covers that come out of the closet this time of year and little angels and Santas lining the mantle. Their tree always looks perfect and the outside of the house is carefully outlined with lights. You know what? It doesn't mean that they're going to have a better holiday than you are.

Zen and the art of Christmas cooking

If you're grating cheddar, answering the phone, and thinking about where Aunt Margaret is going to sleep when she visits, you are not focusing on any of those activities. Next thing you know, you've grated your knuckles along with the cheese, you're "answering" the remote control, and Aunt Margaret has to sleep on the porch. If you concentrate on the one task at hand, not only will you enjoy the process more, but you will end up with yummier food and a lower stress level. Think Zen.

But getting into the spirit does help. Every year, just add one thing. Buy a pretty seasonal pillow. Buy new candlesticks for the table.

And don't forget the post-Christmas sales. Plan for next year and buy your one new item then.

Giving Back

Focusing on presents and elaborate meals to share with family and friends is easy, but remember that others are not as fortunate. You can give back to your community in myriad ways:

- Pick a day near the holiday to work in a soup kitchen.
- If you eat early on Christmas, take leftovers to a shelter later on.
- Make an extra batch of cookies or soup and bring it to a busy or elderly neighbor.
- Shovel snow for a friend.
- Give cookies to the folks who help you all year long, such as bank tellers, hairdressers, postal workers, or babysitters.
- If you have a non-religious or non-Christian friend, offer an invitation. He or she may be thrilled to be included, especially if your get-together is more family oriented than religious.

Chapter 2

Taking Inventory: Ingredients, Tools, and Techniques for Holiday Cooking

In This Chapter

- Stocking your pantry
- Sorting out the cooking tools
- Measuring, whipping, melting — a once-over on technique

You want to get to the recipes, right? This is a cookbook, after all. But since I can't be right there with you in your kitchen, I'm including this chapter, which is the next best thing to an in-person advisor.

Most cookbooks have a chapter that discusses ingredients, tools, and techniques, and it can get boring. Bear with me though, because this is some important information. You just have to read this chapter once, and then you'll know what I mean when I say "insert your probe thermometer" — did that get your attention? Seriously, if you read through this chapter, you will be able to bring out the best in the recipes in this book. And then, if you need to refer to it now and again, it's right here for you. In other words, if you come across a recipe that calls for an offset spatula and you can't quite remember what that is, you can look it up here and you'll be good to go.

Your Basic Pantry

Ah, the joys of a well-stocked pantry. I know that peering into a well-stocked pantry doesn't hold a candle to the rush you get sledding down a big hill, but keeping your pantry stocked makes your holiday cooking easier and more enjoyable. What follows is a list of basic ingredients that you should have on hand, as they are common to so many recipes.

A baker's dozen — more or less

The Christmas holidays mean baking, so that's why the baking pantry comes first. Certain ingredients live in the realm of the baker and if you have them available on your shelf, it will be easier for you to whip up a batch of cookies or make a holiday pie. For instance, sugar and vanilla extract are commonly used baking ingredients, while olive oil would be more of a common cooking item. Here's a list of ingredients that will help you bake right through the Christmas season.

- **Flours.** Make sure that you use the flour that is called for in a recipe. All-purpose flour has a higher protein content than cake flour; these are the two flours called for in the book and they are not interchangeable. The higher protein content in all-purpose flour gives structure to breads — for instance, the Stollen with Marzipan (Chapter 13). On the other hand, you want to keep the cake component in the White Chocolate Bûche de Noël (Chapter 12) as tender as possible. The lower protein content in cake flour helps you achieve that goal.

  All flours attract moisture, so proper storage is crucial. I keep mine in an airtight plastic container at room temperature because I go through it so quickly. The right storage also makes it easy to *dip and sweep,* which is the measuring method used in this book for dry ingredients. When you want to measure your flour, take the appropriate-sized measuring cup, dip it into the flour (the dip), and then level it off with a butter knife or icing spatula (the sweep). If you measure your flour in any other way, such as spooning the flour into your measuring cup or dipping and tamping down before sweeping off the excess, you end up with a completely different amount of flour than what is meant for that recipe. Store your flour in the refrigerator or freezer if you plan to store it for an extended time.

- **Granulated sugar.** This is by far the most commonly used sweetener in these recipes. Use regular white granulated sugar, unless otherwise specified.

- **Brown sugar.** I use light brown sugar and dark brown sugar. The correct one to use is specified in the recipes. They are interchangeable, but the light version has less molasses flavor than the dark brown version.

  If your brown sugar hardens, microwave it briefly or slip a slice of apple in the bag overnight and seal tight. Just remember to remove the apple in the morning.

  When measuring brown sugar, lightly pack it into the measuring cup.

- **Confectioners sugar.** This is very finely powdered sugar that has a small amount of cornstarch added to prevent clumping. It is sometimes labeled as *10X,* which refers to that fact that it is ten times finer than granulated sugar.

- **Vegetable shortening.** Store the vegetable shortening in the refrigerator so that it is cold and ready to go into your crust recipe. Cold fat yields the flakiest crusts.
- **Chemical leaveners.** Baking soda and baking powder are the common leavening agents used in the book. Leaveners help to lighten the batter and create height.

  Double-acting baking powder is the type of baking powder used in the recipes in this book. It's the standard type sold in supermarkets. It is called *double acting* because it works twice — first when exposed to moisture and a second time when exposed to heat.

  In a pinch, you can make your own baking powder by combining two parts cream of tartar and one part baking soda; this mixture is for immediate use only and does not store well.

  Baking soda is used in batters that have an acid component, such as buttermilk, honey, and chocolate. Its addition helps to neutralize the acid. Recipes that are leavened only with baking soda must be baked immediately as the reaction will begin as soon as the acid in the batter and the baking soda are combined.
- **Cream of tartar.** This acidic white powder is a byproduct of the wine making process. It's used in small amounts to help stabilize whipped egg whites. You may not think of cream of tartar as an essential ingredient, but it helps your egg whites whip up perfectly.
- **Vanilla extract.** Use pure vanilla extract only. Neilsen-Massey is a good brand.
- **Pan coating.** While technically not an ingredient, I use pan coating a lot and wanted to insert a few words about it. Products such as PAM are flavorless non stick vegetable oil sprays that make cooking and baking surfaces virtually stick resistant.

Year-round basics

There are certain items that you should always have on hand for any type of cooking, whether it's for Christmas or not. If you have the following on hand, you'll be prepared to cook most of the recipes in this book with very little last-minute shopping.

Remember: The baking ingredients are listed earlier. This section presents items for the basic cook.

- **Olive oil and vegetable oil.** Have extra-virgin olive oil on hand as well as a vegetable oil, such as canola. In this book, extra-virgin olive oil is used when the flavor really counts, such as in salad dressings, and the vegetable oil is used when lightly sautéing, for instance, and in other situations where the flavor of the oil isn't that important.

- **Balsamic and sherry vinegars.** Balsamic vinegar from the supermarket is fine. No need to buy a 12-year-old vintage bottle (they do exist!). Sherry vinegar comes in handy too.
- **Unsalted butter.** Always use unsalted butter. Salted butter has a higher moisture content and has a longer shelf life than unsalted. (It's also, of course, salty.) Use unsalted — it's normally fresher.

  I refrigerate the butter that I need and freeze the rest. Butter keeps frozen for months. Always wrap it well or it will pick up strong flavors and odors from other foods.
- **Eggs.** All of the recipes in this book were tested with large eggs. Do not substitute small, medium, extra-large, jumbo, or any other size! Your results will be radically different — and probably not for the better.

  Store your eggs in the cartons they come in. The packaging absorbs refrigerator odors, which would otherwise end up in the eggs.
- **Milk.** The milk used in these recipes is whole milk. Do not substitute skim, 1 percent, or 2 percent milk. The recipes may become unbalanced.

  Dairy products are quite perishable and should be stored in the refrigerator on the shelves, where it is coldest, not in the door, where it is less cold.
- **Chicken and vegetable broths.** Many holiday recipes use chicken or veggie broths for moistening and flavor. Keep the low-salt varieties on hand. Swanson and College Inn both make good broths. They are used in gravies, soups, and stuffings.
- **Dijon mustard.** Mustards add zip to salad dressings and other recipes. Dijon mustard is a particularly tangy mustard that works well in many preparations.
- **Onions and garlic.** Keep onions and garlic on hand as they are used in numerous recipes. All-purpose yellow onions, bought 5 pounds at a time, are a good way to go. Chopped garlic in oil can be stored in the refrigerator and scooped out a teaspoon at a time as needed. Or you can store whole garlic cloves at a cool room temperature.
- **Dry pasta.** Having dry pasta in the cupboard is an insurance policy against going hungry.

Essential seasonings

You should have a good assortment of seasonings on hand so that you are prepared to make just about any dish. Note that all the herbs and spices in this book are dried unless otherwise stated. The basics include

- **Kosher salt and table salt.** Kosher salt can be found at most supermarkets and is what most of these recipes were tested with. It has a full, round flavor that enhances foods wonderfully. However, when it comes to desserts and baking, table salt is used, as that is the salt most commonly used in baking. You cannot use them interchangeably because they measure out differently. A teaspoon of kosher salt, which is larger grained and lighter than table salt, yields less salt by weight than a teaspoon of table salt.
- **Black peppercorns.** Fresh black pepper has a totally different taste than preground pepper. It's worthwhile to have a pepper mill and keep it filled with whole pepper. The PepperMate pepper mill is a good option — it has an easy-to-turn handle and a clear plastic reservoir on the bottom so that you can grind a quantity and then measure, if you wish, right out of the bottom piece.
- **Bay leaves.** These enhance many stews and soups.
- **Sage.** Sage is a flavor that just seems to say "Christmas." It adds an unmistakable something to a holiday bird and stuffing.
- **Thyme.** Thyme is a delicious, savory flavor that enhances many holiday dishes, like stuffing and turkey.
- **Cinnamon (ground).** Cinnamon is the workhorse of the holiday kitchen and comes into play in beverages and baked goods.
- **Cloves.** A handy spice for holiday baked goods, cloves appear in pumpkin pie, among other dishes.
- **Ginger.** A good spice to have on hand, ginger lends zing to items like gingerbread cookies.
- **Nutmeg.** This is a holiday spice that's often found in pumpkin pie and eggnog.

Chocolate — in a class by itself

For many of us, Christmas wouldn't be Christmas without sweets, and that sweet is often something chocolate. You may have whipped up chocolate chip cookies before, using the chips from the supermarket and the recipe on the bag, but I want to introduce you to some other chocolates that are frequently used when baking.

Did you know that those good old chocolate chips are formulated to hold their shape? That's why they don't melt very easily and why it's best to use other kinds of chocolate when baking desserts other than chocolate chip cookies.

Where to buy it

If you live in or near an urban area, you probably have access to three different types of stores in which you can buy your ingredients. If you familiarize yourself with what they each offer, your shopping will go more quickly and be less expensive.

- **Supermarkets.** Look here for canned goods, most produce, and meats, fish, and poultry. Dairy products and basics such as oil, vinegar, flour, and sugar can be purchased here too.
- **Natural food stores and health food stores.** Many of these stores have bulk sections where you can find dry ingredients such as rice, flour, dried fruit, nuts, herbs, and spices. Sometimes you can find bulk liquid items like olive oil, vegetable oil, and maple syrup. All of these ingredients will be much less expensive if purchased in bulk. Some natural foods stores have high quality bakeries for breads and purchased desserts, and meat, seafood, and cheese departments too.
- **Specialty food stores.** An occasional trip to a specialty store may be in order to obtain that perfect Christmas treat. After all, if you can't splurge at Christmastime, when can you splurge?

If you don't have access to anything other than the local grocery store, don't worry. Most of the recipes in this book use basic supermarket variety ingredients. Also, check out Chapter 17 for some mail order sources. They can send ingredients and tools right to your door.

Unsweetened chocolate

Unsweetened chocolate is also referred to as *chocolate liquor* (even though there is no alcohol in it), *bitter chocolate,* or *baking chocolate.* It is quite bitter and has no added sugar. Do not substitute unsweetened chocolate for semisweet or bittersweet chocolate; these do have sugar added and are not the same thing as unsweetened.

Bittersweet and semisweet chocolates

The difference between bittersweet and semisweet chocolates is that semisweet has more added sugar than bittersweet. The two types of chocolate can, however, be used interchangeably in most recipes.

If you shop at a store where this option is available, think about buying a chunk of chocolate — the chunks normally come in 10-pound blocks, but some stores sell portioned pieces. Blocks offer versatility. You can cut them into chunks for cookies or for melting. And buying this way is often less expensive. Look for bulk chocolate in natural food stores, specialty food stores, and through mail order.

Supermarket semisweet chocolate chips are formulated to hold their shape when exposed to heat. They do not make good melting chocolate. Before using a chocolate in a recipe that requires melting, make sure that the chocolate is meant for that purpose.

Storing your stash of chocolate

Chocolate should be stored at room temperature, wrapped well, in an airtight container free of moisture. Dark chocolates will last at least one year. White and milk chocolates should be used within six months, due to their milk solids content. Do not refrigerate or freeze chocolate.

Most chocolate is bought in *good temper,* which means that the ingredients are stable, yielding a shiny look and sometimes even a snapping sound when you break the chocolate. If the chocolate acquires grayish streaks during storage, it has developed *fat bloom,* which simply means that the cocoa butter has become unstable and risen to the top. Don't worry; it looks ugly, but the cocoa butter will mix back in upon melting. Do not, however, use this type of cosmetically impaired chocolate for any use where you would not be melting it.

Milk and white chocolates

Milk chocolate has had milk solids added to it and usually has higher sugar content than semisweet chocolate. White chocolate also has milk solids added to it. White chocolate is not actually chocolate at all, according to the FDA. High quality white chocolate will contain cocoa butter, however, and is the only type of white chocolate that has a chocolate flavor and aroma. Less expensive white chocolates contain other types of fats that are not indigenous to chocolate, such as cottonseed oil or palm kernel oil. You can find good quality white and milk chocolates in most supermarkets. You can find both domestic and imported brands in 3 to 4 ounce bars.

Couverture (koo-vay-tyoor)

This chocolate (which can be white, milk, or dark) is very fluid when melted and is the coating of choice for professional chocolatiers when making truffles and candies. It must be tempered before being used to get a shiny, beautiful end product. Use it for making perfect shapes, such as the White Chocolate Bûche de Noël's "bark" (see Chapter 12 for the recipe).

Cocoa

Many types of unsweetened cocoa are on the market, both imported and domestic. All cocoas fall into one of two categories: regular or Dutch processed. *Dutch processed* means that the cocoa beans, or their byproducts, are exposed to an alkaline solution. This exposure reduces the acidity of the cocoa, making it mellower, darker, and richer. Do not substitute one cocoa for another. Use the specific cocoa listed in a particular recipe.

Not basic, but useful pantry items

In this section, you find some items that are familiar, like cream cheese, and some that you might not be familiar with, like mascarpone cheese. Both have their uses in this book, as do the other ingredients listed.

- **Cream cheese.** Nationally available Philadelphia brand cream cheese was used to test these recipes. I use the regular type, but feel free to experiment with the reduced-fat variety. I do not recommend the non-fat variety, as it has an unpleasant taste and texture.
- **Crème fraiche.** You can make your own crème fraiche, which is like a tangy sour cream, but for our hectic, I-have-no-time purposes, purchased crème fraiche will do just fine. You can find it in cheese shops, some specialty food stores, supermarkets, and in the cheese department of some health food stores. You could substitute sour cream, but I think crème fraiche has a more interesting flavor. If you've never tried it, but can find it easily, a Christmas party recipe might just be the perfect time to put it to use.
- **Mascarpone.** This is an Italian product, sort of a cross between cream cheese and sour cream. It can be purchased in cheese shops, some specialty food stores, supermarkets, and in the cheese department of some health food stores. The Five-Cheese Spinach Lasagne (Chapter 8) would only have four cheeses without it!
- **Sour cream.** Any commercially available full-fat sour cream is good to have on hand. Experiment with reduced-fat varieties, if you so desire.
- **White truffle oil.** This is used in only one of the recipes in this book (see Chapter 5), but boy does it make a difference! Search it out in specialty food stores. Truffles are a fungus, like the common mushrooms you are familiar with, and they give the oil an earthy, exotic flavor.
- **Dry white wine.** White wine is often used to add flavor to stews and sauces. Most white wines labeled *table wine* are dry, meaning not sweet, as are those labeled *Chardonnay.*
- **Fresh parsley.** This is the fresh herb that is called for in several of the recipes in this book. It is definitely more than a garnish and adds an unmistakably fresh, green flavor to recipes. Use flat-leafed parsley, not the curly parsley. The flat has better flavor and texture.
- **Fresh breadcrumbs.** Whenever you have some leftover bread, process it in the food processor and make crumbs. Store the crumbs in your freezer in a resealable bag so that you have crumbs on hand. Yeah, I know they'll be frozen, but they are still "fresh" breadcrumbs, as opposed to the dry, toasted ones that come in cardboard containers.

Lining Up Your Tools and Equipment

You already have everything that you need to make the recipes in this book, like an oven, a stove, a mixing bowl or two, and some utensils. Some additional tools will help you work in the kitchen with speed and a masterful touch. Maybe look through these lists and add an item or two to your Christmas list?

Almost basic tools

Here are some helpful kitchen tools:

- **Oven thermometer.** Internal oven temperatures can vary from the temperature on the dial by as much as 50 degrees. I strongly suggest you use an oven thermometer and adjust your oven accordingly. In other words, if you set the dial to 350 degrees and the thermometer reads 325, you know you have to set the dial about 25 degrees higher to get the desired temperature.
- **Microwave oven.** I give approximate levels of power for microwave usage in some of the recipes, but follow your manufacturer's directions for specific information. Microwaves have different wattage, so giving exact directions is difficult. I use my microwave for softening butter so that it's ready for creaming, melting dark chocolates and butter, and defrosting various foodstuffs.
- **Food processor.** The recipes were tested with a KitchenAid model, but any food processor with a metal blade and shredding and slicing attachments works. I use my processor for grinding breadcrumbs, chopping herbs and onions, and shredding cheese, among other things. Motor power varies with make and model. Always follow the manufacturer's instructions.
- **Non-reactive pot.** Aluminum reacts with acidic foods. If you cook a cream sauce, for instance, in an aluminum pot, the sauce may develop a metallic taste and turn gray. Some non-reactive materials are stainless steel, glass, and enamel.
- **Rubber spatulas.** The standard-size rubber spatula sold in supermarkets is too small for some cooking techniques. Kitchen supply stores and restaurant supply houses stock extra large spatulas that make it easy to gently fold ingredients together.
- **Whisks.** Perhaps you've used a whisk to combine eggs for a weekend breakfast, but they do have other uses. For instance, try using them to fold ingredients together when a gentle touch is needed. Whisks come in all lengths, diameters, and rigidity. Most likely, you will want to have at least a couple handy.

- **Thermometers.** There are several varieties on the market, but you can get by with a digital probe thermometer for the recipes in this book.

  A digital thermometer with a probe has become my all-purpose thermometer and I think it's a worthwhile investment. The large, easy-to-read digital read-out is magnetized and can sit on your stove or countertop. The stainless steel probe is attached to a long wire that can be inserted into your turkey, sugar syrup, or whatever you're cooking. The range goes from 32 to 390 degrees and there are many functions. The best part is that you can set the thermometer to your desired finished temperature, and when the probe detects that your food has reached that temperature, it lets you know by beeping. You don't have to keep opening the oven to check for doneness. They are battery run and cost about $30. I use a Polder brand thermometer.

Tools for your bake shop

Here are some typical baker's tools. You don't need to have all of these, but having a good assortment of baking tools is sure handy when it comes time to make those elaborate Christmas desserts.

- **Mixer.** I use a freestanding, 5-quart KitchenAid. The KitchenAid not only has a large capacity, it also has a powerful motor, is well built, and will last a lifetime. If you do any amount of baking, a freestanding mixer is a great investment.

  The KitchenAid mixer that I have comes with a stainless steel bowl, a balloon whip, a flat paddle, and a dough hook. The balloon whip incorporates air into whipped cream, buttercream, and eggs; the flat paddle creams butter, cream cheese, and most cake batters. The dough hook is used with yeast dough.

  If you use a hand-held mixer, the mixing times will be longer and you should be prepared to hold the mixer over the bowl for extended periods of time in certain instances.

- **Measuring cups and spoons.** For dry ingredients, use sturdy stainless steel cups that resist denting — dents make for inaccurate measurements. Same goes for measuring spoons. Most cup sets have ¼ cup, ⅓ cup, ½ cup, and 1-cup sizes. Some have a ⅛ cup, which may be helpful. Measuring spoon sets have ¼ teaspoon, ½ teaspoon, 1 teaspoon, and 1 tablespoon (which is equivalent to 3 teaspoons). Some have ⅛ teaspoon. A *pinch* is generally considered to be equal to a ⅛ teaspoon; a *dash* is half of that.

  For liquid ingredients, use standard heatproof glass measuring cups, available at most supermarkets and kitchenware stores. For the most accurate measurements, use a cup that's not much bigger than what you are measuring. For instance, if you need ½ cup of milk, use a one-cup measurer, not a four-cup.

Always have your liquid measuring cup on a flat surface, add the ingredient, and then bring your eyes down to the cup's level to assess the amount. The top line of the ingredient should be level with the line on the cup that marks the desired amount.

Are you used to just throwing ingredients willy-nilly into a pot without accurately measuring them? I bet it works most of the time when it comes to cooking. After all, a little extra chicken broth never hurt anybody. But, and this is a big but, measuring precisely when you're baking is crucial. The difference between a ½ teaspoon of baking powder and 1 teaspoon of baking powder is huge! Trust me on this one.

- **Cookie sheets, baking sheets, and jelly roll pans.** The terms *cookie sheet* and *baking sheet* are generally used interchangeably. They mean a flat sheet of metal, sometimes with a very small lip all the way around it, on which you place whatever you're baking. A jelly roll pan is like a cookie sheet, but it has slightly higher sides. The jelly roll pan that I use measures 16½ inches by 11½ inches (interior dimensions).

Many cookie sheets and jelly roll pans are flimsy and warp, which encourages burning. Purchase high-quality aluminum or stainless steel pans to provide a flat baking surface.

- **Cookie cutters.** Have an assortment of cookie cutters on hand for the holidays. They are inexpensive and building a collection is fun.

  If you don't have any cookie cutters, simply cut out dough with a juice glass. You can also make a template out of cardboard cut to any shape you like. Lay the cardboard on the cookie dough and use a knife to trace the edges of the cardboard figure.

- **Cooling racks.** Properly cooled foods have the best texture. Cooling racks are necessary to help diffuse heat efficiently.
- **Icing spatula, offset spatula.** An icing spatula is a flat metal spatula with a handle. It's often used to apply buttercream or smooth the surface of your food. An offset spatula has a bend along its length, and this angle makes it particularly useful for spreading ingredients in a pan. Having an assortment of spatulas aids you immensely when making desserts. Different spatulas all have their own specific function and can make the difference between a dessert that looks *too* homemade and one that looks professional. Experiment.
- **Chocolate chipper.** This is a heavy-gauge fork that makes quick work of chopping chocolate. It will save your knives and is indispensable if you bake with a lot of chocolate that you buy in bulk.
- **Strainer.** You can use a traditional flour sifter, but you can also use a round-shaped strainer with a handle. Use one that fits over a bowl and sift your dry ingredients right into it.
- **Parchment paper.** Parchment is available in rolls, like aluminum foil, from kitchenware stores, some supermarkets, and mail order sources. Parchment paper provides a non-stick surface upon which to bake and

cook. Cut out circles to fit pan bottoms and use it to line baking sheets. When parchment paper is used in conjunction with a greased pan, your baked goods release effortlessly.

- **Pastry bags.** Some of the recipes in this book require that you use pastry bags. The polyester type made by Wilton is the best. The bags that Wilton makes are called Featherweight Decorating Bags and come in sizes ranging from 8 inches to 18 inches (in 2-inch increments). The 14-inch and 16-inch sizes are the most useful. Trim the opening to allow a large decorating tube to fit, or to fit a coupler, which allows you to change small tips easily.
- **Decorating tips.** Tips are inexpensive (usually less than a dollar) and owning a variety allows you to experiment. For the recipes in this book, all you need is a star tip, such as a Wilton #22, and a round tip, such as a #2 or #10.

Equipment that's nice to have

Sometimes a special piece of equipment, even if it's only used occasionally, deserves a place in the kitchen. The right tool for the job makes the job that much easier and the results that much better.

- **Double boiler.** There are pieces of equipment on the market that are actual double boilers. They are comprised of a larger bottom pot, which you put water in, and a slightly smaller pot that fits snugly on top and that you put your food in. The idea is that the food — like chocolate — should be heated gently, so when it's in a double boiler, it's off the direct heat and is receiving gentle heat from the water, which is being heated directly.

  However, you don't need to buy a double boiler. You can rig up your own. I often use a large pot on the bottom and a stainless steel mixing bowl on top. Just make sure that the top part fits snugly into the base so that no steam escapes from where they meet. Steam burns are no fun and the condensation created from the steam could wreak havoc with your food, especially chocolate. The top bowl should fit down into the bottom pot somewhat so that the contraption is stable. Allow enough room to fill the bottom pot at least a third of the way full with water without the water touching the bottom of the top bowl.
- **Potato ricer.** For the silkiest mashed potatoes and mashed sweet potatoes, a potato ricer does the trick (see Figure 2-1). It looks like one of those machines that you may have pushed Play-Doh through as a kid to make hair and spaghetti strings. If you missed out on the Play-Doh experience, think of it as a giant garlic press.

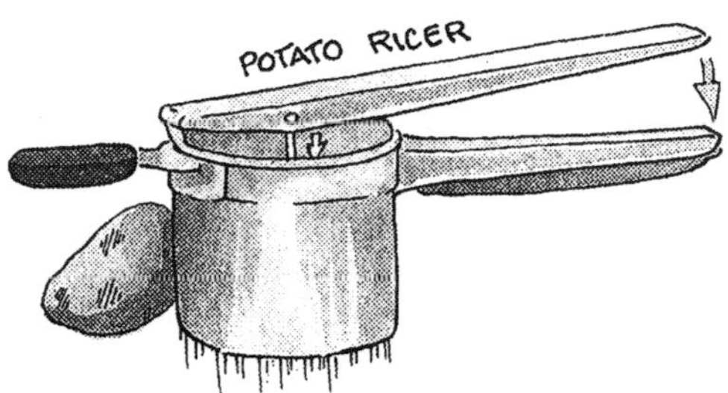

Figure 2-1: Long handles make it easy to push boiled potatoes through a ricer.

- **Shrimp deveiner.** Although a deveiner is unnecessary, it does make quick work out of cleaning shrimp. It looks like a curved knife and it easily slips under the shell, removing the shell and the dark vein that runs along the shrimp (see Figure 2-2).

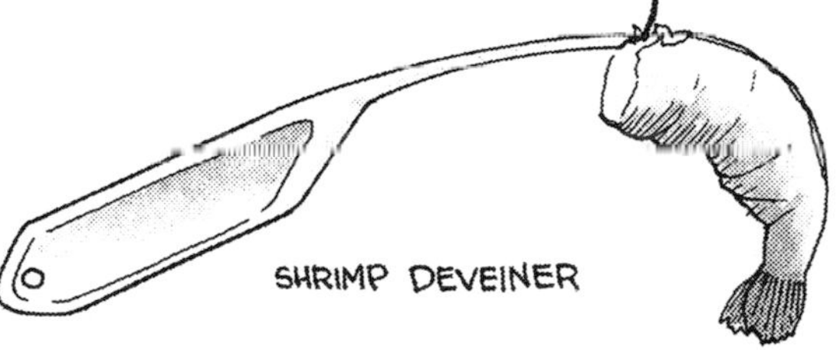

Figure 2-2: Making quick work of cleaning shrimp.

- **Kitchen shears.** You can find many uses for a heavy-duty pair of kitchen shears. Use them to cut up chicken pieces, cut twine, open stubborn packages, and the like. Using your shears saves your knives for the tasks they were intended for.
- **Tongs.** These are great for turning foods and grabbing hot items. If you have them around, you'll find uses for them.
- **Pie server.** These look like a flexible triangular metal spatula. The pointy end slips between your pie and the pie plate, right under the crust, and serves up even the first slice beautifully.
- **Nutmeg grater.** You can certainly purchase ground nutmeg and use it in these recipes, but few things say "Christmas" like the aroma of freshly grated nutmeg. You can find various graters on the market, and they work like a small cheese grater.
- **Fat separator.** These look like a measuring cup with a long spout. The spout reaches all the way down into the bottom of the cup. When you pour your pan drippings into the separator, fat rises to the top and the spout is down in the good stuff. Pour out your drippings to use and the fat is left behind.

- **Carving board.** You can carve your turkey or roast on any cutting board, but carving boards are the best type of cutting board for the task. They have grooves and a well that collect juices, which you can then add to your gravy or use as a natural sauce. They are also usually large enough to handle even a giant turkey.
- **Carving knife and fork.** You can cut up a turkey or a roast with any sharp knife, but a thin, sharp carving knife with a long blade produces slices that maximize the exquisite texture of your beautifully cooked food. A sturdy fork with strong tines helps as well.
- **Warming tray.** This is an electric tray that can sit in the kitchen or on a sideboard. During dinner you can place casseroles and platters on the tray to keep the food warm.
- **Wine bucket and/or ice bucket.** Somewhere along the way, you will want to have a chilled bottle of champagne or white wine. You can keep it in the fridge or fill a bowl with ice, but a wine bucket is attractive and functional at the same time. If you're serving mixed drinks, or even juices and soda, a bucket of ice comes in handy.

(Stop Me If You've Heard These) Common Cooking Techniques

Some recipes are straightforward, but sometimes you might need a reminder about technique, or maybe an introduction to one. Remember that while these ideas may seem exacting and picky, they will help you get the best results from the recipes.

Measuring ingredients

Dry ingredients should be measured with cups specifically calibrated for them. Store your dry ingredients (flour, sugar, and so on) in airtight containers. *Dip and sweep* to measure out the right amount. Dip the correct-sized measuring cup into the container and then, using the blunt edge of a knife or an icing spatula, sweep the excess off the top and back into the container. If you shake or tap the measuring cup, the dry ingredient settles, becoming denser, and therefore skewing your results.

Liquids such as honey, oil, liqueurs, water, or lemon juice should be measured in liquid measuring cups. The common glass cups with spouts that you can find in most supermarkets and hardware stores are fine for this purpose. Place your measuring cup on a level surface and pour your ingredient up to the line that indicates the amount you need.

Use appropriate-sized cups. Don't try to measure ¼ cup of liquid in a 4-cup measurer — you skew the accuracy. When measuring sticky ingredients, like honey or corn syrup, lightly spray your measuring cup with pan coating so that the honey will slip right out of the measurer.

Pan preparation

A cake that releases easily has beautiful sides and all of its crust's integrity intact. A veggie casserole that's been packed into a greased dish is not only easier to serve, but cleanup is faster as well. I use a vegetable oil–based spray such as PAM, which is available everywhere. Check individual recipes for any special pan treatments.

Creaming fat and sugar

Properly creaming fat and sugar together maximizes the amount of air added to your batter and yields a high volume, which in turn gives you the light, tender baked goods you want.

Start with room temperature ingredients. Add your fat (in the form of butter, shortening, or whatever) to your mixer's bowl. Use the paddle attachment and cream on a medium-high speed until smooth and creamy. Add sugar gradually and continue creaming until light and fluffy, before adding the dry and liquid ingredients.

You can do this by hand with a wooden spoon and finish it off with a wire whisk, which adds some air and lightness, but your biceps and triceps better be ready for a workout. Also, make sure that your butter is at room temperature or the creaming process will be nearly impossible to accomplish by hand.

Separating eggs and whipping egg whites

Cold eggs separate easier than eggs at room temperature. The white is stiffer and more viscous and the yolk is less prone to breakage. However, in general, the eggs should be room temperature when they are actually incorporated into your other ingredients or when the whites or yolks are whipped. Room temperature eggs give you maximum volume.

You shouldn't let the eggs stay at room temperature for more than one hour.

Many dessert recipes call for egg whites to be whipped separately from the yolks. Folding whipped whites into a batter lightens the texture by adding air. A bit of cream of tartar can be added to the egg white foam for increased stability. Any grease will prohibit proper whipping. Make sure that absolutely no trace of yolk gets into your mixture and always use scrupulously clean bowls and beaters.

Begin by beating the whites with a balloon whip attachment on low speed. When frothy, add cream of tartar, if you're using it. Increase the speed to medium-high and beat until soft peaks form. Then add sugar gradually, if it's called for in the recipe. Soft peaks are reached when the whites form peaks that fold over on themselves a bit. Stiff peaks stand up straight and are somewhat glossy. You will get grainy, lumpy whites if you overbeat.

Many recipes call for a large rubber spatula to be used when folding in egg whites. I usually start the folding process with a balloon whisk, which really preserves the volume, and finish off the folding with a large spatula.

You can whip whites by hand, in which case you use a wire whisk, but it takes some time and your arms will be so sore you won't be able to do the dishes that evening. Hey, wait a minute, that's not such a bad thing!

Whipping cream

Start with heavy cream (at least 36 percent fat), a chilled bowl, and a balloon whip mixer attachment. Start on medium speed and whip just until you can see marks left in the cream. Proceed with the machine on low speed or finish of by hand with a whisk, only beating until soft peaks form. This keeps the texture silky, which is optimal whether you're serving it alongside a dessert or folding it into other ingredients.

You can whip cream by hand, and if you've been creaming butter and whipping egg whites by hand all your life, you'll have built up enough arm muscles to pull this off easily. Otherwise, share the whipping procedure with a friend, passing the bowl and wire whisk back and forth.

The cream found in most supermarkets is ultra-pasteurized. This means the cream has been exposed to a high heat, which kills off bacteria and therefore extends shelf life. It also has a slightly cooked flavor and does not whip as easily as regularly pasteurized cream because a coagulating enzyme has also been destroyed. See if you can find pasteurized cream.

Sometimes you may need your whipped cream to hold up for a prolonged period of time or hold up without refrigeration. To stabilize cream, a little bit of gelatin dissolved in water can be folded into the whipped cream. Use 1 teaspoon of gelatin to 1 cup of liquid cream. Sprinkle the gelatin over 1 tablespoon of cold water and allow 5 minutes to soften. Heat the gelatin over hot water or in a microwave and stir to dissolve. Cool to a barely warm temperature. Whip the cream until soft peaks form and then fold the gelatin mixture into the cream. Continue whipping until the proper consistency is reached.

Melting chocolate

Chocolate can be melted successfully in a double boiler or in a microwave. Either way, it should first be chopped into small pieces. The best way to do that is with a chocolate chipper (see "Tools for your bake shop" earlier in this chapter). Even if you buy one-ounce squares, chopping them up a bit first makes them melt more quickly and evenly.

To melt in a double boiler, add water to the bottom of the double boiler, but don't add enough to touch the bottom of the top bowl. Place the chocolate in the top bowl and bring the water to a simmer, stirring the chocolate occasionally until it's almost completely melted. Turn the heat off and continue to stir. The residual heat will melt the remaining chocolate.

The two problems with this technique are that steam can get in the chocolate and you may end up overheating the chocolate. Steam is created by the hot water in the bottom pot. If water droplets get into the chocolate, the chocolate will immediately clump and turn into a grainy mass and be unsalvageable for most preparations. Prevention is the best medicine. Make sure that the top and bottom of your double boiler have a tight fit, which lessens the chance of steam escaping.

Overheating will do one of two things. It may separate the fats (cocoa butter or oils) in the chocolate from the rest of the chocolate, which will result in an oily mass, or it will burn the chocolate, which will make it grainy and lumpy. The best way to avoid overheating is to remove the chocolate from the heat before it's completely melted. Residual heat will finish off the job.

To heat chocolate in the microwave, finely chop the chocolate, place it in a microwave-safe bowl, and set the machine at about one-third power. For one pound of chocolate, heat the chocolate, uncovered, for 3 to 5 minutes, checking and stirring at intervals, until the bulk of the chocolate is melted — note that the chocolate may still *look* solid. It's melted as soon as you can stir it. Take it out of the microwave early enough that residual heat completes the melting process.

I do not like to melt milk or white chocolates in the microwave because I don't have the same degree of control over the heat source as on top of the stove and these chocolates are temperamental.

Quick-tempering chocolate

Tempering chocolate is a process usually reserved for candy making. In this book, the spectacular White Chocolate Bûche de Noël (Chapter 12) has an optional chocolate "bark" that requires you to use the tempering process.

How to tell when "It's done!"

Cooking and baking times are approximate; note that I nearly always preface the cooking time with the word "about." That's because even if you made a recipe the exact same way twice in a row, there are bound to be differences that affect the final cooking time. Maybe the butter was a bit softer the second time around, or maybe you kept the oven door closed the whole time, which sped up the cooking time. There are always variables. This is why, in addition to having a time estimate, it's good to also use your nose, eyes, and occasionally your sense of touch.

Here are a few things you can do to help ensure the proper doneness of your dish.

Invest in a high-quality oven thermometer and test your oven temperature. These are thermometers that live in the oven, usually hanging from a rack; you can buy them in the supermarket. If the recipe calls for a 350-degree oven, you'll know whether you are even in the ballpark. Then, get in the habit of assessing doneness before the suggested time is up. Overcooking is very common and easily averted. Some of this is intuition and experience, but begin by checking about 5 to 10 minutes before the recipe is supposed to be ready. Of course, if your dish only takes 5 minutes of boiling, you gotta check after 3 or 4 minutes. Use your judgment.

Use your nose too. Are the cookies starting to smell fragrant? Time is probably drawing near. This is not a conclusive test, just one to use along with the others.

And use your eyes. Does the recipe say the dish will turn golden brown? Then you have something to shoot for. I've strived to bring a multitude of doneness clues to you in each recipe.

Use all the techniques mentioned for the most foolproof result; if you do, your chances of success increase exponentially. And remember, it is better to undercook than overcook — you can usually put undercooked food back in the oven!

Traditional tempering requires a chocolate thermometer, a marble slab, and a long offset spatula (in addition to the chocolate). But you can use a quick-tempering method, which should suffice for the recipes in this book.

Place three-quarters of your finely chopped chocolate in the top of a double boiler and place over hot, not simmering, water. Do not let the hot water touch the bottom of the top pan. Stir constantly until the chocolate is three-quarters of the way melted. You can dab a tiny bit of chocolate on your upper lip; it should feel warm. Do not let it get hot. Remove the chocolate from the heat and add the remaining chocolate. Stir for several minutes until completely melted. Use immediately.

Techniques to Add to Your Talent-Bank

I know your Christmas season is busy, but here are a couple techniques worth knowing that actually save you time when they're called into action. These techniques may not come into play everyday, but knowing them is helpful.

- **Deglazing a pan.** When you make gravies for roasts, a technique called *deglazing* comes into play. It sounds much more exotic than it is; deglazing is really very easy. It is a technique that makes use of those tasty bits that get stuck to the bottom of the roasting pan and incorporates them into a sauce.

  Add wine, water, or another liquid to the pan; bring the contents to a simmer on top of the stove, all the while scraping up those tasty bits. Sometimes you add a thickener like flour, or maybe you add butter to enrich the sauce. Simply follow the specific instructions in individual recipes.
- **Using a pastry bag.** When a bag is new, its opening is small. Cut the bag's tip to allow for the insertion of a coupler, which will then hold your tip of choice. Fill about ⅓ of the way with the desired filling, twist the top closed, and proceed as directed in individual recipes. The important things are to not overfill the bag and to use one hand to keep the top tightly closed. Apply a little pressure from the closed end of the bag while the other hand simply guides the bag. Do not choke the bag with both hands, squeezing it like you're trying to kill it. Be gentle; you will be rewarded with beautiful desserts.

Before You Get Creative, Do It My Way, Please

When you're making a recipe, take every word as gospel. I don't mean to be dogmatic, but I've presented recipes to you with no extra fluff. Every ingredient, every ingredient amount, and every step in the directions is there for a reason. A good reason. Follow the recipe like a map. If you skip point B and try to get from point A to point C, you might get lost. This is particularly important when it comes to baked goods, where the difference between ½ teaspoon and 1 teaspoon of baking powder can mean the difference between complete success and utter failure. Here's my motto: Try the recipe once as it's written. Then, if you have ideas about adding raisins or replacing chicken stock with veggie stock, be my guest.

When making a dish, especially for the first time, make notes about the procedure and the result. How long did it take you to make? How did it taste? Does it need more salt next time? Or maybe a longer baking time? This way, when you make it again, you can better tailor it to your liking.

Avoiding two big pitfalls and several smaller booby traps

The two main reasons that recipes fail are that cooks do not read the whole recipe and do not follow the directions. Pretty simple — what more can I say? For instance, if the recipe calls for room temperature butter, make sure you don't use it straight out of the refrigerator or you may not like your results. Some other common mistakes include

- **Overcooking.** Cooks often leave their dishes in the oven too long. With experience, you learn how to count on *residual heat* — the heat that's left in the item and its container after you pull it from the oven. Cookies are a perfect example of this. They look done, you pull them from the oven, and then you leave them to sit on the pan for 5 to 10 minutes. When you go to remove them, they have darkened appreciably. That's because the residual heat from the cookie sheets continued to cook the cookies even though they were out of the oven.

  Same thing with top-of-the-stove cooking. Residual heat continues to cook whatever is in your pan even after you remove it from the burner, so plan accordingly.

  Overcooking can also occur when cooking on top of the stove if you turn off the burner element but leave the pan on top of the burner. This is particularly true with electric ranges, as the burner element takes a while to cool off.

  The recipes in this book have time ranges and suggest visual clues for doneness to help you avoid overcooking.

- **Burning baked goods.** If your oven has poor heat circulation, the bottoms of your cookies and cakes may routinely burn. Doubling up on pans creates an air pocket that eliminates this problem. Using high-quality, heavy-duty pans also helps. Before you go out and invest in all new pans, try doubling your sheet pans or brownie pans (simply putting one on top of another) and see if doing so doesn't improve your results.

- **Storing inadequately.** Some foods should be refrigerated, some stored at room temperature. Sometimes an airtight container is best, at other times, a loose wrapping is better. Follow the directions I give you in the individual recipes.

When you absolutely, positively have to make a substitution

Although sticking to a recipe is always best, I understand that sometimes you won't have an ingredient and will still want to make a recipe. Here are some substitutions that, while not always giving you the same results as the ingredient that's included in the recipe, will get you through the dish:

- 1 cup chicken broth = 1 cup vegetable broth
- 1 cup beef broth = 1 cup chicken broth
- 1 cup chicken broth = 1 cup boiling water + 1 chicken bouillon cube
- 1 teaspoon vinegar = 1 teaspoon lemon juice
- 1 teaspoon dried herbs = 1 tablespoon fresh herbs
- 1 cup milk = ½ cup evaporated milk + ½ cup water; or 1 cup milk = ¼ cup dry milk + ¾ cup water
- 1 cup heavy cream = ¾ cup milk + ¼ cup melted unsalted butter; or 1 cup heavy cream = 1 cup evaporated milk (neither substitute is good for whipping)
- 1 cup buttermilk = 1 cup milk + 1 tablespoon lemon juice (let this mixture sit 15 minutes before using); or 1 cup buttermilk = 1 cup yogurt; or 1 cup buttermilk = 1 cup sour cream
- 1 pound unsalted butter = 1 pound salted butter less 1 teaspoon salt from elsewhere in the recipe. (This substitution isn't great for baking recipes.)
- 1 cup cake flour = 1 cup short 2 tablespoons all-purpose flour + 2 tablespoons cornstarch
- 1 tablespoon flour (used for thickening) = 2½ teaspoons arrowroot, 2 tablespoons quick-cooking tapioca, or 2½ teaspoons cornstarch. (If you use cornstarch, you can't reheat the recipe because the thickening power will break down.)
- 1 cup light brown sugar = 1 cup sugar + ¼ cup molasses
- 1 cup dark brown sugar = 1 cup sugar + ⅓ cup molasses
- 1 teaspoon baking powder = ½ teaspoon cream of tartar + ¼ teaspoon baking soda
- 1 ounce unsweetened chocolate (1 square) = 3 tablespoons cocoa + 1 tablespoon vegetable shortening

Safety first in the kitchen

Your mind may be on the end result — that golden brown turkey or those perfect gingerbread people — but always keep your wits about you in the kitchen. Here are some easy-to-remember safety tips:

- Wash your hands before you cook and occasionally while cooking to prevent the spread of germs. Contamination happens all too easily.

- Consider having one cutting board that is just for meats, poultry, and fish. This can prevent contamination. Both wooden and plastic boards have their fans. The wooden are more aesthetic and easier on your knives, but the choice is up to you. Many of the plastic ones can go right in the dishwasher, which is a nice feature. I use both. I use the plastic for poultry and stinky things like garlic and onions because I can get the smell out of them either through hand scrubbing or a soak in the dishwasher.
- Use tools correctly — don't hold a piece of fruit in your palm while you slice down towards your hand. I have seen too many people do this — and end up with stitches.
- Dull knives cause more accidents than sharp ones. Keep them sharp.
- Never leave a hot pan with oil in it unattended. If the oil gets hot enough — called the *flash point* — it will burst into flames.
- Have a fire extinguisher easily accessible in the kitchen. Also keep baking soda handy and use it to extinguish small fires. If there is a fire in the oven, always keep the door closed so as not to add any oxygen, which would feed the fire. It might just go out by itself.
- Buy extra-long oven mitts to protect your forearms as well as your hands. Look for these mitts where grills are sold.
- Keep cold foods below 40 degrees and hot foods above 140 degrees to discourage bacteria growth. If you don't have a thermometer handy, use your sense of touch. Our body temperature is in the mid 90s, so, if something feels warm, it's above 100 degrees. A hot tub is about 106 degrees, and it feels pretty hot to most of us, so 140 degrees is going to feel really hot. 32 degrees is freezing, as in ice! So something that is 40 degrees will feel quite cold. It's those in-between regions you've got to watch out for.
- To minimize accidents, keep your hair tied back, remove loose jewelry, and wear close-fitting clothing.
- Cloth towels are a breeding ground for germs. Use one towel for drying clean hands and another for wiping up messes. Replace both frequently. Better yet, use paper towels for food spills and reserve cloth towels for hands.

Avoiding freezer burn

If you're making a recipe that you can make ahead and freeze, by all means do so. Freezer burn is an issue, though. Follow this basic procedure to beat freezer burn. Wrap foods in plastic wrap, preferably a double layer. Then, wrap in heavy-duty foil. Then, if you can, depending on the size of your item, slip it into a heavy-duty resealable bag and seal tight, sucking out any air.

Chapter 3

Making Magic with Christmas Menus

In This Chapter

- Creating a menu
- Writing the shopping list, running the pantry check
- Making the meal step-by-step

Browsing recipes and tasting them in your imagination is a great way to spend time. I'm sure I'd clock a lot of hours skimming cookbooks even if I didn't write them for a living.

But putting together a number of separate recipes into a well-orchestrated menu of harmonious parts — well, that's something else. True confession time: In my household, the main meal on an ordinary day may be a thrown-together affair — filling and nutritious, but lacking much Tinker Bell magic. And that simply won't do at Christmas time.

Christmas-season meals need a spritz of the magical, and conjuring it takes a bit more planning than ordinary. But it's not hard — starting with a menu is one way to go. So to get you started, I've put together nine menus consisting of recipes from this book. Whether you're looking for a quick weeknight dinner, the main Christmas Day meal, or an open house buffet for dozens of guests, you can find what you need in this chapter.

Getting Mileage Out of Menus, Mine or Yours

You can use the menus in this chapter in two ways: as a complete set of directions, including shopping lists and preparation sequence, or as a jump-start to designing magical menus of your own. Either way works.

If you want me to serve as your personal kitchen coach, I'm at your service. The advantage of using one of the menus in this chapter is that everything is planned for you. I even include shopping lists. Each menu has a making-the-meal section that details what you can make ahead and what general order to prepare your foods in so that the meal gets to the table as effortlessly as possible. Sometimes individual recipes are designed to serve eight, but you're cooking for four (or maybe twenty-four). Every recipe in this chapter comes equipped with information on scaling up or down to suit your needs.

The other way to use the menus in this chapter is to tailor them to your tastes and special holiday needs. You can modify the menus here and there, or you can use them as a model and build your own menu. If you don't want to use one of those suggested, then grab a piece of paper and start brainstorming. Writing down exactly what you want to serve is best, from the appetizers to dessert. If you do so, you can use your master list to make your shopping list and note what can be done ahead for maximum efficiency.

Creating your own menus

Creating a menu is very easy. I suggest starting with the main dish. Maybe you always have turkey and want to continue the tradition. Or perhaps you've decided to make a goose this year. So make that decision first. Then determine the flavors that will accompany your main dish. Will it have a maple glaze and a New England theme? Or maybe you want to go Southwestern and rub your turkey with chilies? The main dish then suggests what side dishes to add. (If I were doing Southwestern Turkey, I might have hot chile pepper cornbread stuffing with a mole-style gravy; get the gist?)

Appetizers and desserts come next. If your main dish has a lot of spicy flavors, then you could either complement or contrast that with the appetizers. If you're having a rich, creamy, cheesy cauliflower gratin for dinner, then skip a cheese selection with drinks. You want the meal to be well-rounded — a balanced selection of flavors, some rich items and some light items. Of course, when it comes to dessert at Christmastime, most folks feel the more the better. It usually works to have something fruity and something chocolatey, at the very least. Then think about contrasting textures. Have some crunchy cookies along with a smooth ice cream, for instance.

Blending recipes into shopping lists

Now that you've chosen your recipes, you can make a shopping list. Look for ingredients that are called for in more than one dish. For instance, you might need onions for several dishes, so add those up and make one notation on your list. Put similar ingredients together, such as grouping all of your dairy products, as you'll find them together in the supermarket. Be familiar with your market and write down ingredients in the order in which they appear in the store. And bring a pen to the store to cross off items as you place them in your cart.

Be as specific as possible. Use your recipes and write down exactly what you need.

Getting ahead by making ahead

One of the keys to organizing your holiday cooking is to take advantage of any make-ahead recipes or steps. Look at each of the recipes you have selected for this information and start another list. At the top of the list, write down those foods that can be made way ahead, perhaps even a month before. Then keep going until you've listed what you must do the day of your party or within hours of serving. Again, check things off as you go along; doing so makes you feel like you've accomplished a lot.

The recipe is for 8, but I'm having 4: Scaling up and down

All of the recipes in this book give you a yield. Sometimes the yield is given in terms of how many the recipe will serve and sometimes it's given as a volume or weight. When the yield says that the recipe will serve 8, rest assured that I'm generous with my math; I'm not into skimpy portions. For certain dishes, like the Spiced Cashews in Chapter 5, the yield is given in terms of cups, as it's hard to say how many servings you're really creating.

So you'll always know how much a recipe makes, but what if the recipe yield isn't what you need? You need to take a few things into consideration. Familiarize yourself with the term used in professional kitchens for increasing or decreasing the output of a recipe — it's called *scaling up* or *scaling down.*

In general, you can halve a recipe or double a recipe with no problem. The recipe will still turn out with the right taste and texture. However, there's a point in every recipe where the sum is more than the parts. In other words, 2×4 doesn't always equal a neat, tidy 8. Some recipes just don't scale up or down very well, especially the further you get from the original.

The worst culprit is baked goods. Scaling a recipe way up is very difficult. Leaveners in particular, like baking powder and baking soda, get quite cranky if you mess around with the basic recipe. So for most desserts, stick close to the original. Or at least know that you're venturing into uncharted territory and may or may not like the results.

My suggestion is to avoid scaling up or down too drastically. The first time you make a recipe, always make it as it's written. That way, you'll be familiar with the way it's intended to be. Then stick with halving and doubling and keep an eye out while you're making the recipe. If the soup you've doubled looks a bit thick, for example, add some broth.

There are two big exceptions to doubling and halving: cooking times and seasoning. In general, baking and cooking times are not like ingredients. You might be doubling the amount of sugar, but that doesn't necessarily mean the cooking time is doubled too. And when it comes to seasoning, be conservative. If you've doubled a recipe, don't automatically double the salt. Start with the original amount, and then slowly add more salt to taste. The same for pepper and many herbs and spices. It's best to err on the side of caution, as adding is easier than taking away.

If you've added too much salt to a soup, stew, or a casserole that has a high liquid ratio, you might be able to salvage it. Peel a large raw potato, cut it in half, and add it to the dish. Simmer for awhile, and, with any luck, the potato will absorb some of the salt. Good luck! By the way, throw out the potato. Eating it would be bad for your (or your dog's) sodium intake.

Presenting Nine Christmas Menus

I know — there are 12 days of Christmas, and a list of nine menus looks like it comes from Scrooge & Co. But I know what December is like and I assume that you'll grab a few days of fast food along the way. Besides, the nine menus are infinitely adaptable, and some may win such stunning applause that you'll make them more than once.

Each menu contains five main parts:

- A list of the recipes that make up the menu, with chapter references so that you can find each recipe fast.
- A shopping list of all the items required for the menu.
- A checklist of items that you need to draw from your pantry (if you're short a pantry item, add it to the shopping list).
- Step-by-step suggestions for making the meal in the most organized fashion possible.
- Notes about how you can tailor the menu to the size of your party. If the directions say that a recipe can be scaled up or down directly, you can multiply or divide to your heart's content.

Quick Shopping Night Pasta Dinner for 2

Fusilli with Caramelized Onions (Chapter 8)

***

The Basic Green Salad (Chapter 6)

***

Bread and Cheese

***

Fresh Fruit

This is a great meal to make when you're running around midweek after work hunting down presents. The crowds were oppressive, the traffic could have been better, and you're tempted to just grab a bowl of cereal for dinner. But not only do you deserve more; your body needs more. This meal is quick to put together. Add a bottle of red wine, if you're so inclined.

Shopping list

2 ripe pears or other fresh fruit for dessert

1 small head butter lettuce

1 small head red or green leaf lettuce

1 small head romaine lettuce

½-pound wedge of cheese, your choice

½ pound fusilli pasta

1 French baguette

¼ cup chopped kalamata olives

¼ cup dry vermouth

Pantry items you may already have

Garlic

Onions

Extra-virgin olive oil

Balsamic vinegar

Dijon mustard

Thyme

Making the meal

1. Make the onion sauce for the pasta.
2. Bring the water to a boil.
3. Prepare the salad greens and vinaigrette while the water comes to a boil.
4. Add the pasta to the boiling water.
5. Set out the cheese and slice the baguette while the pasta cooks. Prepare the fruit. Toss the salad with the dressing.
6. Drain the pasta, toss with the sauce, and serve with the remainder of the meal.

Scaling up or down

Every part of this menu can be scaled up or down directly.

60-Minute Weeknight Entertaining Menu for 4

Duck Breasts with Dried Cherry Wine Sauce (Chapter 8)

***

Mashed Sweet Potatoes with Bourbon and Brown Sugar (half the recipe) (Chapter 9)

***

Balsamic Glazed Green Beans (half the recipe) (Chapter 9)

***

Pears and Gorgonzola

During this busy season, we can all use an elegant, delicious meal that can be made in an hour. Here it is. Go ahead, invite friends over; you'll wow them with this quick-to-the-table gourmet meal.

Shopping list

2½ pounds sweet potatoes

1½ pounds green beans

4 ripe pears or other fresh fruit for dessert

2 tablespoons flat-leaf parsley

1 pound Gorgonzola

2 whole Pekin duck breasts

¼ cup demi-glace

¼ cup dried cherries

⅓ cup bourbon

Pantry items you may already have

Orange marmalade

Unsalted butter

Whole milk or half-and-half

Light brown sugar

Thyme

Cinnamon

Cider vinegar

Extra-virgin olive oil

Balsamic vinegar

Dry red wine, such as Merlot

Making the meal

1. Get the sweet potatoes going, or even make them the day before. While they're roasting in the oven, make the rest of the meal.

2. Make the green beans next; they can sit while you make the duck breasts. I think this menu flows best if everything is done and you focus on the duck last, right before you're going to eat.

3. While the duck rests for a few minutes, prepare the fruit and cheese for dessert.

Scaling up or down

Every part of this menu can be scaled up or down directly.

Christmas Day Breakfast for 6

Citrus Breakfast Fruit Salad with Yogurt and Granola (Chapter 7)

***

Overnight French Toast with Maple-Orange Syrup (Chapter 7)

Spinach and Chevre Breakfast Frittata (Chapter 7)

Brown Sugar Bacon with Mustard (Chapter 7)

***

Fruit Smoothies × 3 (Chapter 4)

Orange–Passion Fruit Mimosas × 4 (Chapter 4)

Hot White Chocolate (Chapter 4)

Coffee and Tea

What a great way to start your holiday. Make a hearty breakfast for your family and then sit back, open presents, and enjoy.

Shopping list

4 clementines

3 navel oranges

2 ruby-red grapefruit

3 large bananas

½ pint cherry tomatoes

1 lime

5 ounces cheddar, shredded (about 1⅔ cups)

4 ounces soft chèvre

3 cups half-and-half

2 cups cottage cheese

1 cup heavy cream

⅔ cup vanilla yogurt

1 pound thick-cut bacon

8 ounces white chocolate

3½ cups freshly squeezed orange juice, extra as needed

1-pound loaf challah or egg bread

10-ounce jar (about 1 cup) apricot all-fruit jam

¾ cup vanilla soymilk

⅓ cup granola

1¼ cups maple syrup (real, please)

2 tablespoons orange juice concentrate

½ cup passion fruit–cranberry liqueur (such as Alizé Red Passion)

1 tablespoon honey

1 teaspoon Dutch-processed cocoa

12 slices frozen peaches (or use canned peaches, packed in juice and drained, frozen in a resealable bag)

10-ounce package frozen chopped spinach

¾ cup frozen raspberries (or use fresh raspberries frozen in a resealable bag)

1 standard bottle dry champagne

Pantry items you may already have

Whole milk

Large eggs

Sugar

Light brown sugar

Dijon mustard

Cardamom

Cinnamon

Nutmeg

Vanilla extract

Coffee

Tea

Making the meal

1. The Citrus Breakfast Fruit Salad with Yogurt and Granola can mostly be made the night before, as can the Brown Sugar Bacon with Mustard.
2. The Overnight French Toast is also prepared the night ahead and then just popped in the oven on Christmas morning.
3. First thing in the morning, get the Spinach Chevre Frittata in the oven along with the French toast and bacon. Then, while the dishes in the oven are cooking, make the Maple-Orange Syrup and add the yogurt and granola to the fruit salad.
4. Make the Hot White Chocolate and keep it warm. Make coffee or tea and keep it warm. Then make the Fruit Smoothies and the Orange–Passion Fruit Mimosas.

Scaling up or down

- **Fruit Smoothies:** Can be scaled up or down directly, but you'll have to make them in batches if you increase the recipe.
- **Orange–Passion Fruit Mimosas:** May be scaled up or down directly.
- **Citrus Breakfast Fruit Salad with Yogurt and Granola:** May be scaled up or down directly.
- **Overnight French Toast with Maple-Orange Syrup:** You may halve these recipes, but if you double the French toast, the center will not be baked by the time the edges are. I don't suggest doubling and baking in one large pan. You could double the ingredients and bake it in two pans, though.
- **Spinach Chevre Frittata:** Same as the Overnight French Toast.
- **Brown Sugar Bacon with Mustard:** May be scaled up or down directly.
- **Hot White Chocolate:** May be scaled up or down directly.

Healthy Holiday Meal for 6

Low-Fat Seafood Stew (Chapter 8)

* * *

The Basic Green Salad (Chapter 6)

* * *

Bread and Cheeses

* * *

Cranberry Cider Sorbet (Chapter 11)
Meringue Wreath Cookies (Chapter 11)

With all the rich food you'll be eating this season, it's nice to know that you can eat a healthy meal that's also satisfying. This meal is not about denial. It's a low-fat seafood celebration.

Shopping list

1 fennel bulb

1 small head butter lettuce

½ small head red or green leaf lettuce

½ small head romaine lettuce

1 pound cheese, your choice

Three 4-ounce frozen lobster tails

2 dozen small clams

2 dozen mussels

2 pounds sea bass fillets

2 dozen large shrimp (20 to 25 per pound size)

4 cups bottled clam juice

2 loaves French bread

1½ cups cranberry juice

1½ cups apple cider

28-ounce can plum tomatoes

Pantry items you may already have

Onions

Garlic

Large eggs

Sugar

Cream of tartar

Extra-virgin olive oil

Balsamic vinegar

Dijon mustard

Thyme

Rosemary

Bay leaf

Dry white wine

Making the meal

1. The meringue cookies can be made as far as a month ahead.
2. The sorbet can be made two to three days ahead. Just soften it before

serving by letting it sit at room temperature for 5 minutes; it may become quite hard in the freezer after an extended stay.

3. Get the stew going. While the stew is simmering, before you add the seafood, you have a 10-minute window of opportunity. Take advantage of this break to get the salad together, slice the bread, and set out the cheese.

Scaling up or down

- **Low-Fat Seafood Stew:** No problem here. The stew can be scaled up or down, but if you scale up, make sure that you have a large enough pot — and wallet!
- **The Basic Green Salad:** May be scaled up or down directly.
- **Cranberry Cider Sorbet:** You may scale this up or down, but if you scale it up you'll probably have to make it in batches. Few ice cream machines hold more than 1½ quarts.
- **Meringue Wreath Cookies:** May be scaled up or down directly.

A New England Christmas Dinner for 10

Oyster Stew × 2 (Chapter 6)

Maple-Glazed Turkey (Chapter 8)

Bread Stuffing with Sausage, Apples, and Cognac (Chapter 9)

***

Glazed Winter Squash (Chapter 9)

Brussels Sprouts with Chestnuts × 2 (Chapter 9)

Cranberry Sauce (Chapter 10)

***

Apple Pie (Chapter 12)

Pumpkin Pie (Chapter 12)

I happen to live in New England, so the flavors in this menu are like home to me. For you, they may seem a little exotic. Regardless of where you live, you find flavors to please a crowd in this menu.

Shopping list

8 sprigs fresh thyme

8 stalks celery

6 apples, a mixture of Cortland and Golden Delicious

5 Granny Smith apples

4 carrots

4 flat-leaf parsley stems

4 sprigs fresh sage

3 navel oranges

2 medium butternut squash

Two 12-ounce bags fresh or frozen cranberries

2 pounds Brussels sprouts

2 cups heavy cream

8 dozen shucked oysters, with juices

20-pound turkey, preferably fresh

1 pound bulk pork sausage

6 cups low-sodium chicken broth

3 tablespoons maple syrup

1 pound close-grained (dense) white sandwich bread

1½ cups pumpkin puree

1¼ cups evaporated milk

1 cup low-sodium chicken broth

¼ cup honey

1 pound vacuum-packed, cooked chestnuts

2 tablespoons cognac

Pantry items you may already have

Onions

Whole milk

Butter

Large eggs

Sugar

Light brown sugar

Flour

Shortening

Lemon juice

Bay leaf

Sage

Thyme

Cinnamon

Ginger

Nutmeg

Cloves

Dry white wine

Making the meal

1. I know you've already fainted from the long shopping list. After you've revived, sit down at a table and make your shopping list. Several components of these recipes can be made way ahead.

   If you're buying a frozen turkey, allow at least two days defrosting time in the refrigerator.

2. Make the piecrusts up to a month ahead and freeze them.
3. The cranberry sauce comes next and can be made a week ahead.
4. Two to three days ahead, prep the stuffing and pumpkin pie filling.
5. Make the Brussels sprouts, the chestnuts, and both pies the day before.
6. The day of, concentrate on the turkey, the squash, and the stew.

   If you have two ovens, you can bake the pies the day of your meal, which is all the better. If you bake the pies the day before, warming the apple pie before serving is a nice touch.

Scaling up or down

- **Oyster Stew:** May be scaled up or down directly.
- **Maple-Glazed Turkey:** You're not going to make, or even find, a 40-pound turkey, so forget about scaling this recipe up. Even if you did find a turkey worthy of feeding an army, it wouldn't cook evenly and wouldn't fit in your oven. So if you need to feed a larger crowd, add another main dish, like a ham. If you want to scale down, a smaller turkey will cook very differently, and you can't follow the directions for the Maple-Glazed Turkey. My suggestion is to make this big turkey and then luxuriate in leftovers. You can always freeze the cooked turkey meat for later use.
- **Bread Stuffing with Sausage, Apples, and Cognac:** May be scaled up or down directly.
- **Glazed Winter Squash:** May be scaled up or down directly.
- **Brussels Sprouts with Chestnuts:** May be scaled up or down directly.
- **Cranberry Sauce:** May be scaled up or down directly.
- **Apple Pie:** May be scaled up directly (making additional pies, not a larger pie).
- **Pumpkin Pie:** May be scaled up directly; same as apple pie.

Christmas Tree Trimming Party for 20 Kids and Parents

Classic Eggnog (Chapter 4)

Kid-Friendly Eggnog × 3(Chapter 4)

* * *

Easy Homemade Gravlax (Chapter 5)

Baked Brie with Roasted Apples (Chapter 5)

Caramelized Onion Dip with Crudité (Chapter 5)

* * *

Classic Sugar Cookies (Chapter 11)

* * *

Cinnamon Stick Votives × 4(Chapter 14)

Candy Garlands and Popcorn Cranberry Garlands each × 4 (Chapter 14)

This menu is perfect for a large party. Invite over your friends and neighbors, kids and adults. Set the materials for the votives and candy garlands on a table for everyone to use. The cookies can be baked and decorated, or leave the decorating to do with the guests as part of the fun. Bake the cookies with small holes so that you can hang them as ornaments; consider letting everyone take a cookie ornament home.

Shopping list

6 medium apples (8 ounces each), such as Cortland or Granny Smith

1⅛ cups chopped fresh dill

2.2 pounds Brie (8-inch wheel)

7 cups heavy cream

1 cup sour cream

4 pounds salmon fillet

Three hundred and eighty-four 3-inch cinnamon sticks

3 cups cranberries

10 slices dark pumpernickel bread

4 loaves French bread

8 juniper berries (optional)

Sugar or colored sugar (optional)

½ cup apple cider

4 cups brandy

2 cups dark rum

2 cups bourbon

¼ cup gin

Assorted vegetables for crudité

Craft items

400 pieces wrapped candy, such as sour balls in cellophane

16 votive candles, cinnamon scented

8 yards strong thread, such as nylon or waxed cotton

16 plain-glass, straight-sided votive holders (1.75 inches across the bottom x 2.5 inches tall)

8 yards thin ribbon (optional)

Glue gun with glue sticks

Needle

Pantry items you may already have

Onions

Whole milk

Butter

Sugar

Light brown sugar

Large eggs

Popcorn

Flour

Vanilla extract

Light olive oil

Lemon juice

Nutmeg

Black peppercorns

Making the meal

1. The sugar cookies, undecorated, can be made one month ahead.
2. The roasted apple component of the baked Brie recipe can be made one week ahead.
3. The onion dip can be made two to three days ahead.
4. The gravlax must be started two to three days ahead.

5. The kid's version of the eggnog can be made one day before.
6. Make the adult eggnog the day of the party and prepare the vegetables for the crudité.
7. Bake the Brie right before your guests arrive.
8. Set out the craft items before your guests arrive.

Scaling up or down

- **Eggnog:** Both versions may be scaled up or down directly.
- **Easy Homemade Gravlax:** May be scaled up or down directly.
- **Baked Brie with Roasted Apples:** You can scale the roasted apples up or down, but the Brie is a whole item and can't be halved or doubled as such.
- **Caramelized Onion Dip with Crudité:** May be scaled up or down directly.
- **Classic Sugar Cookies:** May be scaled up or down directly.
- **Cinnamon Stick Votives:** May be scaled up or down directly.
- **Candy Garland and Popcorn Cranberry Garland:** May be scaled up or down directly.

A White Christmas for 20

Warm White Truffle Bean Dip (Chapter 5)
Caramelized Onion Dip (Chapter 5)
Crudité (assorted vegetables)

* * *

Maple-Glazed Turkey (Chapter 8)
Wild Rice Dressing with Golden Raisins and Pecans (Chapter 9)
Creamed Onions and Mushrooms × 2 (Chapter 9)
Cauliflower Gratin × 3 (Chapter 9)
Spiced Cranberry Relish (Chapter 10)

* * *

White Chocolate Bûche de Noël (Chapter 12)
Pear Almond Trifle (Chapter 12)
Sugar-Frosted Fruit (Chapter 11)
Meringue Wreath Cookies (Chapter 11)

Whether you have snow outside or not, throw a white Christmas party right at your table. The foods present an array of off-white and creamy white hues accented by the red of the cranberry relish.

Shopping list

1 pound mushrooms

1 pound shiitake mushrooms

8 stalks celery

8 sprigs fresh thyme

6 firm, ripe pears (about 7 ounces each), such as Bartlett

5 Granny Smith apples

4 sprigs fresh sage

4 carrots

3 navel oranges

2 pounds assorted fruit, such as lady apples, kumquats, grapes, small lemons, small limes, clementines, or small pears

2 cups cranberries, fresh or frozen

3 heads cauliflower

1 bunch flat-leaf parsley

Assorted vegetables to go with dip

1 cup sour cream

24 ounces Gruyère cheese

6⅔ cups heavy cream

⅔ cup Parmesan cheese

20-pound turkey, preferably fresh

1 pound bulk pork sausage

8 cups low-sodium chicken broth

1 pound close-grained (dense) white sandwich bread

15-ounce can cannelini beans

14½-ounce can sour pitted cherries, water packed

12 ounces white or dark chocolate (optional)

2 cups superfine sugar

1 loaf French bread

¾ pound white chocolate

¾ cup canned crushed pineapple

⅔ cup chopped walnuts

½ cup honey

1½ cups fresh breadcrumbs

¼ cup sliced almonds

3 tablespoons maple syrup

3 tablespoons confectioners sugar

1 tablespoon white truffle oil

White peppercorns

8 cups frozen pearl onions

16-ounce pound cake

12 Amaretti di Saronno cookies (6 wrapped pairs)

¾ cup Di Saronno Amaretto liqueur

2 tablespoons cognac

2 tablespoons kirschwasser liqueur

Pantry items you may already have

Onions

Whole milk

Unsalted butter

Large eggs

All-purpose flour

Cake flour

Sugar

Baking powder

Cream of tartar

Vanilla extract

Nutmeg

Cinnamon

Ginger

Cardamom

Cloves

Light olive oil

Sage

Thyme

Sweet paprika

Bay leaf

Dry white wine

Making the meal

1. The meringue cookies can be made a month ahead of time.
2. The cranberry relish can be made one week ahead.
3. Make the stuffing two to three days ahead, along with the onion dip.
4. The mushrooms and onions can be prepped one day ahead, as can the bûche de Noël and the trifle.
5. On the day of the party, make the turkey, bean dip, cauliflower, and sugared fruit.

Scaling up or down

- **Warm White Truffle Bean Dip:** May be scaled up or down directly.
- **Caramelized Onion Dip with Crudité:** May be scaled up or down directly.
- **Maple-Glazed Turkey:** If you can find a 40-pound turkey and cook it to perfection, let me know! I would love to hear how you did it. Seriously, leave this recipe as is.
- **Wild Rice Dressing with Golden Raisins and Pecans:** May be scaled up or down directly.
- **Creamed Onions and Mushrooms:** May be scaled up or down directly.
- **Cauliflower Gratin:** May be scaled up or down directly.
- **Spiced Cranberry Relish:** May be scaled up or down directly.
- **White Chocolate Bûche de Noël:** You may make a small one by halving the recipe or make two by doubling the recipe, but don't try to make one gigantic bûche de Noël.
- **Pear Almond Trifle:** May be scaled up or down directly; just use a very large glass bowl if you scale up.
- **Sugar Frosted Fruit:** May be scaled up or down directly.
- **Meringue Wreath Cookies:** May be scaled up or down directly.

Open House for 25+

Caramelized Onion Dip with Crudité (Chapter 5)

Whole Roasted Garlic and French Bread (Chapter 5)

Cheddar, Port, and Blue Cheese Ball (Chapter 5)

Shrimp Cocktail with Two Sauces X 2 (Chapter 5)

* * *

The Basic Green Salad X 4 (Chapter 6)

* * *

Baked Fresh Ham with Herbs (Chapter 8)

Five-Cheese Spinach Lasagne X 2 (Chapter 8)

* * *

Basic Yuletide Biscuits X 3 (Chapter 13)

Gingered Pear Sauce X 2 (Chapter 10)

Brussels Sprouts and Chestnuts X 3 (Chapter 9)

* * *

Pear Almond Trifle X 2 (Chapter 12)

Pumpkin Toffee Cheesecake X 2 (Chapter 12)

Chocolate Pecan Pie X 2 (Chapter 12)

Assorted Cookies

Bowl of Clementines

* * *

Classic Eggnog (Chapter 4)

Mulled Cider X 4 (Chapter 4)

Most elements of this menu can be made ahead, leaving the day of the party very manageable. With a few chafing dishes, borrowed or rented, and maybe a warming tray, you can just set the food out and forget about it for the duration of the party. (You've seen chafing dishes before; they're those metal containers that have a heat source beneath them that are often used at buffets.)

This is a large party, and some of the recipes need to be doubled, tripled, and even quadrupled.

Here's the optimum situation: Set the shrimp on ice, slice the ham and set it in a chafing dish, and have the lasagne on a warming tray or in another chafing dish. Bake the biscuits as close as possible to when you serve them. Everything else is fine at room temperature.

Shopping list

24 clementines

20 firm, ripe pears (about 7 ounces each), such as Bartlett

4 navel oranges

4 small heads butter lettuce

3 pounds Brussels sprouts

2 pounds fresh spinach leaves

2 small heads red or green leaf lettuce

2 small heads romaine lettuce

½ cup chopped flat-leaf parsley

¼ cup finely chopped celery

Assorted vegetables for dip

Nine 8-ounce packages cream cheese

8 cups heavy cream

6 cups sour cream

5 ounces sharp cheddar cheese

5 ounces blue cheese

2 pounds mozzarella

2 cups mascarpone

2 cups whole-milk ricotta cheese

1 cup grated Parmesan cheese

1 cup grated Romano cheese

4 pounds large shrimp, shell on (20 to 25 per pound)

14-pound fresh ham, bone in (shank and leg portion of pork)

3 loaves French bread

2 gallons apple cider

2 pounds lasagna noodles

4 cups whole pecans

2½ cups gingersnap crumbs

2½ cups light corn syrup

2 cups pumpkin puree

1½ cups fresh breadcrumbs (4 slices bread)

1 cup toffee bits

1 cup chili sauce

½ cup finely chopped crystallized ginger

½ cup cider

½ cup walnuts

½ cup sliced almonds

¼ cup wasabi powder

¼ cup cornstarch

2 tablespoons horseradish

4 ounces unsweetened chocolate

3 ounces (hefty ½ cup) shortening

32 whole allspice berries

24 whole cloves

Twelve 3-inch cinnamon sticks

Assorted cookies, purchased or homemade

Two 16-ounce pound cakes

10-ounce box frozen chopped spinach

1½ pounds vacuum-packed cooked chestnuts

6 ounces sun-dried tomatoes

24 Amaretti di Saronno cookies (12 wrapped pairs)

4 cups brandy

2 cups dark rum

2 cups bourbon

2 cups Di Saronno Amaretto liqueur

⅔ cups port

¼ cup Kahlua or other coffee liqueur

Pantry items you may already have

Onions
Whole garlic
Unsalted butter
Whole milk
Large eggs
Flour
Sugar
Dark brown sugar
Light brown sugar
Baking powder
Vanilla extract
Extra-virgin olive oil
Light olive oil
Lemon juice
Mayonnaise
Dijon mustard
Black peppercorns
Bay leaf
Thyme
Sage
Cinnamon
Ginger
Allspice
Nutmeg
Soy sauce
Dry red wine

Making the meal

1. Make the lasagne and piecrust up to a month ahead and freeze.
2. One week ahead, make the pear sauce.
3. Four to five days ahead, make the cheese ball.
4. The onion dip can be made two to three days ahead. You can prepare the salad now too.
5. The day before the party, prepare the shrimp, Brussels sprouts, trifle, and cheesecake and defrost the lasagne. Bake the chocolate pecan pies if you won't have oven space on the day of the party.
6. On the day of the party, make the roasted garlic, ham, biscuits, eggnog, and mulled cider and bake the lasagne.

Scaling up or down

- **Caramelized Onion Dip with Crudité:** May be scaled up or down directly.
- **Whole Roasted Garlic and French Bread:** May be scaled up or down directly.
- **Cheddar, Port, and Blue Cheese Ball:** May be scaled up or down directly.
- **Shrimp Cocktail with Two Sauces:** May be scaled up or down directly.
- **The Basic Green Salad:** May be scaled up or down directly.

- **Baked Fresh Ham with Herbs:** Keep this recipe as is or make two of them. You'll need two ovens to bake two.
- **Five-Cheese Spinach Lasagne:** Don't make a larger one; make two if you need the volume. You can halve the recipe.
- **Biscuits:** May be scaled up or down directly.
- **Gingered Pear Sauce:** May be scaled up or down directly.
- **Brussels Sprouts with Chestnuts:** May be scaled up or down directly.
- **Pear Almond Trifle:** May be scaled up or down directly; just use a very large glass bowl if you scale up.
- **Pumpkin Toffee Cheesecake:** May be scaled up, making additional cakes, not a larger cake.
- **Chocolate Pecan Pie:** May be scaled up, making additional pies, not a larger pie.
- **Classic Eggnog:** May be scaled up or down directly.
- **Mulled Cider:** May be scaled up or down directly.

Dessert Party for 50

White Chocolate Bûche de Noël (Chapter 12)

Pear Almond Trifle × 2 (Chapter 12)

Eggnog Ice Cream in an Ice Bowl × 2 (Chapter 11)

Chocolate Truffle Tart × 2 (Chapter 12)

Cranberry Cherry Tart × 2 (Chapter 12)

Apple Pie × 2 (Chapter 2)

Pumpkin Pie × 2 (Chapter 12)

Christmas Pudding with Rum Cream (Chapter 12)

Cookie and Truffle Platter — purchased or homemade

Bowl of Clementines

When it comes to dessert, the more the merrier! Make a whole bunch of desserts and invite over a whole bunch of friends. Pour some champagne, offer coffee, if you like, and have a blast. To make this party as easy as possible to throw, use paper or plastic plates and utensils. I draw the line at plastic champagne glasses, though — I say don't use 'em. Rent glass ones if you can.

Shopping list

24 clementines

12 apples, a mixture of Cortland and Golden Delicious

12 firm, ripe pears (about 7 ounces each), such as Bartlett

4 cups fresh or frozen cranberries

Lemon slices, cranberries, and kumquat slices (optional)

12½ cups heavy cream

6 ounces (hefty 1 cup) shortening

4½ cups canned pitted sour cherries, water packed (three 14½-ounce cans)

4 cups chocolate cookie crumbs

3 cups fresh white breadcrumbs (8 slices bread)

3 cups pumpkin puree

2½ pounds bittersweet chocolate

2½ cups evaporated milk

1½ pounds white chocolate

1 cup raisins

½ cup golden raisins

½ cup dried cherries

½ cup diced dried figs

½ cup diced dried apricots

½ cup sliced almonds

¼ cup chopped candied orange peel

¼ cup orange juice

¼ cup honey

¼ cup cornstarch

3 tablespoons confectioners sugar

Cookies and truffles, purchased or homemade

Two 16-ounce pound cakes

24 Amaretti di Saronno cookies (6 wrapped pairs)

1 cup dark rum

1 cup Di Saronno Amaretto liqueur

2 tablespoons kirschwasser liqueur

Pantry items you may already have

Unsalted butter

Whole milk

Large eggs

Sugar

Light brown sugar

All-purpose flour

Cake flour

Baking powder

Lemon juice

Vanilla extract

Cinnamon

Ginger

Nutmeg

Cloves

Making the meal

1. Make the piecrusts a month ahead and freeze them.
2. The ice bowl for the ice cream can be made four to five days ahead.
3. You can churn the eggnog ice cream two to three days ahead.
4. The bûche de Noël and trifle can be assembled the day before; make the steamed pudding the day before too. If you want, you can make the pumpkin pie filling now as well.
5. The day of your party, make the truffle and cranberry tarts, bake the pies, and whip the cream for the steamed pudding.

Scaling up or down

- **White Chocolate Bûche de Noël:** You may make a small one by halving the recipe or make two by doubling the recipe, but don't try to make one gigantic one or to multiply it any more than that.
- **Pear Almond Trifle:** May be scaled up or down directly; just use a very large glass bowl.
- **Eggnog Ice Cream in an Ice Bowl:** Most likely, your ice cream machine will not be able to handle double the amount, but you can always double the ice cream mixture and then freeze it in two batches. If your freezer can handle an extra-large ice bowl, go for it. Otherwise, make one as directed and just refill the bowl with balls of ice cream as it's depleted.
- **Chocolate Truffle Tart:** You can make double the crust at one time and then press it into two tart pans. The filling can be doubled and then divided into the two pans.
- **Cranberry Cherry Tart:** The sweet tart crust recipe already makes enough for two tarts. The filling can be doubled and then divided between the crusts.
- **Steamed Pudding:** You can double this recipe, but you'll need two molds and two steaming setups. It can be halved, but you'll need a smaller mold, and you're on your own as to steaming time.
- **Apple Pie:** May be scaled up directly (making additional pies, not a larger pie).
- **Pumpkin Pie:** May be scaled up directly; same as apple pie.

Part II

Holiday Meals: Opening Acts

"At 1700 hours position yourselves along the perimeter of the living room. As they enter we'll hit them with the nuts and bread sticks. At 1750 hours Dolores will move to their right flank and advance with the drinks, driving them from the kitchen. As they weaken from dancing we'll cut off their supplies and force them into the driveway."

In this part . . .

Well, you've got to start somewhere. Why not the beginning? This part has what I call the "opening acts" — drinks, appetizers, salads, and soups. Look here for ideas on how to get your party, large or small, off to a great start.

Chapter 4

Drinks, Anyone?

In This Chapter

- Stocking the bar for your holiday get-togethers
- Pairing wine with food
- Buying and serving champagne
- Brewing coffee and tea
- Indulging in smoothies
- Fixing the traditional ciders, chocolates, and eggnog

Recipes in This Chapter

- Orange–Passion Fruit Mimosas
- Champagne Punch
- Café Brûlot
- Irish Coffee
- Fruit Smoothies
- Mulled Cider
- Classic Eggnog
- Kid-Friendly Eggnog
- Hot White Chocolate
- Bittersweet Hot Chocolate

We often think exclusively of foods when we plan menus, but the appropriate beverage can make all the difference. In fact, in some situations the beverage of choice takes center stage — think of the steaming cup of cocoa on Christmas morning or the perfect wine that complements your fancy holiday dinner.

In this chapter, I talk about the beverages, both nonalcoholic and alcoholic, that you should have in your holiday repertoire. Most holiday parties, large or small, are a conglomeration of young and old, teetotalers and those who appreciate fine wine. You need to be prepared with a variety of drinks.

The advantage of the drinks in this chapter is that they can enhance your meals and get-togethers considerably, yet they're easy to make. So get out your liquid measuring cups and whip up a smoothie or a sophisticated champagne drink.

Setting Up a Beverage Bar

Certain do's and don'ts exist when it comes to providing the proper beverages for guests. You should have a selection of both alcoholic and nonalcoholic drinks on hand, and by "nonalcoholic" I mean more than water!

On the alcoholic side of the bar, perhaps you just want to serve wine and no hard alcohol. That's one way to go, and it keeps things much simpler. Have at least one white wine and one red wine. Beer is always popular, and having regular as well as light beer is quite generous. If you want to offer champagne, there will always be takers.

If you do want to offer hard-alcohol choices, you don't have to be outfitted like the town pub. Have one light alcohol, like gin or vodka, and one dark alcohol, like scotch or bourbon. Add club soda, tonic, maybe some lemon or lime twists, and ice to the mix and call it a day.

When it comes to nonalcoholic choices, I have a bone to pick: Too many hosts offer sparkling water, and that's it. I end up with a dry evening, and I'm not the only one. So make sure that you have still water, sparkling water, a basic soda, like a cola, and at least one juice, such as orange or cranberry. This way, you'll be covered for the likes of me, and any kids, too.

Always have a pitcher of still water available, either good-quality tap water or bottled water. Plain water is the world's most popular beverage, so you will be able to make many guests happy.

Here's what your beverage selection should look like for a holiday gathering:

Nonalcoholic	***Alcoholic***
Water	Red wine
Sparkling water	White wine
Cola	Beer, regular and light
Fruit juice (100%, not a "fruit drink")	Champagne, if you like
	Light alcohol, like gin or vodka (optional)
	Dark alcohol, like scotch or bourbon (optional)

Buying wine and beer

If you don't have a regular liquor store that you go to for wines, ask around for recommendations. Word-of-mouth can help you find a reputable wine merchant. If you enjoyed a bottle at a friend's house, ask your friend where he shops. There are also online services that offer great deals and helpful information. Sometimes shipping is free or at a flat rate, and the wine is delivered right to your door. Some states have restrictions for ordering alcohol by mail; any of the Internet sites will be able to tell you whether you can order wine and have it delivered.

Designated drivers

Sometimes people overindulge in spirited drinks. At holiday time, letting your guard down is all too easy. So please, as part of being a host who looks out for your guests' enjoyment and well-being, do not let anyone who is intoxicated drive home. Keep the phone numbers of a local cab company handy and arrange for intoxicated guests to be driven home. Or ask a family member to drive the guest home. If you have a spare couch or bedroom, consider letting the person spend the night.

What should you pay for wine? As much as you want. If budget is an issue (and if you're buying prime rib for $100, you're already broke), most wine experts agree that a good bottle can be found in the $10 to $15 range. Find a reputable liquor store and become friends with the staff, who can offer much guidance. If you're buying a case, ask for a case discount. That should take at least 10 percent off the price of the wine.

For beer, search out local breweries; they're cropping up all over the place. They usually have a variety of interesting brews, with the advantage usually being that they're made to the demanding standards of the independent brewmaster. If no breweries are nearby, ask your liquor-store owner for suggestions. They may carry a few regional brands.

Buying champagne

For the purposes of the two recipes in this chapter that use champagne, you don't have to break the bank on your champagne purchases. However, as when cooking with wine, you do want to use a bottle that you would enjoy drinking straight.

True champagne is from the Champagne region of France and is made according to the *méthod champenoise*. However, many domestic American, Spanish, and Italian sparkling wines fit the bill quite well. Look for *brut* champagne, which is the least sweet, for these recipes.

You should be able to find a standard-sized 750 ml bottle of champagne for about $10. Here are some other available sizes (I doubt you'll ever need this info, but it's fun):

- Split = ¼ bottle
- Half = ½ bottle
- Magnum = 2 bottles

- Jeroboam = 4 bottles
- Rehoboam = 6 bottles
- Methuselah = 8 bottles
- Salamanzar = 12 bottles
- Balthazar = 16 bottles
- Nebuchadnezzar = 20 bottles (a lot of money, and you better be strong enough to lift it)

Properly chilling wine, champagne, and beer

There's more to chilling wine, champagne, and beer than just sticking it in the refrigerator. Generally, if you buy something cold, you want to keep it cold and drink it fairly soon. Allowing these beverages to chill, warm, and chill again is likely to degrade the quality.

Here are the details on chilling temperatures for beer, wine, and champagne:

- **Beer:** Most beers should be chilled to 45 degrees; a warmer 60 to 65 degrees is best for stout. Americans tend to like their beers colder than Europeans do — let your own taste buds be your guide.
- **Wine and champagne:** Wines are served at a variety of temperatures. In general, hearty reds should be chilled to 55 to 65 degrees, with lighter reds, like Beaujolais, a bit cooler. White wines, dessert wines, and champagnes should be chilled to 35 to 50 degrees.

Pairing Wine with Christmas Foods

A trip to the liquor store can be overwhelming, but you don't have to have a personal sommelier at your side to make decisions about matching wine with food. Holiday foods tend to be rich and full-flavored, so I have edited the choices down to a few that are surefire:

- **Beaujolais:** This light-bodied red wine is easy to drink; even white wine lovers enjoy it. It has a fruity aroma and pairs perfectly with holiday turkey or pasta dishes. It also works well on a buffet that includes a variety of foods.

  Beaujolais Nouveau is a fresh batch of seven- to nine-week-old wine that's released every third Thursday of November. (Beaujolais being a French product, the French government controls this date.) Many fans eagerly await this day, because these young wines are at their peak when released. So head to the store around Thanksgiving and grab a few bottles to serve over the holidays.

- **Zinfandel:** This California red wine has many fans — so many that it has earned the nickname "Zin." It is a heavier wine with full flavor and a high alcohol content. (Don't confuse Zinfandel with White Zinfandel, which is a light, sweet blush wine made from the same grapes.) It works with turkey, ham, roast beef, and any spicy foods you might be serving.
- **Cabernet Sauvignon:** Here's another red wine with a nickname. When you hear someone speaking of a "Cab," they may not be talking about hailing a ride. This wine is produced both domestically and as an import from France, Italy, Australia, South Africa, and Chile. Cabernets can be medium- to full-bodied and, while rich, can have fruity overtones. This wine goes well with full-flavored foods such as ham, roast beef, duck, and strong cheeses.
- **Pinot Noir:** Another red wine that's quite flexible and goes with the multiple layers of flavors presented at a holiday table. It is smooth and bright and pairs beautifully with turkey recipes.
- **Pinot Grigio:** This Italian white wine is identical to the French Pinot Gris. It is easy to drink, even during the cocktail hour when you may or may not be nibbling. It is clear and refeshing and can cut through many holiday foods.
- **Sauvignon Blanc:** This dry white wine is best suited to the holiday's full-flavored dishes. It is produced all over the world, usually has a light to medium body, and can be quite acidic. It's a good basic white to offer throughout the season.
- **Dessert wines and liqueurs:** This area can even intimidate those who are well versed in the main course reds and whites. Try a port or a Sauternes or ask the wine merchant for something called Muscat Beaumes-de-Venise, which is a very special sweet wine with a wonderful floral flavor. You could also try a clear fruit-based eau de vie, such as blackberry or apple. Offering a dessert wine either with, after, or in place of dessert can set your dinner apart from just another meal.

Are you still confused? Then just go to a reputable wine merchant and tell him that you need help. That's what he's there for! Explain your menu, and you should be guided to just what you need.

Remember, too, that rules are made to be broken. Many experts drink red wine with fish, which you may have heard is a no-no. Follow your instincts, and serve wines that you enjoy.

Hard cider may not be the first thing that comes to mind when you're thinking about what drinks to offer, but its flavor goes beautifully with many holiday foods. Hard cider is sweet cider that has been allowed to ferment. Varieties range from soft and sweet to hard and dry, but any which way, cider's inherent fruitiness will be a welcome surprise for the adventurous drinkers in the crowd. Try it with turkey, stuffing, and cranberry sauce.

Selecting a wineglass

Believe it or not, the choice of wineglass affects your ability to appreciate a wine. Tasting wine involves all the senses. With a clear glass, you can enjoy the wine's color; faceted goblets distract from your visual enjoyment. With a thin glass, no bulky rim gets between you and the beverage. A wineglass with a slightly narrower opening than its bowl concentrates the aromas and funnels them right up into your nose (see Figure 4-1).

Figure 4-1: A flute-shaped glass (left) is the best choice for serving sparkling wines. A large-bowl glass (right) provides headroom for the bouquet. A smaller glass (center) works fine with white wine.

Pouring the right amount of wine

You may want to maximize the volume of your glass, but don't be tempted. A wineglass should seldom be filled more than halfway. This leaves enough headroom to release the wine's *bouquet,* or aroma.

Serving Champagne

Something about sparkling clear champagne glasses filled with effervescent, pale gold champagne is exciting and festive. Here are some tips for opening a champagne bottle and proper chilling and serving.

Opening a champagne bottle

I hope that you're lucky enough to be faced with opening a bottle of champagne during the holiday season. There's a safe and easy way to do it, and then there are reckless ways. The cork can pop out of the bottle at a tremendous speed and inflict damage — not the best way to start a party.

To open a champagne bottle correctly, take a look at Figure 4-2 and follow these steps:

1. **Remove the outer foil covering.**
2. **Untwist the metal cage, holding one hand over the top.**
3. **Remove the cage, immediately placing one hand on the top of the cork.**

   Note that some champagne producers, such as Domaine Chandon, are now telling consumers not to remove the cage (but to remove it along with the cork) to avoid any possibility of the cork flying out.

   This is when the cork can fly. Make sure to keep one hand on top of the cork, and keep the bottle pointed away from guests and family.
4. **Grasp the cork firmly with one hand and twist the bottle with the other.**

   That's right, twist the bottle instead of the cork.
5. **Ease the cork out of the bottle with as small a "pop" as possible.**

   The bubbles that make champagne special are made from carbon dioxide, and you don't want them to exit the bottle in an explosion.

Now you're ready to pour!

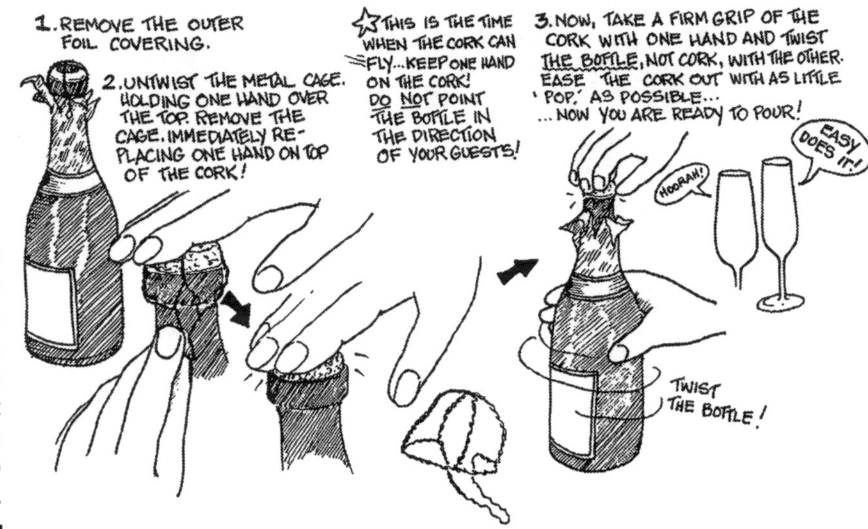

Figure 4-2: How to open champagne without sending the cork into orbit.

Serving champagne straight

Later in this section, I give you some options for blending champagne with other ingredients to make festive drinks, but sometimes serving champagne straight is the most elegant option. Here's what you need to know:

- Make sure that the champagne is chilled thoroughly — it should be at 35 to 50 degrees.
- Figure on five glasses per 750 ml bottle.
- Use flute glasses, which funnel the aroma to the nose and accentuate the bubbles.
- Fill each glass two-thirds full.
- When you drink, hold the stem of the glass, not the bowl. If you hold the bowl, your fingers will warm the champagne.

Don't use those saucer-shaped glasses to serve champagne. The bubbles have a short trip to the surface, so they dissipate quickly, and the lovely aroma will be dispersed into the air.

Making champagne drinks

Straight champagne in a glass works for many occasions, but sometimes you want to be able to extend the bottle to serve more people or just have fun with adding other flavors. Here are two champagne drink recipes.

Orange–Passion Fruit Mimosas

This beverage is ideal for Mom and Dad to enjoy on Christmas morning. You can easily double or even quadruple this recipe if you're having a lot of adults over. One 750 ml bottle of champagne is equal to four splits.

Preparation time: *5 minutes*

Yield: *2 servings*

⅓ cup fresh-squeezed orange juice

2 tablespoons passion fruit–cranberry liqueur (such as Alizé Red Passion)

1 split brut champagne, chilled

Pour half of the juice and 1 tablespoon of the liqueur into each champagne flute. Top with the champagne and serve.

Per serving: *Calories 132; Fat 0g (Saturated 0g); Cholesterol 0mg; Sodium 6mg; Carbohydrate 11g (Dietary Fiber 0g); Protein 0g.*

Kiddie champagne

Christmas is a family holiday, and the kids want to get into the action. If you're serving pâté and they want a taste, why not? Maybe their palates will be expanded and they'll discover the joys of a delicacy. Or they'll think it's disgusting, and you'll still have the whole plate for yourself. You win either way.

Here's a surefire way to thrill the kiddies: Pick up a bottle of nonalcoholic sparkling grape juice or sparkling cider. It's just like champagne, but without the alcohol kick.

If the adults are toasting with champagne, pour some sparkling juice for the kids. If you're worried about them handling your fine crystal flutes, pick up some plastic champagne glasses and everybody's happy.

Champagne Punch

This punch is a great and delicious way to extend a bottle of champagne. It's perfect for a large gathering.

Preparation time: *5 minutes*

Yield: *12 servings*

1¼ cup Grand Marnier, chilled

1 cup cranberry juice, chilled

1 cup fresh-squeezed orange juice, chilled

1 quart ginger ale, chilled

Two 750-ml bottles or 1 magnum brut champagne, chilled

Combine all the ingredients in a large punch bowl and serve immediately.

Tip: *Grand Marnier is an orange brandy liqueur and can be pricey. You can substitute less-expensive Triple Sec with decent results; the punch will be a bit weaker.*

Going All Out: *An ice ring will keep the punch cold and look good doing it. Simply fill any kind of ring mold or bundt mold that will fit in the punch bowl with a mixture of orange juice and cranberry juice and freeze. Place the ice ring in the punch just before serving.*

Per serving: *Calories 217; Fat 0g (Saturated 0g); Cholesterol 0mg; Sodium 14mg; Carbohydrate 24g (Dietary Fiber 0g); Protein 0g.*

Making Great Coffee

You've got to be able to brew a great pot of coffee; coffee comes in handy for breakfast, after lunch or dinner, and for those so inclined, anytime during the day. During the holidays, whether it is at the end of the Christmas Eve meal or for Christmas Day breakfast, offering a great pot of coffee is a gracious gesture.

Buying the right kind of coffee

Yes, you can buy a can of preground coffee at the supermarket, but if you want to make the best possible cup of coffee, start with whole beans. Many supermarkets sell whole beans in bulk, but you may have to go to a specialty store to find them. Many varieties exist; a breakfast blend, which is usually a combination of dark and light roast beans, is a good place to start and makes a fine cup any time of day.

Make sure that your coffee is ground to the proper consistency. If you're making coffee via the drip method, which I explain how to do later in this section, a medium grind is fine.

If you don't own a coffee grinder or don't want to buy one, buy beans that are ground right before you buy them or buy the beans and grind them in the store.

Storing coffee

Whether you buy whole beans or have the beans ground on the spot, store the coffee in an airtight container. If you plan to use it within the week, store it at room temperature. If you need to store it for longer, pop it in the freezer. Placing coffee in the refrigerator will retard spoiling, but the freezer halts it altogether. The pros tell me that freezer burn is a worthwhile tradeoff, as you fight the degradation that occurs otherwise. Coffee's enemies are oxygen and moisture. The trick is to buy fresh, small batches and use them quickly.

Brewing coffee

You can brew coffee in many ways, but the drip method is my favorite. You need a coffeepot, a filter cone, and a filter to fit the cone. Then follow these steps:

1. **Fit the cone on top of the pot with the filter inside.**

   Whether you use a paper filter or a reusable gold filter is a matter of personal preference.

   - With paper, you have a choice of bleached or unbleached. The bleached ones are less expensive, but some connoisseurs claim that they can detect a chemical residue in the coffee that ruins their enjoyment. You can find unbleached filters alongside the bleached versions in supermarkets.
   - A gold filter (really 23 karat gold–covered plastic) can be used for years, which to many people is even more ecologically sound. It also makes a completely different cup of coffee. Paper filters absorb some of the coffee's essential oils, whereas gold filters pass them on into your pot along with a very fine sediment. Some people prefer this, and some find the taste muddy. You decide.

2. **Measure the ground coffee into the filter.**

   The proper proportion of coffee to water is crucial. Here's the formula for a strong cup of coffee: 2 tablespoons of ground coffee beans to 6 ounces of water. (Note that this is not 1 cup of water, which is 8 ounces.)

If you like stronger or weaker coffee, adjust the measurements accordingly.

3. **Slowly pour boiling water over the grounds.**

   You need good water to make good coffee, and the water from your tap may not be good enough. If your water is highly chlorinated or heavily mineralized, your coffee will have off-flavors. Use a water filter or buy bottled water. Don't use distilled water, which makes the coffee taste flat.

   As for temperature, most experts agree that water just under a boil — 195 degrees to 205 degrees — is ideal. You accomplish this by bringing the water to a boil, removing it from the heat, and then waiting a few seconds before pouring it over your grounds.

The brewed coffee drips down into the pot, which is how the drip method got its name. If you drip it into a vacuum pot, the coffee will stay warm for a long time; this is the method of heat retention that most coffee aficionados prefer. If you drip it into a heatproof glass pot, you can place the pot on a flame tamer over very low heat to keep it warm.

A *flame tamer* is a heatproof flat surface device that goes between your heat source and whatever you're protecting from the direct heat. It allows a coffeepot, for instance, to be heated on the stove while reducing the risk of the pot overheating and breaking.

Serving coffee to a crowd

If you need to serve coffee to a crowd of two dozen or more, chances are your home coffeepot won't be large enough. Rather than brewing several pots of coffee, which invariably will cool before your guests can drink it, consider renting a large-capacity coffeepot to use for your get-together. Rental companies usually have at least two sizes available. The company near me has 30-, 55-, 90-, and 100-cup sizes, so I'm prepared for anything.

These pots for rent are usually percolators — not my favorite way of brewing coffee, but it gets the job done. The rental company should be able to supply you with operating instructions, which will include how much coffee and water to use.

Making coffee drinks

Once you know how to make a great cup of coffee, making delicious coffee drinks is easy. With a few extra ingredients and a minimum of fuss, you can offer your holiday guests delicious, warming, and spirited drinks. The drinks that follow are for adults only, as they contain alcohol.

Café Brûlot (flaming brandy coffee)

Orange, cinnamon, and brandy flavors liven up this coffee drink. *Brûlot* means "burnt brandy." This recipe makes enough for a party.

Preparation time: *5 minutes*

Yield: *10 to 12 servings*

3 tablespoons sugar

Zest of 1 orange, cut into thin strips. (See Figure 4-3.)

One 3-inch cinnamon stick

1 vanilla bean

1½ cups brandy

6 cups brewed, hot, strong black coffee

1 Place the sugar, zest, cinnamon stick, and vanilla bean in a large heatproof bowl.

2 In a small pot, heat the brandy over low heat until warm. Pour over the ingredients and ignite carefully by holding a lit match close to the alcohol until it ignites.

3 Douse the flames by pouring the coffee over the brandy mixture. Stir, remove the zest and vanilla bean, and serve immediately.

Per serving: *Calories 48; Fat 0g (Saturated 0g); Cholesterol 0mg; Sodium 3mg; Carbohydrate 4g (Dietary Fiber 0g); Protein 0g.*

ZESTING AN ORANGE
USE A VEGETABLE PEELER TO REMOVE THE OUTER, ORANGE COLORED LAYER ONLY. NOT THE BITTER WHITE PITH!
CUT LARGE PIECES OF ZEST INTO THIN STRIPS!

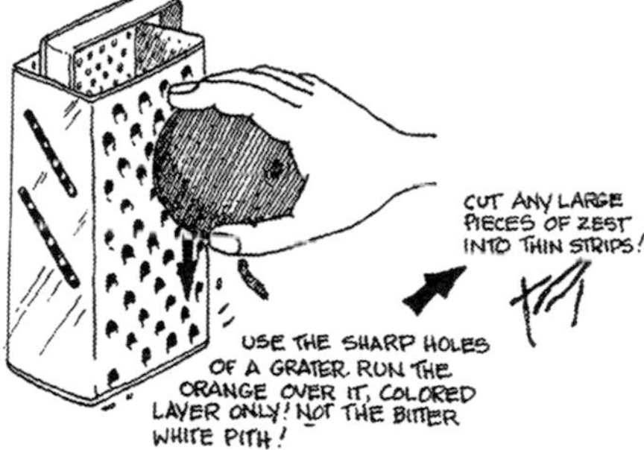

ZESTING AN ORANGE
CUT ANY LARGE PIECES OF ZEST INTO THIN STRIPS!
USE THE SHARP HOLES OF A GRATER. RUN THE ORANGE OVER IT, COLORED LAYER ONLY! NOT THE BITTER WHITE PITH!

Figure 4-3: Two ways to zest an orange.

Irish Coffee

The flavors of coffee, Irish whiskey, and cream combine to make this classic coffee drink. Make sure that your cups or glass mugs are heatproof!

Preparation time: *5 minutes*

Yield: *6 servings*

1 cup heavy cream

2 tablespoons sugar

4 cups brewed, hot, strong black coffee

4 jiggers Irish whiskey

Whipped cream

1 In a medium-sized bowl, whip the heavy cream and sugar until stiff peaks form.

2 Pour the hot coffee into mugs, add a jigger of whisky to each mug, and top with whipped cream.

Tip: *A jigger is a term used in drink making and is equivalent to 1½ ounces of liquid.*

Per serving: *Calories 222 (From Fat 135); Fat 15g (Saturated 9g); Cholesterol 54mg; Sodium 18mg; Carbohydrate 6g (Dietary Fiber 0g); Protein 1g.*

Many different liqueurs can enhance coffee. To 6 ounces of brewed coffee, try adding di Saronno Amaretto, Grand Marnier, Kahlua, or Irish Cream. You can combine liqueurs as well. Coffee (Kahlua) and orange (Grand Marnier) are great together. Let your imagination soar.

Brewing a Proper Pot of Tea

Did you know that after water, tea is the most commonly drunk beverage in the world? I am a tea lover, and while the United States has been catching up with the rest of the world in its per capita tea consumption, most of that tea is the bottled, presweetened variety, which contains all kinds of additives. Brewing a proper pot of tea is not something that the average American learns to do, but I'm here to help you along. It may not become your daily cup of tea, so to speak, but Christmas morning or afternoon is the perfect time to indulge in a cup for yourself or to offer tea to friends and family.

Black tea can make a bracing cup in the morning and take the place of coffee on occasion — or, if you're like me, it is your everyday hot beverage. Brewed black tea tastes nothing like a cup made with a teabag. I also want you to consider green tea, which has become very popular throughout the United

States due to its proven health benefits. Green tea contains antioxidants, which fight free radicals, which have been blamed for cell damage and some cancers. It also reputedly has antibacterial effects.

For either type of tea, look for loose, bulk tea at a specialty store. Buying in bulk is the most economical way to buy tea — you can just buy a tiny amount, which sets you back only a couple of bucks. Make sure that the store has high product turnover. At the very least, smell the tea. Regardless of the type, it should have a bright aroma.

Store loose tea in an opaque, airtight container, away from heat but at room temperature.

Brewing black tea

As with coffee, you need good water to brew black tea. Your tea will be only as good as your water source. You also need a pot and some sort of *infuser* — a device that you insert into the pot to hold the tea leaves (see Figure 4-4). Some pots come with a ceramic or mesh infuser or you can buy one separately. Make sure that it fits the pot. I use a cotton "sock" designed for the task. The purpose of the infuser is to let you remove the leaves when the steeping is done so that the tea doesn't become oversteeped and bitter.

Figure 4-4: Three kinds of tea infusers.

Decide how many 6-ounce cups of tea you want to make, and then follow these steps:

1. **Place the exact amount of cold water — 6 ounces per cup — in a clean pot and bring it to a boil.**
2. **Meanwhile, preheat your teapot with hot tap water.**
3. **Measure approximately 1½ teaspoon of loose tea per 6-ounce serving and place the tea in your infuser.**
4. **Empty your teapot, insert the infuser, and, when the tea water comes to a boil, pour water over the infuser. Immediately set a timer for 4 minutes.**
5. **After the brewing time has finished, remove the infuser and serve the tea.**

Note that these measurements and steeping times are approximate. After you try a pot, you'll know whether you want the tea a bit stronger or less strong. It's all a matter of trial and error. There are variables: the type of tea and your individual preference.

Brewing green tea

To brew green tea, follow the directions for black tea, but heat the water to only 150 degrees. Steep for only two to three minutes, as green tea can develop bitterness. As with black teas, you will learn through trial and error how long to steep your tea. Green tea is traditionally taken without sweetener, milk, or lemon.

Making Smoothies to Order

Smoothies are a great breakfast drink. If they're made without any alcohol, as most are, they will make the kids feel special while the adults are sipping champagne drinks. I for one, am a forty-year-old kid and would probably join in on the smoothie drinking.

One thing I love about smoothies is that they really are the quintessential nonrecipe recipe. What I mean is that most any combination of frozen fruit and liquid or yogurt makes a luscious frozen drink. Try the following concoctions:

- Frozen bananas, cold brewed coffee, soymilk or milk, and sugar to taste
- Cranberry juice, orange juice, and frozen raspberries (plus a splash of Grand Marnier, perhaps)
- Mango nectar, frozen pineapple, and fresh strawberries or raspberries
- Vanilla yogurt, frozen blueberries, orange juice, and a bit of honey
- Coffee yogurt, brewed coffee, frozen bananas, and chocolate syrup

You can also add brewed, chilled green tea to any fruit smoothie. The sky's the limit!

Fruit Smoothies

You need to freeze the fruit for this recipe overnight, so plan accordingly. Please try the soymilk variation at least once; it's creamy and yummy and is the only soy-based thing my kids like. It gives you a nutritional boost and tastes great at the same time.

Preparation time: *5 minutes*

Yield: *2 servings*

4 frozen peach slices (or use canned peaches packed in fruit juice, drained, placed in a resealable bag, and frozen)

1 large banana, peeled, placed in a resealable bag, and frozen

¼ cup frozen raspberries (or use fresh raspberries placed in a resealable bag and frozen)

¾ cup orange juice (plus extra as needed)

¾ cup vanilla soymilk or vanilla yogurt

1 Place all the ingredients in a blender. Process on low speed, increasing to high until blended, smooth, and creamy. Add more juice if necessary to achieve the right consistency.

2 Pour into two tall glasses and serve immediately.

Tip: *To make an all-fruit version, just add extra orange juice in place of the soymilk or yogurt. You could blend juices too and try cranberry juice along with the orange juice.*

Per serving: *Calories 197 (From Fat 18g); Fat 2g (Saturated 0g); Cholesterol 0mg; Sodium 37mg; Carbohydrate 43g (Dietary Fiber 3g); Protein 4g.*

Warming Down to Your Toes with Mulled Cider

Nothing warms you up faster than a steaming cup of hot cider. The aroma fills the house and just says "Christmas."

Read labels and try cider from a local orchard. A green market or farmer's market is a good place to find cider in late fall. You can buy half-gallons, remove an inch or two off the top to allow for expansion upon freezing, and freeze them right in their own plastic containers. Take them out and defrost to enjoy at Christmas time. Defrost completely and shake before serving.

Mulled Cider

Make sure to use cider and not apple juice in this recipe — cider has a much richer flavor and more body. Give this drink to the kids on a cold winter morning while you're sipping coffee or after a day of sledding. It's also perfect to offer guests as they arrive for a Christmas party.

Special equipment: *Cheesecloth, string*

Preparation time: *5 minutes*

Cooking time: *25 minutes*

Yield: *8 servings*

8 whole allspice berries

6 whole cloves

Three 3-inch cinnamon sticks

8 cups apple cider

1 navel orange, peel on, scrubbed, sliced, and seeded

2 to 4 tablespoons sugar (optional)

1 Place the allspice berries, cloves, and cinnamon sticks in a piece of cheesecloth and tie with string to make an enclosed bag (see Figure 4-5).

2 Place the cider in a large nonreactive pot and add the spice bag and orange slices.

3 Bring to a boil over medium heat, reduce the heat to low, and simmer gently for 20 minutes to develop the flavors. Taste and add sugar, if desired. Pour into heatproof glasses or mugs.

Tip: *A nonreactive pot is one that does not react with acidic foods. Stainless steel and tempered glass are examples of nonreactive materials. Aluminum is reactive and should not be used in a recipe like this. Have you ever seen aluminum pots discolor? This is probably because something acidic was cooked in them, like tomato sauce. What is happening is that tiny bits of aluminum are actually being eaten away by the acid and leaching into the food.*

Simplify: *If you don't have cheesecloth, simply place the allspice, cloves, and cinnamon sticks directly in the pot of cider along with the orange slices and strain before serving.*

Going All Out: *For the adults in the crowd, add a couple of tablespoons of apple brandy to each mug.*

Per serving: *Calories 127; Fat 0g (Saturated Fat 0g); Cholesterol 0mg; Sodium 25mg; Carbohydrate 32g (Dietary Fiber 0g); Protein 0g.*

Understanding the difference between cider and apple juice

Although cider and apple juice can be substituted for one another in a pinch, they are totally different beverages.

- **Filtered apple juice** is usually quite processed and is a clear, light golden-brown color. It has a mild apple flavor and is often found bottled on supermarket shelves or as frozen concentrate. Unfiltered apple juice is also available. It is not clear.
- **Cider** is a less-processed drink, sometimes only going through pasteurization, and sometimes not even that. It is a rich, red-tinged brown opaque liquid with much more body on the tongue than apple juice. You usually find it fresh in the supermarket's refrigerated section.

Figure 4-5: Bagging spices for mulled cider.

For a party, stud a few lady apples with cloves and float them in your punch bowl for a decorative look. You could also use cinnamon sticks as stirrers.

Making Eggnog — Traditional and Kid-Friendly

Eggnog is traditionally a very alcohol-rich drink, but many kids like the flavor of a "virgin" version, so I offer both in this section. In its original fortified form, eggnog goes down easy, so make sure that you have designated drivers among your guests if you serve the "real" kind.

Commercial eggnog is available, and I've even seen low-calorie versions, but both pale next to homemade. If you've never had the real thing, try it at least once. My suggestion is to treat eggnog like an indulgence; don't substitute skim milk or try to lighten it up. It's rich in calories, and the original version is rich in alcohol, but either way, a sip of eggnog will put you in the Christmas spirit.

Classic Eggnog

This eggnog version is alcohol rich for the adults in the crowd. This recipe makes a large amount, perfect for an open house party. Feel free to cut the recipe in half.

Preparation time: *15 minutes*

Yield: *30 to 40 servings*

12 large eggs, separated (see Figure 4-6)

1½ cups sugar

4 cups brandy

2 cups dark rum

2 cups bourbon

1 quart whole milk

1 quart heavy cream, softly whipped

Freshly grated nutmeg

1 Whip the egg whites until soft peaks form. Add ¾ cup of the sugar gradually. Beat until stiff peaks form and set aside.

2 In a clean bowl, whip the egg yolks until pale and creamy. Add ¾ cup of the sugar and continue to beat until the sugar begins to dissolve and the mixture thickens.

3 In a large punch bowl, combine the yolk mixture, brandy, rum, bourbon, and milk. Fold in the whipped egg whites and cream. Top with nutmeg and serve.

Tip: *No one can ensure you 100 percent that your eggs are salmonella free, but the American Egg Board (yes, there is such an organization) does make some recommendations for what you should look for when buying eggs. And if you follow these guidelines, along with regular sanitation practices, such as washing hands and keeping preparation surfaces clean, the American Egg Board says that eggs pose no greater food-safety risk than other perishable foods.*

Make sure that your eggs are grade A or AA.

Only buy eggs with uncracked shells.

Buy eggs that have been stored in a refrigerated case.

Refrigerate eggs as soon as you bring them home.

Per serving: *Calories 251 (From Fat 99); Fat 11g (Saturated 6g); Cholesterol 100mg; Sodium 40mg; Carbohydrate 10g (Dietary Fiber 0g); Protein 3g.*

How to Separate an Egg
1.
Hold the egg in one hand over two small bowls
2.
Crack the shell on the side of one bowl

Let the white fall into one of the bowls

4.
Pass the yolk back & forth, each time releasing more white

When all the white is in the bowl, drop yolk in the other bowl.

Figure 4-6: Separating an egg.

Kid-Friendly Eggnog

This "virgin" version of eggnog is great for kids or adults who prefer a nonalcoholic beverage. Cooking the mixture staves off the possibility of salmonella transmission from the raw eggs.

Preparation time: *5 minutes*

Cooking time: *8 minutes*

Yield: *4 servings*

3 cups whole milk

1 cup heavy cream

½ cup sugar

4 large eggs

2 teaspoons vanilla extract

Freshly grated nutmeg

1 Whisk together the milk, cream, sugar, and eggs in a medium-sized nonreactive saucepan.

2 Cook over low heat, whisking constantly, until the mixture thickens slightly and coats the back of a spoon, about 5 minutes. Do not let it boil. Remove from the heat and stir in the vanilla extract.

3 Serve immediately, topped with freshly grated nutmeg to taste. Or you may refrigerate it, serve it cold, or reheat it before serving. If it thickens with refrigeration, simply thin with a little extra milk.

Per serving: *Calories 494 (From Fat 297); Fat 33g (Saturated 19g); Cholesterol 319mg; Sodium 175mg; Carbohydrate 26g (Dietary Fiber 0g); Protein 13g.*

What is eggnog, exactly?

Eggnog, a mixture of eggs and alcohol, has been a traditional American Christmastime drink since the late 1700s. The "nog" in the title possibly comes from the Old English term for ale. Or, quite likely, it was a shortened term of the English word *noggin,* which was a small cup made from birch in which tavern patrons could drink their libations. Although rum, whiskey, and brandy are frequently used, sherry was used back in merry old England. In fact, the term *sack posset* was used to describe such drinks, *sack* meaning "sherry."

As far back as the 1500s, the term *syllabub* was used to describe a fluffy egg white-enriched concoction that also contained milk, cream, sugar, and wine. Milk punches were around, too, but they did not contain eggs.

By the time the 1600s rolled around, recipes for an egg-rich dairy punch existed, but they were not necessarily called eggnog just yet. And they were not so much thought of as celebratory drinks, but as rich beverages that were nourishing for invalids and women. Of course, with the amount of alcohol that most of these recipes included, a sip or two would have made anyone feel better and possibly allowed sickly people to forget their woes. Eggs were often added as an extra ingredient if someone was feeling flush, because eggs were expensive.

Somewhere around 1800, the term *eggnog,* in the usage that we use now, first appeared.

Creating Chocolate Bliss

Chocolate and Christmas, two of my very favorite things in the whole world! Chocolate usually makes at least one appearance at holiday time. Maybe it is in the form of special candies placed in your stocking or maybe it's in the dessert that crowns the holiday meal. I say the more chocolate the better! So here are some chocolate beverages to help make sure that you keep your daily quota up. By the way, dark chocolate has as many, if not more, antioxidants per serving than red wine or green tea, so head straight to the kitchen to make some bittersweet hot chocolate.

High quality white chocolate will have cocoa butter as one of its ingredients and not just palm kernel oil, cottonseed oil, or other fats. It is the cocoa butter that gives it a chocolatey flavor.

Hot White Chocolate

I'm sure you've had dark hot chocolate, but white hot chocolate is creamy and sweet and a bit different.

Preparation time: *5 minutes*

Cooking time: *5 minutes*

Yield: *6 to 8 servings*

3 cups whole milk

1 cup heavy cream

8 ounces white chocolate, finely chopped

1 teaspoon vanilla extract

1 teaspoon Dutch-processed cocoa or freshly grated nutmeg

4 vanilla beans (optional)

1 Heat the milk and cream to a boil in a medium-sized saucepan over medium heat. Remove from the heat and stir in the white chocolate. Let sit for 3 to 5 minutes to melt the chocolate.

2 Add the vanilla extract. Whisk vigorously to a froth and to dissolve the chocolate completely.

3 Pour into four mugs or bowls (very European) and sprinkle with cocoa or nutmeg. Serve with a vanilla bean as a stirrer, if desired.

Tip: *You can find good-quality white chocolate in many large supermarkets. Look on the shelves next to the chocolate chips, in the baking ingredient aisle. Ghirardelli is a good brand.*

Per serving: *Calories 430 (From Fat 288); Fat 32g (Saturated 20g); Cholesterol 79mg; Sodium 115mg; Carbohydrate 29g Dietary Fiber 0g); Protein 8g.*

Bittersweet Hot Chocolate

If you have made hot chocolate or cocoa only with a prepared mix, you're in for a treat. This recipe is rich and very typical of European-style hot chocolate. Try it first thing in the morning or as an afternoon treat; it will pick you up either way. Kids might enjoy the optional peppermint stirrers.

Preparation time: *5 minutes*

Cooking time: *5 minutes*

Yield: *4 to 6 servings*

3 cups whole milk

2 tablespoons Dutch-processed cocoa

1 cup heavy cream

10 ounces bittersweet chocolate, finely chopped

6 peppermint sticks or peppermint candy canes (optional)

1 Mix ¼ cup of the milk and the cocoa in a medium-sized saucepan and stir to a paste. Add the remaining 2¾ cups milk and the cream. Whisk together to blend.

2 Bring the mixture to a boil over medium heat. Remove from the heat and stir in the chocolate. Let sit for 1 to 2 minutes to melt the chocolate. Whisk vigorously to a froth to dissolve the chocolate completely.

3 Pour into four mugs or bowls and serve with peppermint sticks as stirrers, if desired.

Going All Out: *Set out a pitcher of hot chocolate with mugs and a selection of whipped cream, cinnamon, finely shaved chocolate, marshmallows, and peppermint patties. Guests can pick and choose and add what they like to their hot drinks. This cocoa buffet is perfect after a hard day of sledding, ice skating, or shopping!*

Per serving: *Calories 480 (From Fat 315); Fat 35g (Saturated 22g); Cholesterol 73mg; Sodium 77mg; Carbohydrate 35g (Dietary Fiber 4g); Protein 8g.*

Try making a hot beverage with half cocoa and half brewed black tea. Voilà — chocolate tea!

Chapter 5

Appetizers

In This Chapter

- Figuring out appetizer fundamentals
- Three instant and three almost-instant appetizers
- Using cheese to whet the appetite
- Making dips and sauces
- Jazzing up your appetizers with seafood

Recipes in This Chapter

- Herbed Asiago Cheese Crisps
- Cheddar, Port, and Blue Cheese Ball
- Baked Brie with Roasted Apples
- Christmas Salsa
- Warm White Truffle Bean Dip
- Caramelized Onion Dip
- Whole Roasted Garlic with French Bread
- Salted Edamame (Soybeans)
- Spiced Cashews
- Easy Homemade Gravlax
- Shrimp Cocktail with Two Sauces

Sometimes people focus so much on the main meal that making the appetizers seems like an afterthought. But which do you enjoy more, Christmas or Christmas Eve? Christmas is great . . . but the anticipation and excitement of Christmas Eve may be even better. Your appetizers are sort of like Christmas Eve. They don't get as much attention as the main meal, but they may be even more enjoyable and are just as important.

The foods we eat before the main meal are called appetizers because they are supposed to be, well, appetizing and tantalize our taste buds into anticipation of what is to come. Because these are the first foods you will serve to your friends and family at the big Christmas dinner or other holiday event, they should be chosen carefully and arranged artfully to make the best impression.

The appetizers presented in this chapter are for eating around the coffee table. We spend enough time at the dining room table for the main meal, and spending some time in a different room is often appreciated. In the living room or family room, you can play musical chairs and spend some time on the couch with friends before having an intimate one-on-one conversation with Grandma. All the while, these appetizers can be there for you, your friends, and your family to nibble on and enjoy.

Choosing Appetizers

Regardless of the type of party, you want to serve enough appetizers to take the edge off your guests' hunger, but you also need to leave plenty of room for the rest of the meal. A typical cocktail hour for a group of about 6 to 15 people should include three or four offerings, if you are headed to a sit-down meal or larger buffet. If you're just having extended nibbles without a main meal, you would want more choices as well as increased volume. I suggest six to eight offerings if you're having a cocktails-and-appetizers reception or a get-together between lunch and dinner.

Here are a few things to keep in mind:

- Always offer a light choice, like a vegetable-based item.
- Serve something creamy, like a cheese or a dip.
- Consider something unusual, like an exotic cheese, to get the conversation rolling.

As for how much to make of each item, do what caterers do and figure on each guest eating about three or four pieces or servings of every appetizer.

When planning what appetizers to make, consider the logistics. You may have folks coming from out of town and others from around the block. With staggered arrival times, it's best to have foods that can sit out unattended for a lengthy period.

Take advantage of foods you can make ahead. Look for items that can sit out at room temperature for an extended period of time. Recipes from this chapter that can sit out include

- Herbed Asiago Cheese Crisps
- Cheddar, Port, and Blue Cheese Ball
- Christmas Salsa
- Warm White Truffle Bean Dip (the white bean dip will cool to room temperature, but it is just as delicious that way)
- Caramelized Onion Dip
- Whole Roasted Garlic with French Bread
- Salted Edamame
- Spiced Cashews

Have, at most, one last-minute dish, so that you aren't tied to the kitchen. The Baked Brie with Roasted Apples is a good example of a last-minute dish because it's only good when it's still warm and runny.

Variety never hurts when it comes to appetizers. The appetizers don't have to be in harmony with each other, unlike the dishes you serve at the main meal.

One way to create a lot of variety is to invite guests to bring one appetizer each. Use your judgment. If guests are flying in for a Christmas visit, they obviously may not be able to bring any food with them. If it is someone you do not know well, this request may be considered rude. But you're probably inviting family members or close friends who you can ask to pitch in. One warning: If they arrive late, so does the food.

If there's one downfall when it comes to appetizers, it's serving too many in terms of choices and too much in terms of volume. Most holiday meals have a lot to them, and by the time you get to dessert, which is often a highlight, you want your guests to be able to enjoy it. Choose your appetizers and their portions carefully.

Three Instant Appetizers

Sometimes you want to serve a little something before the main meal, but you just don't have a lot of time. Here are three instant appetizers. After you read the list, you'll probably think of a few more.

- Some supermarkets have olive bars where you can mix and match different types of olives for a reasonable per-pound price; check in the deli section. Even if you have to go to a specialty store to find them, it can be worth the trip. All you have to do when you get home is pop them in a bowl to serve. Place them in a pretty bowl — glass is nice — along with a small empty bowl for pits. Try some unusual varieties to pique everyone's interest and palate.
- In the same part of the supermarket where you find the olives or in the cheese department, look for bite-sized fresh mozzarella balls, called *bocconcini.* Bring them home, sprinkle with red pepper flakes and extra-virgin olive oil, and present them in a bowl along with toothpicks. You might have to go to a specialty shop for these, but if you have a few other things to buy, picking some up to have around during the holiday is worth the time.
- NUTS! Easy to find, with no preparation involved. Buy a large amount of one kind of nut to present in an opulent display. I suggest a huge bowl of natural pistachios (as opposed to the ones that are colored with red dye) offered with a small bowl for the shells, or a bowl of beautiful, large, whole cashews, either salted or unsalted. Whole pecans make a statement, too.

  Red pistachios may suit the colors of the season, but they stain your fingertips and lips and you don't need to ingest any extra food coloring.

Three Almost-Instant Appetizers

When you have a little more time but still want to steer clear of recipes, try these ideas for almost-instant appetizers. You can have some appetizers ready in a flash.

- Buy a good-quality chicken salad from the deli (look for chunks of fresh chicken, not just mush). Season to taste at home with herbs such as tarragon or fresh parsley. Take firm white or whole wheat bread and cut out rounds with a small cookie cutter. Place the bread rounds on a cookie sheet and toast in a 350-degree oven until lightly brown. Place a tiny scoop of chicken salad on each bread round and maybe an herb sprig on top.
- Buy one smooth and one rough country-style pâté. Buy a small container of *cornichon* pickles; these are tiny, very tart pickles that are usually found wherever pâté is sold. Arrange the pâté on a platter with fresh, sliced French bread along with a small bowl of cornichon.
- Buy sliced smoked salmon, some pumpernickel bread, unsalted butter, and fresh dill. Cut the bread into small rectangles — no crust. Spread with softened butter and top with a slice of salmon and a sprig of dill. Serve immediately.

Creating an Antipasto Tray

Antipasto means "before the meal" in Italian. Whether you're Italian or not, chances are you have enjoyed an array of antipasto dishes, or will when you taste them! Many Americans have a passing familiarity with antipasti and have encountered this appetizer as a selection of cured meats, cheeses, olives, and pickled vegetables. In Italy, antipasti can include rice dishes, egg dishes, fish and shellfish, and more, but for your pre-Christmas dinner purposes, a lighter selection is just fine. Many dishes that Italians consider as appetizers can easily be found readymade. Just gather together purchased and homemade foods and arrange them on a large platter or on a series of smaller dishes.

- Go to a bakery and buy some *focaccia,* which is a flat bread. It comes with a variety of toppings, from sun-dried tomatoes to pesto to rosemary. All of the varieties are delicious and perfect for this purpose. Just cut the bread into small squares or rectangles and set out in a basket. Or buy a pizza shell from the bread aisle of the supermarket, spread it with pesto, sprinkle with a light layer of shredded mozzarella, and bake until golden. Cool slightly, cut into pieces, and serve.

- Consider buying some thinly sliced *prosciutto,* which is a delicious cured ham, and an assortment of hard and soft salamis. Roll the prosciutto around spears of cantaloupe or steamed asparagus. Serve the salamis on thinly sliced bread rounds or squares.
- Some deli cases have a platter of roasted vegetables that you can buy by the pound. Alternatively, you can roast your own veggies at home. Just toss some vegetables with olive oil and roast in a 375-degree oven until browned and tender. Try sliced bell peppers of all colors (see Figure 5-1 for coring, seeding, and slicing directions), eggplant, zucchini, mushrooms, onion wedges, and fennel. Season with a little salt and pepper, if you like, and arrange on a platter.

  Roasted red peppers, artichoke hearts, pepperocini (pickled hot peppers), mushrooms, and a few other vegetables can be found in jars on the grocery shelves. Some even come marinated in a vinaigrette. These are great timesavers. *Giardiniere* is a pickled vegetable mixture principally made from cauliflower and carrots that can often be found jarred or at Italian delis and will also save you time.
- Marinated vegetables are usually easy to find, but they're easy to make, too. Steam broccoli, cauliflower, green beans, asparagus, beets, or whatever else you like. Steam very lightly so that they retain some crispness and their vibrant colors. Then just toss with a flavorful vinaigrette.
- Don't forget about a selection of Italian cheeses — a wedge of Parmigiano-Reggiano, some fresh mozzarella, a semi-soft fontina, and a sheep's milk pecorino.

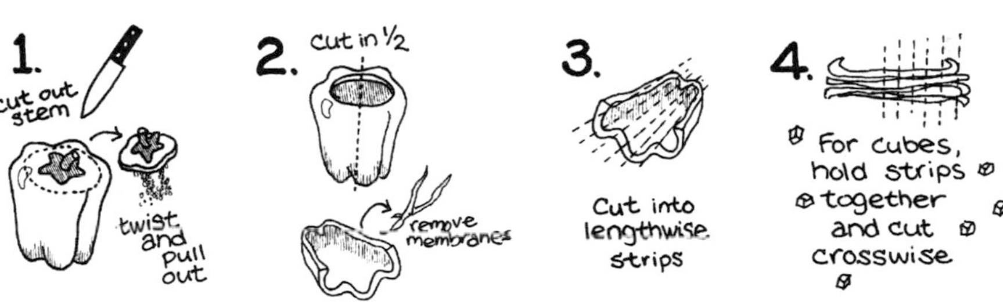

Figure 5-1: Preparing a pepper for roasting. If roasting, stop after the third step.

Say Cheese: Making Cheesy Appetizers

When you read the title to this section, I hope that you knew I didn't mean "cheesy" as in sub-par. I mean appetizers that take full advantage of all the amazing cheeses that are at your disposal.

Arranging the cheese platter

Whether you want to present an array of cheeses as part of the cocktail hour or as a cheese-and-salad course after the entrée, there are a few ways to go about arranging it. For smaller parties, a selection of three or four cheeses is fine. But you have to decide which ones.

My favorite way to decide which cheeses to include is to provide at least one hard cheese, a semi-soft cheese, and one soft cheese. I also like to offer cheeses made from different sorts of milk: cow, goat, and sheep.

How do you tell the cows from the goats from the sheep? Easy: If the cheeses are prepackaged, look at the labels. They might say right there whether they are goat or sheep cheese. If the package doesn't specify, assume the cheese is made from cow's milk.

So you can think in terms of cheese texture or source or both. Or how about a selection of various French cheeses, or take a European trip via the cheese tray and present a French cheese along with an Italian and a Spanish? And don't forget a nice blue cheese, domestic or imported. And the triple cream cheeses, with their rich 75 percent butterfat content! (They are called *triple cream* because of their high fat content.) Take your pick; you have literally hundreds of choices.

The following list is not meant to be scientific or exhaustive, it just includes some suggestions to get you on your way.

Hard cheeses:

Cheddar

Parmigiano-Reggiano

Asiago

Dry jack

Gruyère

Cheshire

Gouda

Semi-soft:

Morbier

Fontina

Taleggio

Chaumes

Port-Salut

Triple crème and soft:

Brie

Camembert

Explorateur

Saint André

Blue:

Stilton

Gorgonzola

Roquefort

Maytag Blue

Goat:

Montrachet

Bucheron

Banon

Valencay

Sheep:

Manchego

Pecorino-Romano

Sheep's milk feta

Making great cheese appetizers

Setting out a fabulous array of cheeses is one way to go, but you can also incorporate cheeses into recipes in many ways. The key when using a good cheese in a recipe is to let the nature of that particular cheese shine through, which these recipes do.

Herbed Asiago Cheese Crisps

These are melted cheese rounds that make a great accompaniment to Christmas cocktails. Older kids can help grate the cheese; younger kids can arrange the cheese on the baking sheets. Kids of all ages enjoy the transformation from grated cheese to lacy, crisp cheese wafers. They are served as you would chips; that is, you just nibble on them straight out of hand.

Special equipment: *Parchment paper*

Preparation time: *5 minutes*

Cooking time: *10 minutes*

Yield: *24 crisps (figure 2 to 3 per person)*

8 ounces Asiago cheese, grated

1 teaspoon finely chopped rosemary, basil, or marjoram

1 Preheat the oven to 350 degrees. Line two baking sheets with parchment paper and spray lightly with cooking oil spray.

2 Toss the grated cheese in a bowl with the herb. Make twenty-four 2-tablespoon-sized mounds and place them about 2 inches apart on each pan. Bake for about 10 minutes. The cheese will melt and will begin to bubble. Do not let the cheese brown or it will be bitter.

3 Let the crisps cool on pans. Serve immediately or store in an airtight container for up to 2 days.

Caution: *Whether the kids or you are grating the cheese, watch out for your knuckles! Skinning knuckles is one of the most common kitchen accidents, and grating cheese is usually the culprit.*

Simplify: *If you can't find Asiago cheese, try Swiss or even cheddar. Just watch carefully during baking, as the timing may be slightly longer or shorter.*

Per serving: *Calories 36 (From Fat 27); Fat 3g (Saturated 2g); Cholesterol 9mg; Sodium 25mg; Carbohydrate 0g (Dietary Fiber 0g); Protein 3g.*

Cheddar, Port, and Blue Cheese Ball

In this recipe, cheddar, port, blue cheese, and walnuts are all rolled into one, literally, in the form of the classic cheese ball, a Christmas tradition in many households. This is a great dish to make ahead. Kids love to play with food, and rolling the cheese ball in the nuts is a perfect step for them to help with. See the color section of this book for a photo of Cheddar, Port, and Blue Cheese Ball

Preparation time: *5 minutes*

Cooking time: *None; 2 hours of refrigeration*

Yield: *10 servings, or one 5-inch ball*

8 ounces full-fat cream cheese

5 ounces sharp cheddar cheese, grated

5 ounces blue cheese, crumbled

1 tablespoon port

½ cup walnuts, toasted and chopped

1 Mix the cream cheese, cheddar, blue cheese, and port together in the bowl of a mixer on low-medium speed, using a flat paddle attachment, until combined. Scrape onto a piece of plastic wrap, form into a ball, and refrigerate until firm, at least 2 hours and up to 4 days.

2 Roll in the nuts and serve immediately.

Tip: *Serve with celery sticks, apple slices, and crackers. You can slice the apples ahead of time and place them in water with a little lemon juice added to keep them from discoloring. This mixture is called acidulated water, in case you come across that term in a cookbook.*

Going All Out: *You can double this recipe and turn it into a large log. Just double the ingredients and follow the instructions as above, but form the mixture into a long log. Proceed as above. It will serve twice as many people and is great for a buffet.*

Per serving: *Calories 228 (From Fat 189); Fat 21g (Saturated 11g); Cholesterol 50mg; Sodium 353mg; Carbohydrate 2g (Dietary Fiber 0g); Protein 9g.*

Baked Brie with Roasted Apples

Brie is probably the most familiar and popular of the French cheeses. It comes in different sizes of flat rounds that are about 1½-inches thick. Some Bries are even produced in the United States. Bries have a range of butterfat content, from 45 percent to 70 percent, and all should be served at room temperature to take advantage of Brie's inherently creamy nature. A ripe Brie will be slightly oozing out of the center when served at room temperature, and it should be uniformly creamy throughout. It should never have any kind of ammonia smell, which signals that it's past its prime. This baked Brie treat is warm, gooey, delicious, and easy to make.

Almost all of the Brie readily found in the United States has a butterfat content of 60 percent. The lower percentages are usually reserved for the unpasteurized versions sold in Europe. Brie with a 70 percent butterfat content is a triple cream style and is richer than the standard Bries. All are delicious. If you can find a few various kinds, have a Brie tasting party!

Preparation time: *10 minutes*

Cooking time: *50 minutes*

Yield: *20 servings*

1 cup Roasted Chunky Apple Sauce (see Chapter 10), made with Granny Smith apples

2.2 pounds brie (an 8-inch wheel)

4 French baguettes, cut into ½-inch slices

1 Have the apples roasted and at room temperature.

2 Preheat the oven to 350 degrees.

3 Slice the Brie in half horizontally. Place the bottom half, cut side up, in a 9-inch deep-dish glass pie plate. Pack the roasted apples over the cheese and put the top half of the cheese back in place, cut side down. Press gently.

4 Bake for 40 to 50 minutes or until the cheese is melted and beginning to bubble gently. Serve immediately with sliced French bread.

Tip: *If you're not able to find a whole Brie, you can order one from many supermarket cheese departments or from specialty food stores.*

Per serving: *Calories 248 (From Fat 135); Fat 15g (Saturated 9g); Cholesterol 50mg; Sodium 359mg; Carbohydrate 19g (Dietary Fiber 1g); Protein 11g.*

Spreading the Joy: Dips, Spreads, and Sauces

There was a time when onion dip meant sour cream and powdered soup mix, and while nothing is wrong with that — it is serious comfort food after all — you probably already know how to make it. Besides, a whole world is out there of dips and spreads and I have a few special ones here that will brighten up your holiday. Dips and spreads are basically the same thing, except that dips are usually a bit thicker. As for sauces, I offer you a salsa that can be served with corn chips, potato chips, veggies, or just about anything else you can use to scoop it up.

Spicing things up with salsa

Salsa is everywhere, and it's not just for chips anymore. Salsas come in a range of prices and in varying degrees of heat. There are basic red salsas that have tomatoes as their main ingredient and green salsas that have tomatillos, a sort of tart green tomato, as their base. Salsas can include roasted tomatoes, grilled peppers, a lot of jalapenos, or no jalapenos at all. Some have a smoky flavor from chipotle peppers. Try them all to see what you like. Basic supermarket salsas are everywhere, but unfortunately they are often mostly tomatoes and aren't very fresh tasting.

Making your own salsa isn't as difficult as you may think and most go together when you combine fresh and readymade ingredients. Mine goes together in a flash and actually uses a jarred salsa as part of the ingredients. Read on . . . your jar of innocent salsa will be transformed.

Crudité, s'il vous plaît

Maybe you've seen the word *crudité* thrown around with abandon in cookbooks and food magazines. Was it clear as to what they were talking about? I am here to clear the air. First of all, how to say it — kru-di-tay. This exotic sounding word simply means raw, and sometimes lightly steamed, vegetables. When you put out some dips with veggies, you are presenting crudité to your guests. It's an easy, one-word name for a whole assortment of vegetables.

Try these veggies with your favorite dip:

- **Raw:** Baby carrots, cucumber slices, cherry tomatoes, radishes, zucchini squash slices, scallions, endive spears, snow peas, bell pepper strips
- **Lightly steamed:** Broccoli florets, green or yellow wax beans, cauliflower florets, small potatoes, asparagus, artichoke leaves

Christmas Salsa

This bean salsa is Christmasized with red peppers and fresh green cilantro. This is a great recipe to make with kids because, after measuring, all you do is mix it together in one big bowl.

Preparation time: *10 minutes*

Yield: *6 cups*

Two 15-ounce cans black beans, rinsed and drained

11-ounce can corn niblets, drained

1 cup prepared salsa, chunky style

1 medium red pepper, diced

3 scallions, sliced, using half of the green part

½ cup chopped fresh cilantro

1 tablespoon lime juice

1 teaspoon cumin

Salt and pepper to taste

Combine all the ingredients in a bowl. You can serve immediately or refrigerate in an airtight container for up to 3 days.

Tip: *Vary the heat of the Christmas Salsa by changing the prepared salsa that you use. The hotter the bottled salsa, the hotter the dish.*

Per serving: *Calories 9; Fat 0g (Saturated 0g); Cholesterol 0mg; Sodium 50mg; Carbohydrate 2g (Dietary Fiber 0g); Protein 1g.*

Here are some quick and easy ideas for serving Christmas Salsa:

- Place chips in a microwaveable dish and top with Christmas Salsa and shredded cheese. Nuke for 1 to 2 minutes for a plate of nachos.
- Roll up pieces of leftover or deli-roasted chicken with shredded cheese and Christmas Salsa in flour tortillas. Warm in the oven or microwave.
- Make a tortilla pie in a 9-inch pie plate. Layer corn tortillas, salsa, sour cream, shredded cheese, cooked ground beef, and refried beans. Finish with a layer of salsa and cheese. Heat through in the oven or microwave.
- Fill an omelet with Christmas Salsa and serve with warm tortillas.

"I thought truffles were chocolate"

There are indeed chocolate truffles. I include a recipe in Chapter 11 of this book. But their small, dark, irregular shapes are meant to suggest the truffles that are a fungus. I know, the word *fungus* shouldn't be in our culinary vocabulary, but that is what mushrooms are, and they're delicious. Truffles just happen to be the most expensive and exquisite of the bunch.

Usually they grow at the base of oak trees. Black and white varieties exist. The black truffles from Perigord in France and the white truffles of Piedmont, Italy are highly sought after. Their expense comes from their rarity and from the fact that they are difficult to find. Specially trained pigs or dogs sniff them out, and then their masters have to dig the truffles up before the animals eat them. Dogs are gaining favor, as they don't seem to want to scarf the prize themselves, whereas the pigs will just go to town! This method of hand-harvesting has never been improved upon and there are teams of man and animal that specialize in this particular hunt.

What taste should you expect? White truffles have been likened to garlic and they are highly aromatic. The black truffles have a fungusy flavor all their own, which is considered more pungent than the white. Some say black truffles taste nutty; others use the word *earthy.* If you like mushrooms and their earthy taste, you just may like truffles. If not, skip to Chapter 11 and make the chocolate ones!

For the first time truffle eater

Truffle oil, which is used in the following recipe, is the most economical way of experiencing truffles. If the quality of the oil is high, it is a good way to introduce yourself to the elusive flavor of truffles. Look at the label. You should see some percentage of real truffles and not just truffle flavor. Buy a small bottle and use the oil soon after opening it to take advantage of the delicate flavor. Buying a bottle of truffle oil is less expensive than buying actual truffles, but, depending on the size of bottle, you will be set back up to $20. If you would like to make this dip without the truffle oil, I give you a variation at the end of the recipe. If you do use truffle oil, the flavor is subtle and elusive — but special.

Warm White Truffle Bean Dip

This creamy white bean dip is so quick and easy, you'll make it more than once a year. The recipe, based on one created by Rozanne Gold and included in her book *Entertaining 1-2-3,* may be made up to 1 day ahead, covered with plastic wrap, and refrigerated. You can find truffle oil at a specialty store. Think of it as an elegant little stocking stuffer — *your* stocking.

Preparation time: *5 minutes*

Cooking time: *3 minutes*

Yield: *1¼ cups*

15-ounce can cannelini beans, drained, liquid reserved

¼ cup heavy cream

Salt and pepper (white, if available) to taste

1 tablespoon white truffle oil

1 Puree the beans until smooth in a food processor fitted with a metal blade. With the machine running, add the cream in a slow stream. Add the bean liquid, if necessary, to attain a smooth texture. Season to taste with salt and pepper.

2 Pack the dip into a microwave-proof dish. Hold at room temperature if using within 2 hours. Otherwise, cover with plastic wrap and refrigerate until needed.

3 Right before serving, heat in the microwave on full power for 2 to 3 minutes or until heated through (you can do this with the plastic wrap still on). Alternatively, heat the dip in the top of a double boiler. Stir in the truffle oil and serve immediately.

Tip: *Serve this dip with cucumber, endive, celery, water crackers, and sliced French bread if you're doing a White Christmas theme. Otherwise, add baby carrots to the mix. Baby carrots work wonderfully with this dip.*

Simplify: *You can eliminate the truffle oil; just make sure to season liberally with salt and pepper and perhaps a little rosemary or sage.*

Per serving: *Calories 33 (From Fat 18); Fat 2g (Saturated 1g); Carbohydrate 3g (Dietary Fiber 1g); Cholesterol 4mg; Sodium 74mg; Protein 1g.*

Delivering an onion dip

Because onions themselves play a primary role in my dip, here's the lowdown on the onions themselves.

Yellow onions are the workhorse of the kitchen and are the most commonly found onion. Two-pound, 3-pound, and 5-pound net bags of onions usually contain yellow onions. White onions can be substituted for yellow in most recipes. Red onions are usually sweeter and are used differently, often raw. All are available year-round.

For my dip, a standard yellow onion works just fine, but feel free to experiment with other varieties.

Caramelized Onion Dip

After tasting this recipe, you will never make onion dip with soup mix again. (Well, *maybe* never!) You do find the traditional sour cream in this dip, but the onion flavor comes from fresh, thinly sliced onions that are cooked nice and slow until they caramelize.

Preparation time: *5 minutes*

Cooking time: *20 minutes*

Yield: *1¼ cups dip*

2 cups chopped onions

3 tablespoons light olive oil

1 cup sour cream

Salt and pepper to taste

1 Cook the onions in olive oil over medium heat in a heavy-bottomed sauté pan to a rich golden brown, stirring about every 4 minutes. This step will take about 20 minutes.

2 Cool to room temperature, and then fold the onions into the sour cream. Season liberally with salt and pepper. Pack into a covered container and preferably refrigerate at least overnight, up to 3 days. The flavor improves if the dip sits overnight. Serve with an assortment of vegetables and chips.

Tip: *In a pinch, you may serve this the same day. But take advantage of the dip's ability to be made ahead and you will not only save yourself last-minute prep time in the kitchen, but will be rewarded with a better-tasting dip.*

Vary It! *To turn this into a low-fat dip, substitute no-fat sour cream.*

Per serving: *Calories 49 (From Fat 36); Fat 4g (Saturated 2g); Cholesterol 5mg; Sodium 36mg; Carbohydrate 2g (Dietary Fiber 0g); Protein 1g.*

Garlic: Delicious and good for you

How many times can we say that a food is both delicious and good for our health? I'm still trying to convince the powers that be that hot-fudge sundaes can dramatically improve one's life. Garlic, on the other hand, has already been found to promote vibrant health while enhancing our cooking at the same time.

Through the ages, garlic has been hailed as everything from a cure for fever to an aid for athletes to maintain their strength. Externally, it can be applied to bug bites for immediate relief. Recently, it has been proven to reduce cholesterol. But as a cook, I'm most interested in how absolutely delicious it is and how it can bring out the best in so many recipes.

Follow these guidelines when you buy a whole head of garlic:

- Choose plump heads with tight-fitting papery outer skin.
- Skin color may be off-white, purplish, or red-tinged.
- Avoid heads with any soft or brown spots.
- Avoid garlic with green sprouts.
- Store in a cool, dark place — not the refrigerator.

You can usually buy garlic in the supermarket in three ways: the whole, fresh heads mentioned above; minced garlic in oil; and whole peeled cloves that are available in the refrigerated produce section. The latter is not as common, but all large supermarkets have the ready-minced garlic in oil and often have both small and large jars of it to boot. I always have a jar of this garlic in my refrigerator. When I'm busy, like at Christmastime, I scoop out a teaspoon of it to take the place of each garlic clove called for in a recipe.

Whole garlic, however, is what you need for the Whole Roasted Garlic with French Bread. Garlic can be transformed into a tasty and fun, albeit somewhat messy, appetizer. I know, you're thinking "What, eat whole garlic cloves before kissing the object of my affection under the mistletoe?" Hey, you'll both be eating this appetizer, so don't worry about it. Besides, folks have been getting around this problem for years when eating onion dip, so the precedent has been set.

Whole Roasted Garlic with French Bread

Garlic becomes soft and sweet after roasting and makes an addictive spread for French bread (see Figure 5-2). You'll need napkins for this mouth-watering appetizer. It's messy, but it's good and surprisingly easy to make.

Preparation time: *5 minutes*

Cooking time: *1 hour*

Yield: *12 servings*

4 whole heads garlic, loose outer skin removed

¼ cup extra-virgin olive oil

French bread

1 Preheat the oven to 400 degrees.

2 Cut off the top quarter-inch of each garlic head. The cloves should be exposed. Place in a small oven-proof pan so that the garlic heads fit without too much spare room. (A metal pie plate works well).Drizzle the tops with olive oil and cover the garlic and pan tightly with aluminum foil and roast for 1 hour.

3 Remove the foil, let cool briefly, and serve warm. Place the garlic heads on a decorative platter surrounded by sliced French bread.

Tip: *Have your guests squeeze the garlic out of its jacket right onto a piece of bread, and make sure to set out a small bowl to collect the garlic skins.*

Per serving: *Calories 135 (From Fat 45); Fat 5g (Saturated 1g); Cholesterol 0mg; Sodium 175mg; Carbohydrate 19g (Dietary Fiber 1g); Protein 3g.*

SQUEEZING ROASTED GARLIC OUT OF ITS JACKET...
...ONTO FRENCH BREAD

1. PREHEAT OVEN TO 450°
2. CUT THE TOP ¼" OFF OF EACH GARLIC HEAD.
PLACE IN A ROASTING PAN AND DRIZZLE THE TOPS WITH OLIVE OIL.
COVER TIGHTLY WITH ALUMINUM FOIL AND ROAST FOR 1 HOUR.
3. REMOVE FOIL. LET COOL BRIEFLY. SERVE WARM. PLACE GARLIC HEADS ON A PLATTER SURROUNDED BY FRENCH BREAD.
☆ HAVE YOUR GUESTS SQUEEZE THE GARLIC OUT OF ITS JACKET RIGHT ONTO BREAD!
VOILA!
SET OUT A SMALL BOWL TO COLLECT THE SKINS.

Figure 5-2: The steps to serving roasted garlic.

Go Ahead, Use Your Fingers: Easy-Eatin' Appetizers

Sometimes we're tempted to eat with our fingers when we shouldn't, but the food is so finger lickin' good, it's hard to resist. Well, here is an assortment of appetizers *designed* for eating out of hand. Nuts are a typical use-your-fingers appetizer, and I provide you with a spiced nut recipe, but don't overlook the delicious cooked edamame. Either way, as host, all you need to provide are napkins.

Salted Edamame (Boiled Soybeans)

You probably don't think of soybeans as a Christmas food. In fact, I'm sure that you don't think of soybeans as a Christmas food. But soybeans are amazing — loaded with protein and healthy Omega-3 fatty acids. They're also tasty. You can find soybeans fresh in some supermarkets or frozen at an Asian food store.

Edamame is the Japanese word for branch beans and is used to describe soybeans that are still in the pod (see Figure 5-3). They're not only delicious and nutritious, but will probably also spark conversation. Guests eat them by squeezing the pod to make the soybean pop right into their mouths. Offer a bowl for discarded pods.

Preparation time: *2 minutes*

Cooking time: *5 minutes*

Yield: *6 servings*

1 pound soybeans in the pod

1 tablespoon plus 1 teaspoon kosher salt

Bring two gallons of water and 1 tablespoon salt to a boil in a large pot and add fresh or frozen edamame. Boil for 2 to 3 minutes (4 to 5 minutes for frozen) and drain. Arrange in a bowl and sprinkle with 1 teaspoon salt. Serve immediately.

Per serving: *Calories 108 (From Fat 45); Fat 5g (Saturated 1g); Cholesterol 0mg; Sodium 191mg; Carbohydrate 8g (Dietary Fiber 3g); Protein 9g.*

Figure 5-3: Edamame, in and out of the pod.

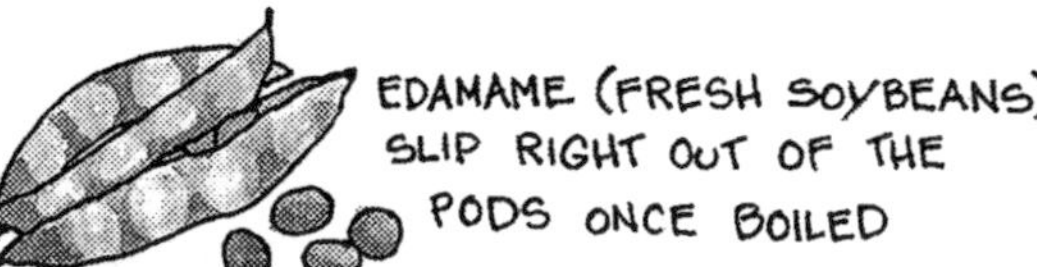

EDAMAME (FRESH SOYBEANS)
SLIP RIGHT OUT OF THE
PODS ONCE BOILED

Spiced Cashews

These are easy to make, and they'll keep for a month in the freezer. Kids can help measure and stir. The flavors are vaguely Indian inspired and the nuts complement your other appetizers.

Preparation time: *5 minutes*

Cooking time: *20 minutes*

Yield: *4½ cups*

2 egg whites

1½ teaspoons ground ginger

1 teaspoon sugar

½ teaspoon cumin

½ teaspoon coriander

½ teaspoon salt

¼ teaspoon turmeric

¼ teaspoon cayenne pepper

⅛ teaspoon black pepper

4½ cups roasted, unsalted cashews

1 Preheat the oven to 325 degrees. Line a rimmed baking sheet with parchment paper and spray with pan coating.

2 Beat the egg whites in a bowl until frothy. Whisk in the ginger, sugar, cumin, coriander, salt, turmeric, cayenne, and black pepper.

3 Stir in the nuts until they're evenly coated. Spread the nuts out in a single layer on the prepared pan.

4 Bake for 20 minutes, stirring once during baking.

5 Cool on the pan. Store in an airtight container at room temperature for up to a week, or freeze for a month.

Vary It! *You can substitute whole almonds, if you like.*

Going All Out: *Toss the cooled nuts with some flaked coconut and dark and golden raisins for a sweet 'n' spicy treat. If you really want to splurge, find some dried mango at a natural foods store, dice it, and toss it with the nuts.*

Per serving: *Calories 191 (From Fat 144); Fat 16g (Saturated 3g); Cholesterol 0mg; Sodium 76mg; Carbohydrate 10g (Dietary Fiber 1g); Protein 6g.*

Nuts!

Nuts can be expensive, but they are universally enjoyed and make such an easy addition to the appetizer array that they are worth considering. But at any price? Probably not. Per pound, they can be as expensive as shrimp!

If you look for nuts in the supermarket, you will probably find them prepackaged in small amounts with high prices. Some are vacuum packed, which somewhat ensures freshness, but some are not. Definitely steer away from those.

Best-case scenario is to find a supermarket or natural foods store that sells nuts in bulk and has a high turnover; the nuts here will probably be the freshest. To tell if nuts are fresh, smell them. There should be no musty or stale odor. Nuts in bulk will be in an open bin, giving you easy access for a sniff. Also, nuts in bulk can cost as little as half of what you'd pay in a grocery store.

As for storing, buy what you need. If you have extra, pack into a resealable plastic freezer bag and freeze for up to a month.

Seafood Appetizers: Let's Party!

Few things say "party" or "holiday" like a big bowl of boiled shrimp or a platter of sliced salmon. While dips and spreads might find their way to even the most casual of events, seafood is usually offered at special parties only, like at Christmastime. They are also the kinds of dishes that people usually don't make for themselves, so you will make your guests feel extra special. Although seafood can sometimes be expensive, these recipes keep the costs under control. I would be surprised if you couldn't find shrimp on sale at Christmastime, and as for the salmon, this home-cured version is much less expensive than buying it smoked.

Salmon

Just as a rose is not just a rose, salmon can be any number of different fish. First there is Atlantic salmon, which is the only kind swimming in the Atlantic Ocean. But there are not many left, so if you end up with Atlantic salmon on your plate, it was probably farm raised. This salmon has a pink-orange flesh with a high fat content.

Pacific salmon comes in four varieties: chinook (or king) salmon, chum, coho, and sockeye. In general, these salmon are leaner than Atlantic salmon. Their colors range the gamut, with sockeye approaching a red color.

There are differences in the tastes of the various salmon, but the most important thing is to buy fresh or appropriately frozen fish. If your fish has been frozen, ask the fishmonger if it was flash frozen on the boat. *Flash frozen* means the fishermen themselves (or should I say fisherpersons?) freeze the fish right after it is caught. This way, when it is defrosted, it is as close to fresh as frozen can be. However, for the Easy Homemade Gravlax, please use fresh salmon. If you are going to be poaching, roasting, or otherwise cooking your salmon, flash-frozen fish is fine.

Gravlax is nothing more than fresh, raw salmon with a few added ingredients that effectively cure it while it sits in the refrigerator. If you like smoked salmon but balk at the price, try this easy to make and much less expensive alternative. Although almost ridiculously easy to make, it's a very impressive appetizer.

Easy Homemade Gravlax

Gravlax is an elegant addition to your appetizer repertoire. Raw salmon is cured for a few days in the refrigerator with sugar and salt; that's about it. See the color section of this book for a photo of Easy Homemade Gravlax.

Preparation time: *15 minutes*

Cooking time: *None; needs to rest 3 days in the refrigerator*

Yield: *20 servings*

4 pounds salmon fillet

8 juniper berries (optional)

2 teaspoons black peppercorns

¼ cup kosher salt

¼ cup sugar

1 cup chopped fresh dill

¼ cup gin

10 slices dark pumpernickel bread

¼ cup (½ stick) unsalted butter

2 tablespoons chopped fresh dill

1 Remove any small white bones embedded in the flesh, called *pin bones,* with needlenose pliers (see Figure 5-4). Locate them with your fingers — they'll feel like a splinter. Grab the end with the pliers and pull out, working with the direction of the bone's insertion angle. They are in one line, so find one and work your way down the fillet.

2 Line a large glass baking dish with enough plastic wrap to cover the bottom completely and with enough to overhang the edges. Place the salmon, skin side down, in the dish.

3 Crush juniper berries and peppercorns with a mortar and pestle or place them on a work surface and crush with the broad side of a heavy chef's knife. Combine with salt and sugar and sprinkle the mixture evenly over the salmon. Spread the dill over the fish. Drizzle the gin over the fish as evenly as possible.

4 Wrap the plastic up and over the fish. Place a pan or plate that fits inside the baking dish over the fish. Weigh down the fish by placing heavy canned goods on top of the pan or plate.

5 Place in your refrigerator for three days; the fish should have lost its translucence by the time you serve it. Unwrap the fish and scrape off the dill, salt, and sugar. Slice the salmon thinly on the bias, leaving the skin behind.

6 Place the gravlax on a serving platter surrounded by a crock of sweet butter and sliced dark bread. Garnish with fresh dill and serve.

GRAB SALMON PINBONES
WITH NEEDLENOSE PLIERS

Figure 5-4: Pulling the pinbones out of salmon.

Tip: *Juniper berries can be found in health food stores or other stores that have bulk herbs. Buying herbs in bulk, by the way, is the most cost-effective way to get them. Although the berries are optional, use them if you can find them.*

Per serving: *Calories 231 (From Fat 117); Fat 13g (Saturated 3g); Cholesterol 60mg; Sodium 477mg; Carbohydrate 8g (Dietary Fiber 1g); Protein 19g.*

Shrimp — yeah, I'm talking to you!

Early on in my life, the word *shrimp* had bad connotations. I am a little over five feet (on a good day), and well, you can see where I'm going with this, can't you? Anyway, as I got older and wiser (but not taller), shrimp took on a whole other meaning. A big bowl or platter of shrimp meant company was coming.

Christmas is a time to indulge both ourselves and our guests, and shrimp does the trick every time. Here's some helpful information on buying and preparing shrimp.

While gazing in the seafood case, you may see many different shrimp sizes. The shrimp have cryptic labels such as "26/30" or "U-15." The former means that there are 26 to 30 shrimp per pound, while the latter means that there are less than 15 shrimp per pound. The shrimp may also be labeled medium, large, and what have you, but this is much less accurate than the accompanying numbers. So go by the numbers.

If a recipe just calls for medium shrimp with no number to indicate what "medium" means, you are at the mercy of your fishmonger. Beware: Not all businesses put their shrimp in the proper categories.

Unless you live near a community that has fleets of shrimp boats, frozen is what you're going to find. But that's okay. The flash-freezing techniques that most fishermen use these days produce very high-quality shrimp and fish. This process, called IQF, is described in the sidebar "What's your IQF?"

Some shrimp, especially shrimp found at wholesale suppliers and at some wholesale buying clubs, comes in a large block. The block may seem to be as heavy as a cinderblock, but in reality these blocks are usually about 5 pounds.

These blocks can be an economical way to buy shrimp, if you need that much. I think it's best to use the whole 5 pounds at a time and not try to partially thaw the block.

Here are a few tips when buying shrimp:

- Non-frozen shrimp may be defrosted previously frozen shrimp. They should also be clearly labeled with something to the effect of "previously frozen."
- Shrimp, like any fish, should have a fresh, briny smell. Avoid shrimp that smells fishy.
- If a recipe calls for 1 pound of shrimp with the shell, you'll end up with ¾ pound shelled shrimp.

If you buy frozen shrimp in bulk from the seafood case or grab a bag from your supermarket's freezer section, chances are that the shrimp will be IQF and therefore all separate from one another. Defrosting these types of shrimp is easy. Simply place the shrimp in a clean resealable plastic bag and place in a bowl filled with cold water. Rotate the bag occasionally until the shrimp defrost.

If you're faced with defrosting a large block of shrimp, plan ahead and do it in the refrigerator. You want the shrimp to defrost slowly and gently. Place the block in a large bowl in the refrigerator overnight or up to 2 days until completely defrosted.

What's your IQF?

IQF means *individually quick frozen*. Many foodstuffs, including shrimp, fruits, and vegetables, are available IQF. You know how sometimes you pick up a bag of frozen blueberries and all the berries are separate and loose? Those are IQF. But if it's a solid block of blueberries, those weren't IQF. They were, as you might expect, *block frozen*.

To make IQF foods, the manufacturers spread out the shrimp or peas or whatever in a single layer and flash-freeze them before packaging. The benefit of this technique is that the food usually retains its shape and integrity. The food will be less bruised by the time you prepare it, and that's a good thing. Buy IQF if you can. Here's what to look for with IQF:

- Each item of food should be separate from the rest, with no large ice crystals.
- Large ice crystal formation indicates that somewhere along the way the food partially defrosted and was refrozen, in which case I would return the batch.
- If some of the food is in clumps, it has also probably been defrosted and refrozen. Go back to the store, tell them what you found, and ask for properly frozen shrimp.

It is best to look carefully at the frozen shrimp while you are still in the store and only buy IQF shrimp that are individually frozen and loose in the bag or container. You can save yourself a trip back to the store and the hassle of going through the exchange.

Resist the temptation to plunge any kind of frozen shrimp in boiling water or to soak it in hot water. These techniques all but guarantee you tough, chewy shrimp.

Never freeze shrimp that have been previously frozen.

Ah, you probably thought I had forgotten to get to the recipe. Here it is, not only a recipe for boiled shrimp but two, count 'em two, dipping sauce recipes. The first is my version of the classic red cocktail sauce. The second is a sinus clearing wasabi (Japanese horseradish) sauce.

Shrimp Cocktail with Two Sauces

There's nothing wrong with a classic cocktail sauce, but offering an option livens up the party. Feel free to buy peeled, cooked shrimp if time is of the essence.

Preparation time: *30 minutes*

Cooking time: *10 minutes*

Yield: *10 servings*

Cocktail Sauce

½ cup chili sauce

1 tablespoon horseradish

1½ teaspoons lemon juice

Salt and pepper to taste

Whisk together all the ingredients in a bowl. Cover with plastic wrap and refrigerate for at least 6 hours for the flavors to develop.

Tip: *Chili sauce is a spicy tomato-based sauce that can be found in bottles right next to the ketchup.*

Creamy Wasabi Dip

½ cup mayonnaise

½ cup sour cream

1 tablespoon soy sauce

1 teaspoon sugar

2 teaspoons freshly squeezed lemon juice

1 to 2 tablespoons wasabi powder

Stir together all the ingredients, starting with 1 tablespoon of the wasabi, in a small bowl. Cover with plastic wrap and refrigerate for at least 6 hours for the flavors to develop. Taste and add more wasabi, if desired.

Shrimp

12 cups water

1 large bay leaf

5 black peppercorns

2 pounds large shrimp, shell on (20 to 25 per pound)

1 Fill a large stock pot with 12 cups water, the bay leaf, and the peppercorns. Cover and bring to a boil over high heat.

2 Add the shrimp, cover the pot, and bring back to a boil, stirring the shrimp up from the bottom once or twice so that they cook evenly. Boil the shrimp until they just begin to turn pink, for about 2 minutes. Keep covered, turn off the heat, and let sit a few more minutes until the shrimp are cooked through.

3 Drain in a colander and rinse under cold water to stop the cooking (see Figure 5-5). Peel and devein the shrimp (see Figure 5-6). You may refrigerate them in an airtight container overnight.

4 To serve, arrange the shrimp in a bowl set in a larger bowl filled with ice. Offer the Cocktail Sauce and Creamy Wasabi Dip in separate bowls, along with lots of paper napkins.

Tip: *When it comes to figuring out the proper amount of shrimp to offer, the only thing you can count on is that the more shrimp you serve, the more your guests will eat. Shrimp is one of those dishes where a bottomless bowl is necessary, but not attainable. Best case scenario is to figure about 4 per person and hope for the best. Some folks will be left wanting more, but all your guests will be thrilled to have had any at all, so you come out ahead.*

Tip: *Wasabi is a Japanese horseradish. You can find it in a powdered form at most Asian food stores or natural food stores.*

Per serving: *Calories 183 (From Fat 108); Fat 12g (Saturated 3g); Cholesterol 120mg; Sodium 541mg; Carbohydrate 6g (Dietary Fiber 1g); Protein13g.*

Create an Icy Bath
1.
Fill a large bowl half with cold water and half with ice cubes and place bowl in sink.
2.
Immediately drain shrimp in a colander (or remove shrimp with a slotted spoon) and stir into ice water bath.
Let stand for 2 minutes!
3.
Drain shrimp, cover and refrigerate if not using IMMEDIATELY!

Figure 5-5: Stopping shrimp from cooking.

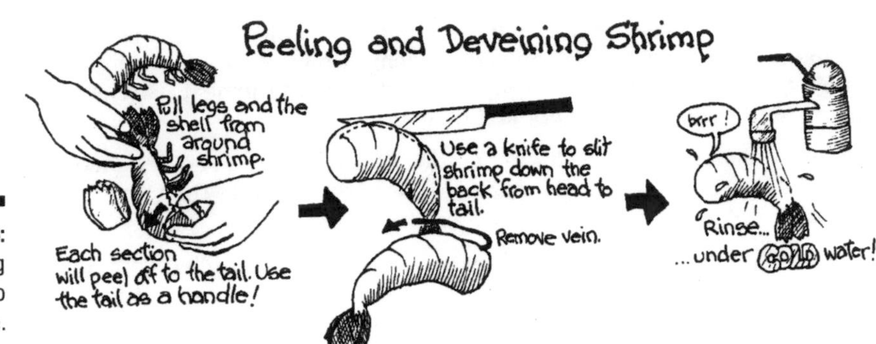

Figure 5-6: Preparing shrimp to serve.

Chapter 6

Salads and Soups

In This Chapter

- Making the perfect salad
- Dressing up — salad dressings
- Mixing up delectable soups

Recipes in This Chapter

- The Basic Green Salad
- Fennel and Orange Salad
- Green Bean Salad
- Balsamic Vinaigrette Dressing
- Sherry Vinaigrette Dressing
- Green Goddess Dressing
- White Bean Soup with Kale and Parmesan
- Roasted Squash Soup
- Corn Chowder
- Day-After Turkey Soup
- Oyster Stew
- Creamy Cheddar Potato Soup

Christmas is not all roast beef and candy canes. Whether you're making the big holiday meal or hosting an open house for the neighborhood, salads can help round out the meal. Soups are important too. They might not be the first thing that comes to mind this time of year, but they are remarkably versatile. I even offer you a hearty turkey soup using leftover turkey, as well as a couple of vegetarian offerings, which can be a boon if you have family members or guests who are so oriented.

Christmas Day dinner comes once a year, but the month of December is filled with opportunities to have a warming holiday meal. On the casual side, consider having a soup-and-salad dinner with immediate family. Most of the soups can be made ahead of time, the salads go together quickly, and guests can even come right up to the soup pot on the stove and serve themselves. Nothing could be easier, and an easy dinner frees you up to have some quality family time during this very hectic season.

Salad Days: Making Salads for the Holidays

Salads play a big role during the holidays because they're often the only dish you prepare with fresh vegetables devoid of cream, cheese, or other delicious but extravagant ingredients. All of the salads in this book are easy to make, and all of the salad recipes have at least some components that can be made ahead of time.

Here are a few things to keep in mind while making your salads:

- When you are preparing greens for a salad, tear the greens into pieces that will be easy to pick up with a fork and eat. I know this book isn't for airing my pet peeves, but this is a big one and I know there are readers out there who will sympathize. I can't stand it when I go to a restaurant and the greens are so big that I can't fit them in my mouth. These are pieces of lettuce that could cover a whole slice of bread. Well, that's where they belong, on a sandwich!
- Salad greens, once they're torn into bite-sized pieces, are easy to measure. Figure on a handful per person. I know that your hand is a different size than mine, but salad making is an imprecise affair. If you really want an exact amount, figure on using about 1 cup of salad greens per person.

  In general, about 1 pound of salad greens equals approximately 24 cups of bite-sized pieces.
- Obviously, there are many ways to make a salad, but the most useful salad to have in your repertoire during the holidays is a salad featuring plain old salad greens. So many holiday foods are rich and heavy — a fresh, light green salad is a welcome addition. If you would like to expand your salad into a heartier and more colorful dish, consider the following additions:
  - Sliced cucumber
  - Cherry tomatoes
  - Sliced radishes
  - Sliced avocado
  - Thinly sliced red onion
  - Croutons
  - Shredded or crumbled cheese

  This list was deliberately kept short, because too many additions make a basic salad into something else. Use discretion. The salad should enhance the rest of the meal, not take it over.
- Next time you walk through the produce aisle, look around and see if there is something near the lettuces called *mesclun* or *salad mix.* It may also be called *baby salad greens.* Whatever it's called, it's a mixture of baby and tender salad greens. It usually includes such exotic-sounding items as mizuna, frisee, baby chard, mache, and baby oak leaf lettuces, among others. Sometimes the mixture also has pieces of more conventional greens like red and green leaf lettuce. What all the salad greens have in common is that they are washed, dried, and already in bite-sized pieces.

  This is truly instant salad, because all you do is toss it with dressing. All the prep work has been taken care of for you. Mesclun is relatively expensive, but there is no waste and no prep time, which is very helpful, especially during the holidays.

- When you wash your salad greens, just make sure to handle them carefully, as they're delicate, and to dry them thoroughly before proceeding. I'm a huge fan of salad spinners — see the sidebar "Salad spinners" for more information.

The Basic Green Salad

This salad is a simple mixture of greens. Make sure that your ingredients are crisp and fresh. Because I hope you will be serving a green salad often during the holiday weeks, I made this salad easy to divide or multiply by factors of 2 or 4.

The recipe calls for different types of lettuce. Most large supermarkets should carry each of the lettuces I mention below. If not, a selection of what is readily available is fine. Iceberg lettuce would be the exception. It is mostly water and, while crunchy, offers little taste, color, or nutrition.

Preparation time: *10 minutes*

Yield: *8 servings*

1 small head of butter lettuce (also known as bibb or Boston lettuce)

½ small head of red or green leaf lettuce

½ small head of romaine lettuce

Approximately ¼ cup salad dressing (your choice)

1 Separate the lettuce leaves from their heads and discard any cores. Place the leaves in a bowl of cold water.

2 Soak the leaves briefly to dislodge any dirt or debris by swishing them around with your hands. Be gentle so as not to bruise the leaves.

3 Drain the clean leaves in a colander. Blot off any excess water with a clean kitchen towel or by using a salad spinner.

4 Tear the greens into bite-size pieces. Toss the greens in a large bowl with the salad dressing until the greens are just lightly coated with the dressing. Transfer to salad plates and serve.

Tip: *Tearing greens is preferable to cutting them. It's easy and gentler on the greens, and it looks better, too.*

Tip: *If you want to get a head start on making the salad, you can clean the greens, wrap them in a clean, dry kitchen towel, and place the towel in a plastic bag. Leave the bag open and refrigerate. The leaves keep for up to one week.*

Going All Out: *Chill your salad plates to keep those greens as crisp as possible.*

Per serving: *Calories 12; Total fat 0g; Saturated fat 0g; Cholesterol 0mg; Sodium 6mg. Carbohydrate 2g; Dietary fiber 1g; Protein 1g;*

Fennel and Orange Salad

This is a very refreshing salad. The citrus makes it a great addition to a rich meal.

Fennel, which looks kind of like celery, is usually somewhere near the lettuce and celery in produce aisles, although not all markets carry it. Celery mimics its texture but not its taste, which has a delicious anise flavor. There really is no substitute.

Preparation time: *15 minutes*

Yield: *4 servings*

1 fennel bulb

2 navel oranges

1 head butter lettuce (also known as bibb or Boston lettuce), leaves separated, washed, and dried; or 2 cups mesclun

2 to 3 tablespoons Sherry Vinaigrette (see the recipe later in this chapter)

1 Trim the fennel bulb by slicing off the stem and discarding. Then trim off the leafy greens on top and any stalks, leaving the round bulb. Quarter the bulb and thinly slice on the diagonal; place in the bowl. Chop leafy greens, measure out ¼ cup, and add to the bowl.

2 Remove the peel and white pith from the oranges. Use a sharp paring knife to cut between the membranes and release the segments. No membranes should be in the salad — just the pulp, but the sections will still retain their shape.Remove any pits and place the segments in the bowl with the fennel.

The salad may be made several hours ahead up to this point. Cover loosely with plastic wrap and refrigerate.

3 When ready to serve, add the vinaigrette and toss gently; you may need an additional tablespoon of dressing. The salad should be just lightly coated.

4 Divide onto plates and serve.

Simplify: *Instead of removing the orange pulp from the membranes, simply peel the orange, remove any white pith, and separate into sections. Toss in with fennel. The salad is not as refined, but it still tastes fine.*

Per serving: *Calories 102 (From Fat 45); Fat 5g (Saturated 1g); Cholesterol 0mg; Sodium 60mg; Carbohydrate 14g (Dietary Fiber 4g); Protein 2g.*

Green Bean Salad

Green beans used to be called *string beans* because they had a stringy component, which has now been bred out of them. You can substitute yellow wax beans in any recipe calling for green beans or string beans.

Look for slender, unblemished beans. They should be crisp and snap when you break them raw. Store them in an open plastic bag in the refrigerator and use within 2 days.

To clean, snap or trim off the stem end. The other end, which is quite narrow and usually tender, does not require trimming.

Preparation time: *5 minutes*

Cooking time: *10 minutes*

Yield: *8 servings*

3 pounds green beans, washed and trimmed

½ cup extra-virgin olive oil

2 tablespoons freshly squeezed lemon juice

¼ cup finely chopped flat-leaf parsley

Salt and pepper to taste

1 Bring a large pot of salted water to a boil over high heat. Drop in the beans and bring back to a boil and cook until the beans are tender but still crisp, about 4 minutes. Drain and immediately place in a serving bowl.

2 Add oil, lemon juice, and parsley and toss well. Season to taste and toss again. Serve immediately, or let sit and serve at room temperature.

Per serving: *Calories 172 (From Fat 126); Fat 14g (Saturated 2g); Cholesterol 0mg; Sodium 78mg; Carbohydrate 12g (Dietary Fiber 5g); Protein 3g.*

Salad spinners

Drying salad greens can be a chore, but a salad spinner can make quick work of the job. A salad spinner is a piece of equipment that is really quite handy. If the spinner makes preparing salad more attractive to you, why not invest in this moderately priced kitchen tool? Or better yet, put it on your Christmas list.

Different varieties are on the market, but they all work basically the same way. They have an outer bowl, usually a heavy-duty plastic, and an inner colander, also usually made of plastic. Then there is a snug-fitting lid, which has some sort of mechanism that can only be activated when the lid is on top of the bowl. The mechanism causes the colander to spin quite quickly. The centrifugal force propels the water off of the leaves, out of the colander, and it eventually gathers on the bottom of the bowl. Just that easy!

Putting on the Ritz: Dressing Up Your Salad

The number one thing that can kill a salad is too much dressing. Even if your greens are as crisp as can be, they lose their freshness if they are drowned in dressing. Follow these steps to make sure that the correct amount of dressing is on your salad:

1. **Place your chosen salad ingredients in a bowl.**
2. **Start with 1 teaspoon of dressing for every 1 cup of salad.**

   Toss gently but thoroughly with tongs, two large spoons, or even your clean hands, until the salad ingredients are coated lightly but evenly with the dressing.
3. **Add more dressing, one teaspoon at a time, until the desired coating is reached.**

   There should never be any dressing left in the bottom of the bowl.

But then again . . . feel free to pour on the dressing if that's to your liking. Some salad ingredients can be rather bland as is and aren't "done" without a dressing. A dressing gives them a spark — so dress accordingly.

All about balsamic

Balsamic vinegar is so rich and flavorful, it really is unlike any other vinegar. It is dark, heavy-bodied, and sweet and tart at the same time. It can also be expensive. Real balsamic is made in the Modena area of Italy, but there are imitations on the market. Let your taste buds be your guide. Try a less expensive brand first to see if you like balsamic's general flavor.

The best balsamic is aged for decades and is extremely expensive. In Italy, balsamic vinegar is used as a potent condiment, dribbled here and drizzled there to enliven the flavor of a dish. Balsamic is even used on strawberries to make an interesting dessert.

Balsamic Vinaigrette Dressing

When you're making a dressing, leave your plain vegetable oil on the shelf. It is great for sautéing, but adds no flavor to your greens. I'm a big fan of using extra-virgin olive oil for salads. You can use lighter olive oils as well for a milder effect.

You can choose from many types of vinegar. Balsamic has a deep, rich, tangy-yet-sweet flavor that I love. You can now find balsamic vinegar in almost any supermarket. Other vinegars to try are sherry, red wine, white wine, cider, and herb infused. (See the sidebar "All about balsamic" for more information on balsamic.)

An *emulsifier* is handy, too, in addition to the basic oil and vinegar. An emulsifier is an ingredient that helps an unstable mixture to blend. Mustard works wonders for the mix in this recipe.

Preparation time: *5 minutes*

Yield: *1 cup*

¼ cup balsamic vinegar

2 teaspoons Dijon mustard

¾ cup extra-virgin olive oil

Salt and pepper to taste

1 Whisk together the vinegar and mustard in a small bowl until well blended and smooth.

2 Drizzle in the oil, whisking all the while. The mixture should stay smooth and never break into its separate components. If the oil and vinegar start to separate, keep whisking before adding any more oil — although with the addition of the mustard, separation shouldn't happen.

3 Season with salt and pepper. Serve immediately or store in an airtight container at room temperature for up to a week.

Tip: *You can make vinaigrette in a small jar with a tight-fitting lid. An old mustard jar is perfect. Shake the vinegar and mustard together vigorously. Add a bit of oil, shake until well blended, and repeat until you've added all the oil.*

Per serving: *Calories 93 (From Fat 90); Fat 10g (Saturated) 1g; Cholesterol 0mg; Sodium 53mg; Carbohydrate 1g (Dietary Fiber 0g); Protein 0g.*

Sherry Vinaigrette Dressing

This vinaigrette goes great with the Fennel and Orange Salad presented earlier in this chapter. The sherry from which the sherry vinegar is made gives the vinegar a complex yet delicate taste that complements the citrus without overpowering it. This recipe makes plenty of dressing, so you'll have some left over.

Preparation time: *5 minutes*

Yield: *Approximately ½ cup*

2 tablespoons sherry vinegar

1 teaspoon Dijon mustard

7 tablespoons light olive oil

Salt and pepper to taste

Whisk together the vinegar and mustard in a small bowl until combined. Very slowly drizzle the olive oil into the mixture, whisking constantly until creamy. Season with salt and pepper, and the dressing is ready to use.

Per serving: *Calories 94; Fat 11g (Saturated 1g); Cholesterol 0mg; Sodium 79mg; Carbohydrate 0g (Dietary Fiber 0g); Protein 0g.*

Choosing and storing parsley

Two kinds of parsley are on the market. Curly parsley is what is put here, there, and everywhere on plates as a garnish. It has minimal flavor and an odd, stiff, curly texture.

For all the recipes in this book, use flat-leaf parsley, which is much tastier and has a delicate texture. It comes in a bunch with long stems. Place the stems in a glass of cold water, cover the parsley and cup with a plastic bag, and refrigerate. The parsley will last up to a week. The moisture from the water nourishes the stems and creates a humid mini-environment to pamper the leaves.

Green Goddess Dressing

Some people just have to have a creamy dressing. This one is basic, but really delicious. You can make it up to three days ahead.

Preparation time: *10 minutes*

Yield: *2 cups*

1 cup mayonnaise

½ cup sour cream or plain yogurt

¼ cup finely chopped fresh flat-leaf parsley

3 tablespoons finely chopped anchovy filets

2 tablespoons finely chopped scallions

2 tablespoons minced chives

1 tablespoon lemon juice

1 tablespoon red wine, white wine, or cider vinegar

Salt and pepper to taste

Combine all the ingredients in a bowl. You can use the dressing immediately, but its flavor improves upon sitting overnight in an airtight container in the refrigerator.

Tip: *The name "Green Goddess" refers to a play put on in the 1920s. The starring actor, George Arliss, dined frequently at the Palm Court Restaurant when the play was in San Francisco. The chef, Philip Roemer, honored the star by creating a green salad with a creamy dressing — which he dubbed "Green Goddess." I have no idea who or what the green goddess was in the play!*

Per serving: *Calories 58 (From Fat 54); Fat 6g (Saturated 1g); Cholesterol 6mg; Sodium 73mg; Carbohydrate 0g (Dietary Fiber 0g); Protein 0g.*

Making Seasonal Soups

Many people enjoy soup year round, but for me, it's all about the cold winter months. There's something about a steaming hot bowl of soup that makes the long, dark days a little brighter. Soup is a definitive comfort food and warms the soul as well as the tummy.

December is the perfect month for soup making and eating. While a big roast beef might take center stage for that one big Christmas Day meal, soup can be worked into many holiday lunches, dinners, and light suppers. Most soups are very easy to make and the most of their cooking time takes place in an unattended pot. Once the soup is done, you can just add a salad, some bread, and maybe a selection of cheeses to complete a meal. This ease of preparation is an added bonus during this busy month. Serving soup makes it possible for you to have a relaxed, informal meal with immediate family members during Christmas week. Or better yet, how about during the week between Christmas and New Year's Day? For many of us, that is sort of a lost week. It's still holiday time, yet it resides in limbo. My prescription? You guessed it, soup! And believe me, most of these soups are hearty enough to stave off any winter blues.

Your Christmas-season soups can precede the main dish or serve as a warm and filling main course on a cold winter night. The soups in this chapter can be used in both ways. In general, these are very easy recipes to make. Many can be made ahead and even improve after a night in the refrigerator. These soups are also pretty adaptable. If a recipe calls for chicken broth, for example, but you only have vegetable broth around, don't worry. Just taste as you go and adjust the seasonings as necessary.

It used to be that if you were going to make soup, you had to first make stock. Some cooks shy away from soup making because they have images of their mothers and grandmothers laboring over stoves for days at a time in order to create the stock. Although soups today are a snap to make, homemade stock does have an unparalleled flavor. With that in mind, I invite you to use your grandma's stock recipe or consult a soup cookbook for a great stock recipe — *Cooking Soups For Dummies* (Hungry Minds), by Jenna Holst, has an entire chapter on stocks — if you have the time to spend on going all out.

However, in this book, I'm assuming that you don't have a lot of time. For that reason, all the recipes that call for broth use ready-made broth. Because the soups in this chapter all use ingredients that have a lot of flavor, a good broth bought at the store is fine.

If you want to make classic clear chicken soup with noodles, you'd better make a homemade stock because it will be the star of the finished product.

When buying broth, try a few different brands. They vary tremendously. Some are rich and dark, and others pale and watery. Most of them are overly salty, so if you find a low-sodium version, try that. You're looking for flavor, not salt.

You can also doctor purchased broths by adding some roughly chopped vegetables and herbs and simmering to blend the flavors. A few carrots, pieces of celery, a quartered onion, and some parsley will do wonders. Start out with an hour's worth of simmering. The freshness and sweetness of the additional ingredients should have brightened the flavors. Continue to simmer a little more, if desired. Strain the liquid and the broth is ready to use; discard the veggies and herbs.

With a few additions, you can turn any soup into a very different phenomenon. Try the following, alone or combined:

- Toast some French bread and spread with goat cheese for an easy, cheesy soup accompaniment.
- Try tossing a thick soup with pasta and topping with cheese.
- Stir some cooked rice or small pasta into the soup.
- Add leftover vegetables.
- Sauté some sausage slices and add before serving.
- Stir in some pesto.
- Add a swirl of sour cream.
- Top with shredded cheese and pop under the broiler.
- Thicken with leftover mashed potatoes or vegetable puree.

White Bean Soup with Kale and Parmesan

This hearty and healthy soup is easy to prepare. Just add a salad, crusty bread, and some cheese for a filling winter meal.

Preparation time: *10 minutes*

Cooking time: *25 minutes*

Yield: *10 servings*

3 tablespoons light olive oil

1 medium onion, diced

1 carrot, peeled and diced

8 cups vegetable broth (use low-sodium if using canned)

Four 15-ounce cans cannelini beans, rinsed and drained

¼ teaspoon sage

¼ pound hunk Parmesan cheese, rind included

6 cups (1 large head) finely chopped kale, rinsed and dried

Salt and pepper to taste

1 Heat the olive oil in a large, heavy-bottomed pot over medium heat; add the onions and carrots. Stir frequently, for about 8 minutes, until the onion is translucent.

2 Add the broth, beans, and sage. Remove the rind from the Parmesan cheese and add the rind to the pot. Bring to a simmer over medium heat and cook for 10 minutes to allow the flavors to blend.

3 Leaving the cheese rind in the pot, remove about 2 cups of the soup and puree it in a blender; add back to the pot. Add the kale, bring the soup back to a simmer, and cook until the kale is tender, about 5 minutes.

4 Season with salt and pepper. Grate the remaining cheese and sprinkle it over soup that you've ladled into bowls. You may refrigerate this soup in an airtight container for up to 4 days, but it does not freeze well.

Tip: *You need to buy the Parmesan whole, not grated, and it needs to have the rind attached, which means the cheese will be cut from an end piece. The rind is the outside of the cheese and is a bit thicker and drier, which works well for the purpose of flavoring the soup. If you can only find a solid piece of cheese without rind, that's okay, just slice off a ¼-inch thick piece and add it to the soup in place of the rind.The cheese might dissolve into the soup a little more, but it will still be delicious. In fact, it might thicken the soup a bit, which you might even like more. Then, just grate the remaining cheese as specified in the recipe.*

Tip: *Kale is a leafy, dark-green vegetable that's often overshadowed by spinach and other more familiar green vegetables. It has large, stiff leaves and hard stems. The stems are removed and the leaves are always cooked before being eaten. When the leaves are added to soup they soften appreciably and add color, a vegetal flavor, and nutrition. They are very high in vitamin A, calcium, and potassium. Kale is a winter vegetable and is usually not even harvested until after the first frost, so Christmastime is a perfect time to cook* *with it. It comes in bunches — look for leaves that have life to them; they should look firm and fresh. Stay away from any kale with yellowed or wilted leaves. Kale does not store well in the refrigerator, so use it the day you buy it or the day after.*

Per serving: *Calories 222 (From Fat 72); Fat 8g (Saturated 8g); Cholesterol 9mg; Sodium 547mg; Carbohydrate 27g (Dietary Fiber 7g); Protein 11g.*

Winter squashes

You have many winter squashes to choose from when you prepare your holiday meals. They all share some qualities, but they differ enough that some are better suited to certain cooking techniques than others. In general, they all store fairly well, unlike summer squashes. In fact, *winter squash* is somewhat of a misnomer. It isn't harvested in the winter at all. It is picked in the fall but can be stored throughout the winter and often into the spring due to its thick skin.

Here are some short descriptions of some of the more popular varieties:

- **Acorn:** This acorn-shaped squash is found in most supermarkets. They come in dark green, orange, and even a creamy white. The dark green, which is the most common, sometimes has an orange blush on the side. Because of their shape and size (they often weigh about 1 pound), they're perfect for splitting in half and serving stuffed, offering half a squash per person. They are sweet but can be a bit stringy, so they aren't the first choice for pureeing or soups; try cutting them into chunks in a casserole.
- **Buttercup:** This squash may be a bit more difficult to find. Look for a squat, round, dark green squash with a turban shape. Sometimes, faint stripes run vertically all the way around. The insides of this squash are dark orange, very sweet, and velvety. Buttercup squash is great for soups and purees if you can find it.
- **Butternut:** This easy-to-find squash is pale tannish-beige in color with a vaguely bell-like shape. It has a brilliant orange-colored interior and makes the creamiest purees and soups. It is featured in the Roasted Squash Soup later in this chapter.
- **Delicata:** This is a fairly tender squash for a winter variety; it usually doesn't store over the entire winter. Typically, it's yellow with green and orange stripes running lengthwise. Use the smaller ones for stuffing or use the flesh in casseroles.
- **Spaghetti:** Not only is there a vegetable called *spaghetti*, but it actually looks like its namesake. The outside of this squash is yellow and oblong in shape with blunted ends. After being cooked, the flesh can be scraped with a fork to make long spaghetti-like strands. Topped with a light tomato sauce or garlic and olive oil, it makes a great vegetarian main dish or a side dish for roasted chicken or meatloaf.

Roasted Squash Soup

This creamy, beautiful, orange soup has a hint of sweetness. Serve it with crusty bread and a green salad to make a light meal.

Preparation time: *10 minutes*

Cooking time: *90 minutes*

Yield: *6 servings*

2 large butternut squash (about 2 pounds each), cut in half lengthwise

¼ cup light olive oil

2 medium onions, chopped

2 garlic cloves, minced (see Figure 6-1)

1 Granny Smith apple, peeled, cored, and diced

1 teaspoon thyme

1 cup dry sherry

5 to 6 cups vegetable broth (use low-sodium if canned)

Salt and pepper to taste

1 Preheat the oven to 400 degrees.

2 Brush the cut halves of the squash with a bit of the olive oil and place, cut side down, on baking sheets or roasting pans. Pierce the squash in a few places using a sharp paring knife; insert the knife halfway through the flesh. Roast for 50 to 60 minutes or until the squash is tender when pierced with a sharp knife. Cool slightly and then scoop out the seeds with a spoon and discard; set the squash aside.

3 Meanwhile, sauté the onions and garlic in the remaining olive oil in a heavy-bottomed pot over medium heat. Stir frequently for about 8 minutes, until the onion is translucent. Add the apples and thyme and sauté for 5 more minutes, or until the apples are soft. Add the sherry and cook for 2 minutes on high heat to reduce the sherry a little bit. Turn the heat back down to medium.

4 Scoop out the squash flesh right into the pot with a large spoon. Add 5 cups of broth; bring back to a simmer for 5 minutes for the flavors to meld.

5 Puree the soup in batches in a blender or food processor, or use an immersion blender if you have one. Season with salt and pepper. Add additional broth if the soup is too thick.

6 Serve immediately. The soup may also be refrigerated in an airtight container for up to 4 days, but it does not freeze well.

Per serving: *Calories 216 (From Fat 81); Fat 9g (Saturated 1g); Cholesterol 0mg; Sodium 123mg; Carbohydrate 34g (Dietary Fiber 7g); Protein 3g.*

Corn Chowder

This delicious soup takes advantage of frozen corn. If you use vegetable broth, this soup makes a great vegetarian offering.

Preparation time: *10 minutes*

Cooking time: *30 minutes*

Yield: *10 servings*

4 tablespoons (½ stick) unsalted butter
2 onions, finely diced
½ large red bell pepper, finely diced
½ large green bell pepper, finely diced
½ teaspoon cumin
½ teaspoon thyme
5 cups defrosted frozen corn kernels
4 large russet potatoes, peeled and cut into ½-inch cubes
6 cups chicken or vegetable broth
1 cup heavy cream
1 cup whole milk
Salt and pepper to taste

1. Melt the butter in a large heavy-bottomed soup pot over medium heat. Add the onion, peppers, cumin, and thyme and sauté for about 10 minutes or until the vegetables are softened.
2. Add the corn, potatoes, and broth and bring to a boil over high heat. Turn the heat down to medium and simmer until the potatoes are tender, about 15 minutes. Use the back of a large, sturdy spoon to crush some of the potatoes against the sides of the pot. This potato mash thickens the soup.
3. Add the cream and milk, season with salt and pepper, and heat over medium heat, but do not let the soup boil. Serve immediately or cool and store in an airtight container for up to 3 days. If necessary, reheat gently.

Per serving: *Calories 288 (From Fat 153); Fat 17g (Saturated 10g); Cholesterol 51mg; Sodium 687mg; Carbohydrate 32g (Dietary Fiber 4g); Protein 6g.*

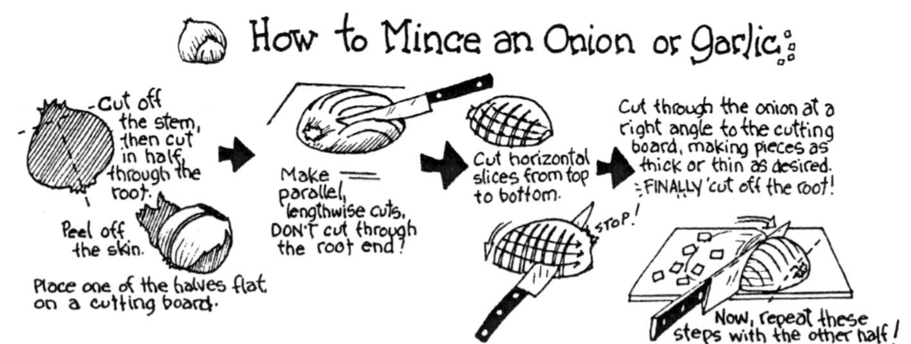

Figure 6-1: Mincing technique.

Day-After Turkey Soup

The day after the big Christmas meal, you just might have some turkey leftovers, if turkey was your main dish. This soup is a creative and easy way to make use of those tasty leftovers, even if they are just scraps.

Preparation time: *15 minutes*

Cooking time: *35 minutes*

Yield: *10 servings*

5 tablespoons unsalted butter

1 onion, chopped

1 garlic clove, minced

3 celery stalks, diced

3 carrots, peeled and diced

1 teaspoon thyme

1 teaspoon sage

3 large all-purpose potatoes, peeled and diced

½ cup frozen corn kernels

½ cup frozen lima beans

6 cups turkey or chicken broth

1½ pounds (about 3 cups) cooked leftover turkey, diced or shredded

½ cup frozen peas

1 cup heavy cream

1 cup whole milk

Salt and pepper to taste

1. Melt the butter in a large, heavy-bottomed soup pot over medium heat. Add the onion, celery, carrot, thyme, and sage and cook until the vegetables soften, about 12 minutes.
2. Add the potatoes, corn, lima beans, broth, and turkey and bring to a boil over high heat. Turn the heat down to medium and simmer until the potatoes are tender, about 15 minutes.
3. Add the peas, cream and milk, season with salt and pepper, and heat over medium heat, but do not let the soup boil. Serve immediately or cool and store in an airtight container for up to 3 days. Reheat gently.

Vary It! *You don't have to use the precise frozen vegetables that I list in this recipe. Use whatever you have — even leftover vegetables from the night before. Just replace with equal amounts. If you use cooked, leftover vegetables, just add them in Step 3 with the cream and milk.*

Per serving: *Calories 294 (From Fat 171); Fat 19g (Saturated 11g); Cholesterol 72mg; Sodium 735mg; Carbohydrate 21g (Dietary Fiber 3g); Protein 11g.*

Oyster Stew

Oysters come in a shell: There's no way to get around it. And somebody has to get those little suckers out of there. You can do it at home, and if you're serving oysters on the half shell, you have to get 'em out yourself. For this Oyster Stew, you can use shucked oysters as long as they come in their own natural juices.

Keep one very important rule in mind when buying fresh oysters, or any seafood for that matter: Buy from a reputable purveyor. The person or company you buy the oysters from should be able to guarantee that the oysters came from safe waters and are fresh.

Safe and *fresh:* Those are the bywords to look for.

Oyster Stew may sound exotic, but it is very simple — just three ingredients, plus seasonings. Serve with French bread to sop up the creamy soup. This soup does not store well, so prepare the amount you wish to serve immediately. You may halve or double the recipe with no problem.

Preparation time: *5 minutes*

Cooking time: *10 minutes*

Yield: *4 servings*

4 dozen shucked oysters, with juices

1 cup heavy cream

½ cup whole milk

Salt and pepper to taste

1 Place the oysters, their juices, the cream, and the milk in a saucepan. Cook over medium heat until the oysters curl up around the edges, about 10 minutes. Do not let the liquid boil. A few small bubbles around the edge of the pan are fine, though.

2 Season liberally with salt and pepper. Ladle into bowls and serve immediately.

Tip: *Rinse out your soup bowls with hot tap water to preheat them. Soups can cool off quickly, especially a soup like the Oyster Stew, which never boils. A preheated bowl helps to slow down the cooling process.*

Per serving: *Calories 339 (From Fat 243); Fat 27g (Saturated 16g); Cholesterol 174mg; Sodium 537mg; Carbohydrate 10g (Dietary Fiber 0g); Protein 14g.*

Creamy Cheddar Potato Soup

This is comfort food in a bowl, and it's easy to make if you use store-bought broth. Use white cheddar cheese if you can find it, unless it's Halloween and you want orange soup! Then the orange cheddar would be perfect. Either way, the flavor works. The soup may be refrigerated in an airtight container for up to four days.

Preparation time: *10 minutes*

Cooking time: *35 minutes*

Yield: *8 servings*

2 tablespoons unsalted butter

1 medium onion, finely chopped

2 large baking potatoes, peeled and diced

2 cups vegetable or chicken broth

5 cups whole milk or half-and-half

2 pounds sharp cheddar cheese, grated

Salt and pepper to taste

1 Melt the butter in a medium-sized saucepan over medium heat. Sauté the onion in the butter for about 5 minutes, until it's translucent, stirring occasionally.

2 Add the potatoes and broth, turn the heat up to high, and bring to a boil. Turn the heat down and simmer until the potatoes are tender, about 15 minutes.

3 Cool until lukewarm. Puree the soup in batches, if necessary, in a blender or food processor. You can also use an immersion blender if you have one.

4 Pour the soup back into the saucepan, add the milk, and cook over medium heat until the soup is very hot but not boiling.

5 Slowly stir in the cheese until it's melted and the soup is smooth.

6 Season with salt and pepper and serve.

Tip: *If the soup separates, don't worry. Throw the soup in the blender and give it a buzz. It will smooth out immediately.*

Per serving: *Calories 624 (From Fat 414); Fat 46g (Saturated 29g); Cholesterol 147mg; Sodium 859mg; Carbohydrate 20g (Dietary Fiber 1g); Protein 34g.*

Part III

Holiday Meals: The Main Event and Sideshows

"I told you not to use a mistletoe as a garnish. Now everyone's kissing the roast beef as it's being passed."

In this part . . .

Here's the meat of the book — pun intended. This part contains main dishes for breakfasts and dinners, as well as side dishes and condiments. Look here for that gorgeous Christmas turkey or roast beef, as well as quick-and-easy breakfast dishes, luscious mashed potatoes, and a couple of versions of cranberry relish. Yum!

Chapter 7

Breakfast Dishes

In This Chapter

- Serving almost instant breakfasts
- Preparing dishes the night before
- Getting into the kitchen on the big day

Recipes in This Chapter

- Citrus Breakfast Fruit Salad with Yogurt and Granola
- Breakfast Baked Apples
- Overnight French Toast with Maple-Orange Syrup
- Apple Raisin Croissant Breakfast Pudding
- Brown Sugar Bacon with Mustard
- Giant Puffed Pancake with Blueberry Syrup
- Spinach and Chevre Breakfast Frittata
- Chunky Hash Browns

It may be Christmas morning, but you and your family still have to eat something. I bet you've worked up an appetite with all the tossing and turning in anticipation of the big day.

On the average weekday, you may just grab a bowl of cereal or a bagel or skip breakfast altogether. Well, all the nutritionists tell us that breakfast is the most important meal of the day. It sets the tone for our eating later on. If you have a good breakfast, you are less likely to snack inappropriately during the day.

When Christmas morning rolls around, most of us are thinking about opening presents, not eating a good breakfast. Now, I know that I'm not going to change your long-held family traditions, but allow me to explain why you should get some decent food into your system before the big day unfolds:

- Breakfast may be the only meal of the day at which you can control what you consume.
- On this busy day, lunch is often overlooked.
- The kids may not fill up on so much junk later on (good luck!).
- Making the kids wait to open their presents is a good way to torment them.
- You need energy to open all of your presents!

Another good reason to eat breakfast together is that this may be your only chance to spend quiet time with your immediate family before getting together with other friends and relatives.

Making Almost-Instant Breakfasts

Nothing in cooking is instant — you even have to boil water for instant soups and hot chocolate mixes. But some foods come close to being instant. Take advantage of quality prepared foods and you can have breakfast on the table in no time.

- Set out a glass bowl of granola, pitchers of juice and milk, a platter of fresh fruit, a bowl of vanilla yogurt, and a basket of muffins or breakfast pastries from the bakery. Make coffee, tea, or hot chocolate and you're ready.
- How about bagels, smoked salmon, and cream cheese? Add a platter of sliced tomatoes, thinly sliced red onion, some lemon wedges, and a sprinkling of capers.
- For a sweet fix, offer some cream cheese mixed with honey, raisins, and chopped walnuts. This is great spread on whole wheat bagels. In fact, making cream cheese spreads is easy. Try chopped sundried tomatoes, fresh herbs, or classic chive — you name it.
- Make a big batch of oatmeal and serve with a buffet of add-ons: dried fruit, nuts, coconut, diced apples or pears, sliced bananas, applesauce, cinnamon, yogurt, milk, sunflower seeds, and mini-chocolate chips, if you're feeling decadent.
- If you just can't handle making breakfast first thing, serve juice and coffee and yell, "PRESENTS!" really loud. No one will notice the lack of food.

Making Breakfast the Night Before

Although it's important for all of your family members to have a good breakfast, I'm sure you don't want to slave over a hot stove Christmas morning for any length of time whatsoever. You may have to put a little effort into the meal on Christmas morning, but you can do most of the work beforehand by taking advantage of dishes you can make ahead. All of the recipes in this section can be made the night before, either in whole or in part. Several just need to be popped into the oven Christmas morning.

Set the table the night before so that you don't have to attend to that in the morning.

Citrus — winter sunshine

Some of the best citrus is available right around Christmastime. Don't overlook the fresh taste and health benefits of these fruits. They are a juicy addition to fall's apples and pears and give you a good dose of vitamin C. In general, you want to look for unblemished fruit that is heavy for its size. Some of the most popular wintertime citrus include

- **White, pink, and red grapefruit.** Try them as is for a snack, or sectioned or sliced for salads and compotes. The dark red tend to be super-sweet, but a combination in a salad offers a nice contrast of colors and flavors.
- **Juice oranges.** These are thin-skinned oranges, often with a bit of green on the skin. They aren't great for eating, but they pack a lot of juice. Valencia oranges are a justly famous juice orange.
- **Navel oranges.** These are thick-skinned and are best for eating or sectioning for recipes. If you need orange zest, navel oranges are a good choice.
- **Blood oranges.** These look like regular oranges with a bit of red blush on the skin. Then, when you open them, the flesh is indeed blood red. They are quite exotic and can be expensive, but wintertime is the best time to buy them. Buy one or two to add to regular oranges in a fruit salad to really jazz it up. Sometimes they are available as early as Christmas.
- **Clementines.** My wintertime staple. These are available late fall through early February and are often sold in their own boxes near the other citrus. They are easily peeled and have no seeds — the perfect snack for kids.
- **Mandarin tangerines.** Clementines are a type of mandarin, but there are others. Look for fruit called *satsumas* (they may also be called just *tangerines.*) All mandarins are usually easy to peel and eat.
- **Tangelos.** These are a cross between a tangerine and a grapefruit. Mineolas are the most common of the more tangerine type and are available during the holidays, while ugli fruit look more like grapefruit and comes to market a little later.

Combine homemade food with prepared food to save time but still get something hot on the table. For instance, make eggs, but serve muffins that you bought.

Citrus Breakfast Fruit Salad with Yogurt and Granola

Be sure to remove the bitter white pith beneath the skin of the citrus fruit. This dish is also good without the yogurt and granola for a simple fruit salad. See the color section of this book for a photo of the dish.

Preparation time: *15 minutes*

Yield: *6 servings*

3 navel oranges

2 ruby red grapefruit

4 clementines

1 tablespoon lime juice

1 tablespoon honey

⅔ cup vanilla yogurt

⅓ cup granola

1 Cut the peel and the white pith from the oranges and grapefruits. Working over a bowl to catch any juice, use a sharp paring knife to cut between the membranes and release the segments. Remove any seeds and cut the sections into quarters and place in a serving bowl. Simply separate the clementine sections and toss them in with the other citrus.

2 Whisk together the lime juice and honey with the citrus juices from the bowl. Pour over the fruit and stir to combine. To this point, the recipe may be made the night before. Just cover with plastic wrap and refrigerate.

3 Divide into 6 bowls and top with yogurt and granola. Serve immediately.

Per serving: *Calories 139 (From Fat 18); Fat 2g (Saturated 0g); Cholesterol 1mg; Sodium 27mg; Carbohydrate 31g (Dietary Fiber 4g); Protein 3g.*

Breakfast Baked Apples

Baked apples make a great breakfast warmed or at room temperature. Kids can help stuff the holes in the middle. Serve with yogurt and granola for a real treat.

Preparation time: *10 minutes*

Cooking time: *45 minutes*

Yield: *4 servings*

4 sweet apples, such as Cortland or Golden Delicious

¼ cup raisins

¼ cup chopped walnuts

½ cup sugar

¾ teaspoons cinnamon

1 cup apple cider

1 Preheat the oven to 350 degrees.

2 Trim a ½-inch strip of skin from the top of the apple. Core the apples almost to the bottom as follows: Insert a sharp paring knife about ½ inch into the top of the apple and cut a small circle just large enough to go around the core. This circle will act as a guide showing you where to cut. Continue to cut around the core, down into the apple, removing the core and seeds as you go. It may take you several steps. Take care not to pierce through the bottom or sides of the apple. After you have removed all of the core and seeds, place the apples in a deep dish 9-inch pie plate.

3 Stir together the raisins, walnuts, sugar, and cinnamon. Fill the apples with the mixture. Pour the cider in the pan.

4 Bake for about 45 minutes, basting two or three times. The apples should be just tender when pierced with a sharp knife. Do not overbake or the apples will burst.

5 Serve warm or at room temperature. The apples may be made a day ahead. If you make them ahead, cover them, along with any sauce, with plastic wrap and refrigerate. Bring to room temperature before serving or reheat in a microwave, if desired.

Tip: *When shopping for apples to bake, look for ones with firm, tight skin. Older apples can have a thicker skin, which will not bake as well. To avoid a chewier apple skin, avoid raw apples that have any wrinkles or bruises or are light for their size — they are older and have dried out a bit.*

Tip: *The cider should become syrupy as it cooks. If it is still liquidy when the apples are done, pour the cider into a small saucepan and boil over high heat until it's slightly reduced and thickened. Serve with the apples.*

Tip: *There are a few ways to go about coring an apple. There is a small, inexpensive tool called an apple corer that's on the market that you can use, but it's not necessary. Other than the sharp paring knife mentioned in the recipe, some cooks have better luck using a butter knife. I've also at times used a tiny spoon to scoop out the core and seeds once the job was started with a knife. Use whatever implements help you get the job done without piercing the skin.*

Per serving: *Calories 289 (From Fat 45); Fat 5g (Saturated 1g); Cholesterol 0mg; Sodium 10mg; Carbohydrate 63g (Dietary Fiber 5g); Protein 2g.*

Marmalade butter

One easy way to make a piece of toast special is to add special butter. Marmalade butter is easy to make and delicious. Just take a softened stick of unmelted butter and ¼ cup of marmalade. Blend them together in a small bowl — you're done! You should have about ½ cup of marmalade butter. Serve in an attractive dish or small bowl.

You can make marmalade butter up to a week before using it. Experiment with different types of marmalade or jam. You may want to add a bit of honey, as well.

If your family members aren't big eaters, you can serve marmalade butter with muffins for a tasty, light Christmas breakfast.

Overnight French Toast with Maple-Orange Syrup

If you love French toast but don't want to be chained to the stove on Christmas morning, this is the recipe for you. You make the French toast the night before, it soaks in the custard overnight, and then you just pop it in the oven Christmas morning. Have the kids whisk together the custard and help with the syrup.

Preparation time: *8 minutes*

Cooking time: *50 minutes*

Yield: *10 servings*

1-pound loaf challah or egg bread, sliced into 1-inch thick slices

One 10-ounce jar (about 1 cup) apricot all-fruit jam

3 cups half-and-half

⅓ cup sugar

4 large eggs

4 large egg yolks

1 teaspoon cardamom

½ teaspoon cinnamon

1 Spray a 15 x 10 x 2-inch pan with pan coating. Spread the jam evenly over the bread slices and arrange them in the pan, jam side up, with each piece overlapping half of the one below.

2 Whisk together the half-and-half and sugar to begin to dissolve the sugar. Whisk the eggs and egg yolks, cardamom, and cinnamon into the half-and-half and sugar combination. You've just created a custard. Pour the custard evenly over the bread. Cover with plastic wrap and refrigerate overnight.

Preheat the oven to 350 degrees. Unwrap and bake the French toast for about 50 minutes or until it's puffed and golden. Serve with Maple-Orange Syrup.

Tip: *If you cannot find challah or egg bread, you can substitute a dense white bread, such as Pepperidge Farm brand bread, if necessary. It will change the dish somewhat, but it will still work.*

Per serving: *Calories 382 (From Fat 135); Fat 15g (Saturated 7g); Cholesterol 220mg; Sodium 294mg; Carbohydrate 53g (Dietary Fiber 2g); Protein 10g.*

Maple-Orange Syrup

Preparation time: *5 minute*

Cooking time: *5 minutes*

Yield: *10 servings*

1¼ cup maple syrup

2 tablespoons orange juice concentrate

1. Heat the maple syrup and orange concentrate together in a small saucepan on the stovetop or in the microwave. Just whisk together and heat.
2. Serve the Overnight French Toast right out of the oven with the warmed syrup.

Per serving: *Calories 110; Fat 0g (Saturated 0g); Cholesterol 0mg; Sodium 4mg; Carbohydrate 28g (Dietary Fiber 0g); Protein 0g.*

Having the right pan size

Using the right pan size is important. If I say use X pan size, and you only have Y pan size and use Y and the dish doesn't come out, there's a good reason for it. Here's an illuminating fact. A 10-inch round cake pan has twice the volume of an 8-inch pan, which is definitely not readily apparent just by looking. You definitely can't substitute the one for the other. Recipes specify pan sizes for the same reason they specify oven temperatures. Even minor variations can really change the final product!

Apple Raisin Croissant Breakfast Pudding

Raisins, as you know, are dried grapes. They are the most popular dried fruit. But there are so many dried fruits on the market that you should consider your other choices. Did you know that prunes have had a facelift? They're now called dried plums! Same fruit, new name, always delicious. Try dried mango, papaya, pineapple, apples, cherries, cranberries, apricots, pears, peaches, and juicy Medjool dates. Any of these can be diced and used in place of raisins.

When chopping dried fruit, try lightly oiling a sharp knife. It will cut through the sticky fruit easily.

In this recipe, the raisins (or other dried fruit) offer a chewy, sweet quality that complements the custardy nature of the dish.

Preparation time: *15 minutes*

Cooking time: *50 minutes; 30 minute resting time*

Yield: *6 servings*

4 croissants, cut into 1-inch cubes (5½ cups)

2 apples, such as Cortland, peeled, cored, and diced

⅔ cup raisins

2 cups whole milk

1 cup heavy cream

⅔ cup sugar

4 large eggs

1 teaspoon vanilla extract

½ teaspoon cinnamon

½ cup chopped walnuts

½ cup lightly packed light brown sugar

2 tablespoons (¼ stick) unsalted butter, melted

¼ cup all-purpose flour

1 Spray a 9 x 13-inch pan with pan coating.

2 Spread the cubed croissants evenly over the bottom of the baking dish. Scatter the apples and raisins over the croissants and toss together lightly, spreading the mixture evenly over the pan.

3 Make a custard by whisking together the milk, cream, and sugar until the sugar begins to dissolve. Whisk in the eggs, one at a time. Whisk in the vanilla and cinnamon. Pour the custard over the croissant mixture; press the croissants down into the custard to submerge, and let sit at least 30 minutes. If you want to, you can cover with plastic wrap and store overnight. Just be sure to remove the mixture from the fridge before you turn on your oven in the morning.

4 Meanwhile, combine the walnuts, brown sugar, melted butter, and flour in a small bowl. Sprinkle evenly over the pudding.

5 Preheat the oven to 350 degrees.

6 Bake for about 40 minutes or until puffed and lightly golden. The custard will be set.

7 Remove the pan from the oven and cool on a rack for 10 minutes. Serve warm, if desired, or at room temperature.

Tip: *If you don't have a bakery nearby, frozen and defrosted croissants are fine.*

Per serving: *Calories 746 (From Fat 351); Fat 39g (Saturated 19g); Cholesterol 243mg; Sodium 390mg; Carbohydrate 89g (Dietary Fiber 3g); Protein 14g.*

Brown Sugar Bacon with Mustard

This bacon is sweet with brown sugar and tangy with Dijon mustard.

If you have a grill pan, use it while making this recipe (see Figure 7-1). Grill pans are pans made from a heavy material, usually cast iron, that have raised ridges all over the bottom. When you cook bacon in a grill pan, the fat drains down below the ridges and the bacon stays up top. These types of pans are great for hamburgers, fish, and chicken breasts as well. The ridges make those nice grill marks like you see in restaurants. You can find these pans in kitchenware stores, but department stores carry them as well. If you don't have a grill pan, just use a flat-bottomed pan.

Special equipment: *Grill pan (optional)*

Preparation time: *5 minutes*

Cooking time: *10 minutes*

Yield: *6 servings*

1 pound thick-cut bacon

2 tablespoons lightly packed light brown sugar

1 tablespoon Dijon mustard

Pepper to taste

1. The night before, cook the bacon in a grill pan over medium-high heat until it's three-quarters of the way done. This should take about 3 minutes on each side. The bacon should be just starting to brown and have released most of the fat. Drain the bacon on paper towels.
2. While the bacon is cooking, combine the brown sugar and mustard in a small bowl to make a paste.
3. Arrange the bacon in an even layer in a 13 x 9-inch baking dish. Spread the paste over the bacon as evenly as possible. Season with pepper. Cover with plastic wrap and refrigerate overnight.
4. Preheat the oven to 350 degrees. Bake the bacon for 5 to10 minutes, or until it's as crisp as you like it. Serve immediately.

Per serving: *Calories 164 (From Fat 117); Fat 13g (Saturated 4g); Cholesterol 21mg; Sodium 463mg; Carbohydrate 5g (Dietary Fiber 0g); Protein 8g.*

PREPARING BACON FOR BROWN SUGAR BACON WITH MUSTARD
1. THE NIGHT BEFORE.... COOK THE BACON IN A GRILL PAN (OR OTHER HEAVY PAN) OVER MEDIUM HEAT UNTIL 3/4 DONE (ABOUT 3 MINUTES EACH SIDE).
DRAIN ON PAPER TOWELS.
2. COMBINE BROWN SUGAR AND MUSTARD TO MAKE A PASTE.

Figure 7-1: A grill pan is ideal for this bacon recipe, but a heavy skillet works okay.

Dishes to Make on the Morning of the Big Day

If you don't have young kids, you might enjoy making a delicious breakfast Christmas morning. Here are some recipes for breakfasts that are guaranteed to get the day started off right.

Giant Puffed Pancake with Blueberry Sauce

Instead of making individual pancakes, try this one large puffy pancake that's baked in the oven. Make the Blueberry Sauce if you have the time. Kids can help whisk together the batter and make the sauce.

Special equipment: *10-inch cast iron pan or other heavy oven-proof pan*

Preparation time: *5 minutes*

Cooking time: *20 minutes*

Yield: *4 servings*

¾ cup whole milk

3 large eggs

¼ teaspoon vanilla extract

¾ cup all-purpose flour

2 tablespoons sugar

Pinch of salt

2 tablespoons unsalted butter

1 Preheat the oven to 400 degrees.

2 Place the cast iron pan in the oven while preparing the batter.

3 Whisk together the milk, eggs, and vanilla extract in a small bowl until they're well blended.

4 In separate bowl, stir together the flour, sugar, and salt. Add the wet ingredients to the dry and whisk just until everything is blended.

5 Remove the pan from the oven and add the butter. Tilt the pan to melt the butter and coat the bottom and sides.

6 Pour the batter into the pan and bake for about 20 minutes, or until the pancake is puffed and golden. Serve immediately with maple syrup or Blueberry Sauce.

Per serving: *Calories 245 (From Fat 99); Fat 11g (Saturated 6g); Cholesterol 181mg; Sodium 106mg; Carbohydrate 27g (Dietary Fiber 1g); Protein 9g.*

Blueberry Sauce

I know blueberries aren't in season in December, but this is a great use of frozen fruit and will be a big hit at your breakfast table.

Preparation time: *5 minutes*

Cooking time: *10 minutes*

Yield: *4 servings*

One 12-ounce bag frozen blueberries, preferably IQF (see definition below)

3 tablespoons sugar

3 tablespoons maple syrup

2 tablespoons water

1 tablespoon lemon juice

Combine all the ingredients in a small non-reactive saucepan and bring to a simmer over medium heat. Cook, stirring occasionally, until the berries have given off some juice and the sugar is dissolved. Serve immediately. Refrigerate any leftover sauce in an airtight container for up to 3 days and reheat before serving.

Tip: *For the sauce, if you don't have any maple syrup in the house, substitute honey or just double the sugar.*

Simplify: *Instead of using syrup to flavor the Giant Puffed Pancake, try a dusting of confectioners sugar and a sprinkling of lemon juice, or a healthy smear of fruit preserves or marmalade.*

Remember: *IQF means individually quick frozen and IQF blueberries are the way to go.*

Per serving: *Calories 120 (From Fat 9); Fat 1g (Saturated 0g); Cholesterol 0mg; Sodium 2mg; Carbohydrate 30g (Dietary Fiber 2g); Protein 0g.*

Spinach and Chevre Breakfast Frittata

Chevre is a type of goat cheese that can be found in many supermarkets. Goat cheese might sound exotic and smelly, but you should at least give it a try. Montrachet is a mild, soft chevre that may tantalize your taste buds.

This Spinach and Chevre Frittata is a great way to feed eggs to a crowd. (See the color section of this book for a photo of the dish. *Frittata* is simply the Italian word for a thick, open-faced omelet. Sometimes they are cooked on top of the stove until firm. This version takes advantage of the oven, freeing you up for other things.

Preparation time: *10 minutes*

Cooking time: *35 minutes*

Yield: *8 servings*

9 large eggs

2 cups cottage cheese

5 ounces cheddar, shredded (about 1⅔ cup)

5 ounces soft chevre (such as Montrachet), crumbled

½ teaspoon salt

½ teaspoon pepper

One 10-ounce package frozen chopped spinach, thawed

½ pint cherry or grape tomatoes, quartered

1 Preheat the oven to 350 degrees. Spray a 9 x 13-inch baking dish with pan coating.

2 Whisk the eggs in a large bowl until they're frothy. Whisk in the cottage cheese, cheddar, chevre, salt, and pepper.

3 Place the spinach in a colander and press any excess water out with the back of a large spoon. Stir the drained spinach and tomato pieces into the eggs and pour into the pan.

4 Bake for about 35 minutes or until the eggs are set. The frittata will be puffed and golden around the edges.

Tip: *Make this first, get it in the oven, then work on the coffee and the rest of breakfast. If you are making the Overnight French Toast and Brown Sugar Bacon with Mustard, they can both go into the oven with the frittata.*

Per serving: *Calories 258 (From Fat 153); Fat 17g (Saturated 9g); Cholesterol 272mg; Sodium 613mg; Carbohydrate 5g (Dietary Fiber 1g); Protein 22g.*

Chunky Hash Browns

For some folks, a hearty breakfast isn't complete without some sort of potato. These hash browns are easy to make for a crowd.

Preparation time: *5 minutes*

Cooking time: *20 minutes*

Yield: *6 servings*

3 large russet potatoes, scrubbed, with the peel on

3 tablespoons light vegetable oil, such as canola

Salt and pepper to taste

Paprika or cayenne (optional)

1 Dice the potatoes to uniform ½-inch cubes.

2 Heat the oil in a large, heavy skillet over medium heat until it's very hot. Add the potatoes; be careful of any splattering. Season liberally with salt and pepper and fry over medium-high heat for about 10 minutes, or until the potatoes are well-browned on the bottom.

3 Flip the potatoes over and season them again with salt and pepper and lightly with paprika or cayenne, if desired. Fry for 10 more minutes, or until the centers are tender and the outsides are crusty. Serve immediately.

Per serving: *Calories 161 (From Fat 63); Fat 7g (Saturated 1g); Cholesterol 0mg; Sodium 104mg; Carbohydrate 23g (Dietary Fiber 2g); Protein 2g.*

Chapter 8

Preparing the Main Dish for the Main Event

In This Chapter

- Choosing your main dish: turkey, goose, roast beef, or seafood
- Making light main dishes
- Vegetarian options

Recipes in This Chapter

- Maple-Glazed Turkey
- Roast Prime Rib
- Baked Fresh Ham with Herbs
- Goose with Apples and Cognac
- Duck Breasts with Dried Cherry Wine Sauce
- Shortcut Cassoulet
- Low-Fat Seafood Stew
- Fusilli with Caramelized Onions and Kalamata Olives
- Five-Cheese Spinach Lasagne

The main dish is often the focal point of the big gathering. Think of a roasted turkey that's presented at the Christmas table for carving, or the aroma of a roasting prime rib of beef or a golden goose with stuffing. All bring smiles to your guests' faces.

When designing a menu for an important meal, the main dish is a good place to start because it's the anchor of the meal — it keeps the menu from drifting. The stuffing and cranberry sauce and other side dishes are important, but play secondary roles.

I mention turkey, goose, and roast beef because they're very popular Christmas foods. Supermarkets and butchers recognize this by running sales on these items at this time of year. Keep your eye out for flyers and advertisements. There's nothing wrong with saving a little money on your chosen dish.

Make sure to take the following into consideration when deciding on a main dish:

- You may have to special order what you want, so plan ahead.
- Buy a probe-type thermometer if you don't have one. These thermometers enable you to keep the oven door closed, with a display outside the oven showing the internal temperature of your dish. They also signal you with a beep when your dish is at the desired temperature.

- If you don't have a butcher or supermarket that can supply you with your chosen item, ask friends for a recommendation of where to go.
- After you find a reputable butcher, either in a specialty butcher store or at the supermarket meat department, don't hesitate to ask for help in regard to size, when to order, and so on.
- Know that the main dish will probably cost you a pretty penny, especially if you're serving a large group. Take a deep breath and remember that this is often a once-a-year luxury and that it's worth every penny. Now is not the time to skimp on quality.
- Make sure that you have a roasting pan large enough.
- Make sure that your oven can hold the bird or roast.
- Always read the recipe all the way through first so that there are no surprises. You've spent quite a bit of money and time on your main dish, so following the directions makes sense.
- The main dish will be in the oven for a good chunk of time, so plan accordingly. You may need to start very early in the day.
- Remember that regardless of what you choose, you won't please everyone. Don't worry. There will be plenty of holiday foods on the table for those who don't care for the main entree.

Following Tradition and Starting New Ones

Many households serve the same main dish every Christmas, be it turkey, roast beef, or whatever. If you and your group still can't wait for that main dish of choice to make its way to the table, why tinker with success? But if you dread seeing turkey one more time, it may be the year for a change. Upholding tradition has its benefits, but maybe it's time for you to establish a tradition of your own.

Even if you're sticking with turkey, nobody says that you can't try a new turkey recipe. The same goes for roast beef or goose. You probably have your tried-and-true methods, but the recipes presented in this chapter just might become your new favorites. I also present some ideas for a nonconventional main course, like seafood stew, and two vegetarian main dishes, one a rich lasagne and the other a pasta with caramelized onions and black olives.

Considering poultry and fowl

Poultry or fowl is a good way to go for Christmas, or anytime you want to please a crowd. Folks eschewing red meat are happy; it's easy to cook; and nothing beats a big bird on a platter.

Just because you're serving a bird, doesn't mean that you have to choose between chicken and turkey. Goose is a classic Christmas dish that makes a dramatic presentation, and its all-dark-meat body provides delicious, rich meat. Just remember that a goose has much more bone in proportion to meat than a turkey does, so buy 2 pounds of goose for every person you're serving.

And having fowl doesn't require that you stick an entire bird in the oven and wait for hours. It can also mean preparing a dish like duck breasts, which are quick to make and are featured in the Duck Breasts with Dried Cherry Wine Sauce in this chapter.

Still, there's nothing like red meat

There's nothing like the smell of beef roasting in the oven; it gets my mouth watering every time. Many people are eating less red meat these days, but when they do eat read meat, they want a good hunk of meat with no skimping. The roast beef in this chapter is a perfect indulgence. It has very little adornment, but it speaks for itself as you carve glistening slices of rare and medium-rare beef seasoned perfectly with salt, pepper, and garlic.

But how about seafood?

Fresh fish and seafood are a light alternative and are more popular than ever. After you purchase your fresh fish, the preparation is fairly simple. The trade-off is that seafood can be a bit pricey. The Low-Fat Seafood Stew in this chapter is a healthy, hearty, and delicious meal that is just as impressive as any other main dish you can think of.

Deciding on Turkey

Turkey is a popular choice for a holiday main dish, and for good reasons. Most people love it, and it definitely has a holiday air about it. This isn't something you prepare every day. And, although it spends a bit of time in the oven, it can do so relatively unattended for periods of time, enabling you to put together the other parts of the meal.

Fresh or frozen?

When it comes to fresh food versus frozen, I usually choose fresh. But I recently read a comparative-tasting review comparing fresh and frozen turkeys, and I couldn't believe the results. The testers loved the frozen turkeys! This was a well-done tasting by professionals whom I trust, and they really enjoyed the flavor and texture of the frozen turkeys. Go figure. I have never roasted 20-some turkeys side by side, so I'll take their word for it.

I still used a fresh turkey for my holiday meal last year, but that's because I have easy access to fresh turkeys and using fresh has been my tradition. So here's what I think: If cost is a big issue, go for frozen: It's cheaper. And if you can't find fresh, don't sweat it. Buy the frozen, defrost it properly, enjoy your holiday dinner, and know that food experts would highly approve.

If you do buy frozen, allow ample time for defrosting. The best approach is to place the turkey in a large bowl and refrigerate it for two days and nights, if it's a large bird. Figure about 2 hours per pound for complete defrosting.

When you shop for frozen turkeys, check the label. Many have all kinds of chemicals injected into them. Personally, I prefer my turkey in all its natural splendor.

Trussing the bird

Trussing a bird is a way of tying the bird into a nice shape, which enables it to roast more evenly and look great at the table. Figure 8-1 shows you how. Even if you're not a sailor or a Boy Scout, you can truss a bird. Doing so doesn't require any fancy knots.

Look in the kitchenware aisle of the supermarket for kitchen twine. You want plain white cotton twine, not twine with a waxy coating or dye.

Making the perfect turkey

What's turkey without stuffing? Not much, right? But make the stuffing on the side. The turkey will not only cook more quickly and evenly, but you also won't be limited by the size of the turkey cavity. See Chapter 9 for a couple of ideas for stuffing. As crucial as the stuffing is, the gravy is probably even more important, so I include a gravy recipe.

Trussing a Turkey

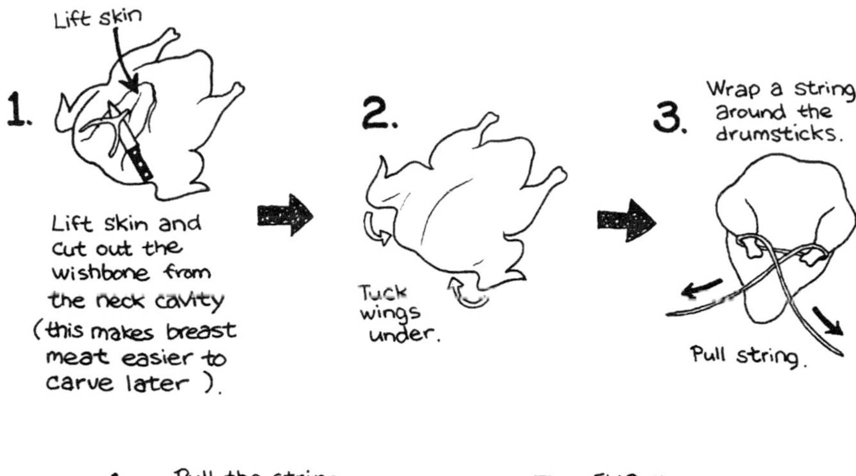

Lift skin

Lift skin and cut out the wishbone from the neck cavity (this makes breast meat easier to carve later).

3. Wrap a string around the drumsticks.
Pull string.

4. Pull the string toward the back.
Catch the tucked wings underneath the string.
5. FLIP the turkey over.
hook the string under the backbone.
Tie the string into a secure knot.

6. Flip it over, and.... VOILA!
beautiful!
Now make a wish with that wishbone you took out!

Figure 8-1: Trussing a turkey forms the bird into a nice shape.

Maple-Glazed Turkey

The bird called for in this recipe is large; make sure that it fits in your oven. See the color section of this book for a photo of the finished product.

Special equipment: *Large roasting pan and rack to fit, instant-read or digital/probe thermometer, fine mesh strainer, fat skimmer (optional)*

Preparation time: *20 minutes*

Cooking time: *5 hours*

Yield: *15 to 20 servings*

20-pound turkey, preferably fresh, giblets and neck removed

2 oranges

½ cup (1 stick) unsalted butter, at room temperature

Salt and pepper to taste

4 sprigs fresh thyme

4 sprigs fresh sage

2 cups low-sodium chicken broth

2 carrots, cut into 2-inch pieces

2 stalks celery, cut into 2-inch pieces

1 onion, cut into eighths

3 tablespoons maple syrup

1 Adjust the oven rack to the lowest setting. Preheat the oven to 250 degrees.

2 Wash the turkey inside and out and pat it dry with paper towels. Roll the oranges on your work surface while applying pressure to release the juices, and then prick the skins all over with a fork. Rub the turkey cavity with 2 tablespoons of the butter and season with salt and pepper. Insert the whole oranges, thyme, and sage.

3 Truss the turkey with kitchen twine. Rub the turkey all over with the remaining 6 tablespoons of butter. Pour the chicken broth into the pan and scatter the vegetables evenly over the bottom. Place the turkey on a rack in the roasting pan, breast side down.

4 Roast the turkey for 3 hours, basting 3 or 4 times. Turn the turkey so that the breast faces up and roast for 1 hour more, basting twice. Increase the oven temperature to 400 degrees, brush the turkey with the maple syrup, and roast until the skin is crisp and a thermometer inserted between the leg and thigh registers 170 degrees, about 1 hour more. While the turkey roasts, make the stock. After the turkey is out of the oven, make the gravy. The turkey should sit for at least 30 minutes before serving.

Tip: *I have you turn the bird periodically so that it roasts evenly — kind of like what you do at the beach to get an even tan. You can rotate yourself, but the turkey can't; it needs your help. Here are some tips to make the rotating process easier: Try wearing clean rubber gloves to insulate your hands from the heat and slippery bird. Or wear hot mitts with pieces of foil between the bird and the mitts. I also have inserted a large stainless steel spoon inside the bird to pick it up and used the other mitt-covered hand to coax it over. If the turkey is browning too quickly at any point, simply cover the browning parts with aluminum foil.*

Stock

Reserved giblets and neck

4 cups low-sodium chicken broth

4 cups water

2 carrots, cut into 2-inch pieces

2 stalks celery, cut into 2-inch pieces

1 onion, unpeeled, cut into eighths

4 parsley stems

4 sprigs fresh thyme

1 bay leaf

Combine all the ingredients in a stockpot. Bring to a boil, uncovered, over medium-high heat. Turn down the heat and simmer until reduced to about 3 cups liquid, about 2 hours. Cool. Remove the giblets and chop finely. Remove any meat from the neck and chop finely. Set the meat aside. Strain the stock and discard the veggies and herbs.

Gravy

Pan drippings

½ cup white wine

5 tablespoons unsalted butter

⅓ cup flour

3 cups Stock (see above)

Salt and pepper to taste

1 Place the turkey on a carving board or serving platter to rest, covering it loosely with foil to keep it warm. Pour the pan drippings from the roasting pan through a fine mesh strainer, and then use a fat separator to eliminate the excess fat (see Figure 8-2). Alternatively, pour the drippings into a measuring cup (after straining them) and skim off the fat. Measure up to 1 cup of the pan drippings and add it back to the roasting pan. Place the roasting pan on a burner on high heat and bring to a boil.

2 Add the white wine to the boiling pan drippings and stir, scraping up any browned bits that are on the bottom of the pan. Boil for about 2 minutes to combine the flavors and thicken the pan drippings. Strain through a fine mesh strainer.

3 In a clean saucepan, melt the butter and stir in the flour. Cook over medium heat for about 2 minutes until golden brown. Slowly add the pan drippings and enough of the stock to make the gravy have the desired consistency — you may not use all of the stock. Whisk to prevent lumping.

4 Stir in the reserved chopped giblets and neck meat, if desired. Season with salt and pepper and serve with the turkey.

Tip: *While the turkey is resting before serving, heat or make side dishes — the oven will be free. You could even bake an apple pie at this time; it will be warm from the oven for dessert.*

Per serving: *Calories 584 (From Fat 261); Fat 29g (Saturated 10g); Cholesterol 258mg; Sodium 203mg; Carbohydrate 4g (Dietary Fiber 0g); Protein72g.*

Figure 8-2: Skimmer separates fat from drippings.

"Is it done yet?"

This is the equivalent of the "Are we there yet?" question that kids and nervous adults assault us with all the time. A thermometer is the way to go to test for doneness.

To test a kitchen thermometer's accuracy, place it in a pot of water and bring the water to a boil. The thermometer should hit 212 degrees when the water boils. If it registers 200 degrees when the water boils, you know your thermometer is registering 12 degrees low, so adjust accordingly. In other words, if you want your turkey thigh to be 170 degrees, your sluggish thermometer must rise to 182 degrees. Get it? Or just go buy a new thermometer.

Insert the thermometer into the deepest part of the thigh, but make sure that it doesn't touch bone, which would give a higher reading (see Figure 8-3). The temperature in this area of the thigh should reach 180 degrees. Do not test the breast area, as it reaches that temperature far sooner than the dark meat in the legs and thighs.

Where to put a Dial (or Oven-proof) Meat Thermometer

Boneless Roast

Insert to core

Poultry

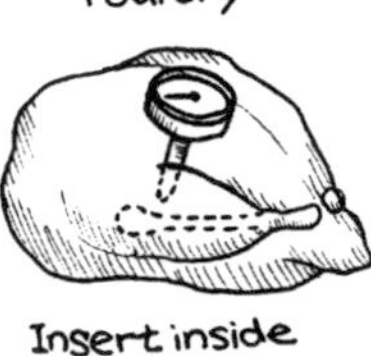

Insert inside of the thigh

Meat with bone

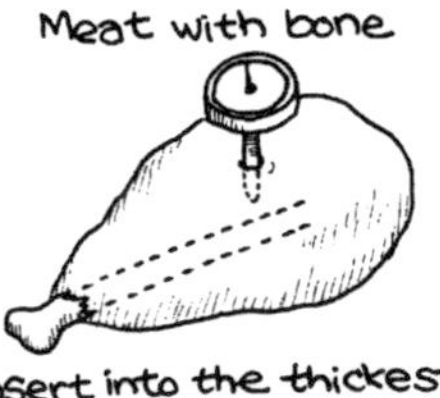

Insert into the thickest part of the meat

* For an accurate reading, do NOT touch the bone, fat, or bottom of the pan with the thermometer

Figure 8-3: A meat thermometer is a must for proper cooking.

If you still need convincing that using a thermometer is necessary, consider this: Every time you check for doneness, you pierce the flesh and let out precious juices, and one of the most common complaints people have with turkey is that it's too dry. Also, every time you open the oven to check, you lose 25 to 50 degrees in oven temperature, and your roasting time gets thrown off. *And* it's dangerous to wrestle with a 20-pound bird with hot fat in the pan. The less you have to fuss with the food, the better.

Meat or poultry, employ that thermometer!

Letting the bird rest

Most recipes for roasted meat and poultry end with a suggestion to let the roast rest out of the oven for 15 to 30 minutes before serving it. When you roast meat or poultry in the oven, the heat draws the juices out of the meat. They try to escape by evaporating through the exterior. So when you first take the roast out of the oven, the juices are pulled toward the edges. By letting the roast sit, you allow the juices to redistribute and you maximize the juiciness of your meat.

So go ahead and put your feet up while the bird is resting. You both deserve it.

Carving the turkey

Figure 8-4 provides a diagram for your carving pleasure. You can buy a carving set, or you can just find a knife and fork that are as close to a real carving set as possible.

- **Carving knife:** You need a long knife so that you minimize the sawing back-and-forth motion. It should have a thin, sharp blade. The thinness makes the blade more flexible and allows you to carve thinner pieces. A sharp blade glides through meat. A dull blade pulls and tears and leaves you with a jagged piece of meat.

  You can use an electric knife if you wish, but you make a much more impressive figure carving the bird if you're not getting help from an electrical appliance.

- **Carving fork:** Yeah, there is such a thing as a carving fork. Try to carve while holding the bird still with a dinner fork, and you'll see why you need a large, strong fork! Carving forks, which are also called meat forks, usually have just two tines. Those parts go into the meat. You don't need a lot of tines — just enough to secure the meat and get the job done. And the tines are long so that they can go deep into the flesh and hold the roast perfectly still while you carve. Carving forks are broad at the base of the tines. The broadness keeps the fork from disappearing into the meat. Sometimes the forks have a small lever that can be flipped up to provide a base, along with or instead of a built-in broad base.

  Any knife and fork with similar figurations should work.

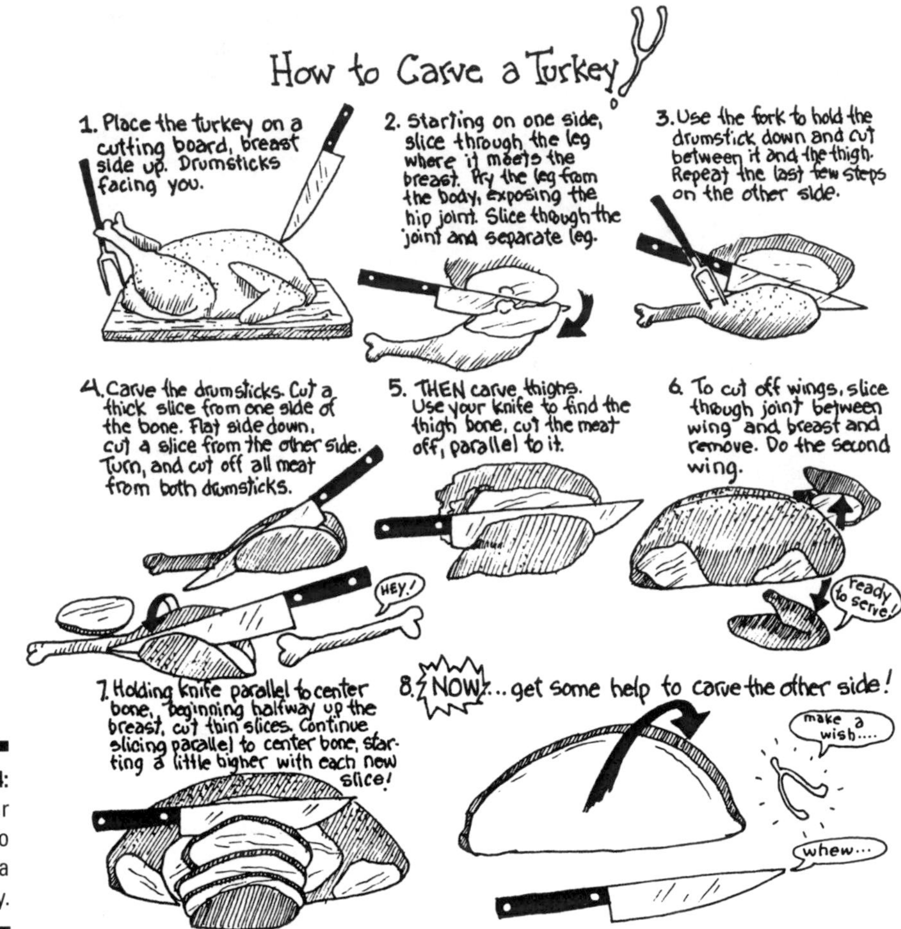

Figure 8-4: The proper way to carve a turkey.

Unstuffing the stuffing

I prefer to cook my turkey without stuffing in it. I think the pros far outweigh the cons. See if you agree:

- Your turkey cooks faster and more evenly.
- You can make as much stuffing as you like — the amount is not dictated by what the turkey can hold.
- You can make two kinds of stuffing.
- If you want turkey juices mingling with your stuffing, you can always baste the stuffing with the pan juices from the turkey during baking.

- If you have vegetarians coming to dinner, you can make a veggie stuffing. Because it is separate, it isn't "tainted" by the turkey — or should I say "fowled"?
- The stuffing doesn't become greasy from the turkey.
- You don't have to worry about bacteria buildup. Bacteria can build up in the stuffing if the stuffing is placed in the raw turkey cavity too early or left in the turkey too long after it comes out of the oven.

When stuffing is cooked on the side, many cooks call it *dressing,* but I like to use *stuffing* as an all-purpose term. Apparently, *stuffing* was the original term, but the Victorians thought the word was a tad offensive and put *dressing* into use. Why they wanted to dress a bird is beyond me. Use whichever term you like.

Many cooks think that day-old or stale bread makes the best bread-type stuffing. If you plan ahead, you can leave the bread out at room temperature overnight. You can also place fresh bread in a single layer on a baking sheet and dry it out in a 350-degree oven for a few minutes.

Instead of white bread, try cornbread, sourdough, or wheat.

Stuffing is very versatile. Take any of your favorite recipes and add the following:

- Dried fruit, such as raisins, dried cherries, apricots, or cranberries
- Chopped apples or pears
- Chopped nuts, such as pecans, walnuts, or almonds
- Sautéed onions
- Sautéed garlic
- Sautéed celery
- Sautéed mushrooms
- Sautéed bell peppers in all colors
- Cooked, chopped greens: spinach, kale, and chard
- A little orange juice or apple cider for moistness — or try a splash of orange liqueur
- A little broth for moistness
- A little wine or sherry for moistness
- Cooked ground sausage, pork, or turkey or cooked, crumbled bacon

As an alternative to the standard sage and thyme, add different herbs: rosemary, savory, marjoram, oregano — experiment!

Disposing of leftovers (as if you needed help!)

Perhaps you have a lot of turkey leftovers. Well, lucky you! You can whip up many, many dishes with this bounty. Simply shred or dice the cooked turkey and create a

- **Turkey omelet:** Whip up an omelet and load the middle with turkey and your cheese of choice.
- **Burrito:** Warm some tortillas and fold up turkey, rice, beans, and cheese. Top with salsa and sour cream.
- **Sandwich:** Yummy! White bread, stuffing, turkey, gravy, and cranberry sauce.
- **Stuffed potato:** Bake a potato, stuff with lots of shredded cheese, steamed broccoli, and turkey, and bake until bubbling.
- **Turkey salad:** Combine cooked turkey with curried mayonnaise, add diced celery and chopped parsley, and season to taste.
- **Caesar salad:** Crown a salad with warm turkey and top with a Caesar dressing.
- **Curry:** Sauté onion and garlic, and then add curry spices, turkey, and some canned tomatoes. Serve with rice and yogurt.
- **Day-After Turkey Soup:** See Chapter 6 for the recipe.

Selecting Prime Rib

When you're spending all that money to buy a beautiful family-size roast, it pays to know a thing or two about meat. There are a few different grades of meat, *prime* being the most desirable. *Choice* is next down the line and is the most commonly found. *Select* meats are the lowest available grade and are best for stewing or braising.

I call my beef recipe Roast *Prime* Rib. The title refers to the preferable grade of beef; however, finding prime beef can be difficult for home cooks. A choice cut is fine; just know what you're looking for and what you're getting.

In general:

- Look for a well-marbled piece of meat. There should be nice ribbons of fat here and there.
- The color should be bright red and not dark brown, although a brownish red is okay.
- The meat should be moist with no hard, dry areas.
- There should be a thin layer of external fat, which should be white, not yellowed.
- If the meat is wrapped in plastic, no red liquid should be on the bottom of the package, which indicates that it has been frozen and defrosted.
- Most of all, if you can get a whiff, the meat should have a fresh smell. Any sour or musty smell is grounds for an automatic rejection.

Browning first — in a hot-hot oven

Many recipes for roasting start with an oven preheated to a very high temperature, much higher than you would, say, bake a casserole in. The reason for the high heat is that it sears the outside of the roast. In other words, the high heat browns the surface quickly, which seals in all the precious juices. This can take anywhere from 10 minutes to about 20 minutes, but the number of minutes that have gone by isn't all that important. The appearance of the roast is what counts. You want it to be browned all over the outside. Keep the heat turned up until the roast is uniformly dark brown, and then turn down the heat to the suggested temperature.

Exceptions arise, of course. A case in point is the Maple-Glazed Turkey, which I prefer to roast in a low-temperature oven for more evenly roasted results because it is so large (20 pounds!).

No matter what your oven temperature, whether it's 350 degrees or 450 degrees, you want to open the oven as little as possible during baking and roasting. The temperature dips by as much as 25 to 50 degrees every time you open the door. This can really throw off your timing and the hinder the results.

Generally speaking, if something has a 30-minute oven time, don't open the oven until about 20 minutes in — that will give the oven a head start at doing what it is supposed to be doing at whatever temperature the recipe called for. Ovens with windows help, but eventually you have to open that oven to get a peek or to check a thermometer.

What is rare and what is well-done

Rare and well-done may seem like subjective terms, but actual temperatures determine whether roast is rare, well-done, or something in between. These are the temperatures that your roast should be when you pull it from the oven; it will continue to cook and its internal temperature will rise while it rests.

- **Rare:** 110 to 112 degrees rising to 120 to 130 degrees after resting.
- **Medium rare:** 115 to 117 degrees rising to 130 to 135 degrees after resting.
- **Medium:** 125 to 128 degrees rising to 140 to 150 degrees after resting.
- **Medium well-done:** 135 to 140 degrees rising to 155 to 160 degrees after resting.
- **Well-done:** 150 degrees, but really, at this point, you're on your own. By the time it rises to 175 or 180 degrees, there's little or no succulence left.

When you do open the oven, do so quickly and remove your roast or whatever and place it on the stovetop and close the oven door. Do whatever you need to do — poke it, takes its temperature — and then quickly put it back inside.

In all likelihood, I know you probably won't do this. You'll probably open the oven and slide out the rack and do what you need to do with the heat pouring out. Guess what? I do that too, even though I shouldn't. Half the time, I am just too lazy to do it any other way.

When a recipe says something should cook for an hour, it is under the optimum situation. The oven hasn't been open three times for a look-see. So if your dish takes one hour and 15 minutes because you did open the oven a few times, that's okay.

Making roast prime rib that melts in your mouth

You might think that a big hunk of mouthwatering roast beef is reserved for ordering in a restaurant. Not so! It's very easy to make and oh so impressive, not to mention incredibly tasty.

Roast Prime Rib

This is it. A big roast beef, bone-in, ready to wow your guests. Many of us are eating less meat, so when we do, we want it to be good — really good. This is the roast beef of your dreams; juicy, rare pieces in the middle and well-done pieces on the ends to give everyone what they want. If you don't buy meat from the butcher very often, just ask for a standing rib roast. The butcher will know what you mean. Have the butcher remove the thick cap of fat and meat from the top and trim the external fat to about ½ inch.

Tools: *Large roasting pan, instant-read or digital/probe thermometer*

Preparation time: *5 minutes*

Cooking time: *2½ hours (plus 2 hours resting at room temperature)*

Yield: *10 to 12 servings*

12-pound standing rib roast

6 garlic cloves, minced

2 tablespoons kosher salt

1 tablespoon coarsely ground pepper

1 Pat the roast beef dry with paper towels. Combine the garlic, salt, and pepper in a small bowl to make a paste. Rub evenly all over the meat and place the meat in a shallow roasting pan, bone side down, fat side up. Let the meat come to room temperature, about 2 hours.

2 Preheat the oven to 450 degrees. Roast for 15 minutes, and then turn the oven down to 350 degrees, without opening the door. Begin checking temperature after 60 minutes. The meat will roast for approximately 12 to 13 minutes per pound for rare meat. For perfectly juicy, rare roast beef, remove the meat from oven at 110 degrees. For medium rare, roast to an internal temperature of 115 to 117 degrees. A thermometer inserted deep into the flesh, but not touching bone, will give you a proper reading.

3 When the meat reaches the desired temperature, remove it from the oven and cover loosely with foil. Let it sit at least 20 minutes, but not longer than 30 minutes. The meat will continue to cook (the internal temperature will rise 5 to 10 degrees) and the juices will redistribute, making the roast as juicy as can be. Do not skip this step.

Per serving: *Calories 537 (From Fat 324); Fat 36g (Saturated 15g); Cholesterol 148mg; Sodium 696mg; Carbohydrate 1g (Dietary Fiber 0g); Protein 50g.*

Carving roast beef

After the roast has rested (see Step 3 of the recipe), carve it by running a knife along the bones and down into the meat to release the bulk of the roast from the bone. Slice to serve and then cut down between the bones to serve them up to the die-hard carnivores. Figure 8-5 gives you the picture.

Easiest Way to Carve a Rib Roast
1. Place the roast on a carving board with the rib bones pointing up. With a sharp carving knife, start slicing where the rib bones meet the eye of the roast and slice along the bone under the eye until meat is realeased in one chunk.

2. Place cut side of meat on cutting board. Slice vertically, about 1/4 to 1/2" thick or thin as desired.
fat side up

3. Slice the rib bones into individual pieces and transfer to a warm platter along with the boneless slices. Your guests will love chewing the crispy, tasty bones!
Yum!

Figure 8-5: The proper way to carve roast beef.

Moving on to roast beef sandwiches and other joys of life

If you're lucky enough to have leftovers, boy, are you in for a treat. Roast beef sandwiches are one way to go. But why not expand your horizons?

- Make the Green Goddess dressing (Chapter 6) and add it to a roast beef, tomato, and lettuce sandwich on wheat bread.
- Try rye bread, roast beef, Russian dressing, and iceberg lettuce with a pickle.

- Toast white bread and cover with roast beef, a layer of mashed potatoes, and gravy to make an open-faced sandwich.
- Pile roast beef onto pumpernickel bread with honey mustard, tomatoes, alfalfa sprouts, and Brie — pop under the broiler until soft and runny.
- Chop it up finely and make a quick chili.
- Cube the roast beef and make a curry.
- Slice, toss small, thin slices with vinaigrette, and serve with salad greens.
- Buy or make an Asian noodle salad with peanut butter or sesame dressing and serve with small slices of beef — make them bite-sized so that you can eat them with chopsticks.

Going Ham for the Holidays, or Pork, if You Prefer

In some households, ham is the Christmas tradition — and I don't mean the ham in a ham-and-cheese sandwich. I'm talking about an ample, succulent cut, made even more appealing through your TLC.

Other than fresh ham, which is often referred to as pork, hams come to you, the consumer, either partially cooked or fully cooked. If it's partially cooked, the label should say, "Cook Before Eating" or something to that effect. These hams should be cooked to an internal temperature of 155 to 160 degrees. Fully cooked hams have "Ready to Eat" labels. All you have to do is warm them and carve away.

If your choice is a cooked ham, make sure to read the label and look for one with a minimum of additives. Many have a lot of water added which plumps them up, but pay a pretty price for the water weight.

Baked Fresh Ham with Herbs

Serve with mashed potatoes, roasted apples or pears, and a green veggie. Modern-day pork is very clean meat. Many old recipes suggest cooking to a very high internal temperature to guard against trichinosis, but that's no longer necessary. After resting, this ham will have cooked sufficiently yet will still be juicy. Kids love to get their hands messy and can help you stuff the ham.

Special equipment: *Large roasting pan, instant read or digital/probe thermometer*

Preparation time: *15 minutes*

Cooking time: *5½ hours*

Yield: *15 to 20 servings*

14-pound fresh ham, bone in (shank and leg portion of pork)

1 tablespoon minced garlic

½ cup finely chopped onion

½ cup chopped parsley

¼ cup finely chopped celery

2 teaspoons dried thyme

2 teaspoons dry rubbed sage

1 teaspoon Dijon mustard

1½ cups fresh breadcrumbs (4 to 6 slices of bread)

⅓ cup (3/4 stick) unsalted butter, melted (3 ounces)

10-ounce box frozen chopped spinach, defrosted and drained

Salt and pepper to taste

1 Preheat the oven to 450 degrees.

2 Trim the fat to an even ⅛-inch thickness. Prick the ham all over and cut 1½-inch-deep gashes evenly over top of the ham (on the side with the fat). This will be the "top" of the ham, where you will "stuff" the stuffing (see Figure 8-6).

3 Place the garlic, onion, parsley, celery, thyme, sage, and mustard in the bowl of a food processor fitted with a metal blade. Process to a paste, then stir together in a bowl with the breadcrumbs, melted butter, and spinach to create the stuffing. Season with salt and pepper.

4 Press the stuffing deep into the gashes; fingers work best. Place the ham fat side up on a rack in the roasting pan. Roast for 20 minutes, then turn the oven down to 325 degrees. Begin checking the ham after 4 hours. Roast until the internal temperature reaches 145 degrees (approximately 5½ hours total cooking time). Let sit at room temperature, covered loosely with foil, for at least 30 minutes. The internal temperature should rise to 155 degrees.

Make the gravy while the roast is resting.

Per serving: *Calories 340 (From Fat 162); Fat 18g (Saturated 7g); Cholesterol 135mg; Sodium 152mg; Carbohydrate 3g (Dietary Fiber 1g); Protein 40g.*

Gravy

Pan drippings (about ¼ cup)
½ cup cider
½ cup Port wine
½ teaspoon sage
½ teaspoon thyme
1 tablespoon unsalted butter, at room temperature
Salt and pepper to taste

1 Pour off any fat and pan drippings and separate out the fat. Place any drippings you have collected (they will be minimal) in a saucepan and add cider. Bring to a boil over medium heat and cook until slightly reduced and thickened, about 3 minutes.

2 Add port, sage, and thyme, reduce heat and simmer for 5 minutes. Season with salt and pepper, whisk in butter, strain into a gravy boat, and serve.

Remember: *Remember to always rest your roast before carving. The down time will allow the juices to redistribute and your meat will be as succulent as it can be.*

Per serving: *Calories 58 (From Fat 36); Fat 4g (Saturated 2g); Cholesterol 9mg; Sodium 61mg; Carbohydrate 5g (Dietary Fiber 0g); Protein 1g.*

MAKING SLITS IN FRESH HAM AND PUSHING IN STUFFING

TRIM THE FAT TO AN EVEN 1/8" THICK. PRICK THE HAM ALL OVER AND CUT 1½" DEEP GASHES EVENLY OVER THE TOP (THE SIDE WITH THE FAT).

PRESS THE STUFFING DEEP INTO THE GASHES WITH YOUR FINGERS.

Figure 8-6: Flavoring fresh ham with an herb stuffing.

Preparing and Serving a Christmas Goose

"Christmas is coming, the geese are getting fat. Please put a penny in the old man's hat." Sounds very English, doesn't it? In fact, goose was the main dish of choice for the Crachit family in *A Christmas Carol* and is favored in England as a traditional Christmas dish.

Although goose has some things in common with other birds, you should take some particulars into consideration. But first, the shared traits. As with all poultry, look for skin that is free of nicks or bruises. The flesh should smell fresh and, if the goose is wrapped in plastic, a minimal amount of juices should be in the bottom of the packaging. Like turkey, if you buy goose frozen, leave ample time for it to defrost in the refrigerator, preferably a few days.

Now, the differences. The goose is an odd-looking bird. Maybe it's just that we're so used to seeing chickens and turkeys, which are round and plump. Comparatively, the goose is long and narrow, rectangular even, and it has these long, bony arms, er, I mean wings. The flesh also sometimes has little bumps — hence the term *goose bumps* (although the goose isn't the only bird that has them).

The most important thing you need to know about buying and serving a goose is that its weight is primarily made up of bone, so you should figure about 2 pounds of raw goose per person. Also, it's all dark meat, so white-meat lovers be forewarned. And it's a very fatty bird, so your cooking technique must take this into consideration.

Goose is expensive, especially when compared to turkey, which can be quite cheap. If you want to make goose, know that it will have a hefty price tag. But the goose is probably a once-a-year treat, so consider that when making your decision.

Knowing when your goose is cooked

The phrase "your goose is cooked" has negative connotations, and I can't imagine why. A properly cooked goose is a culinary wonder and you should try it at least once. So the next time someone throws this term at you, respond by saying, "It most certainly is, and very well at that!" in as bright a tone as possible. Your verbal attacker will look confused and slink away. And now you don't have to share any of your amazingly delicious goose with that negative-thinking person.

Anyway, getting back to that fat issue I mentioned earlier, I've provided you with a cooking technique where the bird is dipped in boiling water. This tightens the skin, which not only helps squeeze out the fat during roasting, but also helps the skin roast up nice and crisp. Don't skip this step because it really does make a difference. Also, please read the recipe thoroughly and note that you must start this recipe one to two *days* ahead of time.

You may notice that I have stuffed this goose, whereas I did not stuff the turkey. That's because some folks love a stuffed bird, and I wanted to provide a recipe to make them happy. We all deserve to be happy during Christmas! Here's my present to you stuffed-bird lovers. Soon you'll be stuffed stuffed-bird lovers.

You may notice that a thermometer is missing from the list of suggested tools. This is because, although you do want the goose to come up to about 170 degrees in the thigh, it will do so rather quickly — and the meat may still be a bit tough. The bird really needs to cook longer; the internal temperature will not rise much more, and due to the high fat content, there is very little chance of the meat drying out. Just take my word for it and understand that the longer cooking time yields more tender meat.

There are four ways to assess doneness with a goose:

- Use the suggested roasting time as your first gauge.
- Use your eyes. The skin should be puffed and taut.
- Use your sense of touch. Gently press the drumsticks. The meat underneath the skin should feel very soft and tender.
- If you want to be absolutely sure, insert a knife at the base of the thigh. If the juices are pink, the goose is not done yet. The juices should run clear. (If there are no juices, the goose is overcooked.)

Carving a goose

If you know how to carve a turkey, you can carve a goose, but there is one big difference. The joints of the goose are much closer together and tighter, which makes cutting between them more difficult. Just use a sharp knife, be aggressive, and don't let the goose win. You've gotten this far; you can do it. Consider carving the goose in the kitchen instead of at the table. There is nothing as comical, or pathetic, as a cook wrestling with his cooked food. The goose may put up a bit of a fight, and it's best experienced by just you and the goose in private.

Goose with Apples and Cognac

This Christmas goose is completed with the Sausage, Apple, and Cognac stuffing from Chapter 9. Read this recipe all the way through — you need to start 24 to 48 hours ahead of time.

Special equipment: *Pot large enough to submerge half of the goose, roasting pan with flat rack, trussing needle and twine, bulb baster*

Preparation time: *15 minutes*

Cooking time: *4½ hours*

Yield: *6 to 8 servings*

Goose — 24 to 48 Hours Ahead

12- to 13-pound goose

1 One or two days before roasting, remove any loose fat and the giblets and neck from the goose cavity. Cut off the first two wing joints if they're still attached. Reserve all of the above.

2 Remove any pin feathers or quills that remain using a small pair of pliers and discard. Flip up the neck fat and locate the wishbone. Using a sharp paring knife, scrape along the wishbone to free it from the meat and remove it. Prick the skin all over using a sharp trussing needle or a skewer, holding the implement horizontally to the bird so that you only prick skin and not the meat.

3 Fill a large pot two-thirds of the way with water and bring to boil over high heat. Submerge half the goose in the water. Hold for 1 minute and then remove. (Wearing clean rubber gloves can help make maneuvering the goose in the boiling water easier. You'll have a better grip than with bare hands.) Repeat with the other half of the goose. Remove the goose from the water and let any extra water drain out. Pat the goose dry inside and out.

3 Place the goose, breast side up, on a flat rack set in the roasting pan. Refrigerate for 24 to 48 hours.

4 Make the stock.

Tip: *Pricking the goose evenly all over takes some time; be patient as it is an important step. Also, rubber gloves can protect your hands while submerging the goose in the boiling water. After its hot bath, the goose will have prominent goose bumps.*

Stock

Reserved giblets and neck

4 cups low-sodium chicken broth

4 cups water

2 carrots, cut into 2-inch pieces

2 stalks celery, cut into 2-inch pieces

1 onion, unpeeled, cut into eighths

4 parsley stems

4 sprigs fresh thyme

1 bay leaf

1 Combine all the ingredients in a stockpot. Bring to a boil, uncovered, over medium-high heat. Simmer until reduced to about 3 cups liquid, about 2 hours. Allow the stock to cool.

2 Remove the giblets and chop finely. Remove any meat from the neck and chop finely. Set aside for the gravy. Strain the stock through a fine mesh strainer and refrigerate in an airtight container until you're ready to roast the goose, between 24 and 48 hours later.

Goose — The Day Of

Prepped goose

Bread Stuffing with Sausage, Apples, and Cognac (see Chapter 9), at room temperature

1 Preheat the oven to 325 degrees.

2 Heat the stuffing in the microwave or toss it together in a large sauté pan over medium heat. Loosely stuff the main cavity and neck cavity of the goose with the warm stuffing until almost full. Sew up the neck and main cavity with trussing needle and twine. Place any extra stuffing in a buttered casserole dish and cover with foil.

3 Place the goose breast side down on the roasting pan with a flat rack and roast for 1¾ hours. Carefully remove the goose from the oven and remove fat with a bulb baster. (Reserve fat for other purpose, if desired). Turn the goose breast side up and roast for 1¾ to 2¼ hours more. To assess doneness, look for puffed, taut skin and gently press the drumsticks. The meat underneath the skin should feel very soft and tender. You can also insert a knife at the base of the thigh. If the juices are pink, the goose is not done yet. The juices should run clear.

4 Turn the heat up to 400 degrees and roast for 15 minutes longer to crisp the skin. Let the goose sit for 30 minutes before carving. Make the gravy while the goose rests. You can also use this time to heat any extra stuffing or side dishes.

Gravy

Stock

¼ cup white wine

1 tablespoon cognac

5 tablespoons unsalted butter

⅓ cup flour

Salt and pepper to taste

1 Pour the pan drippings through a strainer, then into a fat separator or into a measuring cup and skim off the fat. Separate out all the pan drippings; add them back to the roasting pan. Place the roasting pan on a burner and add the white wine and cognac. Set heat to high and bring to a boil, scraping up any browned bits that are on the pan bottom. Boil for about 2 minutes to combine flavors and to thicken pan drippings. Strain.

2 In a clean saucepan, melt the butter and stir in the flour. Cook over medium heat for 2 minutes until golden brown. Slowly add the pan drippings and enough of the stock to make a gravy consistency; you may not use all the stock. Keep whisking for a smooth consistency. Stir in the reserved chopped giblets and neck meat, if desired. Season with salt and pepper and serve with the goose.

Per serving (goose, gravy, and stuffing): *Calories 1,136 (From Fat 648); Fat 72g (Saturated 25g); Cholesterol 259mg; Sodium 914mg; Carbohydrate 48g (Dietary Fiber 6g); Protein 73g.*

Wrapping Another Present for Dark Meat Fans: Duck

I'm a fan of dark meat from poultry. When I make turkey, I go straight for the thigh meat. If you're a dark meat aficionado, goose and duck are a great Christmas present to give yourself. Both birds are all dark meat. They provide a hearty alternative to red meat. Of course, there is a downside. If you're a white meat enthusiast, these might not be the main dishes for you.

With that in mind, consider the following stovetop sensation: Duck Breasts with Dried Cherry Wine Sauce. This dish is guaranteed to impress your family and guests and you can make it in 30 minutes or less. If one of your holiday parties falls on a work night, this dish is perfect.

Duck Breasts with Dried Cherry Wine Sauce

First, you have to make a trip to a specialty food store to buy dried cherries and *demi-glace,* which is a rich, flavorful stock reduction. A butcher can get the duck breasts for you. Different ones are on the market, but Pekin duck breasts (Long Island style) are particularly lean and a perfect size — take a look at the color section of this book for a picture of the finished dish. For the marmalade component, use regular orange marmalade or the Clementine Cranberry Marmalade in Chapter 15.

Preparation time: *15 minutes*

Cooking time: *15 minutes*

Yield: *4 servings*

2 whole Pekin duck breasts, cut in half (the four half breasts should weigh approximately 8 ounces each)

2 teaspoons salt

1 teaspoon pepper

1 teaspoon thyme

¾ cup water

¼ cup demi-glace

¼ cup dried cherries

2 tablespoons orange marmalade

2 teaspoons cider vinegar

¼ cup fruity dry red wine, such as Merlot

2 tablespoons chopped parsley

1 Trim the duck breasts of excess fat; pat the breasts dry. Score the breast meat and skin in a crosshatch pattern into small ½-inch squares. (This will help quickly render the fat when it is in the pan, which will prevent the duck from sticking.) Combine the salt, pepper, and thyme and season the breasts on all sides. Set aside.

2 Whisk the water and demi-glace together in a clean saucepan until they're blended. Add the cherries, marmalade, and vinegar and bring to a boil over medium heat. Turn the heat down and simmer for 5 minutes or until the sauce thickens. Add the wine and return to a boil for 2 minutes. Season with salt and pepper; keep warm.

3 Heat a large heavy skillet over high heat. Add the breasts, skin side down, and cook over high heat for 5 minutes or until the skin has begun to brown and crisp. (The duck fat may smoke as it cooks off.) Turn the breasts over and cook about 3 minutes more, depending on how rare you want the meat to be. Unlike chicken, duck breasts are best a bit pink. Remember that they will continue to cook once removed from the heat.

4 Remove from the skillet onto a plate, let rest for 1 minute, and slice crosswise into thin slices. Fan out the slices on warmed dinner plates and spoon the warm sauce over the top. Sprinkle with chopped parsley and serve immediately. Pass the rest of the red wine.

Tip: *These go great with wild rice or sweet potatoes as a side dish. Make a green veggie too, like broccoli or green beans. This is a pricey main dish, but consider the convenience factor. Time is in short supply this time of year, so a little extra money goes a long way.*

Per serving: *Calories 232 (From Fat 81); Fat 9g (Saturated 2g); Cholesterol 82mg; Sodium 1,717mg; Carbohydrate 23g (Dietary Fiber 1g); Protein 17g.*

Concocting a Christmas Casserole and Stew

The term *casserole* can be used to describe a dish that holds a recipe or can refer to the recipe itself. In general, a casserole is a dish that's made in one pot — a casserole! Because casseroles are assembled and then cooked in one dish, they tend to be easy to make; most of the work is done for you while the flavors and ingredients meld together in the oven.

In this section, I offer you a fancy-sounding but easy-to-make French classic *cassoulet* ("kass-oo-lay") that you can even make a month ahead and freeze, and a seafood stew that you can prepare in mere minutes. Both are perfect for holiday entertaining.

Shortcut Cassoulet

This dish is much quicker to make than traditional cassoulet and actually benefits from an overnight rest in the refrigerator. You can even freeze this dish a month ahead after preparing it through Step 3. This cassoulet makes a complete meal with red wine, crusty bread, and a green salad.

I don't suggest that you add salt, because the ingredients contribute plenty. Taste it before you salt it.

Preparation time: *10 minutes*

Cooking time: *1½ hours*

Yield: *8 to 10 servings*

6 slices bacon, cut into 1-inch wide pieces

2 onions, diced

2 celery stalks, diced

2 carrots, diced

2 garlic cloves, minced

2 teaspoons thyme

1 bay leaf

4 chicken thighs

1 pound cubed lamb (2-inch pieces)

1 pound cubed pork (2-inch pieces)

1 pound kielbasa or garlic sausage, cut into 1-inch thick slices

Two 15-ounce cans Great Northern beans (or other small white beans), drained

14.5-ounce can diced tomatoes in juice

1 cup dry white wine

Pepper to taste

2 cups fresh breadcrumbs, preferably from French bread

2 tablespoons olive oil

1 cup chopped flat-leaf parsley

1. Sauté the bacon in large ovenproof pot over medium-high heat until it's just beginning to crisp, about 6 minutes. Remove the bacon with a slotted spoon and drain on paper towels. Remove all but 3 tablespoons of the bacon fat and discard the rest.
2. Sauté the onions, celery and carrots in the bacon fat over medium heat until the veggies soften and begin to brown, about 8 minutes. Add the thyme and bay leaf and chicken thighs. Brown thighs over medium-high heat for about 5 minutes. Remove the thighs and add cubed lamb and pork. Brown the cubes, about 5 minutes.
3. Preheat the oven to 350 degrees. Add the bacon back into the pot, along with the thighs, sausage, beans, tomatoes, and wine. Season with pepper and bring to a boil over medium heat.

4 Top with the breadcrumbs, drizzle with olive oil, and bake for 1 hour, or until the topping is crisp and the cassoulet is bubbling. Top with parsley and serve immediately.

Tip: *To make this dish ahead, prepare through Step 3 without preheating the oven or bringing the ingredients to a boil. Cool to room temperature, place in an airtight container, and freeze for up to a month or refrigerate overnight. Defrost and/or reheat, bring back to a boil, and proceed with Step 4.*

Tip: *You don't have to cube the pork and lamb yourself. Ask your butcher to make the lamb cubes from the leg and the pork cubes from the loin, both of which are leaner than the shoulder. You should be able to make this request of supermarket meat department butchers.*

Tip: *Two kinds of bay leaf are on the market. Some come from California and have a quite strong flavor. Turkish bay leaf is preferred. It is milder and has a depth of flavor that the domestic variety just can't match. Try using a bay leaf in salt-free dishes to perk up the flavors. And don't forget to remove the bay leaf after cooking. You don't eat it!*

Per serving: *Calories 512 (From Fat 261); Fat 29g (Saturated 9g); Cholesterol 115mg; Sodium 729mg; Carbohydrate 24g (Dietary Fiber 5g); Protein 38g.*

Cooking with wine

An old adage says that if you wouldn't drink the wine, don't bother cooking with it. This is a good rule to live by. There are bottles of cooking wines in the supermarket, but steer clear of them. A good approach is to find a relatively inexpensive wine that you like to drink and stick with it. That way, you won't be wasting time reading labels every time you need a bottle to cook with. A domestic table wine should be fine. Keep a bottle of red and a bottle of white handy for cooking.

Low-Fat Seafood Stew

This satisfying seafood stew is almost a meal in itself. Just add crusty bread and perhaps a salad and cheese course. This is an expensive meal to make, but the time spent in the kitchen is so miniscule and the stew is so impressive that you get a lot for your buck — see the color section of this book for a photo.

Preparation time: *10 minutes*

Cooking time: *25 minutes*

Yield: *8 servings*

¼ cup olive oil

2 large yellow onions, diced

1 fennel bulb, chopped and diced, fennel tops reserved

1 tablespoon minced garlic

1 tablespoon thyme

2 teaspoons crushed rosemary

1 bay leaf

4 cups bottled clam juice

2 cups dry white wine

28-ounce can plum tomatoes, drained and chopped

2 dozen small clams, scrubbed

2 dozen mussels, scrubbed

2 pounds sea bass fillets, cut into 1-inch pieces

2 dozen large shrimp (20 to 25 shrimp per pound size)

Three 4-ounce frozen lobster tails, defrosted, cut into thirds

1 Heat the oil in a large pot over medium heat. Add the onions and fennel and sauté until beginning to soften, about 8 minutes total. Add the garlic, thyme, rosemary, and bay leaf and sauté 3 minutes more, or until the onion is translucent.

2 Add the clam juice, wine, and tomatoes. Cover and bring to a boil over medium-high heat. Turn the heat down and simmer for 10 minutes to blend the flavors.

3 When the liquid is at a simmer, add the clams and mussels and cook 2 minutes. Add the sea bass, shrimp, and lobster tails and cook for a few more minutes until the shrimp is pink and the fish and lobster is opaque. Be careful not to overcook. While the stew cooks, chop the fennel fronds.

4 Ladle into bowls, top with fennel fronds, and serve immediately with crusty bread.

Simplify: *Break up this recipe to make your last-minute preparations as brief as possible. Prepare the recipe through Step 2 either the morning of the dinner or the night before. Just bring the liquid mixture to a boil and proceed from Step 3.*

Per serving: *Calories 387 (From Fat 126); Fat 14g (Saturated 3g); Cholesterol 211mg; Sodium 1,172mg; Carbohydrate 11g (Dietary Fiber 2g); Protein 51g.*

Every Sunday Is Pasta Night

Well, it was when I was growing up, anyway, particularly in the wintertime when we spent every weekend skiing. Sunday night was pasta night because we would be pleasantly exhausted from our exciting weekend and need satisfying food fast. Pasta fit the bill.

Both my parents were wonderful cooks, but pasta seems to be the domain of my dad. He is a very intuitive cook — he takes bits of this and bits of that from the refrigerator and always comes up with a delicious sauce. One day, he sautéed a bunch of thinly sliced onions in olive oil until they were soft, golden, and caramelized. I remember the huge mound he started out with and how he kept the heat fairly low. Slowly, bit by bit, the pile of sharp-tasting onions dissolved into a molten mass of sweet, luscious, caramelized onion sauce. He added a splash of wine and some cracked black pepper and it was done — almost. He took some of the hot pasta water and stirred it into the onions, and they loosened up and turned creamy. Parmesan cheese completed the dish. The Fusilli with Caramelized Onions is inspired by that sauce.

Don't underestimate the power of pasta water. Usually, we disregard the water that we cook food in, but the water from pasta is rich in starch. A little of it stirred into a sauce can not only thin it, but also add body and richness. Sound contradictory? I understand, but when you try it, you'll see than while stirring in this liquid, the sauce will thicken slightly. It's like when you add olive oil to something; it gets thinner from the liquid nature of the oil, but thicker and richer from the properties the oil brings to the dish.

Quick pasta sauces

Pasta is the quintessential busy-night dinner. Here are some ideas for quick sauces:

- A can of light tuna, chopped canned tomatoes, black olives, and capers
- Heavy cream, black pepper, and lots of Parmesan or Romano cheese (add shredded cooked chicken for Chicken Alfredo)
- Butter, garlic, and shucked clams topped with parsley
- Stir-fried veggies with some soy sauce

Also, make sure to check out the prepared sauces that many supermarkets now have in the refrigerator section. You can find everything from pesto to Alfredo. You're probably used to looking for the jarred sauces in the pasta sauce aisle, but the refrigerator case offers options that shouldn't be overlooked.

Tossing pasta with kalamata olives

Sometimes you see kalamata olives spelled with a C instead of a K, but they are one and the same. These are nothing like canned black olives. Canned black olives are okay, but they have a very subtle taste. Kalamata olives are brine-cured, small, black, and so zesty, salty, and delicious that they accent everything you add them to — and they're great if they go straight into your mouth. Served as-is in a small bowl, they make a great addition to an hors d'oeuvre table. In the Fusilli with Caramelized Onions, the saltiness of the olives and the natural sweetness of the caramelized onions make a great combo. You can often find kalamata olives already pitted, which saves you time.

More often than not, high-quality olives come with pits. You can occasionally find pitted, but if you can't, you have to get the pit out of there somehow. Inexpensive olive pitters are on the market. They are handheld devices that work like scissors. One side has a little cup to hold the olive; the other part plunges into the olive and presses the pit out the other side. You pit one olive at a time, but it goes quite quickly. These tools are inexpensive, but you may not want to purchase one as they have limited uses — although you can also use them to pit cherries for pie in the summer. If you don't have a pitter, you can slice olives in half and then use the point of your knife to flick out the pit. Or you can just use your fingers and dig it out. Fingernails help.

Kalamata olives are delicious when mixed with pasta and caramelized onions, as in the following recipe.

Fusilli with Caramelized Onions and Kalamata Olives

Fusilli is a corkscrew-shaped pasta. It's the perfect shape to grab a hold of this caramelized onion sauce. A large wok is the ideal vessel for sautéing the large amount of onions. You need to get your timing down right in this recipe. The pasta should be finishing at the same time the sauce is finishing. This synchronicity will make the best use of your time and produce the best results.

Preparation time: *5 minutes*

Cooking time: *30 minutes*

Yield: *2 servings*

4 cups sliced yellow or white onions

5 tablespoons olive oil

2 minced garlic cloves

1 teaspoon thyme

¼ cup dry vermouth

Salt and pepper to taste

¼ cup chopped kalamata olives

½ pound fusilli pasta

Parmesan cheese to taste

1 Sauté the onions and garlic in the olive oil in a large heavy-bottomed, deep-sided pan over medium heat. Keep the heat low enough to allow the onions to soften slowly and not burn. Stir frequently.

2 After about 20 minutes, add the thyme and put the salted pasta water on to boil; cook the pasta. After about 30 minutes, the onions should be soft and caramelized. Turn the heat to high and add the vermouth. Cook for 2 minutes, stirring constantly. Season with salt and pepper and stir in the olives.

3 Add a little of the hot pasta water to loosen up the sauce, beginning with 1 to 2 tablespoons, drain the pasta, and add the pasta to the onions. Toss and serve; pass the cheese and a pepper mill.

Tip: *Adding pasta water back into a sauce is a "by-feel" kind of procedure. Start with a tablespoon or two, adding more if the sauce seems to need it. You'll know. You want a sauce texture that will combine well with the pasta — not too thin so that it slides off, and not so firm so that it can't be tossed with the pasta.*

Simplify: *Dry vermouth is preferable, but a dry white wine is fine too.*

Per serving: *Calories 796 (From Fat 351); Fat 39g (Saturated 5g); Cholesterol 0mg; Sodium 485mg; Carbohydrate 97g (Dietary Fiber 8g); Protein 16g.*

Concocting a family favorite: Lasagne

Lasagna is a broad, flat pasta noodle that's used for layering with other yummy components to make up a hearty pasta casserole: lasagne. (I know — you think I'm misspelling it. But cooks who know spell the noodle with an *a* and the dish with an *e*. I hope I keep them straight!) It's hard to go wrong with lasagne, which just about everyone loves. The following version combines spinach with a variety of cheeses *and* is a great make-ahead dish that you can freeze and then nuke in the microwave to reheat.

Five-Cheese Spinach Lasagne

This dish is velvety rich and will satisfy the vegetarians and the meat eaters in your crowd. It has a cream sauce enhanced by mascarpone (cheese #1) and sun-dried tomatoes, then layered with pasta, spinach, sautéed onions, red wine, ricotta (#2), mozzarella, (#3), Parmesan (#4), and Romano (#5). The sun-dried tomatoes and spinach give it a delicate red and green Christmas theme. Serve with a big green salad with tangy balsamic vinaigrette and a loaf of crusty bread.

Tools: *4-quart baking dish (15 x 10 x 2 inches)*

Preparation time: *20 minutes*

Cooking time: *45 minutes*

Yield: *12 servings*

1 pound lasagna noodles

¾ cup (1½ sticks) unsalted butter

¾ cup all-purpose flour

4 cups whole milk, at room temperature

3 ounces sun-dried tomatoes, chopped (yields ¾ cup)

1 cup mascarpone

1 pound fresh spinach leaves, stemmed

2 tablespoons olive oil

2 medium onions, sliced

3 cloves garlic, minced

¼ cup dry red wine

1 cup whole milk ricotta cheese

½ cup grated Parmesan cheese

½ cup grated Romano cheese

1 pound mozzarella, grated

Salt and pepper to taste

1 Boil the lasagna noodles per the manufacturer's instructions. Drain and rinse with water to prevent sticking. You can also use no-boil noodles.

2 Preheat the oven to 350 degrees now if you will be baking the lasagne right away.

3 Melt the butter in a large saucepan and add the flour. Whisk until smooth and cook for 2 minutes, whisking often, to remove the raw taste from the flour. Slowly whisk in the milk and chopped tomatoes. Cook over medium heat until it comes to a simmer and thickens, about 3 minutes. Whisk in the mascarpone, season liberally with salt and pepper, and set aside.

4 Heat the olive oil in a skillet over medium-high heat and sauté the onions until they're very soft; add the garlic and continue to cook until the onions begin to caramelize, about 8 minutes total. Add the red wine and cook for 1 minute until the onions absorb the wine. Season with salt and pepper.

5 Rinse the spinach leaves and shake off the excess water. Place in a large pot, cover, and cook over medium heat until they cook down, about 5 minutes. The water clinging to the spinach leaves is enough to steam them. Drain in a colander and squeeze out excess water. Place in large bowl and stir in ricotta, Parmesan, and Romano cheeses. Season with salt and pepper.

6 Layer the lasagna in a 4-quart baking dish (15 x 10 x 2 inches): Spread one-third of the cheese/tomato sauce evenly across the bottom of the dish. Top with one-third of the noodles, cutting the noodles to fit, if necessary. Spread half the spinach mixture on top, then half the onion mixture. Sprinkle with one-third of the mozzarella. Repeat. The final layer is made with noodles, sauce, and mozzarella on top.

7 Bake it immediately in a preheated 350-degree oven for about 45 minutes, or cover it with plastic wrap and refrigerate overnight or up to two days. You can also freeze the uncooked lasagne for up to a month. (Remove the plastic and bring to room temperature before baking.)

If you're oven is full, you can microwave the lasagne, but you will probably have to cut it in half and put the halves in smaller pans; measure your microwave! Nuke it at full power for about 20 minutes. Regardless of how you cook it, the lasagne should be bubbly and lightly browned on the top. Let sit 5 minutes after removing from oven and serve.

Simplify: *Use frozen spinach instead of fresh. Buy a 1-pound bag or a box of frozen whole leaf spinach, cook it according to the package instructions, and drain well; then proceed with the recipe.*

Vary It! *You can substitute skim mozzarella and ricotta for the whole milk versions if you like. Any way you make it, however, this dish is rich. If you can't find mascarpone cheese, substitute an equal amount of ricotta.*

Simplify: *Boiling lasagna noodles is no big deal, but in some markets you can find no-boil noodles. They are somewhere between fresh pasta and dried and can be layered with the other components of the recipe without being boiled first. They cost more but save you time.*

Per serving: *Calories 618 (From Fat 351); Fat 39g (Saturated 22g); Cholesterol 114mg; Sodium 557mg; Carbohydrate 44g (Dietary Fiber 3g); Protein 24g.*

Is the pasta done?

Always use a large pot with plenty of water to cook pasta. The pasta should have room to float around freely to inhibit sticking. Salt the water liberally or the pasta will taste flat. Use about 2 teaspoons of salt per gallon of water. Oil is not necessary if you use enough water; it will make the pasta slick, which will prevent your sauce from adhering.

Cook pasta until *al dente,* which literally means "to the tooth" in Italian. Al dente pasta should be tender but firm. Your teeth should sink into the outer part of the pasta and then hit a spot in the center where there's still a bit of resistance and firmness. If you bite a piece in half and look at it, the center sometimes has a tiny white dot; that's the less-cooked middle. If you want to throw your pasta at the wall to see if it sticks, it's up to you, but I've never gotten the hang of this much-talked-about method and really don't understand how it works. I don't like cleaning walls any more than I have to, either.

Do not rinse pasta after draining it. All the starch on the pasta helps whatever sauce you choose stick to it, making your dish all the tastier. (Lasagna noodles are an exception. You need to rinse lasagna to keep the noodles from sticking to one another, or you will never be able to pick up the individual pieces to layer them in your baking dish.)

Reserve some pasta water in case your sauce needs to be loosened up. The starch in the water can help give body to a sauce as well.

Immediately add the pasta to the warmed sauce in the sauce's pan. Toss the pasta and the sauce together well before serving. This is the best way to properly combine pasta and sauce. If you wait too long to add the pasta to the sauce after the pasta has drained, the pasta will become sticky and impossible to separate. Time is of the essence.

Chapter 9

Complementing the Main Dish with a Chorus of Sides

In This Chapter

- Preparing the ultimate mashed potato
- Making sweet potatoes and yams
- Adding tasty twists to squash and other veggies
- Whipping up a classic white sauce
- Making stuffings that win applause

Recipes in This Chapter

Selecting the side dishes for a Christmas-season meal is a lot like decorating your home for the holidays. You want each bit of décor — each offering on the table — to be part of the overall theme but to still be individually sensational.

Suppose roast beef is the main dish. For side dishes, are you thinking silky mashed potatoes, or creamy, cheesy cauliflower casserole, or an elegant wild rice stuffing? I am, and they're all in this chapter, plus lots more.

I could be mundane and mention the food pyramid. But this is Christmas, so picture the "food tree" shaped like a spruce and save a nice broad mid-section of the tree for vegetables — which are mainly what I think of when I think of side dishes, although I also include a few non-vegetable recipes in this chapter.

Please Pass the Potatoes

If you like mashed potatoes that have some texture, use a hand-held potato masher, which is also the easiest way to make them. The potatoes just go right back in the pot in which they were cooked and you mash away after adding the milk and butter.

However, you will never get completely smooth potatoes if you use a masher. Now, that's not necessarily a bad thing. Some folks just love lumpy mashed potatoes. Others, myself included, can't get enough of the ultra-smooth variety. (Actually, if you make me mashed potatoes, I will eat them any way you dish them up.)

Whichever way you go, you are bound to please some of the folks who you're cooking for and let down others, so don't sweat it. If you like them smooth and have the time, use a food mill or potato ricer. If you like them lumpy or are short on time, use a hand-held masher. No matter your preference, hardly anyone ever turns down mashed potatoes and they usually bring a smile to all the faces at the table.

Note: A potato ricer is sort of like a giant garlic press (see Figure 9-1). You put the boiled potatoes into a cup and then squeeze them out through small holes. A food mill is a sieve-like contraption that has a large, flat rotary mechanism that you turn via a handle and it presses the food through the sieve. But remember: Don't overlook that hand-held potato masher — it works just fine.

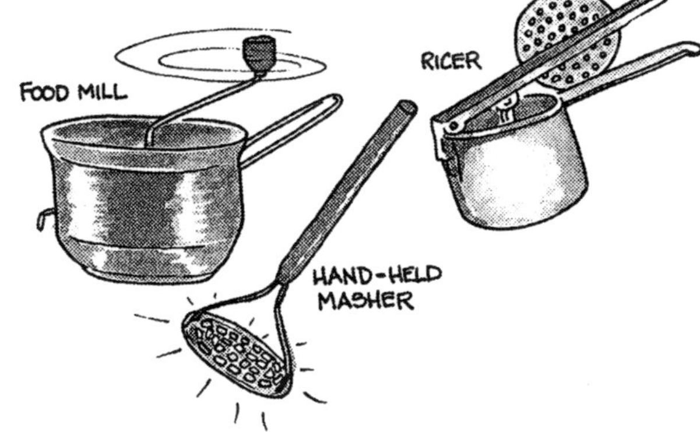

Figure 9-1: Tools for mashing potatoes.

Resist putting potatoes into a food processor, where they will turn gummy. The starch cells in the potatoes swell while cooking, and the action of the food processor breaks them down to such a degree that they burst. The result is a gluey texture.

Classic Mashed Potatoes

Mashed potatoes go with just about every holiday main dish and are universally loved by young and old — they are a definite crowd-pleaser.

Remember that not all potatoes are created equal. Do not try to make mashed potatoes with waxy potatoes. You could try Yukon gold potatoes, which are an all-purpose potato. Their buttery flavor and color make wonderful mashed potatoes.

Special equipment: *Potato ricer or food mill (optional), double boiler (optional)*

Preparation time: *5 minutes*

Cooking time: *30 minutes*

Yield: *10 servings*

Four pounds (about 12 medium) russet potatoes (Idahos)

2 cups hot whole milk or half-and-half

½ cup (1 stick) unsalted butter at room temperature, cut into pieces

Salt and pepper to taste

1 Wash the potatoes well, but don't peel them. Boiling the tubers in their jackets keeps in all that subtle flavor. Place them in a large stockpot and cover with cold water. Bring to a boil over high heat; turn the heat down and simmer until tender, for about 30 minutes (although it may take up to 45 minutes). When the potatoes are done, you should be able to insert a sharp knife tip easily. Drain in a colander and let cool slightly.

2 Peel the potatoes. Cut or break them into large chunks and press them through a ricer or food mill right into the drained pot. Add the hot milk a bit at a time, whisking it in with a heavy wire whisk. If you're not using a ricer or food mill, this is where you use a hand masher or an electric mixer, in which case you would mash or whip to your desired consistency. You may need a little extra milk, or you may not use all of it, depending on how dry the potatoes are. Whisk in the butter and season with salt and pepper.

3 Serve immediately, or keep warm covered in the top of a double boiler. This recipe makes a large amount, so you can make a large double boiler by putting the potatoes in a large bowl set into a large pot filled with hot water. Covered, they may be held for 30 minutes this way.

4 Alternatively, pack the mashed potatoes into a buttered casserole dish, cover with plastic wrap, and refrigerate overnight. Bring to room temperature before reheating. Reheat, uncovered, in the oven or microwave until heated through. Mashed potatoes are pretty forgiving when it comes to reheating, but I recommend an oven temperature of around 350 degrees if you aren't using the microwave.

Per serving: *Calories 246 (From Fat 99); Fat 11g (Saturated 7g); Cholesterol 31mg; Sodium 90mg; Carbohydrate 34g (Dietary Fiber 3g); Protein 5g.*

Mashed Sweet Potatoes with Bourbon and Brown Sugar

This spiked, mashed sweet potato complements many holiday foods — see the color section of this book for a photo. You could peel and boil the sweet potatoes or even cook them in the microwave, but when you bake them in the oven, the high, dry heat brings out the sugars and makes them particularly luscious. Just as with the Classic Mashed Potatoes, these take to reheating very well, and you can reheat them at a variety of temperatures.

Preparation time: *5 minutes*

Cooking time: *60 minutes*

Yield: *10 servings*

Five pounds sweet potatoes

Four tablespoons unsalted butter

¼ cup lightly packed light brown sugar

½ cup whole milk or half-and-half

⅓ cup bourbon

½ teaspoon cinnamon

½ teaspoon salt

1 Preheat the oven to 400 degrees. Scrub the potatoes clean, pierce the flesh in several places, and bake for about 50 minutes, or until they're easily pierced with a knife. You can put them on a sheet pan or right on the oven's rack. Remove from the oven and cool for 10 minutes, until they're easy to handle.

2 Slice the potatoes in half lengthwise and scrape the soft, cooked flesh into a mixing bowl with a spoon. Add 2 tablespoons of butter and begin to mash the potatoes; the butter will melt. Add the sugar and continue to mash. Slowly add the milk, bourbon, cinnamon, and salt and mash until the sweet potatoes are smooth. Serve immediately or proceed with the following steps if you're making them a day ahead.

3 Grease a 2-quart baking dish with 1 tablespoon butter, pack in the mashed sweet potatoes, and dot with the remaining 1 tablespoon of butter. Cover with plastic wrap and refrigerate overnight. Bring to room temperature before reheating.

4 Reheat uncovered in oven or microwave.

Simplify: *You can leave out the bourbon, if you like. If you make them according to the recipe, the sweet potatoes will have a bit of a kick. Adults may like it, but kids might not. You could leave it out and substitute an equal amount of orange juice, cider, or additional milk.*

Per serving: *Calories 228 (From Fat 45); Fat 5g (Saturated 3g); Cholesterol 14mg; Sodium 139mg; Carbohydrate 40g (Dietary Fiber 4g); Protein 3g.*

Making a Great Meal Perfect with the Right Veggies

Vegetables can make any meal memorable. Four things are particularly important:

- **Taste:** As is true whenever you're cooking, taste should be paramount. Always start by choosing quality ingredients and carefully follow the recipe's directions for the best possible results.
- **How the vegetables complement the rest of the meal:** When it comes to Christmas meals, there are often so many tastes and textures on the table that finding the perfect fit might not be easy. Start with the main dish and work from there. If one side dish works with the main dish, the others probably work with it as well and everything will be harmonious. A good place to start is to have one green vegetable and one starch. Also think about complementary flavors. If you have a full-flavored or even spicy main dish, consider having something soothing and calming, like mashed potatoes, as at least one of the side dishes. During the holidays, condiments come into play as well. Consider having something sweet, like a cranberry relish or roasted apples. And remember that all these foods will be sitting on the plate together, so think about color. With a green veggie in there and a relish of some sort, you'll probably automatically end up with a nice variety.
- **Ease of preparation:** Undoubtedly you will be making many different recipes for the Christmas meal. So when you are deciding what side dishes to serve you need to take into consideration how they will be prepared. Do they need oven space or can they be made on top of the stove? Do you even have any oven space to spare? How about side dishes that can be made ahead and warmed in the microwave? Think out all of these things well ahead of time and choose accordingly.
- **Nutrition:** Well, what can I say? Most of us are not thinking about our health front and center this time of year, but the season's rich foods scream for the addition of some simple, healthy foods. Always include something fresh and green such as a salad (see Chapter 6) or the green beans or sautéed broccoli raab from this chapter.

Making Christmas squash

The Glazed Winter Squash recipe is a perfect example of a recipe that becomes something completely different with small additions or substitutions of ingredients. Experiment, or utilize these suggestions. Some of these variations may match your meal better than the primary recipe does:

- **Browned Butter and Herbed Squash:** Cook the butter until it starts to brown, then add 1 teaspoon of thyme. Proceed with the recipe but don't add the honey. Try replacing the thyme with sage or oregano as well.
- **Molasses-Glazed Squash:** Use 2 tablespoons honey and 2 tablespoons unsulphured (not blackstrap) molasses to replace the ¼ cup honey and proceed as directed.
- **Garlic and Olive Oil Squash:** Use ¼ cup light olive oil instead of butter and add 2 teaspoons minced garlic along with the squash. Eliminate the honey and proceed as directed.
- **Glazed Winter Squash with Apples:** Add one peeled and diced apple to the squash as you place it in the pan. You can use sweet or tart apples.
- **Glazed Winter Squash with Dried Fruit:** Add ¼ cup raisins, golden raisins, or currants to the squash as you place it in the pan.
- **Spiced Glazed Squash:** Add ½ to 1 teaspoon of cinnamon or ginger along with the squash to the original recipe. You could also try a pinch to a ¼ teaspoon of allspice. Try the spices alone or in combination.

Glazed Winter Squash

In this recipe, you combine winter squash with butter and honey. Honey not only adds sweetness to the squash, but it adds a lot of flavor as well. Support your local bees!

Special equipment: *Very sharp chef's knife for cutting squash*

Preparation time: *5 minutes*

Cooking time: *20 minutes*

Yield: *8 servings*

¼ cup (½ stick) unsalted butter

2 butternut squash, peeled and cut into 1-inch cubes (6 cups)

¼ cup honey

Salt and pepper to taste

1 Melt the butter in a large sauté pan over medium heat. Add the squash, cover, and cook until tender, about 15 minutes. The squash should yield when pierced with a sharp knife and have begun to color around the edges. The squash may be held at this point at room temperature for 6 hours.

2 Add the honey, turn the heat to medium-high, and toss until the squash is glazed. Season liberally with salt and pepper. Serve immediately. Add a drizzle of honey for added sweetness, if desired.

Tip: *You could use other winter squashes, such as acorn or buttercup, but butternut is preferred; it has the perfect firm-but-creamy texture. You can also turn this into a maple glaze by using maple syrup instead of honey. Any which way, make sure to season well with salt* *and pepper. This is a simple recipe, and all the factors are important to the flavor of the final dish.*

Tip: *Consider using a wok if you have one. It is a perfect size and shape for this sort of dish. If your wok doesn't have a cover of its own, you can use a large lid from another pot.*

Per serving: *Calories 145 (From Fat 54); Fat 6g (Saturated 4g); Cholesterol 16mg; Sodium 80mg; Carbohydrate 25g (Dietary Fiber 4g); Protein 1g.*

Green beans with balsamic — something special!

The bright green taste and color of green beans is quite welcome on the holiday table and this dish is just as good at room temperature as it is warm, making it an excellent addition to the buffet table. The balsamic vinegar adds a bright, tangy flavor.

Balsamic Glazed Green Beans

Fresh green vegetables are infrequently served this time of year. This simple green bean dish can add a colorful, crispy element to your Christmas meal. See the color section of this book for a photo.

Preparation time: *5 minutes*

Cooking time: *10 minutes*

Yield: *8 servings*

3 pounds green beans, trimmed

½ cup extra-virgin olive oil

3 tablespoons balsamic vinegar

Salt and pepper to taste

Bring a large pot of salted water to a boil over high heat. Add the beans and cook until crisp yet still tender, about 5 minutes. Drain. Place in a serving bowl, toss with the oil and vinegar, and season with salt and pepper. Serve immediately or at room temperature.

Per serving: *Calories 181 (From Fat 126); Fat 14g (Saturated 2g); Cholesterol 0mg; Sodium 473mg; Carbohydrate 14g (Dietary Fiber 5g); Protein 3g.*

Now for something completely different — broccoli raab (rhymes with Bob)

There is broccoli and then there is broccoli raab, also known as broccoli rabe, broccoli di rape, and rapini, as well as a few other names. It comes in a bunch, like the broccoli you are familiar with, but it is leafier with smaller, sparser buds. It also has a completely different taste. Broccoli raab is very sharp and is often described as bitter. Now, bitter is not a quality that most Americans enjoy in their food, but please, at least give it a try. It is a great flavor during the holidays as it is assertive enough to cut through many of the rich dishes we enjoy.

When shopping for broccoli raab, look for a bunch with a lot of moist, firm leaves, few buds, no open flowers, and thin stems. The leaves should not be wilted in the least or have any yellow color. The bunch should look like a bunch of fresh flowers, all perky and such. Broccoli raab is very perishable and should be used within a day or two or you will end up with limp leaves and a dead-looking vegetable. Before preparing, trim off the thicker part of the stems. You cook all the leaves as well as the buds. You can then leave the stalks whole or cut them into bite-sized pieces. Broccoli raab is available year-round, but is best during the winter months.

If the flavor is too intense for you, just plunge the broccoli raab in a large pot of boiling water for about 2 minutes, drain, and proceed.

Sautéed Broccoli Raab

Unless you have a huge sauté pan, you may have to divide this in half and make it twice. The recipe steps assume that this is the case. A large wok works well also, if you have one. See the color section of this book for a photo of the finished dish.

Preparation time: *5 minutes*

Cooking time: *20 minutes*

Yield: *10 servings*

4 pounds (4 average bunches) broccoli raab

6 tablespoons light olive oil

6 garlic cloves, thinly sliced

Salt and pepper to taste

1 Wash the broccoli raab, trim away the thick part of the stems, and cut it into bite-sized pieces. Divide it into two batches.

2 Heat half the oil over medium heat in a large sauté pan. Sauté half the garlic gently for about 1 minute, until it's pale golden. Don't let the garlic burn. Add half the broccoli raab, turn the heat to high, and immediately toss with garlic oil in the pan. Cook for

about 5 minutes, tossing occasionally with tongs until the leaves have begun to wilt but they are still a bit crunchy. The broccoli raab will reduce by about two-thirds.

3 Turn out into warm serving dish. Repeat with second batch. Season to taste and serve immediately.

Tip: *Sauté the broccoli raab ahead of time, even the day before, and store it in a microwaveable container. Be sure to stop cooking while the raab is still fairly crisp. Right before serving, nuke the raab for a few minutes until it's warmed through. You can also toss it in a hot wok.*

Per serving: *Calories 106 (From Fat 72); Fat 8g (Saturated 1g); Cholesterol 0mg; Sodium 90mg; Carbohydrate 7g (Dietary Fiber 0g); Protein 4g.*

Mixing chestnuts with Brussels sprouts

Brussels sprouts seem to be one of those vegetables that people like or really don't like. Some people are just turned off by the fact that Brussels sprouts are cabbages, and they have been served overcooked cabbage so many times that they think all cabbage is limp and stinky, I mean aromatic. I'm asking you to try Brussels sprouts one more time, or maybe for the first time.

Whereas large cabbages grow individually, Brussels sprouts grow on a stalk. They look quite odd, actually. A thick stalk grows straight up out of the ground and then these little cabbages are attached to the stalk. Occasionally, you can find Brussels sprouts offered on the stalk, in which case you should look for the smallest stalk, which will be the youngest and the cabbages will be the most sweet. Usually, however, Brussels sprouts come loose, each sprout looking like the tiny cabbage that it is, in which case you can pick and choose the smallest ones with the tightest, most blemish-free leaves.

As with all cabbage, you should cook Brussels sprouts lightly and maintain some of their crisp, green nature. Overcooking Brussels sprouts is a common mistake, and is probably the main reason that they are disliked.

Chestnuts are a classic addition to Brussels sprouts. These glossy brown nuts are harvested in the fall. Before eating, they must be peeled and cooked. They have an earthy, somewhat creamy consistency that accents many other foods and is tasty by itself. If you stroll through New York City in the colder months, you'll see street vendors offering roasted chestnuts to eat out of hand. Many European desserts feature them, taking advantage of their inherent sweetness and their silky texture. In desserts, they are often pureed, sweetened, and sometimes lightened with whipped cream.

The following recipe takes advantage of fully prepared and cooked vacuum-packed chestnuts, but if you find them in their raw state and want to prepare them from scratch, here's what you need to know. Look for firm nuts, heavy for their size and with an unblemished shell. Store them in the refrigerator in a paper or perforated plastic bag for up to 4 days. To prepare the nuts, score an X on the bottom, flat side of the nut with a sharp paring knife (see Figure 9-2). Drop them into boiling water, return the water to a boil, and boil the chestnuts for 5 minutes. Drain and carefully peel the outer shell. Now the chestnuts are ready to be used in your recipe.

One pound of shell-on chestnuts yields about 8 ounces, or 2 cups, of shelled nuts.

Brussels Sprouts and Chestnuts

Here it is, a classic holiday combo that's been around for years. It has stood the test of time because the shape and size of the Brussels sprouts and chestnuts work perfectly together. The creamy, sweet nutty flavor of the chestnuts compliments the slightly bitter, crunchy Brussels sprouts like nothing else. See the color insert of this book for a photo of the dish.

Preparation time: *5 minutes*

Cooking time: *20 minutes*

Yield: *6 servings*

1 pound Brussels sprouts

3 tablespoons unsalted butter

½ pound vacuum-packed, cooked chestnuts, sliced in half

Salt and pepper to taste

1 Rinse the Brussels sprouts and remove any shriveled outer leaves. Trim the woody bottoms with a sharp paring knife and incise an X on the bottom (see Figure 9-2).

2 Fill a large pot with salted water and bring the water to a boil over high heat. Add the Brussels sprouts, bring back to a boil, and cook for about 4 minutes, depending on the size of the sprouts. They should be slightly crisp and just beginning to yield to a knife tip. Drain and rinse with cold water to stop cooking. The sprouts may be held at this point for a few hours or placed in an airtight container and refrigerated overnight.

3 Right before serving, melt the butter in a large sauté pan and add the sprouts and chestnuts. Toss the mixture to coat it in butter and cook for a few minutes until the sprouts and chestnuts are heated through. Season generously with salt and pepper and serve.

Tip: *The X cut into the bottom of the sprouts helps the dense core cook evenly along with the leaves.*

Per serving: *Calories 133 (From Fat 63); Fat 7g (Saturated 4g); Cholesterol 16mg; Sodium 314mg; Carbohydrate 17g (Dietary Fiber 4g); Protein 3g.*

2. FILL A LARGE POT WITH SALTED WATER. BRING TO A BOIL OVER HIGH HEAT. ADD SPROUTS. BRING BACK TO A BOIL AND COOK FOR 4 MINUTES, DEPENDING ON SIZE.
DRAIN + RINSE TO STOP COOKING!
SPROUTS MAY BE HELD FOR A FEW HOURS OR PUT IN AN AIRTIGHT CONTAINER FOR REFRIGERATING OVERNIGHT.

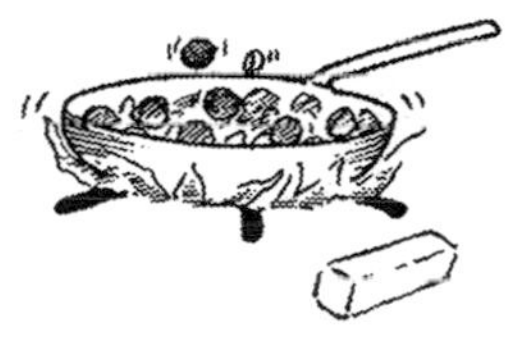

3. RIGHT BEFORE SERVING, MELT BUTTER IN A SAUTE PAN, ADD SPROUTS AND PREPARED CHESTNUTS. TOSS TO COAT IN BUTTER. COOK FOR A FEW MINUTES, TILL HEATED THROUGH!

Figure 9-2: Prepping for the Brussels Sprouts and Chestnuts

Popping carrots raw or roasting them tender

I love baby carrots, even if they aren't real babies but are larger carrots that have been whittled down into uniform pieces. You can find them in most any supermarket and they need no prep work. Although you pay a higher price, you don't have to cut off or scrape away anything. And you save time, which is so precious during the holidays.

Many recipes call for cooking the veggies until "crisp tender" or "crisp yet tender." While this term may seem like a contradiction, it's actually very descriptive. What it means is that when cooking carrots, for instance, you want them to be tender enough to be recognized as cooked, but you want them to still have a little crispness so that they don't become mushy. If you insert a sharp knife tip into a crisp-tender carrot, the knife will go into the cooked carrot, but towards the center will meet with a little resistance. This is the lightly cooked inside where the desired vestiges of crispness remain — the perfect crisp-tender carrot.

Roasted Carrots

These simply prepared carrots are sweet and crunchy. See the color section of this book for a photo.

Preparation time: *5 minutes*

Cooking time: *20 minutes*

Yield: *10 servings*

2 pounds "baby-cut" carrots

¼ cup light olive oil

Salt and pepper to taste

Preheat the oven to 375 degrees. Toss the carrots with the olive oil in a roasting pan and cook until crisp-tender, about 45 minutes. Season with salt and pepper and serve immediately.

Tip: *You can scatter the carrots in the roasting pan of a roast beef and just cook them along with the meat. Remove them when they are done, if they cook faster than the meat. They are pretty forgiving, and can pretty much roast with whatever is in the oven. If oven space is scarce, roast the carrots ahead of time, even the day before, and store them in a microwaveable container. Right before serving, nuke them for a few minutes until they're warmed through. They won't be quite the same, but it is a reasonable compromise.*

Per serving: *Calories 82 (From Fat 54); Fat 6g (Saturated 1g); Cholesterol 0mg; Sodium 90mg; Carbohydrate 7g (Dietary Fiber 2g); Protein 1g.*

Winning cauliflower fans under cover of a classic white sauce

Béchamel sauce, or *sauce Béchamel,* is a creamy, flour-thickened white sauce. It is the workhorse sauce of traditional French cooking, heralded primarily for its smooth texture and neutral flavor. After you learn how to make a white sauce, you can turn it into a variety of sauces with the addition or alteration of a few ingredients. A little more milk and the sauce thins out. A little less and you are rewarded with a thicker, more velvety sauce.

In the following recipe for Cauliflower Gratin, the proportions of butter, flour, and milk make a fairly thin sauce. For an average texture, try 2 tablespoons butter, 2 tablespoons flour, and 1¼ cups of milk and follow the technique described in the recipe.

Cauliflower Gratin

This creamy, easy casserole will delight even non-cauliflower lovers. Don't be put off by the term *gratin*. It's simply used to alternately describe a baking dish and a recipe that is baked under a crust. In this case, we have cauliflower in a creamy cheese sauce under a crust of breadcrumbs, which is a classic gratin topping.

Special equipment: *13 x 9-inch ovenproof dish*

Preparation time: *10 minutes*

Cooking time: *40 minutes*

Yield: *6 servings*

3 tablespoons unsalted butter

1 head cauliflower, cut into bite-sized florets (about 5 cups)

2 tablespoons all-purpose flour

2 cups whole milk at room temperature

2 cups grated Gruyère cheese (about 8 ounces)

Salt and pepper to taste

Pinch of nutmeg

½ cup fresh breadcrumbs

3 tablespoons Parmesan cheese

1 Preheat the oven to 375 degrees. Use 1 tablespoon of the butter to butter a 13 x 9-inch ovenproof dish.

2 Fill a large pot with salted water and bring the water to a boil over high heat. Add the cauliflower, bring the water back to a boil, and cook for about 7 minutes, or until the cauliflower is crisp yet tender.

3 Meanwhile, melt the remaining 2 tablespoons of butter in a medium-sized saucepan and add flour. Whisk constantly, cooking over medium heat for a few minutes to remove the raw taste from the flour. Slowly add milk, whisking all the while. Cook over medium heat for about 3 minutes; the sauce will come to a simmer and begin to thicken. Continue whisking until smooth and then stir in the cheese until it's melted. Season to taste with salt and pepper and a pinch of nutmeg.

4 Place the cauliflower in the buttered dish, then pour the cheese sauce uniformly over the cauliflower. Sprinkle breadcrumbs and Parmesan cheese evenly over the top.

5 Bake for about 40 minutes, or until the breadcrumbs have lightly browned and the cheese sauce is bubbling. Let sit for 5 minutes before serving.

Tip: *After you pour the cheese sauce over the cauliflower in Step 4, you can cover the dish with plastic wrap and refrigerate it overnight. Bring to room temperature while the oven preheats, unwrap, and proceed with the recipe.*

Per serving: *Calories 302 (From Fat 198); Fat 22g (Saturated 13g); Cholesterol 69mg; Sodium 348mg; Carbohydrate 11g (Dietary Fiber 2g); Protein 17g.*

Creamed Onions and Mushrooms

Take advantage of frozen pearl onions. They are easy to find, don't have any additives, and are a perfect example of a convenient product that does not compromise quality.

Preparation time: *10 minutes*

Cooking time: *40 minutes*

Yield: *10 servings*

6 tablespoons (¾ stick) unsalted butter

8 ounces mushrooms, sliced

8 ounces shiitake mushrooms, sliced

¼ teaspoon sweet paprika

4 cups frozen pearl onions, defrosted

1 cup low-sodium chicken broth

1 cup dry white wine

1 cup heavy cream

¼ cup chopped flat leaf parsley

Salt and pepper to taste

1. Melt the butter in a large sauté pan. Add both types of mushrooms and sauté over medium heat until soft, about 8 minutes. Stir in the paprika, season with salt and pepper, remove from the pan, and set aside.
2. In the same saucepan, combine the chicken broth and wine with the onions and bring to a boil over medium-high heat. Turn the heat down and simmer, uncovered, for 20 minutes or until the onions are tender and the liquid has evaporated and reduced by about one third.
3. Add the mushrooms back in along with cream, bring back to a boil, and simmer for 5 more minutes until the sauce has thickened. Remove from the heat, stir in the parsley, and season with more salt and pepper, if desired.
4. Serve immediately or pack the Creamed Onions and Mushrooms in a microwaveable serving dish, cover with plastic wrap, and refrigerate overnight. Microwave right before serving. The dish may also be reheated on top of the stove over low to medium heat.

Tip: *Make sure that you have sweet paprika, not hot paprika. They are very different. The former provides a wonderful flavor, while the later adds a lot of heat, which you do not want in this recipe.*

Tip: *Make a vegetarian version by substituting veggie broth for the chicken broth.*

Per serving: *Calories 190 (From Fat 144); Fat 16g (Saturated 10g); Cholesterol 52mg; Sodium 83mg; Carbohydrate 11g (Dietary Fiber 2g); Protein 2g.*

Exotic mushrooms

The shiitake (shee-TAH-kay) mushrooms called for in the Creamed Onions and Mushrooms recipe are exotic mushrooms that are getting easier to find every day. For many years now, my supermarket has offered an array of mushrooms right next to the common button mushrooms. Some people mistakenly believe that these are wild mushrooms, but they are really exotic mushrooms that have been commercially grown. Look for other unusual varieties such as bolete, chanterelle, enoki, morel, and oyster mushrooms. A simple sauté of any mushroom, or even a mixture of different mushrooms, in butter or olive oil with a sprinkling of salt and pepper is a great accompaniment to roast meats, poultry, or fish.

Harvesting mushrooms in the wild is not something to do yourself, even if you have a book with pictures and descriptions. Mushroom identification is extremely difficult and must be left to the experts. Many poisonous mushrooms look like edible ones, so mistakes are common. Please do not venture out on your own.

Letting Your Stuffings Run a Bit Wild

Stuffing — or dressing, if you prefer — ranks right up there with mashed potatoes on the list of favorite Christmas foods. And it isn't just for stuffing into turkeys. Consider making a stuffing as a side dish to your favorite main dish, even a weekday simple roast chicken. You can bake any stuffing in a casserole dish, in which case, because it is outside of the bird, it is sometimes called a dressing. No need to limit your stuffing intake to only when a turkey is around.

Stuffings can be based on a grain, such as rice, or come in the more familiar bread-based version. I give you one of each. First up is a wild rice dressing with fruit and nuts.

Wild rice is actually a grass and is only distantly related to rice. You prepare it like rice, although it takes longer to cook, and it never gets quite as mushy as rice can.

Wild rice retains a wonderful, chewy texture that seems to accent its nutty flavor. It is expensive, and prices go up for longer, more intact grains. I suggest splurging on the best quality you can afford. Look for it in bulk sections of natural food stores or at specialty stores where it sometimes comes prepackaged in small amounts.

The second recipe, a bread stuffing, is quite versatile. See the sidebar below for a whole mess of variations.

Wild Rice Dressing with Golden Raisins and Pecans

The sweet and savory flavors in this dressing accent many main dishes (see the color section of this book for one possible combination). Yes, I confess to dressing up the basic rices (white as well as wild) with a large supporting cast of ingredients. But after all, it's Christmas — bring on the Rockettes!

Preparation time: *10 minutes*

Cooking time: *45 minutes*

Yield: *16 cups (approximately)*

3½ cups low-sodium chicken or vegetable broth

4 cups water

1½ cups wild rice

2 cups white rice

3 tablespoons light olive oil

3 celery stalks, diced

1 medium onion, diced

½ teaspoon thyme

1½ cups golden raisins

1 cup orange juice

1 cup toasted, chopped pecans (see note for toasting instructions)

1 cup chopped flat-leaf parsley

Salt and pepper to taste

1 Combine the wild rice with 2 cups broth and 2 cups water in a large saucepan, cover, and bring to a boil over medium-high heat. Turn the heat down and simmer for about 45 minutes or until the liquid is absorbed and the rice is cooked.

2 Meanwhile, combine the white rice with 2 cups broth and 1½ cups water in a saucepan, cover, and bring to a boil over medium-high heat. Turn the heat down and simmer for about 20 minutes or until the liquid is absorbed and the rice is cooked.

3 While the rices are cooking, heat the olive oil in a large sauté pan and cook the onions and celery over medium-high heat until they begin to soften, about 5 minutes. Season with thyme, salt, and pepper. Add the raisins and orange juice, turn the heat up to high, and cook until the juice becomes syrupy, about 3 minutes.

4 Toss the wild and white rice together in a large bowl with the onion mixture and the pecans and parsley. Season with salt and pepper if necessary and serve immediately. You can also cool the dressing to room temperature, place in an airtight container, and refrigerate for up to 3 days. Cover with foil and reheat in the oven or reheat using the microwave.

Tip: *Toasting nuts brings out their flavor. You can toast nuts in the oven or in a heavy sauté pan. Either way, watch carefully. Try the oven at 350 degrees and the stovetop heat at medium. Check every couple of minutes. You should just start to smell the nuts' aroma and they should just be beginning to be tinged with a light golden color.*

Per serving: *Calories 147 (From Fat 36); Fat 4g (Saturated 1g); Cholesterol 0mg; Sodium 39mg; Carbohydrate 25g (Dietary Fiber 2g); Protein 3g.*

Bread Stuffing with Sausage, Apples, and Cognac

For many of us, the stuffing we grew up with and are familiar with is a bread stuffing. What I love about bread stuffing is the way that you can endlessly vary it. This classic bread stuffing has apples for moistness, while the sausage and cognac add flavor. You can substitute brandy for the cognac, if you like.

Preparation time: *10 minutes*

Cooking time: *20 minutes*

Yield: *10 cups (approximately)*

1 pound close-grained (dense) white sandwich bread, cut into ½-inch cubes

1 pound bulk pork sausage

4 tablespoons (½ stick) unsalted butter

2 cups chopped onion

1 cup chopped celery

3 cups diced, peeled Granny Smith apples (about 4 apples)

½ cup chopped flat-leaf parsley

2 tablespoons cognac

1 teaspoon sage

1 teaspoon thyme

Salt and pepper to taste

1 cup low-sodium chicken broth

1 Preheat the oven to 350 degrees. Spread the bread cubes in single layer on a jelly roll pan and toast them until they're just turning light golden brown, about 5 minutes. Do not overbrown. Pour into a large mixing bowl.

2 Meanwhile, break up the pork sausage and cook it in a large sauté pan over medium heat until browned, about 5 minutes. Remove the sausage with a slotted spoon and add it to the bread cubes. Pour out all but 2 tablespoons of fat.

3 Add the butter to the pork fat left in the pan and melt over medium heat. Add the onion and celery and cook for about 7 minutes, stirring occasionally, until soft. Add the apples, cognac, parsley, sage, and thyme and cook 5 minutes more, stirring frequently. Pour over the bread/sausage mixture and season with salt and pepper.

Add ¼ cup of the broth and stir to moisten. Add more broth as necessary to make the bread cubes moist, but not soggy.

Per serving: *Calories 144 (From Fat 63); Fat 7g (Saturated 3g); Cholesterol 15mg; Sodium 247mg; Carbohydrate 17g (Dietary Fiber 2g); Protein 4g.*

Tailoring your bread stuffing to fit the table

Making your own bread stuffing is easy, and you can add flavors that you like and tailor the stuffing to the other dishes on your table. For example, you can take the Bread Stuffing with Sausage, Apples, and Cognac in a number of different directions:

- **Cranberry Orange Stuffing:** Omit the apples, cognac, and ½ cup of the chicken broth and add 1 cup dried cranberries, 2 tablespoons Grand Marnier, and ½ cup orange juice.
- **Bacon Cornbread Stuffing:** Replace the white bread with cornbread, add 6 slices of cooked crumbled bacon, and remove the apples and cognac.
- **Whole Wheat Pear Stuffing:** Omit the white bread, apples, and cognac and use whole wheat bread, 3 cups peeled, diced pears, and 2 tablespoons pear liqueur, if desired.
- **Pecan Fig Stuffing:** Omit the apples and add 1 cup of chopped toasted pecans and 1 cup of finely chopped dried figs.
- **Vegetarian Dressing:** Omit the sausage, add 1 cup of chopped dried fruit of your choice and 1 cup chopped toasted nuts and use vegetable broth in place of chicken broth. Bake in buttered casserole alongside, not inside, your turkey.

Chapter 10

Relishing the Season with Sauces Sweet and Savory

In This Chapter

- Making scrumptious cranberry sauces
- Roasting fruit to make fruit sauces
- Topping off desserts with dessert sauces

Recipes in This Chapter

- Cranberry Sauce
- Spiced Cranberry Relish
- Horseradish Sauce
- Roasted Chunky Apple Sauce
- Gingered Pear Sauce
- Bittersweet Chocolate Sauce
- Raspberry Apricot Sauce

Chances are you'll come across a sauce — cranberry, perhaps? — at least once during the Christmas season. And what a difference it makes! Sauces add moistness to the foods they accompany and are usually flavor packed and quite colorful, so they truly bring another dimension to a meal. Everyone knows that turkey and cranberry sauce go together, but in this chapter I want to encourage you to think outside that familiar box.

All of the sauces in this chapter are easy and quick to make, using readily available ingredients. They all keep for at least a week, making them handy to have around during this festive season. You can also package them up in a pretty jar and use them for host gifts.

In addition to the dinner sauces, I include a couple of dessert sauces that have a myriad of uses. The Bittersweet Chocolate Sauce goes great with many, many foods. The Raspberry Apricot Sauce uses one frozen fruit and one canned fruit for a quick-to-make sauce from ingredients that you may already have in your kitchen.

Making Cranberry Sauce Yourself Even Though It Comes in a Can

Of course cranberry sauce comes in a can! You can buy chunky cranberry relish made with whole berries or the jellied type (the sort that comes out of the can looking like the can). Some kids I know will eat only the jellied type.

The suppliers are smart, and they make the jellied kind in two sizes — the tiny can is perfect for a couple eating alone or a family with two very picky kids.

My suggestion is to make homemade cranberry sauce this year. If you're worried about cautious eaters, pick up a small can of jellied cranberry sauce and offer both.

Because so few ingredients are in a sauce, the quality of each ingredient really counts

Cranberry Sauce

This is a classic cranberry sauce, sweet and tart at the same time. It compliments all of your holiday dishes. This version has a hint of orange. (See Chapter 4 for zesting technique.)

Preparation time: *5 minutes*

Cooking time: *10 minutes*

Yield: *4 cups*

1 navel orange, washed

1½ cups sugar

½ cup water

Two 12-ounce bags fresh or thawed frozen cranberries, washed and picked over

1 Peel the orange in a few broad pieces and scrape or cut off any white pith from the skin. Discard or eat the orange; reserve the zest. The zest should be in a few large pieces; you're not going to eat it, just use it for flavor.

2 Stir the sugar and water together in medium-sized saucepan. Add the cranberries and orange zest. Bring to a boil over medium-high heat. Turn the heat down and simmer until most of the cranberries pop, about 7 minutes.

3 Let the mixture cool to room temperature; remove the orange zest before serving. You can refrigerate the sauce in an airtight container for up to one week.

Remember: *Anytime you need zest, use a thick-skinned navel orange. Wash the orange really well. You want to remove any dirt, pesticides, and wax. Use warm water and scrub with an abrasive sponge. And I don't mean the dish sponge. You should keep a scrubby-type sponge handy just for washing your fruits and vegetables.*

Per serving: *Calories 24 (From fat 0); Total fat 0g (Saturated 0g); Cholesterol 0mg; Sodium 0mg; Carbohydrates 6g (Dietary Fiber 0g); Protein 0g.*

In the Spiced Cranberry Relish, the two spices called for, cardamom and cloves, are fairly potent spices with flavors that pack a real punch. You only need a little bit. In fact, I can't even think of a recipe that calls for a full teaspoon of cloves.

Spiced Cranberry Relish

This is a spiced relish made with raw cranberries, orange zest and pulp, pineapple, and honey. It is very different from the cooked relish above and it's nice to serve in addition or as an alternative. Make it the day before, as the flavor improves while the relish sits. Try the relish right after you make it, then let it sit overnight and try it again — I think you'll taste an improvement. And see the color section of this book for a photo of the relish.

Special equipment: *Food processor fitted with medium shredding disk*

Preparation time: *8 minutes*

Yield: *3 cups*

2 cups cranberries, fresh or frozen

1 navel orange, washed, quartered, seeded, if necessary

¾ cup canned crushed pineapple

⅔ cups chopped toasted walnuts

½ cup honey

½ teaspoon cinnamon

½ teaspoon ginger

¼ teaspoon ground cardamom

¼ teaspoon ground cloves

Fit your food processor with a medium-sized shredding disk. Shred the raw cranberries and the whole orange, including the skin. Scrape the mixture into a mixing bowl. Stir in the remaining ingredients, pack into an airtight container, and refrigerate overnight. Will keep for up to a week, but best eaten within 3 days.

Tip: *Note that the measurement of nuts is for after they're chopped. If you measure out ⅔ cup of whole nuts and then chop them, you get a very different amount.*

Per serving: *Calories 27 (From fat 9); Total fat 1g(Saturated 0g); Cholesterol 0mg; Sodium 1mg; Carbohydrates 5g (Dietary Fiber 0g); Protein 0g.*

Cardamom

Cardamom is not one of the most commonly used spices, but after you experiment and taste its warm, exotic flavor, you'll want to find reasons to use it. The spice originates in southern India and is a relative of ginger. Cardamom comes in a few different forms. It can be found as a pod about ½-inch in size with a pale green, creamy brown, or white soft shell. Inside are brownish or blackish seeds; these seeds are ground to make the powdered form. Cardamom is quite perishable and quite expensive, so many authorities suggest buying small quantities of either the pod or seed and grinding it yourself. You can do so with an electric coffee mill if you have one; clean it very well before and after using. And speaking of coffee, a Middle Eastern culinary tradition is to drop a few of the seeds into brewed coffee — try it!

Cranberries and the tradition of cranberry sauce

Cranberries are a small, round, deep-red fruit that are primarily cultivated in North America, although some varieties are found in other areas of the world. In fact, along with Concord grapes and blueberries, they are one of the United States' primary native fruits. My home state of Massachusetts has a huge crop, as do New Jersey, Oregon, and Wisconsin. The cranberry bogs are something to see. Ocean Spray is the largest grower, with headquarters in Plymouth, Massachusetts, where you can visit a museum dedicated to all things cranberry.

Cranberries had already enjoyed a long history with Native Americans by the time the Pilgrims arrived. Cranberries were mixed with dried buffalo or deer meat to make *pemmican,* which was a protein source that could be stored for long periods of time — kind of like a beef jerky with fruit. Native Americans also squeezed juice out of the berries and used the juice to dye blankets, rugs, and clothing and used cranberries medicinally in the form of poultices of mashed berries that were used to fight infections externally as well as to draw poison out of wounds.

German and Dutch settlers named the fruit *crane berry,* after its vine blossom's resemblance to the neck, head, and bill of the crane. Eventually, the name became the easier *cranberry.* Cranberries are also sometimes referred to as *bounceberries,* but more about that later.

The first documented harvest goes back to 1816 in Dennis, Massachusetts. Cranberries grow in very wet, sandy soil. When harvest time comes, they're gathered in one of two ways. Most of the cranberries that are sold whole, either fresh or frozen, are harvested by the dry method. A mechanical picker that looks like a lawn mower goes over the plants and its metal teeth comb through the plants, removing the berries. The cranberries flow up onto a conveyor belt and into a holding bin. Then, they're emptied into other bins by hand or removed from the bogs by helicopter, at which time they're transported to the processing plant.

The wet method involves flooding the bogs with about 18-inches of water. Machines float about and loosen up the berries, which float to the surface. Then the berries are gathered in large nets, sort of like fishing for fruit! Wet harvested berries are mostly used for juice, sauce, and relish production. Either way, wet or dry, harvesting begins mid-September and usually lasts right up to Thanksgiving.

Harvested berries all end up in a central receiving station, where they are sorted by size, color, and freshness. One way you can detect their freshness at home is to drop one on the floor. Or maybe just the counter, for sanitation purposes. A fresh cranberry has a pocket of air inside it, which not only makes it float, but also bounce — hence the aforementioned name bounceberry.

True story: In the early days of commercial growing, there was a cranberry grower in New Jersey by the name of John "Peg-Leg" Webb. He did indeed have a wooden peg leg, which prevented him from carrying the berries down from a loft area where they were stored. So, his preferred method of transfer was to just dump the cranberries down the stairs. He noticed that the older and bruised berries would land with a thud on the stairs and stay put, while the firm and fresh berries would bounce merrily along. This is such a good way of sorting berries that Ocean Spray uses a bounceboard separator to this very day.

Dealing Tearlessly in Horseradish

Most of us, if familiar with horseradish at all, are used to seeing it in small jars, all ground up and possibly colored with beets, which makes it a wild, magenta color. The natural white version is what's called for in the recipe below, in which you blend store-bought horseradish with other ingredients to make a delicious sauce.

Horseradish starts as a root. The plant has large, wavy-edged leaves, but the root is what holds the flavor. The root is scrubbed clean and then the outer part is grated. The core is discarded.

You can try to make horseradish from scratch, if you like, but watch out for the fumes. They can be quite pungent and reduce you to tears. A gas mask isn't overkill.

Horseradish Sauce

This tangy, creamy sauce is a perfect foil to roast beef. Make it the morning of your meal so that the flavors have time to meld.

Preparation time: *5 minutes*

Yield: *1¼ cups (approximately)*

1 cup crème fraiche or sour cream

⅓ cup prepared white horseradish

1 teaspoon Dijon mustard

Salt and pepper to taste

Whisk together all of the ingredients in a small bowl. Refrigerate in an airtight container until needed; store up to 1 week.

Per serving: *Calories 27 (From fat 18); Total fat 2g (Saturated 2g); Cholesterol 5mg; Sodium 54mg; Carbohydrates 1g (Dietary Fiber 0g); Protein 0g.*

Roasting Fruit for the Perfect Sauce

The technique of roasting works fantastically when applied to fruit because the high heat caramelizes the sugars in the fruit. Roasting fruit is simple enough to do and requires only simple preparations: peeling and slicing the fruit, tossing the fruit with some sugar, and throwing it in the oven. You know it's done when the fruit exudes juices and a rich amber caramelization occurs.

The two recipes below use apples and pears and are designed as meat sauces. But as you get creative this Christmas season, think about the possibilities of other fruit sauces and other applications for other times of the year. For example:

- Cubed pineapple with brown sugar. Add a splash of lime juice.
- Sliced and peeled peaches with sugar. Make shortcakes!
- Sliced plums with sugar. Add a bit of lemon juice.
- Sliced bananas, brown sugar, and butter. Add some dark rum.
- Strawberries, raspberries, or blueberries with sugar and lemon juice. Use as a spread for toasted pound cake.
- Sweet or tart pitted cherries with sugar. Drizzle over vanilla ice cream with hot fudge.

Roasted Chunky Apple Sauce

This sweet, chunky sauce complements many roasted meats. Try it with ham.

Preparation time: *10 minutes*

Cooking time: *45 minutes*

Yield: *3 cups*

6 medium apples (8 ounces each), such as Cortland or Granny Smith, peeled and cored

½ cup apple cider

⅓ cup lightly packed light brown sugar

1 tablespoon freshly squeezed lemon juice

1 Preheat the oven to 400 degrees.

2 Slice the apples into eighths. Toss all the ingredients together in a 15 x 10-inch roasting pan. Roast for about 45 minutes, gently tossing once or twice, until just tender. The apples will be golden brown and will have begun to caramelize. Pay more attention to the caramelization and tenderness, not the roasting time. Drier and older apples might take longer.

3 Serve warm or refrigerate overnight in an airtight container. Rewarm over low heat on the stove top or in the microwave. May be made one week ahead.

Remember: *There's a difference between cider and apple juice. You could use either, but cider has a fuller, richer flavor. You should have no trouble finding cider in the supermarket this time of year. In my market, it's in the produce section, for some reason, and not with the refrigerated juices. Ask if you can't find it.*

Per serving: *Calories 65 (From fat 0); Total fat 0g (Saturated 0g); Cholesterol 0mg; Sodium 3mg; Carbohydrates 17g (Dietary Fiber 1g); Protein 0g.*

Gingered Pear Sauce

Make sure the pears are ripe to take advantage of their flavor, which will intensify upon roasting. This sauce goes great with ham.

Tools: *13 x 9-inch roasting pan*

Preparation time: *10 minutes*

Cooking time: *45 minutes*

Yield: *2 cups*

4 medium juicy, ripe pears (8 ounces each), such as Bartlett, peeled and cored

¼ cup brown sugar

2 tablespoons water

1 tablespoon freshly squeezed lemon juice

¼ cup finely chopped crystallized ginger

1 Preheat the oven to 400 degrees.

2 Cut the pears into ½-inch cubes. Toss the pears, brown sugar, and water together in a 13 x 9-inch roasting pan. Roast for about 50 minutes, gently tossing once or twice, until tender. The pears will be golden brown and have begun to caramelize. Stir in lemon juice and ginger.

3 Serve warm or refrigerate overnight in an airtight container. Rewarm over low heat on the stove top or in the microwave. May be made one week ahead.

Per serving: *Calories 23 (From fat 0); Total fat 0g (Saturated 0g); Cholesterol 0mg; Sodium 1mg; Carbohydrates 6g (Dietary Fiber 0g); Protein 0g.*

Saucing Desserts — the Festive Final Touch

The following sauces are for desserts. Having these around is like owning insurance. Just grab some sauce, add some ice cream or cake, and you've got instant dessert. Like the other sauces in this chapter, these are easy to make, keep well, and make great host gifts.

Make some of these and have them in the refrigerator even if you don't have a specific use in mind. Occasions will come up during the holidays when you'll be thrilled to have them on hand.

Bittersweet Chocolate Sauce

You'll find many uses for this easy-to-make sauce. Have some on hand for last-minute dessert embellishment (and general pleasure — see Figure 10-1). The recipe may be scaled up or down directly and can be made a week ahead and stored in the freezer for up to a month.

Preparation time: *5 minutes*

Cooking time: *5 minutes*

Yield: *5 cups*

12 ounces unsweetened chocolate, finely chopped

3 cups heavy cream

1½ cups sugar

4 tablespoons (½ stick) unsalted butter

Pinch of salt

1 teaspoon vanilla extract

1 Place all the ingredients, except the vanilla extract, in a heavy-bottomed pot. Cook over low-medium heat, whisking frequently, until the chocolate is melted. Take care to not scorch the chocolate. Whisk gently until the mixture is smooth. Remove from the heat and stir in the vanilla extract.

2 Store in an airtight container in the refrigerator for up to a week or freeze for one month. Warm briefly in the microwave at a medium power or on top of the stove over low heat before using.

Remember: *Unsweetened chocolate is not the same as other dark chocolates. It has no sugar added whatsoever. If you substitute bittersweet or semisweet chocolate in its place, you will have completely different results. Unsweetened chocolate has a shelf life of at least one-year, so keep a box in the house. It can be found in the baking ingredient aisle of the supermarket with the other chocolates and usually comes in a box with eight individually wrapped one-ounce blocks.*

Per serving: *Calories 52 (From fat 36); Total fat 4g (Saturated 2g); Cholesterol 6mg; Sodium 4mg; Carbohydrates 5g (Dietary Fiber 1g); Protein 1g.*

HEY!
FINGER DIPPING.....ONE OF THE MANY PRACTICAL USES OF CHOCOLATE SAUCE!

Figure 10-1: Be sure it's cool enough!

What can you do with chocolate sauce?

My answer to this question is "Almost anything!" Chocolate sauce can be used in many, many ways. Here are just a few:

- With ice cream
- Over cake
- With cake and ice cream — add whipped cream and a cherry
- Banana splits
- Drizzled over roasted bananas
- Over pancakes and waffles to satisfy a real sweet tooth (kids will love you)
- Warmed and used as a fondue for fruit
- Used as a dip for your finger!

Raspberry Apricot Sauce

This delicious and brilliantly colored sauce is very quick to make and stores for up to a week. Use this over ice cream or pound cake for an instant dessert.

Preparation time: *5 minutes*

Cooking time: *5 minutes*

Yield: *2½ cups*

¼ cup sugar

2 tablespoons water

One 15-ounce can juice-sweetened apricot halves, drained

One 12-ounce bag defrosted unsweetened frozen raspberries

1 teaspoon freshly squeezed lemon juice

1 Combine the sugar and water in a small saucepan, stir to wet the sugar, and bring to a boil over high heat. Boil for 30 seconds, swirling the pan, making sure the sugar is dissolved.

2 Meanwhile, place the apricots and raspberries in a food processor fitted with a metal blade and process until smooth, about 1 minute. Add sugar syrup and lemon juice and pulse on and off to blend.

3 Refrigerate in an airtight container until needed. Will keep for one week.

Going All Out: *This sauce is great as is, but for a further refinement, you can remove the seeds. Simply pass the sauce through a fine meshed strainer set over a bowl. Scrape the sauce back and forth over the strainer's mesh using a rubber spatula. You will end up with 1¾ cups of sauce as you loose some volume from the discarded seeds. The strained sauce will be as smooth as red velvet.*

Per serving: *Calories 13 (From fat 0); Total fat 0g (Saturated 0g); Cholesterol 0mg; Sodium 0mg; Carbohydrates 3g (Dietary Fiber 1g); Protein 0g.*

Choosing frozen fruit

In most supermarkets, you can find frozen raspberries, strawberries, and blueberries, at the very least. Raspberries and strawberries, in particular, usually come in a sweetened version or an unsweetened one. Buy the unsweetened so that you can control the amount of sugar that's added.

When shopping for frozen fruit, look for packaging that says IQF (individually quick frozen). IQF fruit is the way to go. It will be loose, easy to measure, and less bruised than fruit that's frozen in a solid block.

If you have some frozen fruit handy, making those smoothies from Chapter 4 is a lot easier.

Buying canned fruit — it's okay

When I was little, a dessert of canned mandarin orange sections or peach halves was a common occurrence. My Mom would sometimes add sliced banana. In my mind, canned fruit had associations with these humble beginnings of my culinary education. For years, I shunned canned fruit as an inferior product. I am woman enough to now admit I was wrong.

Do not turn your back on canned fruit. Sometimes a canned fruit is even better then fresh, such as in the Raspberry Apricot Sauce. Very few of us can even find ripe fresh apricots, and if we did we'd have to poach them before using them in the sauce — not an impossible task, but what's an easy recipe now would turn into a laborious one.

Most canned fruit, such as apricots, peaches, and pears, come in either heavy syrup or fruit juice — the consumer gets to choose. I prefer the juice-packed so that I can determine the sweetness level. If you can only find fruits in syrup, drain them and rinse them with water before using.

Canned fruits can be used to great effect in smoothies. Use them straight out of the can or freeze them first. Just drain them and place them overnight in a resealable bag in the freezer. See Chapter 4 for more on smoothies.

Part IV

Holiday Meals: Finishing Touches

"We're currently in a state of weightlessness. Amazingly, everything has begun floating except Doug's Christmas fruitcake."

In this part . . .

Ah, the finishing touch! This part offers you a sleigh full of choices for dessert, from cookies to pies to cakes to ice cream and candies. And if you are looking for Yorkshire pudding to go with your roast beef, Part IV also has just what you need. Same goes for muffins and biscuits.

Chapter 11

Visions of Sugarplums . . . Christmas Cookies, Candies, and Confections

In This Chapter

- Fixing Santa's cookie plate
- Experiencing the bliss of chocolate truffles
- Hitting the road to Baked Alaska

Recipes in This Chapter

- Snowdrop Cookies
- Classic Sugar Cookies
- Royal Icing
- Gingerbread People
- Chocolate Shortbread
- Meringue Wreath Cookies
- Cherry-Orange Florentines
- Bittersweet Chocolate Truffles
- Sugarplums
- Sugar-Frosted Fruit
- Cranberry Cider Sorbet
- Eggnog Ice Cream
- Mocha Baked Alaska

This chapter and the next are chock-full of Christmas dessert recipes. I start with a section on cookies because, for many of us, a batch of cookies is our introduction to the world of baking. This chapter also includes a section on candies and confections — the holidays seem to bring out the sweet tooth in all of us. And I give you a few frozen desserts that are easy to make and add a new dimension to your dessert repertoire. Baked Alaska — it doesn't get more dramatic than that!

As you browse in Chapters 11 and 12, remember that baking is not the same as cooking, the subject of most other chapters. Improvisation rules in cooking. You can add a bit more salt here and a little more sage there. Maybe you want the finished product to be a tad less well-done or a little crispier than the recipe suggests. That's what makes cooking so much fun — you can tailor a recipe in endless ways.

Baking is a bit different. Although the freewheeling ways of cooking may attract certain people into the kitchen, the exactitude of baking is what thrills others. It truly is miraculous the way a wet batter can go into the oven and come out as a high-rising cake. The way chocolate and cream can combine to give you deep, dark, silken truffles.

Baking recipes are written as is for a reason. An extra egg or two will completely change that cake, and probably not for the better. Additional chocolate will leave those truffles as leaden as buckshot; well, maybe not that bad, but you get the idea. It isn't that baking is more difficult than cooking; it's just that the recipes are precise formulas that should be followed closely for the best results. End of sermon.

A word about butter and margarine: A lot of us are trying to cut down on fats, but they play a necessary role in cooking and baking. They add moisture and help carry a flavor throughout a dish. The recipes in this book use butter and not margarine because I believe that butter has better flavor and, when used judiciously, isn't harmful to health. However, you can try substituting margarine. On to the cookies.

Producing Cookies for S. Claus and All His Helpers

Cookies are fun to make. They're a great project to do with kids and they're probably the most versatile dessert item during the holidays. All of the cookie recipes in this book can be scaled up or down directly and many of the cookies freeze well. Check the individual recipes for freezing instructions.

Snowdrop Cookies

These snowdrops are a buttery cookie enriched with ground pecans. Many cookies are out there that are similar to these, and all the variations are popular during Christmas. For a photo of my Snowdrops, see the color section of this book.

Preparation time: *10 minutes*

Cooking time: *15 minutes*

Yield: *36 cookies*

⅔ cup pecan halves

1 cup confectioners sugar

Pinch salt

1 cup (2 sticks) unsalted butter at room temperature

½ teaspoon vanilla extract

1¾ cups all-purpose flour

Coating

1¼ cup confectioners sugar (approximately)

1 Place the pecans, confectioners sugar, and salt in the bowl of a food processor that's been fitted with a metal blade. Pulse on and off to break up the nuts, then process until the nuts are finely ground.

2 Add the butter a few pieces at a time, pulsing on and off to incorporate, then run the machine until the mixture is smooth.

3 Add flour and pulse the machine on and off until the mixture is blended, scraping the dough down once or twice. Process until the dough begins to form a ball. Scrape the dough out onto a piece of plastic wrap, form it into a ball, cover with wrap, and refrigerate for 2 hours or until the dough is firm enough to roll.

4 Preheat the oven to 350 degrees. Line two jelly roll pans with parchment paper.

5 Roll the dough with lightly floured hands into 1-inch balls and place the balls 2 inches apart on the pans.

6 Bake the cookies for about 15 minutes or until they're light golden brown on the bottoms and around the edges. For even baking, rotate the sheet pans once halfway through baking. Place the pan on a rack to cool for 5 minutes, then remove the cookies to the rack to cool completely.

7 Place the cookies on a sheet pan and sift a heavy coating of confectioners sugar over the cookies.

8 Store the cookies at room temperature in an airtight container for up to two weeks or freeze for one month.

Tip: *After storing, the confectioners sugar may have worn off. Feel free to give the cookies another powdery coat before serving.*

Tip: *A jelly roll pan is like a cookie sheet, only it has sides that are about an inch high. You can get them through just about any mail order source or baking-supply store. When you make recipes such as this one, where the cookies could roll off as you place the sheet in the oven, you will see why it helps to use a jelly roll pan.*

Per serving: *Calories 106 (From fat 63); Total fat 7g (Saturated 3g); Cholesterol 14mg; Sodium 5mg; Carbohydrates 11g (Dietary Fiber 0g); Protein 1g.*

Classic Sugar Cookies with Royal Icing

The various shapes of sugar cookies say "Christmas" like little else. They can be made way ahead and frozen, and you can lightly sprinkle them with granulated sugar or elaborately ice them with different colors of icing. Kids love helping to roll them out and, of course, they enjoy helping to decorate.

The Royal Icing can be piped onto the cookies for a traditional Christmas look. You can tint the icing any color you like and vary its consistency for a variety of effects. Kids can help make the icing and love to apply it to the cookies. However, these cookies are great even without the icing — and if you're going to freeze them, please freeze them undecorated.

Classic Sugar Cookies

Preparation time: *10 minutes*

Cooking time: *8 minutes; 2 hours cooling time*

Yield: *Thirty-six 3-inch cookies*

1½ cups (3 sticks) unsalted butter at room temperature

1½ cup sugar

½ teaspoon salt

3 large eggs

1½ teaspoons vanilla extract

3¾ cups all-purpose flour

Sugar or colored sugar (optional)

1. Beat the butter in a mixer until it's creamy. Use a flat paddle attachment on medium-high speed. With the mixer running, add the sugar gradually and continue to beat until the mixture is light and fluffy, about 5 minutes.
2. Beat in the salt and the eggs, one at a time. Mix well after each addition. Scrape down the bowl once or twice.
3. Turn the machine off and add about one-third of the flour. Incorporate the flour on low speed, adding the rest of the flour in two batches. Beat just until blended.
4. Scrape the dough out onto a large piece of plastic wrap. Use the wrap to help shape a large, flat disk. Refrigerate the dough for at least 2 hours or until it's firm enough to roll. At this point, the dough may be refrigerated for up to two days or frozen for up to one week. (If you freeze the dough, allow it to defrost overnight in the refrigerator. If it's very firm, allow it to sit at room temperature until it's the proper consistency for rolling).
5. Preheat the oven to 350 degrees. Line two cookie sheets with parchment paper.
6. Roll out the dough on a lightly floured surface to ¼-inch thickness; cut out cookies with the cookie cutters of your choice. Transfer the cookies to the prepared sheets. Sprinkle with plain or colored sugar, if desired. Bake for about 8 minutes or until the edges have

just begun to turn golden. For even baking, rotate the sheet pans once while the cookies are baking.

7 Cool the cookies for 5 minutes on pans set on cooling racks, and then transfer the cookies directly to the racks to cool completely. Repeat with your remaining dough, cooling the pans between uses.

8 Store the cookies at room temperature for up to two weeks or freeze for up to one month.

Tip: *Make sure to use real vanilla extract in this recipe. You should almost always use real extract instead of imitation vanilla. Here, where vanilla is the principle flavor, using the good stuff is all the more important.*

Remember: *Always use large eggs for the recipes in this book, or the balance of the recipe will be thrown off.*

Royal Icing

Preparation time: *8 minutes*

Yield: *⅔ cup*

1 cup confectioners sugar, sifted

1 large egg white (or an equivalent amount of reconstituted powdered egg white)

1 Using a balloon whip attachment, combine the confectioners sugar and the egg white in a mixer's bowl on low speed. Turn the speed up to high and whip until the icing is thick and creamy, about 5 minutes. Add a little water for a thinner consistency or more sugar for a thicker consistency.

2 Use the icing immediately or refrigerate it in an airtight container for up to one week. You will need to re-beat the icing before using.

Tip: *Although Royal Icing can be stored, I think it's best used fresh. It's so quick to make that preparing it right before you use it isn't difficult.*

Caution: *If you have a compromised immune system or are very young or elderly, your doctor may suggest not eating raw eggs. Meringue powder, which can be purchased at craft stores and anywhere cake decorating ingredients are found, can be used in place of egg whites. Substitute 5 tablespoons meringue powder, reconstituted per the manufacturer's instructions, for one egg white.*

Per serving: *Calories 154 (From Fat 72); Total fat 8g (Saturated 5g); Cholesterol 38mg; Sodium 39mg; Carbohydrates 18g (Dietary Fiber 0g); Protein 2g.*

Gingerbread People

Gingerbread, in the form of cookies or cake, is often associated with Christmas. The spice ginger, which is the common ingredient in all gingerbread recipes, originated in the Middle East and reached Europe by the 11th century. Its warm, spicy taste was only part of its appeal. It was, and is, used medicinally to soothe stomach disorders and motion sickness. But you're interested in it for its delectable taste. If you're very fond of its flavor, feel free to up the amount in the cookies.

For a thick, chewy gingerbread cookie, follow the instructions and make sure not to overcook. If you like a crispier gingerbread cookie, roll these out a bit thinner and bake an extra minute. The crispier version is best for ornaments.

Preparation time: *10 minutes*

Cooking time: *8 minutes; 2 hours cooling time*

Yield: *Forty-five 3-inch cookies*

1 cup (2 sticks) unsalted butter at room temperature

¾ cup lightly packed brown sugar

½ cup unsulphured molasses

1 large egg

3¼ cup all-purpose flour

2 teaspoons ginger

1 teaspoon cinnamon

1 teaspoon baking soda

¼ teaspoon nutmeg

¼ teaspoon cloves

¼ teaspoon salt

Cinnamon Red Hots candies (optional)

Currants (optional)

1. Cream the butter with a flat paddle attachment in a mixer on high speed until the butter is soft, about 3 minutes. Beat in the sugar and continue beating until the sugar is light and fluffy, about 2 minutes. Beat in the molasses. Beat in the egg, scraping down the bowl once or twice.
2. Sift together the flour, ginger, cinnamon, baking soda, nutmeg, cloves, and salt. Add the dry ingredients in three batches, mixing just until each batch is blended. Shape the dough into a large, flat ball by hand, kneading a few times until it's smooth. Wrap the dough in plastic wrap and refrigerate it at least 2 hours or until it's firm enough to roll out.
3. Preheat the oven to 350 degrees. Line two cookie sheets with parchment paper and spray lightly with pan coating.
4. Roll out the dough on a lightly floured surface to ¼-inch thickness. Cut the dough into shapes as desired. Transfer the cookies to the cookie sheets, using a spatula. Leave at least 2 inches between each cookie. Place similar-sized cookies on the same sheet. To make hanging ornaments, punch holes in the tops of the shapes with the blunt end of a chopstick.
5. For decoration, place Red Hots or currants on the gingerbread people to make eyes, noses, mouths, and buttons.

6 Bake the cookies for about 12 minutes, depending on their size. Rotate the cookie sheets once during baking. The cookies should have just begun to brown around the edges and feel firm to the touch when you remove them. Cool the pans on racks for a few minutes. Transfer the cookies to the racks to cool completely. Let the pans cool completely before proceeding with the next batch of cookies; you may reuse the parchment. Store the cookies in an airtight container at room temperature for up to two weeks or freeze for up to one month.

Tip: *Carefully soften the butter in the microwave if you've forgotten to bring it to room temperature.*

Going All Out: *Decorate your Gingerbread People with the Royal Icing from the Classic Sugar Cookies with Royal Icing.*

Per serving: *Calories 95 (From Fat 36); Total fat 4g (Saturated 3g); Cholesterol 16mg; Sodium 46mg; Carbohydrates 13g (Dietary Fiber 0g); Protein 1g.*

Royal Icing — the perfect cookie topper

Royal Icing may not be imperial, princely, or even exalted (I have no idea where the name came from), but it is the perfect icing for decorating cookies. It's easy to make, can be tinted to any color you like, and hardens to a solid finish, making cookies decorated with Royal Icing perfect for hanging on the tree, stacking in tins, or mailing to friends. Here's what you need to know about making and working with Royal Icing:

- You can use food coloring to color Royal Icing. Paste colors are best. They can be found at craft stores that have a cake-decorating section or they can be bought through mail order companies. Use tiny bits at a time, as the coloring is very concentrated. Just add a dab, beat it in, assess the color, and then add a bit more coloring, if desired.

  Very dark colors can be difficult to achieve. If you add too much color, the icing begins to taste a bit off. Be judicious.

- To completely cover a cookie with icing, make a thick icing and pipe an outline all the way around the border of the cookie. Use a pastry bag with a #2 tip. Allow the border to dry, then flood the cookie with a thinner icing.
- Two colors of icing can be marbled together. Make an outline in one color. Partially flood the interior with that color and the rest with an alternative color. Draw a toothpick this way and that through the two colors to create a marbled appearance.
- Flavoring may be added as well as coloring. Vanilla extract is an obvious choice, but it adds color. Look for colorless vanilla extract. This is the only case in which I ever suggest using artificial vanilla. Another option is almond extract, which is clear.
- After making Royal Icing, keep it covered with a damp cloth or a crust will form.
- While the icing is wet, you can sprinkle colored sugars on top for color, texture, and sparkle.

Chocolate Shortbread

These cookies are deep and chocolaty. They don't have to be chilled before rolling, so they're very quick to make. As with all cutout cookies, kids love to help.

Preparation time: *15 minutes*

Cooking time: *20 minutes*

Yield: *4 dozen 3-inch cookies*

2 cups (4 sticks) unsalted butter at room temperature

1¼ cups sugar

4¼ cups all-purpose flour

¾ cup Dutch-processed cocoa

1 teaspoon instant espresso powder or instant coffee

¼ teaspoon salt

1 Preheat the oven to 325 degrees. Line two cookie sheet pans with parchment paper.

2 Beat the butter in a mixer on medium speed until it's creamy, using a flat paddle attachment. Add the sugar gradually and continue beating until light and fluffy, about 5 minutes.

3 Stir the flour, cocoa, espresso powder, and salt together in a bowl. Add the mixture to the creamed butter and sugar and beat on low speed just until incorporated. Go easy when adding the flour. It can fly out of the bowl and cover your walls if you're too vigorous, and overmixing toughens the cookie.

4 Roll the cookies out on a lightly floured surface to ⅓-inch thickness and use the cookie cutter of your choice to cut out cookies. The baking directions in this recipe are for cookies that are 3 inches across, so aim for that when you choose a cookie cutter or, if you use a different size, monitor the cookies closely while they're in the oven. Transfer the cookies to pans.

5 Bake the cookies for about 20 minutes. These are so dark that seeing if they're beginning to color is impossible. Check to see if the edges and bottoms are completely dry. You should be able to lift a cookie up with a spatula to peek at the bottom; the cookie should be baked enough to remain stiff and not break. For even baking, rotate the sheet pans once halfway through baking.

6 Take the cookie sheets out of the oven and set them on a wire rack for 5 minutes to cool. Then remove the cookies to the rack and let them cool completely. Store the cookies at room temperature in an airtight container. The cookies are best if eaten within one week; they can be frozen for up to one month.

Tip: *The cookie sheets must be cooled completely between batches, but you can probably reuse the parchment paper. Try flipping it over and making use of both sides.*

Per serving: *Calories 131 (From fat 72); Total fat 8g (Saturated 5g); Cholesterol 21mg; Sodium 14mg; Carbohydrates 14g (Dietary Fiber 1g); Protein 1g.*

Meringue Wreath Cookies

Baked meringues have a lot going for them. They are crisp, sweet, low-fat egg white–based cookies; they contrast nicely with sugar cookies and gingerbread cookies. They have an interesting wreath shape, so they look good on your cookie plate, and they can be made way ahead. Plus, they're fat free.

Preparation time: *12 minutes*

Cooking time: *30 minutes*

Yield: *3 dozen wreaths*

4 large egg whites

¼ teaspoon cream of tartar

1 cup sugar

1 Preheat the oven to 250 degrees. Line two cookie sheets with parchment paper.

2 Place the egg whites in the bowl of a mixer and whip with a balloon whip attachment on low speed until frothy. Add the cream of tartar and turn the speed to high. Continue to whip until soft peaks form.

3 Gradually add the sugar and continue whipping until stiff peaks form and the mixture is glossy, about 5 minutes.

4 Fit a pastry bag with a coupler and a star tip, such as a #22. Fill the bag halfway with the meringue mixture and pipe a wreath of rosettes directly onto a prepared sheet. Pipe rosettes that touch each other until you've got a small wreath that's about 3 inches across. The wreaths themselves should not touch one another.

5 Bake the cookies for about 40 minutes or until they're completely dry to the touch. Set the cookie sheets on racks and allow the cookies to cool completely. Store in an airtight container at room temperature for up to one month.

Tip: *Some bakers like to use extra-fine sugar when making meringues, as this special sugar dissolves more easily with the egg whites. You can make extra-fine sugar by buzzing normal sugar in a food processor fitted with a metal blade for a minute or two.*

Per serving: *Calories 23 (From fat 0); Total fat 0g (Saturated 0g); Cholesterol 0mg; Sodium 6mg; Carbohydrates 6g (Dietary Fiber 0g); Protein 0g.*

Cherry-Orange Florentines

These cookies are chewy and crunchy with caramel, chocolate, orange, cherries, and almonds. (See the color section of this book for a photo.) If you have a candy thermometer, making them will be easier, although I do give instructions as to how to make these without a candy thermometer.

Tools: *Candy thermometer*

Preparation time: *20 minutes*

Cooking time: *12 minutes*

Yield: *Eighteen 4-inch cookies*

6 tablespoons (3⁄4 stick) unsalted butter, cut into large pieces

2⁄3 cup granulated sugar

1⁄3 cup heavy cream

3 tablespoons honey

1⁄3 cup dried cherries

1⁄3 cup water

3 ounces (about 1 cup) sliced almonds, blanched or natural, half of them chopped

1⁄3 cup diced candied orange peel

1⁄4 cup all-purpose flour

6 ounces semisweet or bittersweet chocolate, finely chopped

1 Preheat the oven to 350 degrees. Line two cookie sheet pans with parchment paper.

2 Melt the butter in a medium-sized saucepan. Add sugar, cream, and honey and bring to a simmer over medium heat. Cook to 230 degrees. If you dip a spoon into the mixture and dribble it in a glass of cold water, it will spin a thread. It also becomes a very light brown.

3 Meanwhile, place the cherries and water in a microwave-proof bowl, cover with plastic wrap, and microwave on high for 2 minutes. This will plump the cherries. (Alternatively, bring the cherries and water to a boil in a small saucepan for 1 minute.) Drain if any liquid remains. Stir the cherries, almonds, orange peel, and flour into the cream mixture.

4 Drop by mounds onto the cookie sheets. Each mound should be about 2 teaspoons. Dampen your hands with cold water and flatten the cookies.

5 Bake for about 12 minutes. The cookies will spread, the edges darken, and the centers will bubble. The cookies should be a light golden brown and caramelized.

6 Place the pans on a rack. Some of the cookies may not have a nice round shape. Immediately, while they're still hot, coax them into a rounder shape. Use a round cookie cutter that is larger in diameter than the Cherry Orange Florentines. Place the cookie cutter over a misshapen cookie. Use the inside edges of the cookie cutter to draw in the edges of the cookie. A circular motion is good for making the Florentine into a nice round shape. Completely cool the cookies on pans. The cookie sheets must be cooled completely between use, but you will probably be able to reuse the parchment paper.

7 Meanwhile, quick temper the chocolate (see Chapter 2 for information on tempering chocolate).

8 Carefully remove the cooled cookies from the baking sheet with a spatula. Using a small offset spatula, spread chocolate over the bottoms of the cookies. Place the cookies, chocolate side up, back on sheet pans. Place in the refrigerator until the chocolate is set.

9 Store in single layers, separated by waxed paper or parchment, and refrigerated in an airtight container. Best eaten within 4 days.

Simplify: *No need to plump the cherries. If you're short on time, or just care to skip this step, use them unplumped.*

Per serving: *Calories 180 (From fat 108); Total fat 12g (Saturated 6g); Cholesterol 16mg; Sodium 7mg; Carbohydrates 20g(Dietary Fiber 1g); Protein 2g.*

Techniques and Tips for Baking Cookies

If you bake anything this holiday season, I bet you bake cookies. Take a moment to acquaint yourself with these cookie-baking tips.

Cookie cutters, templates, and more

If you want to make cookies in the classic shapes of angels and Christmas trees, you'll be able to find endless varieties of cookie cutters to choose from. If you want to make a cookie in an unusual shape, you may have better luck if you forego hunting for the right cookie cutter and simply make a template. To make a template, draw whatever shape you like on a piece of cardboard and cut it out. Place the template over the rolled-out cookie dough and cut out the shape, using a very sharp paring knife. Follow the template's edges all the way around.

Kids love seeing their drawings come to life. Have them draw shapes on cardboard, which you can help them cut out. No censoring! Their shapes might not be what you would choose, but the shapes are the kids' creations.

When I was in second grade, we got a new art teacher who was very strict. We were working with clay and I made what I thought was a beautiful turtle. The teacher didn't think it had enough merit to take up room in the kiln, so she smashed it, threw the wad of clay back into the tub, and walked away. Ever since, I have had a love of turtles and a fear of women wearing smocks! Let the kids discover their inner artist.

Preparing cookies for freezing

When it comes to making dishes ahead and freezing them, some foods survive the frost better than others do. Typical rolled cookies or cookies with a high fat content tend to do just fine. But you have to prepare them properly before you freeze them.

The cookies should have cooled completely. Stack them on a piece of cardboard to provide support and double wrap them tightly with plastic wrap. Pop this whole package into a large resealable freezer bag, remove the air, and place in the freezer. Allow the cookies to defrost while they're still all wrapped up.

In the recipes, I include tips on freezing the specific type of cookie that the recipe is for.

Using brown sugar and making your own

Brown sugar can become hard, and I mean rock hard. You could use it as a doorstop. But hard brown sugar is salvageable. First of all, always store the sugar in an airtight container to prevent hardening. But if that fails, there are a few approaches you can take:

- Add a slice of apple to the brown sugar container, close up tightly, and let sit overnight. The sugar should soften.
- Add a few drops of water and microwave in a covered dish on medium power for about 5 minutes. Repeat if necessary until softened.
- Add a few drops of water and heat for about 15 minutes in a covered dish in an oven at 200 degrees. Repeat if necessary until softened.

Do not try to break up rock-hard brown sugar in a food processor or blender. It's so hard that you may damage the appliance.

If you get caught with no brown sugar in the house, but have granulated white sugar and a jar of molasses, brown sugar is near at hand. Simply stir a couple of tablespoons of molasses into one cup of white sugar. Add a little more for dark brown sugar. (Molasses has an indefinite shelf life, so it pays to have a jar around.)

The cookie swap

Now, I did not make this idea up, but what it lacks in originality it makes up for in impact. Suppose you want to make a big batch of Classic Sugar Cookies, but would love to have some gingerbread around for variety's sake. Hold a cookie swap. Invite a bunch of friends over, the more the merrier. Each one brings a different extra-large batch of cookies. To make this effective, you need to have a fairly large amount of each kind of cookie.

Then you swap. You each give some of your own batch to everyone else. Ideally, all the guests end up with a dozen of each kind of cookie.

Have you ever heard the phrase "catch as catch can"? It means that whatever will be, will be. You can take this approach and just let all your guests show up with whatever cookie they want to make. You might get lucky and end up with a varied assortment, but it's a crapshoot. You could take a middle-of-the-road approach and suggest one person make a chocolate cookie, another make a gingerbread cookie, and what have you. Or you can get really organized and mail out specific recipes along with invitations, which guarantees results . . . assuming that your friends know how to bake!

Troubleshooting cookie problems

Even when you follow a recipe, sometimes something goes wrong. When it comes to cookies, there are a few things to look for and a few techniques that you can employ to save your next batch.

- **Cookies are dark or burned on the bottom.** This is a common problem. First, check your cookie sheets. If they are thin, flimsy, and warped, the heat will not be conducted properly. Use thick, solid sheets. Try stacking two sheets on top of one another or buy an air-cushioned baking sheet. Also, try rotating the sheets from front to back during baking. Your oven could be too hot as well; use an oven thermometer.
- **Cookies spread and thin out while baking.** Make sure that your cookie dough has been chilled first, if the recipe suggests this step. Putting too much grease on cookie sheets can cause this problem, too; use parchment paper. Also, do not put unbaked dough on a hot sheet.
- **Cookies run into one another.** You've placed the cookies too close together on the cookie sheet. An average of 2 inches apart is standard and can eliminate this problem most of the time. Follow the instructions in the recipe.
- **Cookie dough is too sticky to roll.** If the dough is supposed to be chilled before rolling, make sure it has chilled long enough. You possibly also added too little flour. If the dough is still too soft after chilling, knead in a little flour, a couple tablespoons at a time.
- **Cookie dough is dry and cracks when rolled.** Just like I said, it's dry! Knead in a teaspoon of water at a time until the dough achieves the proper consistency.

- **Cookies break upon removing them from cookie sheets.** Let the cookies cool on the sheet according to the individual recipe's instructions. If you remove them too soon they may break.
- **Cookies stick to sheet.** Two words: Use parchment.

Explaining my fondness for parchment paper

You may have noticed that I'm a big fan of parchment paper. It not only provides a non-stick surface for baked goods and other foods, but it also makes cleanup that much easier. All you do is fold up the parchment and throw it away.

You can find parchment paper in rolls in many large supermarkets, in the same aisle as plastic wrap and aluminum foil. Alternatively, check specialty foods or kitchenware stores. Parchment paper is one of those products that, if you have it on hand, you'll find more uses for it as time goes by.

When it comes to cutting parchment paper to fit pans, sometimes how to do so is obvious, like when it's a rectangular sheet pan. Sometimes you want to cut out a round piece of parchment, and that's a bit trickier. But as you can see in Figure 11-1, there are just three easy steps: folding the rectangle of paper into quarters; tracing the radius of your pan onto the paper; and cutting on the dotted line.

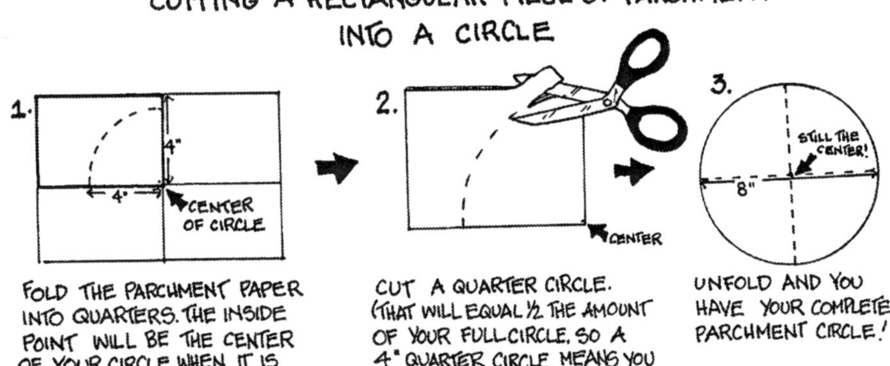
CUTTING A RECTANGULAR PIECE OF PARCHMENT INTO A CIRCLE
1.
4"
4"
CENTER OF CIRCLE
FOLD THE PARCHMENT PAPER INTO QUARTERS. THE INSIDE POINT WILL BE THE CENTER OF YOUR CIRCLE WHEN IT IS UNFOLDED.
2.
CENTER
CUT A QUARTER CIRCLE. (THAT WILL EQUAL ½ THE AMOUNT OF YOUR FULL CIRCLE. SO A 4" QUARTER CIRCLE MEANS YOU GET AN 8" CIRCLE!
3.
STILL THE CENTER!
8"
UNFOLD AND YOU HAVE YOUR COMPLETE PARCHMENT CIRCLE!

Figure 11-1: Cutting parchment paper to fit a round pan.

Separating and whipping egg whites and yolks

Sometimes a recipe calls for just egg whites (like the Meringue Wreath Cookies) or egg yolks (like the Mocha Baked Alaska) instead of whole eggs. Cold eggs separate most easily because the white is stiffer and the yolk is less prone to breakage. However, in general, eggs should be at room temperature when they're incorporated into your recipe or when the whites or yolks are whipped individually. Room temperature eggs give you maximum volume. But bear in mind that sanitation codes suggest not letting eggs stay at room temperature for more than an hour.

Many dessert recipes call for egg whites to be whipped separately from the yolks. Folding whipped whites into a batter lightens the texture by adding air that's provided by the whipped whites. A bit of cream of tartar can be added for increased stability in the egg white foam. The acid in cream of tartar affects the protein strands in the whites and makes for a more stabilized foam.

Any grease inhibits proper whipping. Make sure that absolutely no trace of yolk gets into your egg white and always use scrupulously clean bowls and beaters.

Begin by beating the whites with a balloon whip attachment on low speed. When the whites are frothy, add cream of tartar, if you're using it. Increase the speed to medium-high and add sugar gradually, if sugar is called for in the recipe. Soft peaks are reached when the whites form peaks that still fold over on themselves a bit. Stiff peaks stand up straight. Do not overbeat or you'll produce grainy, lumpy whites.

Instructions often say, "Beat until creamy" or, "Until a ribbon forms." As the yolks are whipped, they become pale and creamy and expand in volume. To tell if the ribbon stage has been reached, lift the beaters or whisk and allow the mixture to fall back upon itself. If it is thick enough to create a ribbon on top of the bulk of the eggs, even just for a moment, then the ribbon stage has been reached. If it dissolves immediately back into itself, the whites have not been whipped enough.

When you combine egg yolks and sugar, do so right before whipping. If sugar sits too long on top of egg yolks, the sugar can "burn" the yolks. They become crusty and combining the sugar and yolks properly becomes difficult.

Copper bowls are often suggested as the bowl of choice for whipping egg whites. The metal reacts with the protein in the egg whites, helping to create a stable foam. It does work really well, but you don't need a copper bowl to get the job done. A bit of cream of tartar does the same thing.

Baking with kids

Kids love to bake and there's plenty of baking to do at Christmastime. One key to working with children is to keep in mind that they may not be able to accomplish some tasks as well as adults. The results may be less than picture perfect. That's okay. Allow them to try their best and use their creativity. If they enjoy the process, they will want to bake again and learn more and more.

Here are some tasks that kids can help with and enjoy doing:

- **Measuring:** You can teach even small children to measure dry and wet ingredients. The kids don't know it, but they learn math in the process.
- **Stirring and whisking:** If there's one problem with kids doing the stirring and whisking, it's that they tend to be a little overly enthusiastic. To prevent flour from flying out of the bowl, give them a brief demonstration first. Just telling them to stir gently doesn't do the trick. Their concept of "gently" is bound to be a bit different than yours.
- **Pan preparation:** Kids can easily help with spraying pans with pan coating. They can use child-safe scissors to cut pieces of parchment paper.
- **Rolling:** When you're making piecrust and rolled cookies, children can help with the rolling pin. In fact, their light touch may be a boon as many doughs need a delicate hand.
- **Cutting cookies:** Kids of all ages love to use cookie cutters. You can also provide kids with cardboard, pencils, and scissors so that they can create their own shapes.
- **Decorating:** There are so many different types of dessert decorating that kids can help with, and decorating is also the part they usually like best. Whether it's sprinkling colored sugars, spreading icing on cookies or cakes, or rolling cookies in powdered sugar, kids can decorate well.

You also need to be aware that the kitchen can be a dangerous place for children. The best suggestion is to keep your eye on the kids and guide them all the way. In particular, watch out for sharp knives and other sharp implements. Even some cookie cutters can be sharp enough to cut or scrape. As for hot pots on top of the stove or hot pans in the oven, these are best tended to by adults.

Observing the fine line between ground nuts and nut butter

I'm sure you've tasted peanut butter. It's ground peanuts (basically) — you could make it yourself by grinding peanuts in a food processor. But there are many times when you want finely ground nuts, and the last thing you want them to do is turn into nut butter.

By grinding nuts with some flour or confectioners sugar, the dry ingredient absorbs some of the nut oils, preventing nut butter from forming. Of course, if you process it long enough, you might still get nut butter, so be careful.

Also, some nuts are oilier than others. Macadamias, which are very high in oil, are very hard to process to a fine meal. Almonds, which are a much drier, harder nut, are easier to work with.

Making Christmas Candies and Confections

What would Christmas be without a little sweet treat, or two, or three?

You may think of Valentine's Day and Halloween as candy-centric holidays, but believe me, Christmas is right up there. People who never have candy dishes out at any other time set them out during December. Boxes of candies are given as gifts and children receive treats, many of the candy variety, in their stockings. Stroll down the grocery candy aisle this time of year. It's a visual assault of special boxes and packaging for the holiday. Chocolate drops normally wrapped in silver foil are now red and green. Chocolate candies come in holiday colors. Candy canes in a rainbow of colors rule the shelves.

But, as with most foods, store-bought candies don't hold a candle to homemade. Perhaps you've never made candies. Well, making candy is really no more difficult than making other types of food. In some instances, candies are actually quite easy to make. In this section, I present a selection of fruity and chocolaty sweets.

Bittersweet Chocolate Truffles

These are little nuggets of pure chocolate bliss. They're easy to make, albeit a tad messy, and even easier to eat. See the color section of this book for a photo of the finished product.

Preparation time: *15 minutes*

Cooking time: *5 minutes*

Yield: *40 truffles*

14 ounces of finely chopped bittersweet chocolate

⅔ cup heavy cream

½ cup Dutch-processed cocoa (approximately)

1. Place 10 ounces of the chocolate in a heatproof bowl. Bring the cream to a boil in a small saucepan over medium heat. Immediately pour the cream over the chocolate.
2. Let the chocolate and cream sit for about 5 minutes, then whisk gently until smooth and combined. Chill the mixture for at least 4 hours or overnight.
3. Line a jelly roll pan with parchment paper. Use a regular teaspoon to scoop up small amounts of the chilled mixture. Cover your hands with cocoa and roll 1-inch balls using your hands. Place the truffles on the pan. Refrigerate while proceeding with the recipe.
4. Melt the remaining 4 ounces of chocolate in a double boiler or microwave. Place the remaining cocoa in a small bowl. Remove the truffles from the refrigerator. Use your clean hands to pick up some melted chocolate, that's right, pick up the melted chocolate, and rub it between your palms. Pick up a truffle and roll it around between your palms until it is lightly coated with chocolate. Immediately drop the truffle into the cocoa and toss it back and forth using two forks. Remove the truffle from the cocoa and place it on the pan. Repeat with remaining truffles.
5. Refrigerate the truffles in an airtight container for up to one month. Bring to room temperature before serving.

Tip: *I know you've been looking for an excuse to cover yourself in chocolate, and here it is. There is a reason for the messy technique, however. Some recipes have you dip the truffle centers into melted chocolate using forks to insert and remove the truffle from the liquid chocolate. This method might be less messy, but it also gives the truffle a much thicker, less-delicate outer chocolate shell. Try it my way at least once; you even get to lick your fingers at the end!*

Tip: *The quality of your truffles depends on the quality of your chocolate. This is the time to splurge on high-quality chocolate and not use supermarket brands. Also, the truffles will not even be half as good it they are eaten cold. They must be brought to room temperature before serving.*

Going All Out: *These truffles are easy to vary. Instead of the cocoa dusting, have separate bowls of finely chopped toasted pistachios and hazelnuts, sweetened shredded coconut, or chocolate sprinkles at hand. As soon as you roll the truffles in the chocolate coating, roll them around in these colorful and flavorful toppings instead of the cocoa. Measurements are approximate, but start with 1 cup of each so you don't get caught short.*

Remember: *These truffles are of the chocolate persuasion. For more information on fungus truffles, see Chapter 5.*

Per serving: *Calories 72 (From fat 45); Total fat 5g (Saturated 3g); Cholesterol 6mg; Sodium 2mg; Carbohydrates 6g (Dietary Fiber 1g); Protein 1g.*

Precautions concerning raw eggs

In recent years, there have been some health scares in regards to salmonella and raw eggs. Traditionally, raw, whipped whites are used in many applications in the baker's kitchen. Chocolate mousse comes to mind, as well as dishes where the whipped whites, with or without added sugar, are added to increase volume and provide an ethereal texture.

Often when we eat in restaurants or buy treats from bakeries, the eggs that are used are pasteurized. Pasteurized eggs aren't readily available to the home cook.

Most doctors and health officials suggest that if you're very young or old or if your immune system is compromised, you should steer away from dishes that may contain raw eggs. If you are the one making the recipe, you have a choice. You can use raw eggs or, if the recipe specifically requires egg whites, you can buy powdered egg whites, sometimes called *meringue powder.* I've seen meringue powder in supermarkets in recent years in the baking ingredient aisle, so you might not have to go far to find it. The egg white powder is reconstituted with water.

Personally, I buy fresh whole eggs from a supermarket with high turnover and use the real deal.

Sugarplums

These are the sugarplums of children's dreams. Sugarplums are small candies made from dried fruit; kids love making them. If you're making them for adults, try the spirited version; otherwise, use orange juice as the liquid. The color section of this book contains a photo of my Sugarplums.

Preparation time: *10 minutes*

Yield: *Thirty-six 1-inch sugarplums*

½ cup finely chopped dried figs

½ cup finely chopped pecans

¼ cup finely chopped dates

¼ cup finely chopped dried cherries

¼ cup finely chopped golden raisins

¼ cup unsweetened grated coconut

2 tablespoons rum, orange liqueur, or orange juice

1 cup confectioners sugar (approximately)

1 The various fruits and nuts should be uniform in size. Place the dried fruits, nuts, coconut, and liquid in a bowl and mix together thoroughly by hand or with a wooden spoon. Roll into 1-inch balls, lightly compressing the mixture so that it sticks together.

2 Roll the balls in confectioners sugar and place in small fluted paper cups, if desired. A nice touch is to roll the ball so that half of it is covered in sugar and half of it is plain.

3 Place in airtight container and refrigerate for up to one month.

Tip: *You can chop the fruits and nuts by hand or chop the fruits one by one in a food processor fitted with a metal blade. Pulse on and off until the fruit is uniform in size.*

Tip: *You know how when you buy a box of fancy candy or chocolate, each piece is nestled in a little paper cup? These fluted paper cups can be found easily at craft stores and specialty food stores. The small ones, which are a little over 1 inch across, are perfect for candies such as these and give them a professional appearance. They also keep the candies from sticking together and make packaging them up for gifts much easier. And, well, they just look darn purty that way.*

Simplify: *If you want to give the candies a nice finish, but don't have any confectioners sugar around the house, simply roll them in granulated sugar. Another way to simplify the recipe is to use whatever dried fruits are easily accessible. Dark raisins are great, as are apricots.*

Going All Out: *To gussie these treats up, dip them in melted and lightly cooled chocolate, let the excess drip off, and then place them on a parchment-lined pan and refrigerate until set. Store in the refrigerator in an airtight container for up to a week. For this recipe, melt about 1 pound of chocolate. I suggest semisweet.*

Per serving: *Calories 35 (From fat 18); Total fat 2g (Saturated 0g); Cholesterol 0mg; Sodium 1mg; Carbohydrates 5g (Dietary Fiber 1g); Protein 0g;.*

Visions of what, exactly?

Have you always wondered what sugarplums are? They are sugary and originally they did contain green plums (or black figs). In Portugal, where some say they originated, these fruits were boiled and reboiled in sugar syrups until the mixture became candied. Nowadays, the term usually refers to many kinds of confection made from dried fruit and rolled into small balls. They can be served in a small bowl or placed in small fluted paper cups.

Sugar-Frosted Fruit

Sugar-Frosted Fruit is simply fresh fruit that's coated with egg white and then coated with sugar. The fruits are crystallized and look beautiful mounded in a glass bowl or on a pedestal. They can be eaten or used as a centerpiece decoration — or both!

Special equipment: *Small artist's paintbrush*

Preparation time: *15 minutes total*

Yield: *10 servings*

2 pounds assorted fruit, such as small apples, kumquats, grapes, small lemons, small limes, clementines, or small pears

3 large egg whites, lightly beaten, placed in a large bowl

2 cups super-fine sugar, placed in a large bowl

1 Place a cooling rack over a sheet pan and set aside.

2 Wash and thoroughly dry all of the fruit.

3 Using the paintbrush, cover each piece of fruit thoroughly but lightly with egg white. Then, holding the fruit over the bowl of sugar, sprinkle sugar over all the surface. Place the fruit on a rack to dry.

4 Arrange the fruit in a bowl or on a pedestal. Eat or display the same day.

Tip: *Buying super-fine sugar is better than making it yourself. When you spin granulated sugar in a food processor, it does do the job of reducing the size of the sugar grain, but it also takes away some of the sparkly nature of the sugar. The grains become a bit powdery as well. When you're shopping for super-fine sugar, it may be labeled bar sugar; the smaller grains dissolve easily in drinks, making it popular with bartenders.*

Per serving: *Calories 203 (From fat 0); Total fat 0g (Saturated 0g); Cholesterol 0mg; Sodium 18mg; Carbohydrates 52g (Dietary Fiber 3g); Protein 2g.*

Preparing Frozen Desserts for Yuletide Tastes

Along with pies, cookies, cakes, and candies, frozen desserts hold their own in the pantheon of desserts. Cool and creamy ice cream is not only a dessert unto itself, but it can also accent a pie or elevate a slice of cake into a sublime dessert.

I include recipes for homemade ice cream and sorbet as well as a baked Alaska that uses purchased ice cream. For the-made-from-scratch versions, you'll need an ice cream maker.

Cranking up the ice cream machine

Many ice cream machines are on the market, ranging in price from quite reasonable to ultra-extravagant.

Inexpensive models have canisters that go in your freezer to chill. Then the canister is placed in a housing that comes equipped with either a hand-crank or electric-crank mechanism that churns the ice cream. The hand-crank models can be bought for as little as $25, while the electric ones can cost twice as much. The hand-operated ones are easy to use. You don't have to continuously crank the machine, just occasionally. The problem I've seen these types of ice cream machines have is that the chemical that's inside the canister that's supposed to provide the chill degrades over time and doesn't seem to get as cold as it did when first purchased.

You can still buy old-fashioned ice cream machines that use salt and ice to chill the ice cream. They'll set you back at least $100. They look like they belong in a country store and have that nostalgia factor working for them. You can find these in both hand-operated and electric versions.

The Cadillac of ice cream machines is the type with a built-in compressor, just like your refrigerator at home. All you do is add your ice cream or sorbet mix to the bowl and turn the machine on. The dasher, which is the part that is down in the ice cream turning and churning around, does the rest. About 20 minutes later, you have ice cream ready to scoop out and serve. You can expect to pay $300 to $1,000 for the privilege of owning such a machine. Many ice cream connoisseurs, myself included, think these machines do a better job than the lesser models. The premium model's method of operation, which involves a gentle continuous churning along with a very fast chilling time, produces a dense, creamy ice cream.

Cranberry Cider Sorbet

This sorbet is easy to make and fat free. It makes a refreshing end to a meal.

Preparation time: *10 minutes*

Cooking time: *4½ hours chilling time*

Yield: *About 1 quart*

1½ cups cranberry juice

1½ cups apple cider

1¼ cups sugar

2 tablespoons freshly squeezed lime or lemon juice

1 Combine the cranberry juice, cider, and sugar in a medium-sized saucepan. Whisk together and place over medium heat, whisking occasionally until the sugar is dissolved. Remove the pan from the heat and stir in the lime or lemon juice.

2 Pour the mixture into a clean container and refrigerate until very cold, at least 4 hours or overnight.

3 Pour the mixture into an ice cream maker and follow the manufacturer's instructions.

4 The sorbet may be served immediately or scraped into an airtight container and chilled in the freezer for 2 to 4 hours to firm it up.

Tip: *When you pack your ice cream or sorbet into a container and freeze it after churning, you're ripening the dessert. The rest in the freezer allows the texture to firm up and the flavors to meld. Some people like their ice cream or sorbet fresh from the machine, others prefer it after ripening. Hold a mini taste test and see which you prefer. It's a tough job, but someone's got to do it.*

Simplify: *You can make this sorbet with just cranberry juice or just cider; either way, it's a great holiday dessert.*

Going All Out: *To gild the lily, serve in chilled bowls.*

Per serving (½-cup): *Calories 172 (From fat 0); Total fat 0g (Saturated 0g); Cholesterol 0mg; Sodium 6mg; Carbohydrates 44g (Dietary Fiber 0g); Protein 0g;.*

Eggnog Ice Cream

You can never have too much eggnog at Christmastime; here it is in a frozen version.

Preparation time: *20 minutes*

Cooking time: *6½ hours chilling time*

Yield: *1½ quarts*

2 cups whole milk

2 cups heavy cream

6 large egg yolks

1 cup sugar

2 tablespoons dark rum (optional)

½ teaspoon vanilla extract

½ teaspoon nutmeg

1 In a medium-sized, heavy-bottomed, non-reactive saucepan, combine the milk and cream and bring to a boil over a medium-high heat.

2 Meanwhile, whisk together the egg yolks and the sugar in a medium-sized heatproof bowl. Slowly add a little of the warm liquid into the egg mixture, whisking all the while, to temper the eggs. Add the remaining liquid, stirring until smooth.

3 Return the mixture to the saucepan and cook over medium heat, stirring constantly, until the custard has thickened slightly and coats the back of a spoon, about 7 minutes. Do not boil.

4 Pour through a fine strainer and stir in the rum, if you're using it, and the vanilla extract and nutmeg. Cool almost to room temperature, stirring occasionally. Transfer the mixture to a storage container and refrigerate 6 hours or overnight. Pour into an ice cream maker and follow the manufacturer's instructions. Freeze in an airtight container. Eat within 4 days, preferably.

Per serving (½-cup): *Calories 257 (From fat 171); Total fat 19g (Saturated 11g); Cholesterol 166mg; Sodium 39mg; Carbohydrates 20g (Dietary Fiber 0g); Protein 4g.*

Ice Bowl

An ice bowl isn't a new idea, but it is an easy and beautiful way to serve sorbets and ice creams.

Tools: *One 8-inch diameter stainless steel bowl, one 10-inch diameter stainless steel bowl, duct tape*

Preparation time: *10 minutes total*

Cooking time: *Must chill overnight*

Yield: *1 bowl*

Water

Lemon slices, cranberries, kumquat slices (optional)

1 Make sure that you've cleared a space in your freezer that's large enough to hold the larger bowl.

2 Place the larger bowl on the counter in front of you. Place the smaller bowl inside the larger one and tape them together along the rims, keeping the gap between them even all the way around, including on the bottom.

3 Carefully pour water into the gap and fill up the space between the bowls until the water is about 1 inch shy of the top.

4 If you like, slide fruits here and there down into the water.

5 If the smaller bowl tries to rise up, fill it with some water to weigh it down.

6 Freeze overnight. To unmold, pour some warm water into the smaller bowl. Remove all the tape, grip the smaller bowl's edges, and gently twist. It should come free from the ice bowl. If not, add some more warm water and try again.

7 Run some warm water over the outside of the larger bowl and carefully remove it from the ice bowl.

8 To use the ice bowl, fold a small cloth napkin in quarters and place it in the center of a pretty plate. Place the bowl on the napkin; doing so keeps the bowl from sliding around as it melts. Place balls of ice cream in the bowl and serve.

Tip: *An ice bowl is a great way to serve ice cream on a buffet, as it helps to keep the ice cream cold.*

Simplify: *You don't have to pull out the measuring tape. Just use two bowls that are approximately the suggested sizes and have at least a 2-inch difference.*

Assembling a polar special: Mocha Baked Alaska

Long recipes can look intimidating. In reality, following a long recipe isn't necessarily more difficult than following a shorter recipe. The next recipe is a case in point. It has four components, plus assembly time, and the recipe goes on and on. But it's really not that hard to make. Just take it one step at a time. One component can be made a month ahead, and the others can be made ahead as well. The entire dessert can be assembled the night before. So, it's actually an easy dessert to make ahead, with no last minute requirements. So don't let a long recipe put you off. Always read a recipe first, all the way through, before passing judgment.

Mocha Baked Alaska

Here's a surprisingly easy-to-make baked Alaska comprised of chocolate cake, purchased ice cream, meringue, and warmed chocolate sauce. It can be made ahead and kept in the freezer until you need it. The ingredient list is long, but the actual time spent on the dessert is reasonable.

Special equipment: *You need a metal bowl to mold the baked Alaska. I have one that is 7 inches in diameter on the bottom and is 5 inches deep, which is a beautiful proportion. A 4½ or 5 quart KitchenAid mixing bowl is perfect. Make sure the diameter fits the 8-inch cake as closely as possible. You also need a 10-inch ovenproof platter and a candy thermometer.*

Preparation time: *30 minutes*

Cooking time: *25 minutes and overnight freezing time*

Yield: *10 servings*

Cake

2 large eggs at room temperature

2 large egg yolks at room temperature (reserve the egg whites for the meringue and save a pretty shell half)

½ cup sugar

2 tablespoons butter, melted

1 teaspoon vanilla extract

⅓ cup cake flour

¼ cup Dutch-processed cocoa

¼ teaspoon baking powder

Pinch salt

1 Preheat the oven to 350 degrees. Spray an 8 x 2-inch round cake pan with pan coating and line the bottom with parchment paper.

2 Whip the eggs, egg yolks, and sugar with a balloon whip attachment in a mixer until a ribbon forms. Meanwhile, whisk together the melted butter and vanilla extract; set aside.

3 Sift together the flour, cocoa, baking powder, and salt and fold into the whipped egg mixture until completely combined. Start with a whisk and finish with a large rubber spatula.

4 Fold in the butter and vanilla mixture. Scrape the cake into the prepared pan and bake for about 25 minutes, or until a toothpick comes out clean. The sides will just be coming away from the edges of the pan and the top should spring back when lightly touched.

5 Cool the cake in the pan on a rack for 15 minutes, then remove the cake from the pan and cool it completely on a rack. The cake may be used the day it's baked or wrapped in plastic wrap after it's cooled and stored at room temperature overnight. Make the sauce while the cake is baking and cooling.

Chocolate Sauce

12 ounces semisweet or bittersweet chocolate, finely chopped

1 cup heavy cream

Place the chocolate in a heatproof bowl. Heat the cream in a heavy-bottomed pot over medium heat until it comes to a boil. Immediately pour the hot cream over the chocolate. Let sit for 5 minutes, then whisk to melt the chocolate. The mixture may be held at room temperature for 2 hours. Alternatively, you can make it up to one month ahead and freeze it in an airtight container; otherwise, refrigerate for one week. Rewarm in a microwave or on a stovetop before using.

Ice Cream Filling Assembly

5 pints (10 cups) premium coffee chip or coffee Heath Bar ice cream, softened

1 Take your ice cream bombe mold, or whatever bowl you're using to mold the ice cream, and line it with a large piece of plastic wrap. You may need two overlapping pieces. Doing so helps you to unmold the bombe later on. Smooth out the plastic as well as you can so that it adheres to the inside of the bombe with as few wrinkles as possible. Have the ends of the wrap hang over the outside. The inside should be completely covered.

2 Using a large, strong spoon, scoop and pack the ice cream into the mold. Place a piece of plastic wrap on top of the ice cream and freeze it solid. The ice cream should be in the freezer at least overnight. This can be done up to one week ahead. Just make sure to wrap the ice cream airtight so that no flavors get picked up from the freezer.

Meringue

1¼ cups plus ⅓ cup sugar

½ cup water

8 large egg whites at room temperature

1 teaspoon cream of tartar

1 teaspoon vanilla extract

1 Combine 1¼ cups sugar and the water in a small, heavy-bottomed saucepan and bring to a boil over medium-high heat. Brush down any sugar crystals from the sides of a pan with a pastry brushed dipped in warm water.

2 Meanwhile, whip the egg whites until they're frothy with a balloon whip attachment on low speed. Add the cream of tartar, increase the speed to high, and whip until soft peaks form. Gradually add ⅓ cup sugar and continue whipping until stiff peaks form, about 5 minutes.

3 Cook the sugar syrup to 248 to 250 degrees. Use your candy thermometer to measure. The mixture should thicken and large bubbles will be rising slowly to the surface. Do not let it begin to caramelize, which is when the mixture will turn golden. Pour the syrup slowly over the meringue and continue beating until stiff peaks form. Beat in the vanilla extract and use immediately.

Caution: *The sugar syrup is very hot and can burn, so be careful.*

Assembly

2 tablespoons vodka or brandy

1 Have a 10-inch ovenproof platter ready. Preheat the oven to 450 degrees after setting the oven rack to the lowest setting. Have the chocolate sauce warmed and ready to go.

2 Peel the plastic away from the open end of the mold in which you've placed the ice cream and place the cake on top of the exposed ice cream. Place the platter on top of the cake and invert the entire dessert. The ice cream should pop right out of the mold. If it does not, place a warm washcloth around the outside of the bombe mold for a minute and try again. Peel off the plastic.

3 Use a large spoon to spread the meringue all over the ice cream and cake all the way down to join the surface of the serving tray. Use the outside of the spoon to make nice peaks of meringue all over the dessert, working quickly. Place an eggshell half on the top of the bombe with the open half facing up. The meringue will hold it in place. Freeze overnight, or proceed immediately.

4 Bake until lightly browned, approximately 5 minutes. Remove the cake from the oven as soon as the meringue is browned in spots here and there. Watch carefully. Remember that you're putting ice cream in the oven.

5 While the dessert is browning, warm the vodka slightly in a small pan over low heat. Do not overheat. When the Mocha Baked Alaska is done, remove it from the oven, pour the vodka into the eggshell, and ignite with a match.

6 Present the cake under dimmed lights. The alcohol will burn out in a couple of minutes. Serve immediately in large, thin wedges and pass the chocolate sauce or spoon it over each serving.

Tip: *This is not the prettiest cake to slice and serve. It does look like a bit of a mess on the plate, but I've never heard any criticism of it and have always garnered much astonished praise from those lucky enough to have this magical dessert made for them.*

Tip: *Use all the meringue and make sure that the meringue completely covers the ice cream and cake and comes all the way down to meet the plate. It insulates the ice cream from the high heat of the oven — you don't want to end up with a pool of melted ice cream. I guarantee that you won't if you follow this advice.*

Per serving: *Calories 1,089 (From fat 585); Total fat 65g (Saturated 33g); Cholesterol 414mg; Sodium 313mg; Carbohydrates 117g (Dietary Fiber 2g); Protein 17g.*

Chapter 12

Cakes, Pies, Puddings, Tarts, and Trifle

In This Chapter

- Making desserts at home
- Baking an amazing bûche de Noël
- Finding shortcuts to yule yum desserts

Recipes in This Chapter

- White Chocolate Bûche de Noël
- Pumpkin Toffee Cheesecake
- Basic Piecrust
- Sweet Tart Crust
- Apple Pie
- Pumpkin Pie
- Chocolate Pecan Pie
- Chocolate Truffle Tart
- Cranberry Cherry Tart
- Christmas Pudding with Rum Cream
- Pear Almond Trifle

The title of this chapter sounds like a law firm, don't you think? *"Cakes Pies Puddings Tarts & Trifle . . . Good morning!"* (I think I'll start answering my phone that way.)

I'm thankful at Christmastime and every other time of the year that there is no law against dessert, my favorite part of the meal! Dessert often takes center stage, right next to the main dish. In some families, dessert is the starring attraction.

If you're a dessert fanatic, the holidays are the time to indulge in whatever your heart desires. Cookies, candies, and confections are covered in Chapter 11. Cakes, tarts, pies, and other wonderful things are assembled in this chapter. Have them all! In fact, even though you may present just one main course with a Christmas meal, a bevy of desserts is never out of the question.

Besides, the cold winter months are a great time to get into the kitchen and bake. The oven warms the house, the aromas are inviting, and the results are worth all your efforts. Of course, you *can* buy dessert in a bakery, but when you bake at home you are assured that the quality of ingredients is the best it can possibly be. Nothing can take the place of fresh eggs, high quality chocolate, fresh nuts, and real vanilla extract. As with all cooking, the quality of ingredients greatly affects the finished product.

It's true that baking things like cakes and pies is more of an exact science and more demanding than preparing other dishes, but recipes are your road map.

If you follow the recipes in this chapter word for word and step by step, I promise great results.

Can't quite remember the difference between a jellyroll pan and a cookie sheet? Not sure how to temper chocolate? Check out Chapter 2, in which I discuss all sorts of helpful equipment and techniques.

Three Almost-Instant Desserts

These desserts aren't instantaneous, but they're almost so. When you need dessert in a hurry:

- Buy pound cake, your favorite ice cream, some chocolate sauce, and whipped cream. Layer them up and serve.
- Buy a fruitcake, poke holes in it and soak it in sherry or dark rum. Serve with a scoop of vanilla ice cream.
- Buy brandied fruit in a jar at a specialty food store and serve over ice cream or cake.
- Place defrosted, sweetened strawberries or raspberries in an ovenproof dish. Cover with lightly sweetened sour cream. Sprinkle with an even layer of brown sugar and broil until the sugar caramelizes. Serve immediately.
- Make ice cream sandwiches with purchased chocolate chip cookies. Try using coffee ice cream.
- Speaking of coffee ice cream, serve it with caramel sauce, whipped cream, and toasted walnuts.

Almost everything is improved by the addition of whipped cream and chocolate sauce — in my opinion, anyway.

Baking a Christmas Cake or Two

A homemade cake can grace your holiday table with drama — a show-stopping centerpiece that elicits oohs and aahs from your guests. I have a couple for you to try, starting with the classic French Christmas dessert, the bûche de Noël, and then on to a creamy and crunchy cheesecake. As with many of the recipes in this book, take note of what components you can make ahead and take advantage of anything that you can do ahead.

Bûche de Noël is French for *Christmas log.* This dessert with the fancy name is found in every pastry-shop window in France during the month of December. It's simply a rolled cake decorated to look like a log, which is quite whimsical and pleases both young and all alike. Don't let the moniker deter you; this is one of those desserts that will establish you as a dessert-maker extraordinaire. Just follow the instructions carefully, and the finished product is certain to be wonderful.

White Chocolate Bûche de Noël

This dessert consists of a yellow sponge cake rolled around a white chocolate and cherry filling. You can start this the day ahead and let it sit overnight. See the color section of this book for a photo of the finished dish.

Preparation time: *45 minutes; 8 hour cooling time*

Cooking time: *20 minutes*

Yield: *10 servings*

Sponge Cake

¼ cup whole milk

2 tablespoons (¼ stick) unsalted butter

½ teaspoon vanilla

¾ cup cake flour

1 teaspoon baking powder

Pinch salt

3 large eggs

3 large egg yolks

1 cup sugar

1 Preheat the oven to 350 degrees. Spray a jellyroll pan with pan coating, line with parchment paper, and spray again.

2 Place the milk and butter in a saucepan over medium heat to melt the butter, or melt the butter together with the milk in a microwave. Stir in the vanilla extract; set aside, keeping warm. Sift together the flour, baking powder, and salt; set aside.

3 In a mixer's bowl, beat the eggs, yolks, and sugar on high speed using a balloon whip attachment until the mixture is light and fluffy and a ribbon forms, about 2 minutes. Resift the dry ingredients onto the egg and sugar mixture in three batches, folding after each addition. Start folding with a whisk, and finish up the last batch with a large rubber spatula.

4 Drizzle the warmed milk and butter mixture over the batter a little at a time, folding all the while. If you add the liquid too quickly, it will sink instead of becoming incorporated. You'll end up with a rubbery layer in your cake. Pour the batter onto a jellyroll pan, using an offset spatula to spread evenly. The cake will be thin.

5 Bake for about 12 minutes, rotating front to back once during baking. The cake should be puffed and light, golden brown. A toothpick will test clean. Do not overbake or the cake will loose its flexibility. Place on a wire rack and allow the cake to cool completely while still in the pan. Use immediately or wrap in plastic wrap and store at room temperature for up to 24 hours.

Whipped White Chocolate Ganache Filling and Frosting

¾ pound white chocolate, finely chopped

2⅔ cups heavy cream

Place the chocolate in a large bowl. Bring the cream to a boil in a medium-sized pot and immediately pour the cream over the chocolate. Let sit for 3 minutes to melt the chocolate. Stir until the chocolate is melted and smooth. If many unmelted chocolate pieces remain, let sit for about 10 minutes, stirring occasionally; the residual heat will melt any remaining chunks. Cover with plastic wrap and refrigerate at least 6 hours or overnight.

Cherry Filling

14½ ounce-can sour pitted cherries, water packed

3 tablespoons cherry liquid (from the canned cherries)

3 tablespoons sugar

2 tablespoons kirschwasser liqueur

Drain the cherries, reserving 3 tablespoons of the liquid. Place the liquid in small saucepan. Place the cherries in small mixing bowl; set aside. Add the sugar to the cherry juice and stir together. Bring to a boil over medium-high heat, stirring occasionally to dissolve the sugar. Remove from the heat and add kirschwasser. Pour over cherries and reserve until needed.

Assembly and Decoration

3 tablespoons confectioners sugar

1 Begin assembly the day before serving or very early on the day of serving. Have ready a large, flat serving platter. It must be at least 18 inches long and 6 inches wide, and must be able to fit in your refrigerator. You can also create a tray by covering cardboard with aluminum foil.

2 To unmold the cake, use a knife tip to loosen all the edges. Lay out a clean piece of parchment on your work surface and dust lightly with confectioners sugar; invert the cake onto the parchment. Remove the pan and very gently peel the parchment off of the cake. Have the cake horizontally in front of you. Using a pastry brush, dip down into the cherry marinade and dab all over the surface of the cake.

3 Using an electric mixer and balloon whip attachment, beat the white chocolate filling on medium-high speed until the mixture just starts to thicken. Watch the filling constantly and whip just until soft peaks form. The filling should not slide off the balloon whip. If you prefer, remove the bowl from the mixer as soon as the mixture thickens and finish off by hand with a large whisk. Do not overbeat.

4 Using an offset spatula, spread 3 cups of the filling evenly over the cake, going all the way to the short edges. Leave ¼-inch border along the top edge. Scatter the reserved cherries evenly over the filling. Press them into the filling slightly by running over them with the spatula.

5 Using the bottom parchment to help, roll the cake, starting with the long side that's nearest to you. Roll firmly, separating the parchment from the cake as you go so that it doesn't get rolled up inside. Carefully transfer the roll onto a serving platter, seam side down.

6 Trim one end on a 45-degree angle, just trimming the very end (taste the scrap!). Trim the other end on a similar angle about 4 inches down the log. Take this piece and lay it a third of the way down the side of the log using the angled end to nestle against the log. Doing so makes a "branch." If you need help visualizing the finished product, note that there's a photograph in the color insert.

7 Spread the remaining white chocolate mixture all over the log using the icing spatula. A small offset spatula might help you to get the corners and the edges that are resting on the platter. Cover the ends with frosting as well. If serving as is, use a small, narrow icing spatula to make long ridges in the frosting to simulate bark. Use a fork to make concentric rings on the ends. Refrigerate at least 2 hours or overnight. Let sit at room temperature for 30 minutes before serving.

8 If desired, place pine boughs around the cake and dust with confectioners sugar to mimic snow.

Remember: *Using cake flour makes your cake tender. All-purpose flour can be substituted in a pinch, but replace the ¾ cup cake flour with ⅔ cup all-purpose plus 2 tablespoons cornstarch.*

Remember: *You can find good-quality white chocolate in many large supermarkets. Look on the shelves next to the chocolate chips, in the baking ingredient aisle. Ghirardelli is a good brand to look for. Callebaut brand is found in specialty shops.*

Going All Out: *Cover a large cookie sheet tightly with aluminum foil, smoothing out any wrinkles. Quick temper 12 ounces of white, milk, or semisweet/bittersweet chocolate and spread it evenly over the foil using an offset spatula; the chocolate will be about ⅛-inch thick. Refrigerate for about 15 minutes or until firm. Break up the chocolate in long irregular strips from ½ inch to 1 inch wide. Press the strips against the cake to mimic bark. Refrigerate 2 hours or overnight and follow the directions above.*

Per serving: *Calories 627 (From fat 369); Total fat 41g (Saturated 24g); Cholesterol 229mg; Sodium 140mg; Carbohydrates 58g (Dietary Fiber 1g); Protein 8g.*

Pumpkin Toffee Cheesecake

This creamy pumpkin cheesecake sits on a gingersnap crust and is crowned by a creamy sour cream topping and a sprinkle of crunchy toffee. (Take a look at it in the color section of this book.) A springform pan is used here to facilitate serving. A springform pan is comprised of a solid, round bottom with a spring-loaded band that fits around the bottom to form the side. When the spring is locked in place, the pan is tight and can be filled up with batter. To release a cake, the spring is sprung, the sides can be lifted away, and the cake is almost automatically unmolded. Figure 12-1 shows a springform pan.

Special equipment: *9-inch springform pan, roasting pan at least 11 inches wide*

Preparation time: *25 minutes*

Cooking time: *1 hour and 30 minutes*

Yield: *12 servings*

Crust

1½ cups gingersnap crumbs

3 tablespoons unsalted butter, melted

1 Preheat the oven to 350 degrees. Spray the insides of 9-inch springform pan with pan coating. Wrap the outside of the pan with heavy-duty aluminum foil, coming at least halfway up the outside.

2 Combine the gingersnap crumbs and butter in a small bowl and stir until blended. Press the crumbs evenly onto the bottom of the pan. Bake for about 8 minutes or until the crumb crust is just beginning to brown. Cool on a wire rack. Turn the oven down to 325 degrees.

Cheesecake

Four 8-ounce packages cream cheese at room temperature

¾ cups sugar

¾ cups lightly packed light brown sugar

4 large eggs

1 cup solid pack pumpkin

2 tablespoons cornstarch

1 teaspoon vanilla extract

1 teaspoon cinnamon

1 teaspoon ginger

¼ teaspoon allspice

1 Beat the cream cheese until creamy in a mixer's bowl using a flat paddle attachment on medium speed. Add the sugar and brown sugar gradually and continue beating until light and fluffy, about 3 minutes.

2 Add eggs one at a time, beating well after each addition and scraping down the bowl once or twice. Beat in the pumpkin, cornstarch, vanilla extract, cinnamon, ginger, and allspice just until well blended.

3 Pour the filling onto the cooled crust. Place the cake in a roasting pan and add hot tap water to come 1 inch up the pan's sides.

4 Bake in a 325-degree oven for about 1 hour and 20 minutes. The cheesecake will look slightly puffed and the center will still be loose and a bit wobbly. Proceed with the topping.

Topping

2 cups sour cream

3 tablespoons sugar

½ cup toffee pieces

1 Quickly whisk together the sour cream and sugar and spread gently and evenly over the top of the cheesecake. It will probably be level with the top of the pan or near to it; that's okay.

2 Place the cake back in the oven and bake for 3 minutes. Cool to room temperature on a rack. Refrigerate overnight.

3 To serve, run the tip of a sharp paring knife around the outer edge of the cake to separate it from the pan. Release the springform, remove the outer ring, and place the cheesecake on a serving platter. Sprinkle toffee bits over the top right before serving.

Remember: *Make the cookie crumbs by placing crispy ginger cookies in a food processor fitted with a metal blade and process until the mixture is finely ground.*

Caution: *Do not use low-fat versions of cream cheese; the cake will not come out properly.*

Tip: *Cheesecake can be sticky to cut and serve. Use a very sharp, thin-bladed knife and dip it in very hot water before slicing; doing so works wonders. Some people even use dental floss to cut the cake! Cut a long piece of floss, at least 2 feet long. Wind the ends around your fingers, hold tight and use it to slice through the cake. Just don't use mint flavored!*

Per serving: *Calories 648 (From fat 396); Total fat 44g (Saturated 26g); Cholesterol 187mg; Sodium 431mg; Carbohydrates 55g (Dietary Fiber 1g); Protein 11g.*

Figure 12-1: Use a springform pan for cheesecake.

Be prepared

"Be prepared" is the Boy Scout motto, but it may as well be the motto of the baker. Whether you're baking a pie, cookies, or a cake, some sort of baking pan must be prepared so that your baked goods brown properly but don't stick and so that they serve as easily as possible. Here's a rundown of the available pans and how to prepare them:

- **Cookie pans/sheet pans:** Line cookie sheets with a sheet of parchment paper cut to fit.
- **Jellyroll pan:** Line the bottom of the pan with a piece of parchment paper cut to fit and spray the paper and the edges of the pan with pan coating.
- **Cake pans:** Line the bottom of the pan with a round parchment paper cut to fit and spray the paper and the edges of the pan with pan coating.
- **Pie plates:** Spray the insides of a pie plate with pan coating.
- **Tart pans:** Spray the insides of a tart pan with pan coating.
- **Miscellaneous pans:** Whether you're using an oblong casserole dish for a deep-dish pie or a pudding mold, spray generously with pan coating.

Walking Hand in Hand through Pie and Tart Land

Pies are the most popular desserts during the Christmas season. Tarts, which are just like pies but are slightly shallower, should be considered in this upper echelon as well. Now, I know you may have never made a pie before, probably because you've been afraid of making the crust, but I'm going to hold your hand, the best I can anyway, and take you through the crust-making process step-by-step. But that comes a little later; right now I want to talk about all the reasons why you should make a pie.

First of all, there's the nostalgia factor. When we think of home cookin', we think pies. Secondly, many of the components can be made ahead. Piecrusts can be made way ahead and frozen. Many pie fillings can be made a few days ahead. Putting the components together the day of your meal takes only minutes.

I find that glass pie plates work the best for pies. Pyrex is a good brand name to look for. For tarts, experiment with different shapes of loose-bottomed fluted tart pans. Always spray pie plates and tart pans with spray coating for easy dessert removal and bake the pies and tarts on a parchment-lined baking sheet to handle any overflow and for ease of handling.

Preparing a basic piecrust and sweet tart crust

You should have two crust recipes at your disposal: a classic piecrust and a sweet tart crust. Well, maybe three. The third would be a purchased crust. Yes, you can buy a frozen crust already in a ready-to-bake aluminum pan or refrigerated crusts that you unfold and place in your own pan. They're convenient, but they don't hold a Christmas candle to homemade. So, in the holiday spirit of giving, I'm asking you to give homemade crust a go.

If you choose to use frozen, preformed pie shells, you will probably have leftover filling. Watch the baking time, because bought pie shells will probably bake more quickly than homemade crusts.

The tart dough is a bit sweeter and crisper and is fitted into decorative tart pans for a shallower dessert, such as the Chocolate Truffle Tart. Piecrusts should be tender and flaky. They can afford to be delicate because a pie plate supports them. Tarts are usually removed from their pans, so the crust needs to be firmer. The techniques for making these crusts are a little different. The directions are lengthy, but that's just because I have taken the time to explain every little step. Read through the directions thoroughly at least once. The next time you use the recipes, you can look them over to reacquaint yourself.

Freeze ahead? Yes, way ahead! Pie and tart doughs freeze very well. It pays to make them ahead. Wrap the dough well in a double layer of plastic wrap and then slip the covered dough into a resealable freezer bag. Remove all the air and freeze for up to a month. Defrost in a refrigerator overnight.

Basic Piecrust

Here it is, the workhorse of the pie world.

Preparation time: *5 minutes*

Cooking time: *2 hours chilling time*

Yield: *2 piecrusts, enough for one 9-inch deep-dish double-crust pie*

2½ cups all-purpose flour

1 teaspoon salt

10 tablespoons (1 stick plus 2 tablespoons) chilled unsalted butter, cut into large pieces

3 ounces (hefty ½ cup) chilled shortening

3 to 4 tablespoons ice water

1 Measure the flour and salt into a mixing bowl and place in the freezer for 15 minutes.

2 Cut the butter and shortening into tablespoon-sized pieces and scatter over the dry ingredients. Cut the butter and shortening into the dry ingredients using a pastry blender or two butter knives until the fats are the size of flat raisins. Do not overwork or you'll end up with a mealy crust.

3 Sprinkle the water over the flour mixture. Toss with two forks or your fingertips until the dough begins to come together.

4 Scrape the dough onto a tabletop and knead briefly, just to bring the crust together into a ball. Divide into two pieces and press into flat disks. Wrap both in plastic wrap and refrigerate for at least two hours or overnight. The crust may also be frozen for a month and defrosted in the refrigerator overnight. The rest in the refrigerator is necessary to relax the protein, or gluten, in the dough. When you mix the dough, the gluten is activated and the dough is temporarily too tough and springy to roll.

5 To roll out the dough, lightly flour your work surface and rolling pin. Begin to apply pressure, starting at the center of the dough and rolling towards the top of the circle. Then pick up your pin, place it in the center of the dough, and roll towards the bottom. Do the same for the sides and all the in-between angles. Check to see that the dough remains free from sticking to the work surface by spinning in quarter turns. Keep rolling until the desired size and thickness is reached. A ¼-inch thickness is standard, if no other thickness is specified.

Tip: *I know it adds 15 minutes to your preparation time, but chilling the flour first goes a long way towards helping your crust come out the best it can be. Keeping the mixture cold while mixing is the name of the game and this is a good way to get the job done.*

Per serving: *Calories 363 (From fat 225); Total fat 25g (Saturated 12g); Cholesterol 39mg; Sodium 75mg; Carbohydrates 30g (Dietary Fiber 1g); Protein 4g.*

Pie plate materials

Pie plates are made from many different materials, from metal to glass to ceramic, with different kinds of interiors and finishes. You want to consider many things when choosing a pie plate. There's heat conductivity — you want the crust to brown well — and if you want to serve the pie at the table, the plate should be pretty enough to show off.

I've had great luck with glass pie plates. Pyrex brand makes good glass plates. They conduct heat well, you can see through them to check on the color of the crust, and they blend in well with any décor. These recipes were tested with glass plates, so I can assure you success if you use them. The deep-dish 9-inch plates have little handles to make moving the pie around easier.

Pie plate sizes

The pies in this book call for a 9-inch deep-dish pie plate, which has a 5-cup capacity. You would think that the diameter measurement is the only thing you need to be concerned about. But some 9-inch pie plates hold a skimpy 2½ cups. Measure the volume of your pie plate by filling it with water and measuring the water.

How to produce an edible Christmas fruitcake

For many people, Christmas wouldn't be Christmas without a fruitcake, and it's not necessarily a pleasant association. Too many fruitcakes are made with candied fruit that bears no resemblance to its original form. Candied cherries practically glow in the dark — some of them are even green! Anyway, I haven't included a fruitcake recipe in this book because there are just too many recipes out there.

But in the spirit of the season, I do have some suggestions if you decide to dig out that tattered old fruitcake recipe handed down from Uncle Oscar's household. Replace the artificially flavored and colored candied fruit with equal amounts of dried fruit. The exceptions are candied lemon and orange peels, which are great. Be aware that some dried fruits are sugared almost as heavily as the candied variety, so use your judgment. Many of the kinds I list here can be found in the bulk foods sections of natural food stores. Also, some dried fruits aren't a good addition to a classic fruitcake.

Here's a list of great additions:

- Dried cherries
- Dried cranberries
- Dried, diced pineapple
- Dried, diced papaya
- Dried mango
- Dried apricots
- Dried figs
- Dried dates
- Dark raisins
- Golden raisins
- Dried currants
- Candied orange or lemon peel

Steer clear of candied cherries, angelica, citron, dried apples, dried peaches, candied pineapple, and diced, multicolored, mixed candied fruit.

Sweet Tart Crust

The Sweet Tart Crust is a tad sweeter and a bit sturdier than the Basic Piecrust. The fat is cut into smaller pieces, which makes the crust less flaky but gives it more structure. The crust is just as tender.

Preparation time: *5 minutes*

Cooking time: *None; 2 hours chilling time*

Yield: *Two 10-inch tart crusts*

3 cups all-purpose flour

¼ cup granulated sugar

¼ teaspoon salt

1 cup (2 sticks) unsalted butter, chilled and cut into large pieces

2 large egg yolks

¼ cup heavy cream, cold

1 Measure the flour, sugar, and salt into a mixing bowl and place in the freezer for 15 minutes.

2 Scatter the butter in tablespoon-sized pieces over the dry ingredients. Cut the butter in using a pastry blender or two butter knives until the mixture resembles a coarse cornmeal or finely ground nuts.

3 Whisk together the egg yolks and cream, then drizzle the liquid over the dry ingredients. Toss in with two forks or your fingertips until the dough begins to come together.

4 Scrape the dough onto the tabletop and knead briefly, just to bring the crust together into a ball. Divide into two pieces, roll into disks, and flatten. Wrap both pieces of the dough in plastic wrap and refrigerate for at least two hours or overnight. The crust may also be frozen for a week and defrosted in the refrigerator overnight.

5 To roll out the dough, lightly flour your work surface and rolling pin. Begin to apply pressure, starting at the center of the dough and rolling towards the top of the circle. Then pick up your pin, place it back in the center, and roll towards the bottom. Do the same for the sides and all the in-between angles. Check to see that the dough remains free from sticking to the work surface by spinning it in quarter turns. Keep rolling until the desired size and thickness is reached. A ¼-inch thickness is standard, if no other thickness is specified.

Tip: *There are many ways to make a tart crust. Some bakers swear by the food processor and a pat-in method, which eliminates the need for a rolling pin. Place the dry ingredients in the bowl of a food processor that you've fitted with a metal blade. Pulse to combine. Add the pieces of butter and pulse on and off until the mixture is the texture of coarse sand. With the mixer running, add the yolks and cream in a thin stream and keep processing until the dough begins to clump. Now, you can directly press the dough into the prepared* *pan. Freeze it for 15 minutes while the oven preheats and you're ready to go. This method is very easy and your hands stay clean, but the dough might be a tad tougher than if it's made by hand. Most people won't notice the difference though.*

Per serving: *Calories 363 (From fat 225); Total fat 25g (Saturated 12g); Cholesterol 39mg; Sodium 75mg; Carbohydrates 30g (Dietary Fiber 1g); Protein 4g.*

Working with pie and tart doughs

You can place pie or tart crusts into their pie plates and tart pans in different ways, depending on whether you are making a single-crusted or double-crusted pie and whether or not your crust needs to be prebaked. (A double-crusted pie has a layer of pastry on the top — think of a classic apple pie.)

Single-crust pies

To partially bake a single crust, spray the pie plate or tart pan with pan coating and then fit the crust into the pan.

- For pie, trim the edges to about 2 inches and fold back under the crust. Crimp with your thumb and index finger to make a decorative edge.
- For tarts, trim the crust about 1 inch above the edge; fold inwards and press to create a thick lip. Alternatively, use your rolling pin to roll over the edges, using the tart pan's edge to cut the dough perfectly even with the top edge. If you're patting in a tart crust, make sure that the top edge doesn't get too thin. Use your fingers to build up the thickness.

To partially bake a single piecrust or tart crust, first freeze it for 30 minutes. Preheat the oven to 375 degrees. Line the crust with foil and fill it with *pie weights.* These are small metal or ceramic nuggets that can be purchased from any kitchenware store. Or use pennies, rice, or dried beans. You just need weight to keep the crust down. Always place the pie or tart on a sheet pan before baking. To partially bake, bake the pie or tart for about 10 minutes, remove the foil and weights, and bake for about 8 minutes more. The crust should be dry but not completely cooked and just lightly colored. To prebake completely, bake the crust for about 10 minutes with the foil, then bake it for about 12 minutes without. The crust should be completely dry and just turning golden brown.

Double-crust pies

When it comes to a double-crusted pie, the top crust must be sealed to the bottom. The bottom crust should be placed in the pie plate, fitted along the bottom, and the edges trimmed to about 2 inches beyond the plate's lip. If the crust has softened, chill briefly at this point. Fill the crust with whatever filling you're using. Lay the top crust over the filling and trim its edges to match the bottom crust. Then, fold both crusts' edges underneath the bottom layer and tuck just inside the pie plate's rim. Now you can crimp a ruffled edge by using your fingers or you can use a fork to seal the edge, pressing the edge with the tines of the fork. The pie can be frozen for 15 minutes to firm up the crust while you preheat the oven.

Including a steam vent is important when you make a double-crusted pie. Make a center hole in the crust using a sharp knife, or make slashes in a decorative pattern across the crust. If steam can't escape, the filling will make the crust soggy.

Matching your touch to a rolling pin

Your choice of rolling pin is important. A large, heavy, double-handled rolling pin with ball bearings is good, as is a tapered French pin or a straight, nonhandled pin. It's really a matter of preference. Some work better with your touch than others, but all get the job done. Figure 12-2 shows an assortment of pins.

Figure 12-2: Choose a rolling pin that feels good.

Thin-sliced fruit solves the air problem

Have you ever sliced into a double-crusted fruit pie and found a large amount of air between the cooked-down fruit filling and the top crust? If so, the raw fruit was inserted into the pie in large chunks, creating a lot of air space between the pieces of fruit when they were assembled in the bottom crust. Using thin slices of fruit eliminates this problem. You get more fruit bang for your buck, and fruitiness is why we eat fruit pies in the first place.

Apple Pie

This apple pie features a blend of two apple varieties, which I think is the way to go. The flavors and textures of each apple type combine to make for one amazing pie. This is a juicy pie with very little flour to bind the filling.

Preparation time: *20 minutes*

Cooking time: *60 minutes*

Yield: *8 servings*

Basic Piecrust (from the recipe in this chapter)

Apple Filling

6 apples (6 cups sliced); use a mixture of Cortland and Golden Delicious

⅔ to 1 cup granulated sugar

1 tablespoon all-purpose flour

1 teaspoon freshly squeezed lemon juice

½ teaspoon cinnamon

2 tablespoons (¼ stick) unsalted butter, cut into small pieces

Crust Topping

1 tablespoon whole milk

1½ tablespoons granulated sugar

¼ teaspoon cinnamon

1 Spray a 9-inch deep-dish pie plate with pan coating. Roll out the bottom crust and fit it into the pie plate. Refrigerate the crust while assembling the remaining ingredients.

2 Peel and core the apples (see Figure 12-3). Slice into ¼-inch slices by hand or machine. Place in a mixing bowl with sugar, flour, lemon juice, and cinnamon. Toss to mix.

3 Pile the apples into the piecrust. Dot with butter. Refrigerate while rolling out the top crust.

4 Roll out the top crust and place it on top of the apples. Seal and crimp the edges. Make a steam vent by cutting a 1-inch hole in the center or a few slashes here and there. The steam vent keeps the pie from getting soggy. Brush the pie with milk. Combine the sugar and cinnamon and sprinkle over the pie. Freeze for 15 minutes while you preheat the oven to 400 degrees. The freezing firms up the fat in the crust and helps make it flaky.

5 Place the pie on a parchment-lined baking sheet. Place the baking sheet, with the pie on it, in the oven and turn the oven down to 375 degrees. Bake for 45 minutes. Check to see how the pie is browning. Continue to bake for about 15 more minutes or until the crust is golden brown and the filling is bubbling.

6 Cool at room temperature for 30 minutes before serving to allow the juices to thicken.

Going All Out: *Serve with ice cream for an à la mode treat.*

Per serving: *Calories 523 (From fat 261); Total fat 29g (Saturated 14g); Cholesterol 47mg; Sodium 77mg; Carbohydrates 64g (Dietary Fiber 3g); Protein 5g.*

Figure 12-3: Create a dense filling for the Apple Pie by slicing the apple quarters into smaller strips.

Peeling and Coring an Apple
1. Quarter apples
2.
Peel skin with a paring knife

3. Cut out the core
①
②

Pumpkin Pie

This lightly spiced pie goes beautifully with many holiday meals.

Preparation time: *10 minutes*

Cooking time: *45 minutes; 2½ hours chilling time*

Yield: *8 servings*

½ Basic Piecrust (The Basic Piecrust recipe makes two crusts; for this recipe, you need only one)

1½ cups pumpkin puree

¾ cup lightly packed light brown sugar

3 large eggs

1¼ cups evaporated milk

1 teaspoon cinnamon

1 teaspoon ginger

¼ teaspoon nutmeg

¼ teaspoon salt

Pinch cloves

1 Spray a 9-inch glass deep-dish pie plate with pan coating.

2 Roll out the dough on a lightly floured surface and fit it into the pie plate, making a high crimped edge. Freeze for 30 minutes. Meanwhile, preheat the oven to 375 degrees and make the filling.

3 Place the piecrust on a parchment-lined baking pan, line the crust with foil, add pie weights, and prebake for 15 minutes. Remove the foil and weights and bake for 5 minutes more. Remove the crust from the oven and leave the door open for about 3 minutes to quickly reduce the oven temperature. Reset the oven to 350 degrees.

4 Place the remaining ingredients in a food processor fitted with a metal blade or blender and process for at least 2 minutes, until blended and very smooth. The mixture may be refrigerated in an airtight container up to 2 days.

5 Pour the filling into the crust and bake for about 50 minutes. The filling will be set, but should still be a little soft and wiggly in the center. It will firm up tremendously upon cooling.

6 Cool on a wire rack for at least 30 minutes before serving. The pie can be made a day ahead, but it's best made the day you plan to serve it.

Tip: *If you try to cook your own pumpkin puree, it will be much more watery and much less smooth than the canned. Stick with the canned — in this case, the canned is better than anything that can be made at home. Just make sure it's pure pumpkin and not pumpkin pie filling, which has spices and sugar and other ingredients that you don't need.*

Tip: *You may not be familiar with evaporated milk. It's canned milk that has some of its water content removed, yielding a denser, creamier liquid. You can keep a can or two, along with a can or two of pumpkin puree, in the pantry for last-minute use.*

Remember: *This pie perfectly showcases the need for prebaking a crust. The prebaking technique is a good one to master. Here you have a custard-style pie that is very wet and could leave you with a soggy crust. Prebaking eliminates the soggy-crust problem.*

Per serving: *Calories 355 (From fat 153); Total fat 17g (Saturated 8g); Cholesterol 112mg; Sodium 186mg; Carbohydrates 43g (Dietary Fiber 3g); Protein 8g.*

Peeling apples

Peeling apples by hand with a paring knife is certainly doable, but apple peelers are on the market that make quick work of the job. Some have a vice-like clamp that attaches to a table; others have a broad, suction-cup base. I prefer the latter version. Both have a rotating spit that holds the apple. When the spit is turned via a crank, the apple is pushed against a sharp peeler. The apple is cored, peeled, and cut into ¼-inch slices in one action. This tool is not cheap (about $40), but when fresh apples appear in the fall, it can make the difference between being motivated to get into the kitchen with a few pounds of apples or only dreaming about how great it would be to have freshly baked apple pies.

Chocolate Pecan Pie

This is not your average pecan pie. It's still rich and gooey, but it has chocolate added for good measure. Serve with softly whipped cream or ice cream to cut the richness.

Preparation time: *10 minutes*

Cooking time: *60 minutes; 2½ hours chilling*

Yield: *10 servings*

½ Basic Piecrust (The Basic Piecrust recipe makes two crusts; for this recipe, you need only one)

4 tablespoons (½ stick) unsalted butter

2 ounces unsweetened chocolate, finely chopped

1 cup lightly packed dark brown sugar

1¼ cups light corn syrup

4 large eggs

2 tablespoons Kahlua or other coffee liqueur

2 teaspoons vanilla extract

¼ teaspoon salt

2 cups whole pecans, toasted

1 Spray a 9-inch glass deep-dish pie plate with pan coating.

2 Roll out the dough on a lightly floured surface and fit it into a pie plate, making a high crimped edge. Freeze 30 minutes. Meanwhile, preheat the oven to 375 degrees and make the filling.

3 Place the piecrust on a parchment-lined baking pan, line the crust with foil and weights, and prebake for 15 minutes. Remove the foil and weights and bake for 5 minutes more. Remove from the oven and leave the door open for about 3 minutes to quickly reduce the temperature. Reset the oven to 325 degrees.

4 To make the filling, melt the butter and chocolate together in the microwave or in the top of a double boiler. Whisk in the sugar and corn syrup. Then whisk in the eggs, one at a time. Stir in the Kahlua, vanilla extract, salt, and pecans.

5 Pour the filling into the crust and bake for about 55 minutes. The filling will be puffed and have a few cracks along the edges, but it should still be a little soft and wiggly in the center. It will firm up tremendously upon cooling.

6 Cool on a wire rack for at least 20 minutes before serving. This pie can be made a day ahead, but I think it's best made the day you plan to serve it. Serve with whipped cream.

Remember: *Always handle pastry dough lightly — handle it just enough to get the job done. Overhandling makes it tough.*

Per serving: *Calories 595 (From fat 315); Total fat 35g (Saturated 11g); Cholesterol 113mg; Sodium 173mg; Carbohydrates 70g (Dietary Fiber 3g); Protein 7g.*

Making whipped cream

I know you can buy whipped cream in a can, but the only place canned whip cream belongs is at a kid's ice cream–sundae party. Whipping cream is very easy, and real whipped cream adds so much to holiday desserts that it's worth preparing.

First, you need heavy cream or whipping cream; I prefer heavy cream. Look for cream that is at least 36 percent butterfat. If you can find regular pasteurized and not ultra-pasteurized, so much the better. Ultra-pasteurization is when the cream is exposed to a brief blast of very high heat. The heat kills bacteria and extends the shelf life, but it also leaves the cream tasting slightly cooked and has the unfortunate byproduct of making the cream harder to whip.

To maximize the whipping efficiency of any heavy or whipping cream, place the cream in a chilled bowl, along with a little granulated sugar if you like (try 2 tablespoons of sugar for every 1 cup of cream). Whip with the balloon whip attachment of a mixer on medium speed until the cream starts to thicken. Turn the speed to high and whip just until soft peaks form. Do not whip any longer. If you do overwhip, just add some liquid cream and stir gently. It should smooth out.

Of course, you can make whipped cream by hand with a whisk, but make sure that your biceps are up to the job.

Whipped cream can be enhanced with a couple tablespoons of liqueur. Try Kahlua, Grand Marnier, Di Saronno Amaretto, or dark rum, to name a few.

Always whip cream according to the recipe's instructions. Read recipes carefully. In general, cooks tend to overwhip, so err on the side of caution.

Chocolate Truffle Tart

This is a chocolaty, decadent, rich dessert. Serve in small slices with a cup of coffee. This tart may be made one day ahead. See the color section of this book for a photo of the tart.

Special equipment: *10-inch loose-bottomed, fluted tart pan (see Figure 12-4)*

Preparation time: *10 minutes*

Cooking time: *12 minutes*

Yield: *12 servings*

Crust

2 cups chocolate cookie crumbs (use Nabisco Famous Chocolate Wafers to make the crumbs)

6 tablespoons (¾ stick) unsalted butter, melted

1 Preheat the oven to 375 degrees. Spray a 10-inch, loose-bottomed, fluted tart pan with pan coating and place it on a parchment-lined sheet pan.

2 Combine the chocolate cookie crumbs and butter in a small bowl and stir until blended. Press the crumbs into the tart pan evenly over the bottom and up the sides.

3 Bake for 10 minutes. Cool completely on a wire rack.

Filling

19 ounces bittersweet chocolate, finely chopped

1½ cups heavy cream

1 Melt the bittersweet chocolate with the cream in a double boiler or microwave. Whisk just until smooth and pour into crust.

2 Chill to set the filling, about 2 hours. May be covered with plastic wrap and refrigerated for up to 2 days.

3 Unmold the tart from the pan. Serve cold, in thin slices.

Tip: *Make the cookie crumbs by placing crispy chocolate cookies in a food processor fitted with a metal blade and processing until the mixture is finely ground.*

Going All Out: *This tart could use a side serving of softly whipped cream. If you like, you could add a little of your favorite liqueur to the whipped cream. Or, you could cover the top of the tart with some milk chocolate or white chocolate shavings.*

Per serving: *Calories 502 (From fat 315); Total fat 35g (Saturated 21g); Cholesterol 60mg; Sodium 175mg; Carbohydrates 43g (Dietary Fiber 4g); Protein 5g.*

Figure 12-4: Tart pans.

Chopping dried fruit

Dried fruit is a great addition to the kitchen. It adds sweetness, color, and flavor to everything from stuffings to scones to desserts. But chopping dried fruit can be a challenge. Dried fruit is sticky, making the job difficult. Here are a few tips to make the job easier:

- Oil it: Rub flavorless oil on the blade of your knife before chopping by hand.
- Spray it: Spray a pan coating on the blade of your knife beforc chopping by hand.
- Flour it: Flour your knife blade before chopping by hand.
- Process it: Toss the fruit in a food processor fitted with a metal blade and pulse on and off until the desired texture is attained. Be careful not to overdo it or you'll end up with a paste.

Cranberry Cherry Tart

Sweet and tart, this tart has it all. The cranberries can be fresh or frozen; the canned cherries are available nationwide. Extra dough is cut into stars to place on top of the open-faced tart.

Special equipment: *10-inch, loose-bottomed, fluted tart ring; star-shaped cookie cutter (optional)*

Preparation time: *10 minutes*

Cooking time: *12 minutes*

Yield: *12 servings*

Half the Sweet Tart Crust recipe

2 cups fresh or frozen and defrosted cranberries

1½ cups canned pitted sour cherries, water packed (one 14⅘-ounce can Thank You Brand, available nationwide)

2 tablespoons cherry liquid (from the canned cherries)

1 cup sugar

2 tablespoons cornstarch

1 Spray a 10-inch, loose-bottomed, fluted tart pan with pan coating. Roll out the dough and fit it into the pan, bringing the edges of the dough even with the top of the pan's sides; alternatively, pat the dough into place. Place the dough in the freezer for 15 minutes. Roll out extra dough and cut into half a dozen various size stars, if desired. Place these on a parchment-lined sheet pan and freeze for 15 minutes.

2 Preheat the oven to 375 degrees. Place the tart crust on a parchment-lined sheet pan, line the crust with foil and weights, and bake for 10 minutes.

3 Remove the foil and weights and bake for about 8 minutes more. The crust should just be turning golden around the edges and the bottom should be dry and beginning to crisp. Bake the stars for 5 to 10 minutes total, depending on their size. Place the tart crust and stars on a wire rack to cool. Meanwhile, make the filling.

4 Wash and sort the cranberries, removing any stems or leaves. Drain the cherries, reserving 2 tablespoons of the juice. Combine the cranberries, cherries, and sugar in a saucepan. Bring to a boil over medium heat. Turn the heat down and simmer for about 5 minutes or until the cranberries have popped, the fruit has broken down a bit, and the mixture has begun to give off some juice. Combine the cornstarch and reserved cherry juice and stir the mixture into the fruit mixture. Boil for 2 minutes or until the mixture thickens.

5 Remove the filling from the heat and scrape it immediately into the tart shell. Use an offset spatula to spread the filling evenly across the bottom of the tart. Cool on a wire rack.

6 Store the tart at room temperature for up to 6 hours; set the star cookies on top right before serving. Serve at room temperature.

Going All Out: *This tart just begs for vanilla ice cream. Splurge on the good stuff.*

Per serving: *Calories 234 (From fat 81); Total fat 9g (Saturated 6g); Cholesterol 42mg; Sodium 28mg; Carbohydrates 36g (Dietary Fiber 1g); Protein 2g.*

Pudding and Trifle: Carrying on a Fine Christmas Tradition

Few holiday dishes are as steeped in tradition as Christmas pudding. It's a classic English dessert, but it's enjoyed all over the globe in one form or another.

Trifle is a kind of pudding consisting of cake, pastry cream, liqueur, whipped cream, and fruit, all layered up in a pretty glass bowl (see Figure 12-5). The Pear Almond Trifle has quite a bit of liqueur, so plan on serving it to an adult crowd.

Christmas Pudding is also called plum pudding because plums, specifically dried plums, are often included. The inclusion of beef suet is traditional as well, which makes it a very heavy dessert. Occasionally, it's served flaming with a sprig of holly on top.

Old English custom calls for adding little metal charms to the batter of Christmas puddings. Some American households carry on the tradition. (Note that I don't include these little lawsuits in my recipe — you're on your own.) If one of these surprises lodges in your bridgework, it is said to indicate what type of fortune is ahead for you in the coming year. Finding a ring means you are to be married. A coin signifies wealth. A button heralds spinsterhood and a thimble bachelorhood.

One superstition attached to plum pudding says that it must be made with 13 ingredients in order to be lucky. Another says that a person who doesn't eat any will be sure to lose a friend in the coming year. Better at least take a bite!

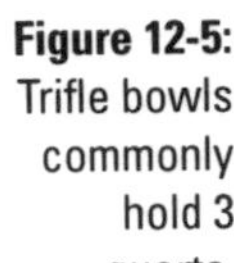

Figure 12-5: Trifle bowls commonly hold 3 quarts.

Christmas Pudding with Rum Cream

A classic steamed Christmas pudding contains suet, which is animal fat. This recipe excludes the suet and is much lighter as a result. Dried fruit and rum provide the rich flavor. Start this at least one day before serving. Kids can help measure and stir.

Special equipment: *2-quart pudding mold or heatproof glass bowl, large pot with lid able to hold mold, flat rack to fit inside pot*

Preparation time: *20 minutes*

Cooking time: *2 hours; overnight rest*

Yield: *8 servings*

1 cup raisins

½ cup golden raisins

½ cup dried cherries

½ cup diced dried figs

½ cup diced dried apricots

¼ cup chopped candied orange peel

1 teaspoon cinnamon

1 teaspoon ginger

¼ cup nutmeg

⅔ cup dark rum

¼ cup orange juice

¼ cup honey

1 teaspoon vanilla extract

3 cups fresh white breadcrumbs (8 slices bread)

⅓ cup all-purpose flour

½ teaspoon baking powder

½ teaspoon salt

½ cup (1 stick) unsalted butter at room temperature

½ cup lightly packed brown sugar

3 large eggs

1 Combine all the dried and candied fruit with the spices, rum, orange juice, honey, and vanilla extract in a large bowl. Stir together well, cover with plastic wrap, and let sit at room temperature overnight.

2 The next day, generously grease a 2-quart pudding mold.

3 Stir together the breadcrumbs, flour, baking powder, and salt; set aside.

4 Beat the butter until it's creamy in a large bowl with a flat paddle using an electric mixer on medium speed. Gradually beat in the sugar until the mixture is light and fluffy. Beat in the eggs one at a time, scraping down the bowl once or twice.

5 Stir the fruit mixture, including any liquid, into the butter and egg mixture. Stir in the dry mixture just until combined.

6 Scrape into a pudding mold, smoothing the top. Attach the lid or, if using a bowl, cover tightly with aluminum foil.

7 Place on a rack set in a large pot. Add enough boiling water to come halfway up the sides of the mold. Cover the pot and simmer gently on the lowest heat that maintains the simmer for about 1¾ hours or until a toothpick inserted in the center of the pudding comes out clean.

8 Remove the pudding from the pot; set on cooling rack for about 5 minutes. Unmold the pudding onto a serving platter and serve immediately with rum cream. Alternatively, let the pudding cool completely, wrap it in plastic wrap, slip it into a large resealable bag, and refrigerate for up to one week. Bring back to room temperature before serving and reheat gently in a microwave on low power or insert back into the mold and re-steam until heated through.

Rum Cream

1 cup heavy cream

2 tablespoons sugar

1 tablespoon dark rum

Beat the heavy cream and sugar until very soft peaks form. Whip in the rum.

Per serving: *Calories 481 (From fat 135); Total fat 15g (Saturated 8g); Cholesterol 111mg; Sodium 295mg; Carbohydrates 85g (Dietary Fiber 5g); Protein 7g.*

Pear Almond Trifle

Pears are a wonderful winter fruit. Roasting them brings out their natural sugars and concentrates their flavor. Make this recipe the day before through Step 2 of the assembly instructions.

I call for a trifle bowl, which looks like a gigantic stemmed glass, but any glass bowl will do. It's classic to be able to see all the layers. Actually, I'm not much of a classicist — use any kind of bowl that you like!

Special equipment: *3-quart glass trifle bowl or similarly sized bowl.*

Preparation time: *30 minutes*

Cooking time: *50 minutes*

Yield: *14 servings*

16-ounce pound cake, thawed if frozen

12 Amaretti di Saronno cookies (6 wrapped pairs)

¼ cup sliced almonds, toasted

Tip: *The amaretti cookies can be found in specialty stores.*

Roasted Pears

6 firm, ripe pears (about 7 ounces each), such as Bartlett, peeled and cored

2 tablespoons sugar

2 tablespoons Di Saronno Amaretto liqueur

1. Preheat the oven to 400 degrees. Cut the pears into ½-inch chunks. Toss the pears, sugar, and liqueur in a roasting pan. Roast for about 40 minutes or until the pears are tender and have begun to caramelize.
2. Make the other components of the trifle while the pears are in the oven.

Amaretto Syrup

½ cup water

¼ cup sugar

⅓ cup Di Saronno Amaretto liqueur

Combine the water and sugar in a small pot. Stir to wet the sugar thoroughly. Place over medium heat and bring to a simmer. Cook for 1 minute. Remove from heat and add liqueur. Use immediately or refrigerate in an airtight container for up to a month.

Pastry Cream

2 cups whole milk

7 large egg yolks

½ cup granulated sugar

¼ cup all-purpose flour

Pinch salt

2 tablespoons (¼ stick) unsalted butter at room temperature

2 tablespoons Di Saronno Amaretto liqueur

1 Bring the milk to a boil over medium heat in a medium-sized non-reactive saucepan. Meanwhile, whisk together the egg yolks, sugar, flour, and salt in a medium-sized, non-reactive, heatproof bowl. Dribble warm milk over the egg mixture, starting with just a few tablespoons, to temper the eggs. Whisk in the remaining milk.

2 Return the mixture to the saucepan and bring to a simmer over low-medium heat. Stirring continuously, simmer for about 2 minutes to remove the raw flour taste. Immediately pour through a fine strainer into a storage container and stir in the butter. Stir occasionally until the mixture comes to cool room temperature. The cream may be used immediately. If storing, cover with plastic wrap that you press onto the surface of the cream to prevent a skin from forming and refrigerate for up to 4 days.

Topping

2 cups heavy cream

3 tablespoons sugar

Beat the heavy cream and sugar until relatively stiff peaks form.

Assembly

1 Slice the pound cake horizontally into three layers, then cut vertically into eighths. Using a 3-quart glass trifle bowl or regular glass bowl, line the bottom with a third of the pound cake. Crush four of the amaretti cookies and sprinkle them over the cake. Drizzle with one-third of the amaretto syrup. Spread with one-third of the pastry cream and a layer of one-third of the pears. Repeat two more times. The trifle may be made ahead up to this point. Simply cover tightly with plastic wrap and refrigerate overnight. Proceed if serving immediately or within 6 hours.

2 Top with a layer of sweetened whipped cream. May be refrigerated up to 6 hours, if desired. Top with toasted almonds immediately before serving.

Simplify: *You can leave out the amaretti cookies if you like, but they do add some crunch and a unique flavor.*

Per serving: *Calories 481 (From fat 234); Total fat 26g (Saturated 12g); Cholesterol 181mg; Sodium 176mg; Carbohydrates 56g (Dietary Fiber 3g); Protein 6g.*

Dashing through the Snow — Desserts without Delays

I want you to have your dessert and eat it too. Let me help you with some ideas that will get dessert on the table in a flash.

Purchased piecrusts

Ready-made piecrusts are on the market in a couple different forms. Some piecrusts come ready to use in a disposable aluminum pie plate, crimped edges and all. You can find these in the freezer section of your supermarket. The problem with them is that the tin plate doesn't look so great on your holiday table, but that's up to you. Some come in a box all folded up; you can find them in the refrigerator case. You just take out the crust, which is rolled out into a large circle, unfold it, separate it from the plastic wrap that has protected it in its packaging, and proceed with your recipe. These crusts have the advantage of being able to be placed in your own pie plates.

Purchased piecrusts don't use any real butter, just shortening. As a result, their flavor isn't as good as homemade. But, if this is the only way to get a fresh-baked pie on your table, go for it. You don't have to feel guilty if someone sees them in your cart.

Topping off store-bought cookies with homemade decorations

If you don't have time to make cookies, you can still put cookies on the table that have a homemade element. You can buy slice-and-bake cookies and proceed from there, or you can go to a bakery and buy fairly plain sugar cookies. Then you can apply your own personal touch:

- Dip the cookies halfway into melted chocolate, whether white, milk, or dark.
- Apply royal icing in various colors and add colored sprinkles.
- Sandwich thin cookies together with icing, chocolate, or jam.
- Make faces and designs by affixing raisins, Red Hots candies, and currants with dabs of icing
- Buy icing that comes in a tube to apply directly to the cookies.

Sweet solutions using confectioners sugar

Confectioners sugar can be used in a myriad of ways. If you have a small dredger, put the sugar in that and sprinkle away to your heart's content. If you don't have a dredger, you can make one. Take a glass, even a paper cup, and fill it one quarter of the way with confectioners sugar. Stretch a piece of foil over the top and affix the foil to the cup with a rubber band. Using a toothpick, poke as many small holes in the taut foil as you can manage. Now you're ready to shake.

- Sprinkle plates with confectioners sugar before placing a piece of cake or pie on top.
- Just dust the edges of a plate for a more precise look.
- Make a template out of cardboard, place it over a pie (pumpkin works well), and shake sugar over the top. For instance, you could make a pretty leaf or pumpkin shape out of cardboard and have it appear as the undusted portion of your pie. Do this right before serving or the sugar might melt into the moist surface.
- Confectioners sugar looks like a carpet of snow and can be used to that effect, such as for a bûche de Noël.

Chapter 13

Baking Breads, Scones, and Muffins for the Holidays

In This Chapter

- Making and varying quick breads
- Baking up some scones and biscuits
- Creating stollen

Recipes in This Chapter

- Cranberry-Orange Quick Bread
- Buttermilk Lemon Cherry Scones
- Basic Yuletide Biscuits
- Gingerbread Muffins
- Popovers/Yorkshire Pudding
- Stollen with Marzipan

I'll bet you bake more at Christmas than you do at any other time of the year. If so, you're not alone. For many people, December is the peak of the baking season. December brings the marvelous aroma of cookies, pies, cakes, and breads wafting through their homes.

But even if you *only* bake at Christmas, don't worry. The recipes in this chapter are not about becoming an expert, and I'm definitely not training you to open your own bakery. But what these recipes *will* do is get good bread, biscuits, and treats on your Christmas table to enhance your holidays.

Flavored butters enhance most any bread in this chapter and they are so easy to make, why not at least try one? See the Marmalade Butter in Chapter 7 for an example.

Starting with a Quick Bread (And It Really Is)

I know that you don't have a lot of time to spend in the kitchen as Christmas gets closer and closer. This quick bread is simple to prepare and, as the name of the bread suggests, it doesn't take up much of your time.

Quick breads are so easy to make that you can use your bare hands without straining yourself. Bare hands holding a wooden spoon, that is. You melt butter and combine it with the other wet ingredients in one bowl, you whisk the dry ingredients together in another, and then you gently stir the dry and wet together until they're blended; that's the quick bread method. That's it. Even if you've never made bread before, you can do this. After you master the technique, you can vary the bread endlessly.

When reading a recipe, look at it with a creative eye. In the case of the Cranberry-Orange Quick Bread, think about how you could substitute chopped dried apricots, diced fresh apples, or add other grated citrus rinds.

Cranberry-Orange Quick Bread

This is the easiest bread you'll ever make. The recipe doubles very easily, so make extra loaves for gifts. Kids can help measure and stir.

Special equipment: *9 x 5-inch loaf pan*

Preparation time: *5 minutes*

Cooking time: *35 minutes*

Yield: *1 loaf, 12 slices*

¾ cup buttermilk

¼ cup orange juice

Grated zest of one orange

6 tablespoons (¾ stick) unsalted butter, melted and cooled

1 large egg

2 cups all-purpose flour

1 cup sugar

1 teaspoon baking powder

½ teaspoon salt

¼ teaspoon baking soda

1½ cups cranberries, fresh or frozen, roughly chopped

½ cup chopped toasted walnuts

1 Preheat the oven to 350 degrees. Spray a 9-x-5-inch loaf pan with pan coating and lightly coat with flour.

2 Whisk together the buttermilk, orange juice, zest, and melted butter. Whisk in the egg.

3 In a large bowl, whisk together the flour, sugar, baking powder, salt, and baking soda. Add the wet ingredients and stir just until combined. Gently stir in the cranberries (unthawed if bought frozen) and nuts.

4 Scrape the batter into a loaf pan and bake for 55 minutes. When the bread is done, a toothpick will come out clean when it's inserted into the center, the top will be golden and risen, and the edges will just be pulling away from the sides of the pan.

5 Cool the pan on a rack for 10 minutes, and then turn the bread out and cool completely on a rack. Wrap the bread in plastic wrap and let it sit at room temperature at least overnight before slicing. It needs to rest so that the texture can come together.

Tip: *Any buttermilk will work, but low fat, as opposed to non-fat, is preferable.*

Going All Out: *Sometimes when you chop nuts, you're left with some powdery pieces and flecks of skin along with the nuts. You can place the nuts in a strainer and shake out the powdery residue. This isn't necessary, but it is a refinement that adds a professional touch to your quick bread.*

Per serving: *Calories 245 (From Fat 136); Fat 14g (Saturated 4g); Cholesterol 34mg; Sodium 178mg; Carbohydrate 36g (Dietary Fiber 2g); Protein 4g.*

One basic recipe, many breads

I absolutely love the Cranberry-Orange Quick Bread. But as good as it is, you can add different fruits and nuts and flavors to make a whole new quick bread. Try these variations:

- Use pecans instead of walnuts.
- Substitute dried cranberries and lemon zest for the fresh or frozen cranberries.
- Substitute fresh blueberries and lemon zest for the cranberries and orange zest.
- Substitute dried cherries and lemon zest for the cranberries and orange zest.
- Substitute chopped dried apricots and chopped whole almonds for the cranberries and walnuts.
- Substitute lemon zest for the orange zest, leave out the cranberries, and add ¼ cup finely chopped crystallized ginger.
- Substitute lemon zest for the orange zest, leave out the cranberries and walnuts, and add ½ cup finely chopped pistachios.
- Use yogurt or sour cream in place of the buttermilk. Try different flavors of yogurt.
- Leave out the cranberries and nuts, use coffee yogurt instead of buttermilk, substitute brewed coffee for the orange juice, and add ½ cup mini semisweet chocolate chips.

- Try a blended orange juice beverage instead of straight orange juice, such as orange-banana or orange-pineapple.
- Replace half the flour with whole-wheat flour.
- Try brown sugar instead of white.
- Add spices if you like, such as cinnamon, ginger, nutmeg, or cardamom.

Lighter-colored pans make paler loaves

The quick bread recipe in this chapter calls for a 9 x 5-inch loaf pan, which is considered a standard size for a loaf pan. But so many different pans are out there, made from so many different materials and with so many finishes, that choosing can be confusing.

In general, the lighter the pan, the less pronounced the browning properties are. Some very light-colored aluminum pans leave your loaves with a pale look and pasty texture. Glass loaf pans similarly do not brown the crust very efficiently. Some browning is desirable because it means that the sugars are at work, giving your crust a nice color and texture.

I've had the best results with aluminum pans or tin-coated steel pans with a nonstick coating. Several varieties are on the market and you can pick one up for less than $10. They brown the crust just enough. Very dark pans can overly darken your loaves, so steer clear of those.

Getting your mitts on 'em

One nice feature on a loaf pan is handles on either end (or, at the very least, a pronounced lip). Because of the handles, the pan is easy to get on and off the counter and in and out of the oven, even when you're wearing oven mitts.

Even if you do a minimal amount of cooking or baking, you're going to need at least two oven mitts. You have many choices. Some are small, flat squares, sometimes with a pocket. Many are glove shaped. The glove-shaped ones come in varied lengths.

Here's what I think. The better protection you have, the better. But thicker is not necessarily better. You have to take into consideration the material the mitt is made of. Some materials are coated and flame retardant, which is great. Steer clear of plain, padded cotton. Also, if a mitt is too thick you won't be able to get a good grip on your pots and pans. As far as length goes, why not go for the most protection? My choice is a long mitt that protects up to the elbow.

As soon as a mitt develops a hole, throw it out! That's probably obvious; this may not be: If you begin to feel heat through your mitt, the interior padding is probably worn and the mitt needs to be replaced.

Swayed by suede?

Some mitts aren't padded at all and are made from sturdy suede. These can work very well as far as heat insulation is concerned, but they can be stiff, making it difficult to feel handles and pots. Use your judgment and buy what is comfortable for you. The good news is that many of these are washable suede. Read the label and buy those. I ain't gonna dry-clean an oven mitt. Are you?

Baking Scones and Biscuits — Close Relatives

Scones and biscuits are both made from flour that has had fat cut into it. Liquid components are added at the end of the mixing and the ingredients are combined gently to maximize the delicate texture of both of them. The primary difference is that most contemporary scones contain eggs, while biscuits do not. Scones are also often sweeter than biscuits.

Take all this information with a grain of American salt. In other parts of the world, altogether different terminology exists. In England, if you ask for a biscuit, you'll get what we call a cookie or a cracker.

The important thing to keep in mind is that scones and biscuits are both very quick and easy to make, even if you've never baked before. As always, just follow the recipes and you'll have warm baked goods on the table in no time.

Buttermilk Lemon-Cherry Scones

These are quick to make and are best eaten while still warm from the oven. Kids can help measure and mix.

Preparation time: *5 minutes*

Cooking time: *15 minutes*

Yield: *12 scones*

2 cups all-purpose flour

¼ cup sugar

2 teaspoons baking powder

½ teaspoon baking soda

½ teaspoon salt

Zest of ½ lemon

8 tablespoons (1 stick) unsalted butter, cut into ½-inch pieces

1 cup dried cherries

⅔ cup buttermilk

1 large egg

1 Preheat the oven to 375 degrees. Line a baking sheet with parchment paper.

2 In a large bowl, whisk together the flour, sugar, baking powder, baking soda, salt, and lemon zest.

3 Cut the butter in with a pastry blender or two knives until the mixture is uniform and has the texture of coarse sand. Stir in the cherries.

4 In a separate bowl, whisk together the buttermilk and egg. Combine the wet mixture with the dry and stir just until combined and a soft dough forms.

5 Turn the dough out onto a lightly floured surface, knead gently, and separate into two halves. Shape each half into a flattened round and place on a prepared sheet so that they're not touching. They should each be about 6-inches across and 1-inch thick. Cut each round into 6 wedges, but do not separate the wedges.

Topping

1 tablespoon milk

1 tablespoon sugar

1 Brush the tops of the scones with milk, using a pastry brush, and sprinkle with sugar.

2 Bake for about 20 minutes. The scones should be lightly browned around the edges. The tops should be dry, but not too highly colored. Place the pan on a rack and cool for 5 minutes.

3 These are best served warm and eaten the day they are made. Simply separate the wedges and serve.

Tip: *Prepare the dry mix the night before and combine the buttermilk and egg in a bowl, then cover and refrigerate. In the morning, just cut in the butter, stir in the dried cherries, and mix the batter together. It goes very quickly.*

Simplify: *If you can't find dried cherries, substitute an equal amount of raisins.*

Going All Out: *This is a small embellishment, but it adds a delicious nuance: Simply plump the cherries. Place them in a small microwaveable bowl with ½ cup water and nuke on high power for about 1½ minutes. The cherries should absorb the liquid and become quite plump. Then just incorporate the cherries as directed in recipe.*

Per serving: *Calories 233 (From Fat 117); Fat 13g (Saturated 5g); Cholesterol 39mg; Sodium 236mg; Carbohydrate 35g (Dietary Fiber 2g); Protein 4g.*

Basic Yuletide Biscuits

Tender, melt in your mouth biscuits require a light hand during mixing — in other words, mix them delicately! Serve with most any dinner or brunch.

Preparation time:*10 minutes*

Cooking time: *10 minutes*

Yield: *10 biscuits*

2 cups all-purpose flour

1 tablespoon baking powder

½ teaspoon salt

8 tablespoons cold unsalted butter, cut into ½-inch pieces

¾ cup whole milk

1 Preheat the oven to 450 degrees. Line a baking sheet with parchment paper.

2 Whisk together the flour, baking powder, and salt in a large bowl. Cut the butter in with a pastry blender or two knives until the mixture is uniform and has the texture of coarse sand. Gently stir in the milk until the dough just comes together.

3 Turn the dough out onto a lightly floured surface and knead briefly to bring the batter together. Gently pat out into a ½-inch thick rectangle (approximately 10 x 7 inches). Cut into 10 squares using a sharp, floured knife.

4 Transfer the biscuits onto a baking sheet; you may gently shape them into rounds if desired. If you like biscuits with browned sides, set them on the sheet so that they're not touching. If you like soft sides, place them very close to one another so that they're just touching.

5 Bake the biscuits for about 10 minutes, until they're lightly browned on the top and bottom. Serve immediately.

Per serving: *Calories 184 (From Fat 144); Fat 16g (Saturated 6g); Cholesterol 27mg; Sodium 241mg; Carbohydrate 20g (Dietary Fiber 1g); Protein 3g.*

Accenting the taste of a scone or biscuit

After you get the hang of making biscuits and scones, you can add and subtract ingredients and end up with some deliciously different variations. Here are some ideas for you to try; all these add-ins are gently added at the very end of mixing.

For scones:

- Substitute any dried fruit you like: Try chopped apricots, golden raisins, moist dates . . . your choice.
- Add chopped fresh fruit, such as apples, pears, or peaches.
- Fold in raspberries or blueberries.
- Add spices: cinnamon, nutmeg, cardamom, ginger, or allspice.
- Add some chopped and toasted nuts.
- Substitute brown sugar for granulated sugar.
- Add candied orange or lemon peel.
- Fold in some mini or standard-sized chocolate chips, any flavor.

Want something more daring than a single addition? Try a theme:

- Cinnamon Chocolate Chip Scones
- Brown Sugar Nut Scones
- Lemon Pistachio Scones
- Apricot Almond Scones (chopped dried apricots and sliced almonds)

For biscuits, try these additions:

- Dried herbs or minced fresh herbs; try thyme or rosemary dried, chives and tarragon fresh
- Finely chopped sun-dried tomatoes
- Finely chopped black olives
- Any kind of grated citrus zest
- A good dose of cracked black pepper
- A couple slices of crisp bacon, crumbled
- Prepared or dry mustard

Here are some biscuit combinations for you to consider:

- Rosemary Black Olive Biscuits
- Basil Sun-Dried Tomato Biscuits
- Lemon Black Pepper Biscuits

Gingerbread Muffins

These muffins contain ground ginger and crystallized ginger, so they really wake you up in the morning. Look for crystallized ginger in a specialty food store. Kids can mix and stir and seem to love placing the paper liners in the muffin cups. See the color section of this book for a photo of Gingerbread Muffins.

Special equipment: *Muffin tin, paper muffin liners (optional)*

Preparation time: *8 minutes*

Cooking time: *25 minutes*

Yield: *12 muffins*

2 cups all-purpose flour

2 teaspoons baking soda

1 tablespoon ginger

1 teaspoon cinnamon

¼ teaspoon salt

Pinch ground cloves

6 tablespoons (¾ stick) unsalted butter at room temperature

⅓ cup sugar

½ cup unsulphured molasses

1 large egg

¾ cup boiled water (let sit off the heat for a minute to cool)

¼ cup finely chopped crystallized ginger

1 Preheat the oven to 350 degrees. Spray 12 standard-size muffins cups with pan coating or line the cups with paper liners.

2 Stir together the flour, baking soda, ginger, cinnamon, salt, and cloves in a bowl.

3 Beat the butter in a mixer with the flat paddle attachment until the butter is creamy. Add the sugar gradually and beat on medium speed until light and fluffy, about 2 minutes. Scrape down mixture and add molasses; beat 30 seconds. Beat in the egg.

4 Alternate stirring in the flour mixture and hot water just until mixed. Fold in the crystallized ginger.

5 Divide the batter equally among the muffin cups and bake for about 20 minutes. A toothpick inserted in the center of a muffin should come out clean. Cool pan(s) on cooling rack. Serve warm or at room temperature.

Tip: *Stir together the dry ingredients the night before to give yourself a head start. The other ingredients can be measured out ahead of time as well.*

Tip: *Make these way ahead of time and pop them into a resealable freezer bag. Freeze for up to a month, defrost and warm in the microwave.*

Going All Out: *Stir together butter that's at room temperature and orange marmalade to make a tasty orange butter to serve with the muffins.*

Per serving: *Calories 204 (From Fat 54); Fat 6g (Saturated 4g); Cholesterol 33mg; Sodium 272mg; Carbohydrate 34g Dietary Fiber 1g; Protein 3g.*

Reheating breads

Many foods, including many of the recipes in this chapter, can be made ahead of time and frozen. While fresh food is always better than reheated, you can maximize the taste of your reheated breads by following a few guidelines.

In the oven

Whether you're reheating a room-temperature muffin or yeast bread, preheat the oven to 250 degrees. Place the bread directly on the rack or on a sheet pan. Use your judgment: You can place larger items right on the rack, but small items, like biscuits, work much better on a sheet pan. The length of time in the oven depends on the size and density of the bread. Start checking after 10 minutes; you may need to leave your bread in the oven a little longer. These directions work with toaster ovens, too.

In the microwave

Try 5 seconds at full power. Check the muffins, biscuit, or whatever, and see if you need to try another 5-second blast. Even if you have to stop and start a couple of times, this is a fast way to go.

Some microwave manufacturers suggest you place breads on paper towels while microwaving them. The paper will absorb any excess moisture. Food scientists I have spoken with suggest using very moist paper towels, as the water in the towel attracts the microwaves, thereby deflecting their onslaught of energy away from your lowly little muffin. In other words, the muffin will have a gentler ride as it gently steams.

Maximizing the Pop in Your Popovers

The recipe for Popovers is the same as the recipe for Yorkshire Pudding. The main difference is what the batter is poured into for baking: Yorkshire Pudding is baked in one pan and cut into pieces for serving, but Popovers rise to their luscious golden crowns in individual baking tins.

You can definitely do a few things to ensure that your popovers "pop" and come out large, airy, eggy, almost creamy in the middle, and crusty on the outside. The way a liquid batter can go into an oven and come out so large and puffed is almost magical. Every one of these suggestions, if implemented, makes a big difference, so take this list seriously. All these suggestions are easy to follow.

- Make sure that your oven is preheated to the proper temperature. Use an oven thermometer and give the oven at least 15 minutes to preheat.
- Use dark popover or muffin tins; dark tins maximize the heat.
- Don't over-fill or under-fill the muffin cups. Two-thirds full is about right.
- Once the popovers are in the oven, don't open the oven until the full 35 minutes have gone by.
- Serve the popovers immediately.

These tips should do the trick. But if you feel like making extra sure, here's a technique that some chefs swear by: After 30 minutes, pierce the side of each popover. Doing so allows steam to escape during the last minutes of cooking, which can help dry out the insides a little bit. You can even pierce the sides as soon as the popovers come out of the oven to create the same effect.

One pitfall that many cooks fall into is not cooking the popovers long enough; the insides need to dry out or they'll be soggy and deflate almost immediately. Bake the popovers until they're a deep golden brown, or even mahogany-colored, and quite popped.

New pairings for a classy old pudding

You're probably familiar with the classic pairing of Yorkshire Pudding and roast beef. But don't stop there; airy, eggy Yorkshire Pudding (or Popovers) can be used to great advantage in a variety of ways:

- Serve it alongside eggs for breakfast.
- Add just a smear of orange marmalade and eat as a snack.
- Try it with soft butter and honey — YUM!
- Split and fill with tuna fish salad, chicken salad, or egg salad for an elegant brunch or lunch item.
- Serve with soups.
- Split and fill with ice cream and hot chocolate sauce — it's like a giant cream puff.
- Split and fill with strawberries and whipped cream.

Popovers/Yorkshire Pudding

Whether you make the batter into Popovers or Yorkshire Pudding, you'll have the perfect foil to roast beef. You'll see what I mean when you sop up the juices from your roast beef with a perfect popover (see Figure 13-1). See the sidebar "New pairings for a classy old pudding" for more serving ideas. And check out the photo of Popovers in the color section of this book.

Special equipment: *12-cup muffin tin*

Preparation time: *5 minutes*

Cooking time: *35 minutes*

Yield: *12 popovers*

¼ cup reserved beef fat or melted unsalted butter

4 large eggs

1½ cups milk

1½ cups all-purpose flour

½ teaspoon salt

1 Preheat the oven to 450 degrees. Have ready a 12-cup muffin tin.

2 Divide the beef fat into the muffin cups and place the tin in the oven to heat.

3 Whisk together the eggs and milk in a 4-cup measuring cup or a bowl with a spout. Sift the flour and salt right into the bowl and whisk until smooth.

4 Carefully divide the batter into the muffin cups, filling about two-thirds full. Watch for sputtering hot fat!

Bake for 20 minutes without opening the oven door; turn the oven down to 350 degrees. Bake for about 15 minutes more, or until a rich golden brown. Serve immediately.

Per serving: *Calories 139 (From Fat 63); Fat 7g (Saturated 3g); Cholesterol 80mg; Sodium 133mg; Carbohydrate 14g (Dietary Fiber 0g); Protein 5g.*

Figure 13-1: Wow — this should be scratch-n-sniff!

Enriching Your Life with Loaves of Rich Stollen

Stollen with Marzipan is such a Christmas-season specialty that I've saved it for last.

I know that you're used to seeing a recipe read precisely, 1 tablespoon of this and 2 cups of that. But when it comes to yeast breads like stollen, there's a certain amount of touch and feel that must be relied upon. You want the dough to be smooth and springy, but not sticky or wet. Sometimes you need a little more or a little less flour to get your dough the way it needs to be. So don't be put off by the range of flour; if you follow the recipe, you'll know when you've added enough.

Stollen with Marzipan

This stollen is a yeast bread that's filled with a fruit-and-almond paste. The recipe makes three loaves, so you have one or two to eat and at least one to give as a gift — or store in the freezer for up to a month later. See the color section of this book for a photo of Stollen with Marzipan.

Preparation time: *3 hours*

Cooking time: *50 minutes*

Yield: *3 loaves, 10 slices per loaf*

⅔ cup dried cranberries or cherries

⅔ cup golden raisins

⅔ cup dark raisins

⅔ cup candied orange peel

⅔ cup dark rum, brandy, or orange juice

½ teaspoon vanilla extract

½ teaspoon almond extract

Grated zest of 1 lemon

1¼ cups warm (about 115 degrees) milk

1 tablespoon active dry yeast

12 tablespoons (1½ sticks) unsalted butter, melted

½ cup sugar

1 teaspoon salt

3 large eggs

¾ cup toasted sliced almonds, natural or blanched

5 to 6½ cups all-purpose flour

Vegetable oil

8 ounces almond paste or marzipan

1 Combine the dried fruit, candied orange peel, rum (or other liquid), extracts, and zest in a small bowl; set aside to soak.

2 Stir together ¼ cup of the warm milk and the yeast in a large bowl; set aside in a warm place for the yeast to proof, about 5 minutes.

3 Add the remaining milk, melted butter, sugar, and salt to the yeast mixture and stir to combine. Whisk in eggs, one at a time. Stir in the soaked fruit and nuts. Stir in 4 cups of flour to make a very soft dough. Gradually add more flour, using your hands to stir, until the dough comes together and forms a smooth, springy, elastic ball. Knead the dough for about 8 minutes.

4 Place dough in an oiled bowl and turn it over a few times to coat all sides. Cover with plastic wrap or a clean, damp towel and place in a warm, draft-free area to rise for at least 2 hours or until it's almost doubled in size.

5 Line two baking sheets with parchment paper. With an open palm, roll the almond paste into three logs about 6-inches long. Let them lie there for the time being.

6 Punch down the dough, turn it out onto a lightly floured surface, and knead briefly. When you "punch" the dough, just push it down fairly gently — no roundhouses! Divide into three equal pieces. Pat out each piece until it's about ½ inch thick and 9 inches around. Returning to the almond paste, use a rolling pin to roll out each log to a circle 1 inch smaller than the dough, and place the almond paste on the dough; fold the top half over the bottom half, leaving a 1-inch strip of the bottom edge exposed.

7 Place the breads on sheet pans, cover with clean, damp towels, and set in a warm, draft-free area to rise for about 1 hour.

8 Preheat the oven to 350 degrees. Bake the breads until they're golden brown, about 45 minutes, rotating the pans front to back once during the baking time. Cool breads directly on rack for 10 minutes before proceeding with topping.

Tip: *You will know that the yeast has proofed when the yeast and warm water mixture has expanded and becomes foamy.*

Tip: *During the first rise, the dough may not quite double in size. This is a very dense dough and it does not rise high like some others. After rising, look for a softness and springiness when you touch it.*

Tip: *Telling whether a yeast dough is thoroughly baked is a little different than with other baked goods. Try this trick of the trade employed by professional bread bakers. Pick up the baked loaf and knock the bottom with your knuckles. It should sound hollow. If it's under-baked, the interior will still be moist and it will sound like a dull thud.*

Coating

8 tablespoons (1 stick) unsalted butter, melted

2 cups sugar

2 cups confectioners sugar

Brush the cooling, but still warm, breads with melted butter and then roll the breads in sugar. Cool completely, then roll the breads in confectioners sugar. Store for up to 1 week at room temperature in airtight plastic bag.

Tip: *Don't skimp on this last basting and coating step. When I owned my bakery, we used to melt pounds and pounds of butter. The melted butter was 2 feet deep in a big bucket. We would literally submerge the entire stollen in the butter to coat it completely. Then we would let the excess butter drip back into the bucket before rolling the bread in a large bowl filled with sugar. At this point, the bread must be cooled completely before it's rolled in the confectioners sugar. If, during storing, the confectioners sugar loses its powdery texture, don't be afraid to reroll the bread in confectioners sugar right before serving. This is rich, indulgent bread, so go for the full experience.*

Per serving: *Calories 288 (From Fat 117); Fat 13g (Saturated 6g); Cholesterol 43mg; Sodium 96mg; Carbohydrate 40g (Dietary Fiber 3g); Protein 5g.*

Almond paste versus marzipan

Although almond paste and marzipan are similar and are interchangeable in some instances, there are some important differences between the two. First, the similarities. Both are made from finely ground almonds and are sweetened with sugar. They have the texture of malleable clay that can be rolled out, like a piecrust, or formed into logs or even animal shapes.

The main difference is that almond paste is considered the raw ingredient, while marzipan, which has extra sugar and sometimes egg white or corn syrup added for texture, is what is usually used as an end product. The marzipan animals, fruits, and vegetables that you can find in some bakeries, particularly German and Italian bakeries at Christmastime, are made out of marzipan and not almond paste because the former has a more refined texture.

You can usually find both almond paste and marzipan in the baking aisle, side by side, in small, tightly wrapped plastic tubes packaged in boxes. If you can't find the one your recipe is calling for and can only find the other, substituting is okay. Either works for the Stollen with Marzipan. Using marzipan instead of almond paste just makes the final dish a bit sweeter.

Part V

It's Looking a Lot Like Christmas: Decorations and Gifts

"Why do I sense you're upset? Because you're piping that cake with hand grenades instead of sugar plums."

In this part . . .

The Christmas season is more than just good food. It's decking the halls, sending greetings, and selecting special gifts for special people. In that spirit, this part contains suggestions for making simple food-based decorations that the kids can help with, and constructing a landscaped gingerbread house that's a real knockout. Chapter 15 contains recipes for easy food gifts — suitable for home consumption, too!

Chapter 14

Simple Decorations from the Kitchen

In This Chapter

- Creating a head-turning gingerbread house
- Decorating the inside of your home
- Making Christmas decorations for outdoors

Decorations in This Chapter

- Landscaped Gingerbread House
- Simmering Scent
- Candy Garland
- Cinnamon Stick Votives
- Pomander Candles
- Ribbon-Wrapped Gilded Walnut Ornaments
- Cookie Wreath Centerpiece
- Popcorn Cranberry Garland
- Cranberry Kumquat Ice Wreath

Just look around — Christmas is everywhere. Tinsel garlands hang from lampposts. Store windows are filled with holiday-themed displays. Trees, inside and out, shimmer with sparkling decorations. The colors of Christmas — red, green, gold, and silver — herald the season. Colored and white lights twinkle and glow everywhere, outlining houses and trees and beaming from windows. Decorations and decorating are part of what makes the season fun. Although I'm sure that you'll want to use some store-bought decorations as you dress up your home for the holidays, you can also create many decorations in your own kitchen.

Making decorations is satisfying and economical. Your personal touch can't help but be in evidence. Just as cooking for friends and family is more than just making food, embellishing your home with homemade decorations is more than just decorating. When you craft something yourself, it is not only *from* you, it is *of* you.

In this chapter, you find out how to add a wonderful scent to the air in your home, how to make decorative candles for every room, how to put together a spectacular gingerbread house, and much more. (I also have some suggestions for you on hosting a Christmas gathering. Check out "Setting the Stage for Christmas Entertaining" at `http://www.dummies.com/bonus/christmascooking/index.html`.)

Having a Christmas tree decorating party

My family and I had just moved into a new home and my husband was determined to take advantage of the 18-foot-high ceiling in the living room. He decided that we should have a huge tree. Just because we could. He went out into the woods and cut down a 15-foot-high tree that we were barely able to fit through our sliding doors. And we hadn't even thought about how wide it would be — it was at least 8 feet wide! We put the tree up and stabilized it with strong nylon filament that held it to the walls. We decorated it, but we only had enough ornaments to put one about every 5 feet. The tree looked completely bare.

We decided to have a party and invite everyone to bring something to hang on the tree. If you're in need of ornaments for your tree, do likewise. Make some food and invite a slew of people over. After the party, you will be left with ornaments given to you by all of your friends, which you will cherish forever. Every year when you unwrap your decorations, you will think about your friends.

Take a look around your kitchen. You probably have some items that can be quickly put to work as simple decorations:

- Oranges, lemons, and limes piled in a beautiful bowl make a great centerpiece or accent piece.
- Pineapples are a traditional American symbol of hospitality — you could build a centerpiece around one with other fruits and greenery.
- Any dessert can be used to grace a side table — a home-baked pie, a Bûche de Noël . . . anything you can think of.

Bring in the Realtor: Making a Gingerbread House

If you've never made a gingerbread house, you'll be glad to know that it's not hard (although it does take time). You don't have to be an architect; if you can bake cutout cookies (the walls and roof), you can make a gingerbread house. The mortar is an easy-to-make two-ingredient icing. Then the fun begins. Buy all the different types of candy that you normally deny yourself and go to town. Needless to say, making this with kids, grandkids, or borrowed kids is the way to go.

Because making a gingerbread house does take some time, being organized can really make your life easier. Here are a couple of tips to make the project more approachable:

- Make the dough up to three days ahead and refrigerate it, or make it up to a month ahead and freeze it.
- Bake the gingerbread pieces one day, assemble and decorate them the next day.

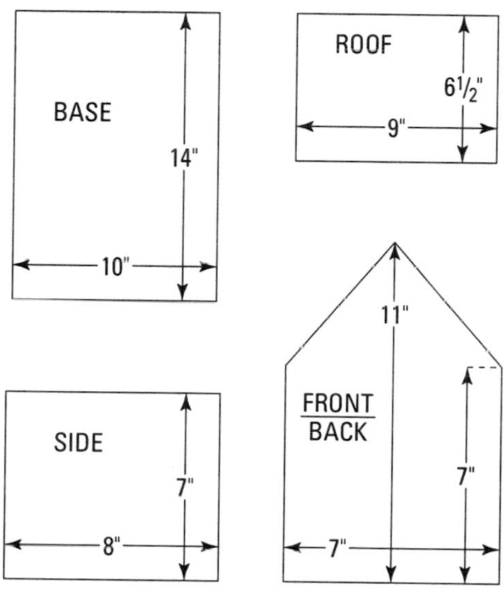

CHIMNEY PIECES

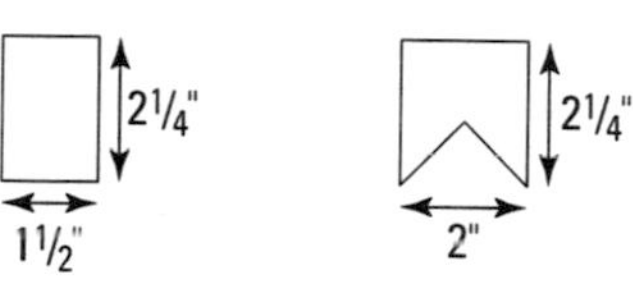

Not to scale

Figure 14-1: Templates for the gingerbread house. You need one base piece and two of all the other pieces.

Landscaped Gingerbread House

This gingerbread is not for eating; it's for construction. It's edible, but it's a deliberately sturdy, and therefore drier, version of gingerbread. The recipe makes a large batch — you'll have some left over for trees or other shapes to add to the landscape. If you don't have a 5-quart standing mixer, make it in two batches. Kids can help cut out the templates and the house pieces and, of course, can decorate the house. (For a vision of what it could look like, see the color section of this book. And if you want a tasty gingerbread, see the Gingerbread People recipe in Chapter 11.)

Special equipment: *Stand mixer, large flat platter, pastry bag, coupler, #10 decorating tip, offset spatula*

Preparation time: *2 hours*

Cooking time: *24 minutes (two 12-minute shifts in the oven)*

Yield: *1 amazing, gorgeous gingerbread house*

2 cups pure vegetable shortening

2 cups sugar

2 cups unsulphured molasses

1 tablespoon cinnamon

1 tablespoon ginger

2 teaspoons baking soda

1 teaspoon salt

9 to 10 cups all-purpose flour

1 Cream the shortening in a mixer with the flat paddle attachment until it's smooth. Add the sugar and beat on high speed until light and fluffy, about 4 minutes. Beat in the molasses until the mixture is smooth. Whisk the dry ingredients together and add to the mixer, 1 cup at a time, mixing until the dough comes together but is not dry.

2 Turn the dough out onto a lightly floured surface, gather it together, and press it into a large, flat disc. Wrap it in plastic and refrigerate at least 2 hours, or until it's firm enough to roll.

3 Cut out the templates, following the diagrams; poster board or cardboard works well. Figure 14-1 shows the template plan.

4 Preheat the oven to 375 degrees. Have two sheet pans ready and several pieces of parchment cut to fit the pans. (If you have more sheet pans, by all means use them. You will need several, or just rotate them as they come out of the oven, cooling between uses.)

5 Roll out the dough on a lightly floured piece of parchment paper to a ¼-inch thickness. Use the templates to cut out the pieces from the dough. You may also cut out a small door shape from one of the ends. Save the piece that you cut out and bake it alongside on the sheet. Transfer the parchment paper, with the gingerbread on it, to the sheet pan. Bake about 12 minutes or until the gingerbread pieces have begun to color and are firm to the touch.

6 Remove the gingerbread from the oven and immediately place your templates back on top of the pieces and trim any protruding edges. Do this while the dough is warm. Cool on pans set on cooling racks. Repeat with the remaining dough; this will take you a few cycles depending on your oven size and how many pans you have.

Tip: The pieces of gingerbread may lose their shape a little bit during baking, which is why you might need to trim them. If you wait until the pieces have cooled to trim them, they may crack. If the pieces have cooled and you really need to trim a piece, try a gentle sawing motion with a serrated knife.

Mortar (Royal Icing)

8 large egg whites (or equivalent meringue powder reconstituted per manufacturer's directions)

8 cups confectioners sugar

Make the mortar in two batches. For each batch, whip 4 egg whites in a mixer with the balloon whip attachment until frothy. Slowly add 4 cups of confectioners sugar and whip until thick and fluffy and stiff peaks form, at least 8 minutes. Add a little more sugar if too thin, or a little water if too thick. Place a damp towel over the bowl until you're ready to use the mortar. Repeat with the remaining ingredients.

So you've got the pieces of your gingerbread house and you've got the icing. Now you need to put the house together. So put on your hard hat and whip out a pastry bag with a #10 tip, if you have one. If not, just use a table knife and glop the icing onto the gingerbread.

1 Place the gingerbread base on a large, flat platter or a stiff piece of cardboard that you've covered with foil. The platter or cardboard should be large enough to leave room for a yard. Fill a pastry bag fitted with a #10 round tip halfway with icing. Apply a strip of icing to the bottom of the front of the house and place it 2 inches in from one short end of the base. Prop the front upright with a canned good. Now apply the icing to one of the sides and connect to the propped-up front. Prop this piece up too. Continue with the back of house and the other side. Allow 10 minutes for the icing to firm up. You can reinforce the icing "cement" by going over all the lines on the inside of the house one more time.

2 Meanwhile, decorate the roof pieces. You could spread icing on the roof and apply wheat cereal pieces, sugar side facing out, to make a thatched roof or use any other decoration you can think of.

3 Remove the cans from the inside of the house and apply icing to the roofline all the way around and press on the roof. Hold in place for a minute or so. Glue on the chimney and the door. The door can be slightly ajar if you like.

4 Now the fun begins. Let the kids loose to decorate the house. Use icing to affix candy pieces all over the house. Rim the windows. Place a doorknob on the door. Make a candy walkway winding from the edge of the tray to the door. The sky is the limit.

Of all the projects in this chapter, this is the most personal. Gingerbread houses are truly individual projects, which is the way it should be!

Here are my favorite landscaping ideas:

- Cover cone-shaped ice cream cones with green-tinted frosting. Make peaks in the frosting and small pine trees appear before your eyes. Press on small candies for ornaments.
- Use two candy canes to form the runners of a sled. Place a graham cracker across the candy canes to form the base of the sled, gluing the graham cracker into place with frosting. Load up the sled with candy and place on the lawn. One of my 10-year-old twins came up with this idea.
- Build a snowman with marshmallows and toothpicks, using various candies to make the eyes, nose, and mouth. Straight mini pretzels make great arms.

The important thing is to have fun and be creative. Here are some types of candy, and what you can possibly use them for:

- **Licorice sticks:** Outline walls, use as fence posts
- **Licorice whips:** Sled ropes, windowpanes
- **Large pretzel sticks:** Logs, beams, sled runners
- **Mini pretzel sticks:** Windowpanes, wheel spokes, stack of firewood
- **Candy canes:** Gateposts, lampposts
- **Candy wafers:** Roof tiles, wheels
- **Sweetened flaked coconut:** Snow for roofs and lawn
- **Chocolate bars:** Shingles, doors, shutters, patio bricks
- **Redhots:** Ornaments on trees
- **Confectioners sugar:** Snow
- **Sheet gelatin:** Window glass
- **Candied fruit slices:** Stained glass windows
- **Flat lollipops:** Road signs
- **Round lollipops:** Tops of lampposts

- **Slivered almonds:** Shingles, paving stones
- **Rock candy:** Ice chunks
- **Shredded wheat cereal:** Bales of hay

Though the house lasts for weeks, the candy will probably get picked off and it will start to look like a rundown shack. But that's part of the fun.

Gingerbread and possums

I have a wonderful memory of the first gingerbread house I ever made. I was in high school and a friend of mine, Gordon Wands, had worked in a bakery. He was the first bakery worker I had ever met and, as far as I was concerned, that made him an expert. I had always been a home baker, but I had never tackled something like this before. I knew that with Gordon at my side I would have success.

Well, we got it done. My mother, as always, was extremely understanding — good thing, because there was flour all over the kitchen. I decided to give the decorated house to my friend Katie Webb as a Christmas present.

After Christmas vacation, Katie told me she had taken a photograph of the gingerbread house. I hadn't thought of doing that myself, so I was eager to see it. She handed me the photograph, and there was her pet possum taking a bite out of the roof of the house like Godzilla attacking a skyscraper.

I guess I should explain. Katie had a pet possum named Priscilla who literally hung around her apartment in empty hanging planters. The possum cohabited with a cat and Dachshund and ate cottage cheese and either dog or cat food (I don't remember which). She ate gingerbread too. Bear in mind, we lived in NYC — what a scene!

Dressing Up the Inside of Your House with Homemade Decorations

In this section, you find decorations for every room of your home or apartment; there's even a natural fragrant potpourri that will welcome all who cross your threshold. No matter how large or small, formal or informal your home is, these decorations make it festive and merry.

Simmering Scent

Smell is a powerful sense. In fact, scientists say that our earliest memories are often olfactory. So decorate the air for Christmas! You may bring this to room temperature, cover, refrigerate, and use again. Eventually the scent will dissipate. Make a new batch!

Preparation time: *5 minutes*

12 whole allspice berries

Three 3-inch cinnamon sticks

1 orange, cut into eighths

1 lemon, cut into eighths

1 whole nutmeg

1-inch piece of fresh ginger, sliced

½ cup whole cloves

Combine all of the ingredients in a non-reactive, medium-sized saucepan and cover with cold water. Bring to a boil over medium-high heat, and then turn the heat down to the lowest simmer. Keep the pot simmering for as long as you'd like the aromas wafting through the house. Add additional water as needed.

Vary It! *This is one of those non-recipes that can be varied without much damage. Throw in an extra cinnamon stick or leave out the lemon, if you don't have one. Experiment.*

Candy Garland

Kids love to help make these garlands. The garland can be draped on the tree, over a mantel or a doorway, or any other place where you would like a colorful accent. You can make the garland as long as you want, and you can vary the color scheme depending on what types of candy you choose to use.

Special equipment: *Strong thread, such as nylon or waxed cotton; needle*

Preparation time: *15 minutes*

100 pieces wrapped candy, such as sourballs in cellophane, per 3 to 4 feet of thread

1 Place the candy in a bowl for easy access.

2 Thread the needle and make a large knot about 6 inches from one end.

3 Start sewing the candy together, inserting the needle through the cellophane, stringing the candies together (see Figure 14-2). Insert the needle close to the candy, not the end of the cellophane where the thread might rip through it. Place a knot after the last piece. Use the thread on the ends to tie the garland to branches or whatever else you choose to attach it to.

Tip: *Children can be shown how to use the needle safely. They really like working with candy — as long as you let them have some, which is a just reward for being Santa's helper.*

Tip: *You can approach this project in many ways. You can use multicolored candies or ones that fit your color scheme, if you like — red and green, silver and blue, and so on.*

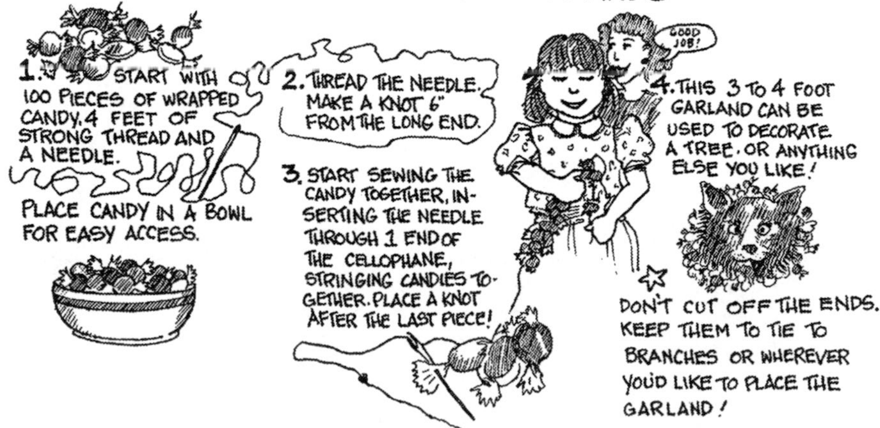

STRINGING CANDY GARLANDS
1. START WITH 100 PIECES OF WRAPPED CANDY, 4 FEET OF STRONG THREAD AND A NEEDLE.
PLACE CANDY IN A BOWL FOR EASY ACCESS.
2. THREAD THE NEEDLE. MAKE A KNOT 6" FROM THE LONG END.
3. START SEWING THE CANDY TOGETHER, INSERTING THE NEEDLE THROUGH 1 END OF THE CELLOPHANE, STRINGING CANDIES TOGETHER. PLACE A KNOT AFTER THE LAST PIECE!
GOOD JOB!
4. THIS 3 TO 4 FOOT GARLAND CAN BE USED TO DECORATE A TREE, OR ANYTHING ELSE YOU LIKE!
DON'T CUT OFF THE ENDS. KEEP THEM TO TIE TO BRANCHES OR WHEREVER YOU'D LIKE TO PLACE THE GARLAND!

Figure 14-2: Organizing a garland-stringing session for the kids.

Cinnamon Stick Votives

Candles bring a room to life with an elegant glow. These inexpensive glass votives are decorated with cinnamon sticks. They make nice presents for the kids' teachers.

Special equipment: *Glue gun and glue sticks (optional)*

Preparation time: *15 minutes*

Yield: *4 votives*

4 plain glass, straight-sided votive holders (1-¾ inches across the bottom x 2- ½ inches high)

Glue gun with glue sticks

Ninety-six 3-inch cinnamon sticks

2 yards thin ribbon (optional)

4 votive candles (cinnamon scented, if you like)

1. Wash the votive holders inside and out and remove any labels.
2. Load the glue gun with a glue stick and apply a thin strip of glue to 2 inches of a cinnamon stick, along the seam. Immediately press the stick against the votive, lining up the base of the stick where the glue begins with the bottom of the votive. The rounded side of the cinnamon stick should face out. Hold the cinnamon stick against the votive for a few seconds until the bond is solid. Repeat until you've covered the votive all the way around. You will use approximately 24 sticks per votive.
3. Cut the ribbon, if you're using one, into 18-inch lengths and tie the ribbon around the cinnamon sticks, making a small bow. Insert the votive candles.

Simplify: *You can make the votives without a glue gun. Just make sure to buy a heavy-bodied, clear glue that's suitable for use with glass.*

Vary It! *The ribbon you choose can make a big difference here. A gingham pattern gives the votive a country look, while a gold or silver ribbon can look quite elegant.*

Glue guns: You don't need a license

Glue guns may sound scary, but they aren't. You can pick one up for less than $5, with no waiting period. Anyone can use one — even children, with supervision. They look like water guns. Glue sticks, which are long, skinny, solid inserts, go into the gun. When you pull the trigger, the liquified glue comes out of the nozzle, allowing for very easy application. The glue dries fairly quickly. You can find glue guns in craft stores and in some hardware stores. They're worth seeking out.

Pomander Candles

These old-fashioned fragrant balls of citrus and cloves scent a room. The embedded candles create a great atmosphere via flickering light. To make these candles, you need to use *tealights,* which are half-dollar size candles about 1 inch thick. Make sure that your tealights come in small metal cups (most do).

Special equipment: *Very sharp paring knife with a short blade, a few round toothpicks (optional)*

Preparation time: *30 minutes*

Yield: *6 pomander candles*

6 thick-skinned oranges

1 cup whole cloves (or more or less, depending on your preference)

6 tealights in metal cups

1 Slice a thin piece of skin from the stem end of the orange to create a stable base. On the opposite end, use a sharp paring knife to cut out a hole that's just large enough to fit the tealight into. The tealight should fit down in the orange with the top of the tealight even with the skin of the orange. Do not insert the tealight yet.

2 Insert cloves into the fruit in any pattern, even covering the whole fruit if you like. If the cloves are not going in easily, poke holes with a toothpick first and then insert the cloves.

3 Place one pomander on a small plate, or a bunch of them on a tray. Insert the tealights, light, and enjoy.

Vary It! *You can use any citrus fruit. Try small grapefruits, lemons and limes, or an assortment of citrus. Kumquats, while a bit more difficult to work with because of their tiny size, make adorable little pomanders. These would not be hollowed and filled with candles, but just left as is and used for their spicy scent. Pile the kumquat pomanders in a small bowl and place them in the living room or bathroom or tie a thin ribbon around them and hang them on your tree.*

Ribbon-Wrapped Gilded Walnut Ornaments

With little time and effort, you can turn a simple walnut into beautiful Christmas ornaments. Red, burgundy, or green ribbons look particularly striking against the metallic background. Hang on trees or anywhere you need a tiny, elegant ornament. ***Caution:*** These nuts are not edible due to the spray paint, glue, and pins.

Special equipment: *Glue gun and glue sticks (optional)*

Preparation time: *30 minutes*

Yield: *12 ornaments*

Newspaper

12 whole walnuts in the shell

Gold or silver spray paint

6 yards thin ribbon (1/8-inch to 1/4-inch width), cut into 18-inch lengths

12 straight pins

1 Set out the newspaper in a well-ventilated area. Lay out the walnuts so that they don't touch one another. Spray the nuts, following the spray paint manufactuer's instructions, rotating as they dry so that all the surfaces are covered. Let the nuts dry completely.

2 Place a drop of glue on the center bottom of a walnut's shell. Affix the center point of a length of ribbon over the glue so that the ribbon can be pulled up along the seam of the nut. Insert a straight pin through the ribbon, into the nut right through the glue. Using the small gap between the shell halves allows you to do this easily. Let the glue dry.

3 Bring the ribbon up around the nut and tie a tight knot at the top of the nut. Place a drop of glue under the knot, if desired. Let dry. Tie a bow, using the ends of the ribbon, to create a large loop about the size of a bracelet between the nut and the bow. Use the loop to hang the ornament. Repeat with the remaining nuts.

Tip: *Some walnuts are so tightly built that you may not be able to insert the pin. Look for walnuts that have a visible seam.*

Tip: *You don't need to use a glue gun. Just make sure to buy a heavy-bodied, clear glue that dries fairly quickly.*

Simplify: *You can make these ornaments without the spray paint. Just let the natural beauty of the nuts shine through.*

Cookie Wreath Centerpiece

Kids love cookies and they also like to build things with food. You or one of your helpers makes this centerpiece by gluing a batch of cutout cookies together with icing to make an edible 10-inch wreath made of cookies. Place a large pillar candle in the middle for a beautiful centerpiece. You can use any shape of cookie cutter you like. I often use stars. For best results, use cookies with perfectly flat bottoms.

Tools: *Large 12-inch flat plate or platter, small offset spatula*

Preparation time: *15 minutes*

50 to 60 Classic Sugar Cookies (Chapter 11)

1 large egg white

1 cup confectioners sugar

1 Bake and cool the cookies per the instructions in Chapter 11. They may be decorated with sugar, candies, or icing, or they can be plain.

2 Make the "glue" by whipping the egg white in a large bowl with a balloon whip attachment until the egg white is frothy. Slowly add the confectioners sugar and whip the mixture until it's thick and fluffy and stiff peaks form, at least 5 minutes. Add a little more sugar if it's too thin, or a little water if it's too thick. Place a damp towel over the bowl until you're ready to use the frosting.

3 Arrange the cookies on a plate as follows: Place a cookie along the outer edge of the plate and place a dab of icing, using the offset spatula, near the bottom left of the cookie. Glue a second cookie onto the first, pressing it against the glue. Glue a third cookie slightly to the lower right of the second cookie, creating an alternating zigzag pattern; work counterclockwise around the plate. Create a wreath by forming a circle with the cookies. The icing should act as glue and be hidden beneath the cookies.

4 Set the wreath out on a table and fill the center with a pillar candle, a small floral arrangement, or a bowl of ornaments. The wreath lasts 5 days and the cookies may be eaten.

Tip: *A dark-colored plate shows off the wreath to its best advantage. Try a red glass plate if you have one.*

Caution: *If you have a compromised immune system or are very young or elderly, your doctor may suggest not eating raw eggs. Meringue powder, which can be purchased at craft stores and anywhere cake decorating ingredients are found, can be used in place of egg whites. Substitute 5 tablespoons meringue powder, reconstituted per the manufacturer's instructions, for one egg white.*

Simplify: *If you like the idea of a cookie wreath, but don't have the time to bake, buy several dozen flat cookies (you can even use chocolate chip) and shape a wreath right on a platter, without the glue. This kind of wreath is particularly easy to disassemble and eat.*

Decorating the Outside of Your Home

When you take such care to prepare the inside of your home, don't forget the outside. This is the first thing guests see, and first impressions do count! For many children, even just viewing outdoor decorations around the neighborhood can weave memories. In this section, you find decorations for the outside of your home.

Popcorn Cranberry Garland

Making these decorations is a great, easy-to-do project to share with the kids. Drape the garlands over the bushes and trees in your yard and the birds will thank you; the garlands last however long the birds allow them to. Use fresh cranberries; frozen and defrosted cranberries are too soft and wet.

Special equipment: *Strong thread, such as nylon or waxed cotton; needle*

Preparation time: *15 minutes*

1 cup popped popcorn per 3 to 4 feet of thread

¾ cup cranberries per 3 to 4 feet of thread

1 Place the popcorn in one bowl and the cranberries in another for easy access.

2 Thread the needle and make a large knot about 6 inches from the end of the thread.

3 Sew a garland of popcorn and cranberries, in any pattern you like. Place a knot after the last piece.

Tip: *Air-popped popcorn is less greasy and more pleasant to handle than oil-popped popcorn.*

Remember: *You can make this garland as long or as short as you like. Provided that there's adult supervision, kids should be able to sew this garland together.*

Cranberry Kumquat Ice Wreath

The only requirement for this project is that the temperature outside be below freezing. This ice wreath is beautiful and unusual and will last as long as the temperature stays low. Remember to make room in the freezer for your ring pan before you begin.

Tools: *10 to 12 cup Bundt pan or other ring pan*

Preparation time: *10 minutes; 4 hours chilling time*

1 cup cranberries

10 kumquats, sliced

24-inches of 2-inch-wide red ribbon

1 Fill the ring-shaped pan a third of the way with cold water. Sprinkle half of the cranberries and half of the kumquats over the water. Freeze until firm.

2 Add cold water to the mold so that it is about three-quarters full. Sprinkle in the remaining fruit. Freeze again.

3 Remove the wreath from the mold. Thread the ribbon through the center and tie a knot and bow near the ribbon's end, resulting in a large loop underneath the bow.

4 Immediately hang outside.

Tip: *Kumquats are small orange citrus fruit available at this time of year. You can leave them out, or use slices of a small diameter orange, lemon, or lime if you like.*

Tip: *If you don't have room in the freezer, but have room on your porch or in your garage, just freeze the ring out there. You wouldn't be making this unless it were freezing outside!*

Going All Out: *Use distilled water to make the frozen ring as clear as possible, or, boil and cool your tap water.*

Reindeer on rooftops

If your kids are like mine, they like the homes that have the most lights and decorations — on the lawn, in the windows, on the trees and bushes, and on the roofs. Sometimes we'll come upon a house with a whole set of reindeer on the roof pulling Santa in a sleigh. Of course, I'm a lesser Mom for not having this display on our roof, but where does this tradition come from?

Apparently, an American book written in 1821 called *The Children's Friend* not only mentioned Santa's reindeer but also showed, in illustration, one reindeer pulling Santa in a sleigh. Then, in 1823, Clement Clark Moore presented his "A Visit from St. Nicholas," in which the reindeer were expanded to eight in number and given names — Dasher, Dancer, Prancer, Vixen, Comet, Cupid, Donder, and Blitzen.

In some cultures, Santa uses other means to get around. In Australia, large white kangaroos carry Santa. In some areas of Louisiana, it's alligators and a red-nosed werewolf. Donkeys and horses carry Santa in some parts of the world, and inanimate objects, like a broom, a dugout canoe, and a golden cord, get Santa around in other parts. Brazil seems to lead the way in terms of technology — the Brazilian Santa, known as Papai Noel, uses a helicopter.

Chapter 15

Edible Gifts

In This Chapter

- Gifts from the kitchen and from the heart
- Creative packaging for your food gifts

Recipes in This Chapter

- Chocolate-Covered Pretzels
- Hot Chocolate Mix
- Chocolate Peppermint Bark
- Chocolate-Caramel Apples
- Super-Easy Fudge
- Cranberry Liqueur
- Clementine-Cranberry Marmalade
- S'mores Graham Crackers
- Marshmallows
- Edible Clay
- Pumpkin Butter
- Caramel Sauce

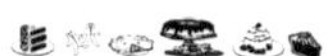

Edible gifts? You know what I mean. When your mom made your favorite type of cake on your birthday, the cake was an edible gift — and a gift of love. Christmastime is a perfect time to head into the kitchen and create delicious edible gifts. In this chapter, you find chocolate covered pretzels, an orange and cranberry marmalade, chocolate fudge, homemade s'mores — and much more! I also give you some ideas for creative, decorative packaging.

That you need to get presents for your parents and brothers and sisters might be obvious, but whom else should you get a present for? The list could go on and on and the last thing you need is the stress of buying more gifts. That's where homemade presents come in.

Making presents in your kitchen is not only immensely satisfying, but it's economical as well.

Here's a list of people you may want to remember this time of year:

- Your neighbors
- Your boss and coworkers
- Your childcare provider
- Your mail carrier, garbage collector, and anyone who helps you around the house

- Your children's teachers and principals
- Your doctor and dentist — don't give the dentist the fudge!
- Friends who are alone for the holiday
- Hosts of the parties you've been invited to

Making Food Gifts

Anyone can go out and buy a gift, but when you offer a gift that you've made in your own kitchen, it does mean more. You have thought about what the person would enjoy, chosen the recipe, shopped for the ingredients, and taken the time to make the present. Perhaps you've even taken the extra step of packaging the present beautifully. All this adds up to a very powerful and personal statement.

Chocolate treats

Who doesn't love chocolate? I know, there are some chocolate abstainers out there, but for most of us, a treat made from chocolate is the absolute best. Here are four chocolate recipes that are sure to satisfy chocolate fanatics.

Chocolate-Covered Pretzels

Kids and adults alike appreciate a gift of chocolate-covered pretzels. Adults seem to like them unadorned, but kids like them heavy on the decorations. Chocolate-covered pretzels may seem odd to you if you haven't tried them, but think about it: They combine crunchiness and saltiness with sweet creaminess. Go ahead and try them; you may really like them. Have the kids sprinkle on the decorations.

To measure out the 6 ounces of chocolate, you can use a scale or use two 3-ounce candy bars.

Preparation time: *15 minutes, plus 10 minutes cooling time*

Yield: *18 pretzels*

Eighteen 7-inch long pretzel rods

6 ounces chocolate (dark, milk, or white), finely chopped

Assorted decorations (options include chocolate and colored sprinkles, toffee bits, chopped nuts, shredded coconut, mini chocolate chips)

1. Cover a sheet pan with aluminum foil. Melt the chocolate in a tall, narrow container in a microwave or double-boiler. Place whatever decorations you are using in small bowls.
2. Dip the pretzels about ⅔ of the way down into the chocolate. Use a spoon to help coat the pretzels, if necessary, or tip the container to allow for better access to the chocolate. Let the excess chocolate drip back into the container and lay the pretzel down on foil. Sprinkle with the toppings of your choice. Repeat with other pretzels; don't let the pretzels touch on the tray while drying. Place the sheet pan in the refrigerator until the chocolate is set, about 10 minutes. Store pretzels at room temperature in an airtight container for up to one week.

Tip: *You can use any shape pretzel you like, but try these large rods first. They are the easiest to handle and make for a great ratio of pretzel to chocolate and candy.*

Going All Out: *If you like, you can wrap the pretzels individually in clear or colored plastic wrap or cellophane. These are great to give to teachers and young friends.*

Per serving: *Calories 85(From Fat 27); Fat 3g (Saturated 2g); Cholesterol 2mg; Sodium 131mg; Carbohydrate 13g (Dietary Fiber 1g); Protein 2g.*

Hot Chocolate Mix

Why bother making hot chocolate mix? After all, you can buy it easily and relatively inexpensively. But come on, there's the cachet factor of being able to say, "I made this!" All the neighborhood kids will think you are way cool. And, when you make your own, you can make sure that you use the highest quality cocoa and chocolate, raising this treat into the realm of the almost gourmet. Kids can help measure and stir.

Preparation time: *5 minutes*

Yield: *Approximately 10 cups of mix*

3 cups non-dairy creamer

2 ½ cups sugar

2 ¼ cups nonfat dry milk

1 ½ cups Dutch-processed cocoa

8 ounce block of bittersweet chocolate, grated

1 Stir together all the ingredients in a bowl. Ladle into five pint-size jars and cover. The dry mix will last for 6 months.

Include a card that gives the directions: For each serving, place 3 tablespoons dry mix in a large mug and add 8 ounces of boiling water. Stir together well and serve.

Tip: *You can grate your chocolate on a cheese grater. But don't try this with chips — start with a whole block of chocolate.*

Going All Out: *Place in a basket along with a tin of homemade marshmallows, some mugs, and decorative teaspoons. The recipe for homemade marshmallows is included in this chapter.*

Per serving: *Calories 103; Protein 2g; Carbohydrates 17g; Dietary fiber 1g; Total fat 3g; Saturated fat 2g; Cholesterol 1mg; Sodium 17mg.*

Chocolate Peppermint Bark

Chocolate and peppermint are combined in this easy homemade candy. Place large shards of the bark in cellophane bags and tie with a ribbon for a perfect gift for teachers and neighbors.

Chocolate bark gets its name because when extra ingredients are added to melted chocolate, the chocolate becomes textured, like tree bark.

Preparation time: *10 minutes*

Cooking time: *25 minutes*

Yield: *About 1 pound*

⅓ cup crushed candy canes (approximately 6 standard, 6- to 7-inch candy canes) or crushed peppermint sticks

1 pound chocolate (bittersweet, semisweet, milk, or white), melted and tempered (see Chapter 2 on tempering chocolate)

1 Line the bottom of a sheet pan with aluminum foil and smooth out any wrinkles.

2 Break the peppermint sticks or candy canes into pieces and place the pieces in a food processor fitted with metal blade. Pulse on and off until finely chopped; pieces will vary from matchhead size to pea size. Pour into a strainer fitted over a bowl and shake out all the powder; measure out ⅓ cup of the pieces that are still in the strainer.

3 Spread the melted and tempered chocolate over the foil lined pan using an offset spatula; it will be about ⅛ of an inch thick. Sprinkle the crushed peppermint evenly over the chocolate.

4 Refrigerate for about 12 minutes or until the chocolate is set. Lift large pieces off of the foil; break them into irregular shards. Store at room temperature in an airtight container for up to 3 weeks.

Tip: *Try making two batches, one with white chocolate and one with either milk or dark chocolate; the assortment will be most appreciated by friends and family.*

Tip: *Don't throw away the peppermint powder that you shake out in Step 2. Keep it around to add to hot chocolate or sprinkle on cookies.*

Per serving: *Calories 346 (From Fat 171); Fat 19g (Saturated 12g); Cholesterol 2mg; Sodium 6mg; Carbohydrate 40g (Dietary Fiber 4g); Protein 4g.*

Chocolate-Caramel Apples

Rich chocolate, sweet caramel, and tart, juicy apples make a perfect combination. Make these for the kids or for friends, but I have to warn you — this caramel actually pulled a baby tooth out of my son's mouth. Fortunately, the tooth was loose at the time, and being an 11-year-old boy, he thought this was very cool. Kids love to help dip the apples and add the decorations (see Figure 15-1). See the color section of this book for a photo.

Even if you've never made candy before, give these apples a try. Kids and adults love 'em. Making these apples is a great project to do with kids; if you have a child with a December birthday, these are a fun party project.

Special equipment: *Candy or probe thermometer, 6 wooden chopsticks, 6 large muffin pan liners, 6 cellophane bags, ribbon*

Preparation time: *10 minutes*

Cooking time: *50 minutes*

Yield: *6 apples*

6 medium Granny Smith apples

2 cups sugar

1⅓ cups light corn syrup

2 cups heavy cream

1 tablespoon unsalted butter

2 teaspoons vanilla extract

¼ teaspoon salt

1 pound chocolate, finely chopped (white, milk, or dark)

Assorted decorations: chocolate sprinkles, chopped nuts, mini-chocolate chips, and toffee bits are all options

1. Cover a sheet pan with aluminum foil and spray the foil with pan coating. Wash and dry apples and insert chopsticks into stem ends.

2. Stir together the sugar, corn syrup, and cream in an 8-quart heavy-bottomed saucepan. Cook over medium-high heat to a boil without stirring. Brush down any sugar crystals from the pan's sides with a pastry brush dipped in warm water.

3. Boil until a thermometer registers 255 degrees, about 30 to 40 minutes. Remove from heat and stir in the butter, vanilla extract, and salt. Plunge the bottom of the pan into a bowl of cold water to stop cooking. Allow the caramel to sit for a few minutes to thicken for better adhesion to the apples.

4. Holding the apples by the chopsticks, submerge the apples three-quarters of the way straight down into the caramel, letting any excess drip off back into the pan. Tilt the pan, if necessary, to gain access to the caramel. Place the apples on a foil-lined pan to harden — chopstick end straight up, no apples touching. If a large rim of caramel forms around the bottom of the apples, either press it against the apples or trim it off — kitchen shears work well for this.

5 Melt the chocolate in a double boiler or in the microwave and dip the hardened caramel apples into chocolate to cover three-quarters of the caramel. Let the excess chocolate drip back into the pan, and then place the apple back on the foil-lined pan — again, chopstick end up.

6 While the chocolate is still wet, sprinkle the apple with decorations of your choice. Let the chocolate completely harden before serving. You may let the chocolate harden at room temperature or place the pan in the refrigerator for 10 minutes or until chocolate is set. Set each apple in a paper muffin liner. To store, wrap in clear cellophane bags and tie with ribbon. May be stored at room temperature for up to 2 days or refrigerated for 4 days. Bring to room temperature before serving. These apples are easiest to eat if they're sliced before serving.

Caution: *Although this is a great project for kids, the hot caramel can be dangerous. Supply plenty of adult supervision when making these with kids. With younger children, you might help guide their hands while dipping the apples to ensure that no stray fingers dip into the pot or get burned.*

Per serving: *Calories 1,270 (From Fat 531); Fat 59g (Saturated 35g); Cholesterol 130mg; Sodium 297mg; Carbohydrate 189g (Dietary Fiber 4g); Protein 7g.*

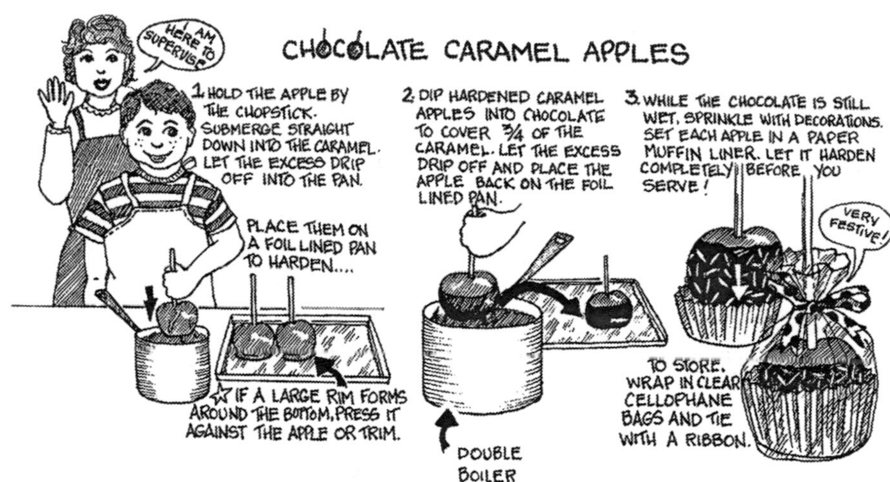

Figure 15-1: With supervision, kids can have fun dipping apples.

Super-Easy Fudge

This recipe is foolproof and kids love to help make it (almost as much as they love to eat the result).

Preparation time: *5 minutes*

Cooking time: *10 minutes*

Yield: *2 pounds; 40 pieces is reasonable*

2 pounds bittersweet or semisweet chocolate, finely chopped

4 tablespoons unsalted butter

Two 14-ounce cans sweetened condensed milk

1 teaspoon vanilla extract

1 Spray a 9 x 13-inch pan with pan coating.

2 Melt the chocolate and butter together in the top of a double boiler or in the microwave, stirring until smooth. Remove from heat and stir in the condensed milk and vanilla extract, again stirring until smooth.

3 Spread the mixture in a pan and refrigerate 2 hours or until set. Cut into squares and store in an airtight container, separating the layers of fudge with parchment paper or waxed paper. Store at room temperature for up to 1 week.

4 If you're giving the fudge as a gift, package it in a decorative tin lined with plastic wrap or parchment paper.

Tip: *You can use regular, low-fat, or nonfat sweetened condensed milk. Personally, I think fudge should be loved for what it is, which is a special treat. You shouldn't be thinking about dieting while indulging. So I say go for the regular full-fat variety; it will be a tad creamier. Just be moderate in your portion sizes.*

Tip: *Fudge is sweet, so if you can find and use bittersweet chocolate, which has less sugar than semisweet, I think the results will be better. Unless you have an intense sweet tooth, in which case you should go for the semisweet. You could even try milk chocolate, but in that case up the chocolate amount to 2⅛ pounds.*

Per serving: *Calories 201 (From Fat 99); Fat 11g (Saturated 6g); Cholesterol 11mg; Sodium 27mg; Carbohydrate 24g (Dietary Fiber 2g); Protein 3g.*

Grandma labored over her fudge, and even then it sometimes ended up grainy. The basic recipe I include in this section is delicious, but definitely think of it as a jumping-off point.

These variations are just some of my favorites — go on, experiment!

- Make Rocky Road Fudge by adding 1½ cups mini marshmallows and 1½ cups chopped walnuts or pecans.
- Add 2 cups chopped nuts (almonds, walnuts, pecans, or macadamias).
- Add 2 cups chopped hazelnuts and 1 tablespoon hazelnut liqueur.
- Add 2 cups toffee bits to make Toffee Fudge. Stir the toffee in at the end or sprinkle the top of the fudge with the bits and gently press them in.
- Add 2 cups chopped chocolate-covered raisins.
- Add 2 cups chopped peppermint patties.
- Add 2 cups chopped chocolate-covered coconut bars.
- Make Cherry Chip Fudge by adding 1 cup dried cherries and 1 cup chopped nuts.
- Make Milk Orange Fudge by using milk chocolate and adding 1 tablespoon orange liqueur and 1 cup finely chopped candied orange peel.
- Make Coffee Walnut Fudge by adding 2 teaspoons of instant coffee powder to the melted mixture (try it with milk chocolate) and then stirring in 2 cups chopped walnuts.
- Make Triple Chocolate Fudge by making half the recipe with milk chocolate and spreading that half into the pan. Make the other half with dark chocolate and spread on top. While the fudge is still warm, sprinkle 1 cup of mini semisweet chocolate chips evenly over the top. Gently press the chips into the fudge using an offset spatula.

You know how when you see a photo of chocolate chip cookies the cookies are just bursting with chips? That's because the cookies have been styled by a food stylist. A food stylist is sort of like a beauty consultant for food. When food is being prepared for a photo shoot, a stylist makes sure it looks the best it can be. You can steal a trick from stylists to make the fudge look as good as possible.

Take the Rocky Road version as an example. The recipe calls for 1½ cups of both marshmallows and nuts. When you measure them out, set ¼ cup of each aside. Fold the bulk of the marshmallows and nuts into the fudge, spread the fudge into the pan, and then sprinkle the reserved marshmallows and nuts over the top and gently press them into the fudge. The fudge will look like it is just exploding with goodies!

You can use this technique for any of the add-ins. Just reserve a bit of the chopped candy, nuts, or dried fruit and sprinkle them over the top. You will have the most beautiful fudge, worthy of a picture postcard. (This works for your favorite chocolate chip cookies, too.)

Cranberry-accented gifts

Cranberries are seasonal, and they play a large part in the winter holidays. You're probably familiar with their appearance in cranberry sauce, but they're really quite versatile. In this section, I have included a deep red cranberry liqueur and a jewel-toned marmalade. Both are great to make as gifts or to have around the house to offer guests. If you make them as gifts, keep some for yourself too. You deserve a little present!

Cranberry Liqueur

This gorgeous, sparkling red liqueur looks spectacular in a clear bottle; it's perfect for a host gift. Make this at least one month ahead. It's a great Thanksgiving weekend project. Use a recycled wine bottle or purchase a decorative one. New corks and paraffin for the optional decoration can be found at the hardware store.

Special equipment: *Large glass container, one 750- milliliter clear glass wine bottle with new cork, 8-inch bamboo skewer*

Preparation time: *15 minutes; 25 minutes with packaging*

Cooking time: *5 minutes; 10 minutes with packaging*

Yield: *about 1 quart*

2 cups sugar

1 cup water

3 cups cranberries, washed and sorted

3 cups vodka

10 cranberries

1 Place the sugar and water in a medium-sized saucepan and stir to wet the sugar. Bring to a boil over medium heat. Stir in the 3 cups of cranberries. Turn the heat down to low and simmer for 1 minute. Remove from the heat and cool to room temperature.

2 Pour into a glass container and add the vodka; stir to combine. Store in a cool, dark location for 1 to 2 months. Stir the contents twice a week.

3 Strain out the berries, collecting the liqueur in a bowl. Press down on the berries to extract as much liquid as possible. Discard the berries. Strain the liqueur again through cheesecloth or through a very fine strainer into a 4-cup measuring cup. Repeat, if necessary, until clear.

4 Using a funnel, pour the liqueur into clean glass wine bottle, leaving a 2-inch space at top. Any extra can be reserved for you, the deserving cook. Thread 10 cranberries onto a skewer and slip it into the bottle; cut down the skewer to fit, if necessary. Insert the cork. The liqueur is ready to serve, or it may be stored for up to 3 months.

Optional Decorative Packaging

4-ounce block of paraffin

1 crayon, your choice of color, paper removed

8-ounce empty tin can

Decorative self-adhesive label

1 Place the paraffin and the crayon in the tin can and place the can in a small saucepan. Add water to the saucepan until the water comes one-quarter up the sides of the can. Heat over medium heat until the paraffin and crayon melt, stirring occasionally with a metal spoon. Turn off heat.

2 Invert the corked bottle and dip it into the wax to cover cork and go about an inch down the bottle. Remove from the wax and cool for a minute, then dip again. Repeat until the wax is opaque and you can no longer see the cork. Cool completely.

Wipe the bottle dry and affix the label printed with the name of contents.

Per serving: *Calories 101 (From Fat 0); Fat 0g (Saturated 0g); Cholesterol 0mg; Sodium 0mg; Carbohydrate 14g (Dietary Fiber 0g); Protein 0g.*

Clementine-Cranberry Marmalade

This jam is easy to make — and beautiful. The golden color of the citrus fruit and the red of the cranberries will bring a smile to your face and to your English muffins. Just make sure to read through the directions so that you acquaint yourself with the canning procedure. It's not difficult to do, but you do have to follow the directions carefully. See the color section of this book for a photo of this dish.

Special equipment: *Eight 1-pint glass jelly jars with lids and screw bands*

Preparation time: *15 minutes*

Cooking time: *60 minutes*

Yield: *Eight 1-cup jars*

15 clementines (3 pounds)

2½ cups water

5 cups sugar

2 cups fresh cranberries

1. Sterilize the jars by filling them with boiling water. Leave them filled with the water until you need them. Sterilize the lids and screw bands by dropping them in a pot of boiling water. Immediately remove the pot from the heat and let the lids and screw bands soak for 10 minutes.
2. Place a small ceramic plate in the freezer. Fill a pot that's large enough to hold all of the jars with enough water to cover the jars by two inches. Place a thick folded towel on the bottom of the pot, in the water, and set aside.
3. In a separate pot, blanch whole clementines in boiling water for 1 minute; drain. Slice the clementines in half through the stem end and remove any seeds. Then slice crosswise as thinly as possible. Combine sliced clementines, peel and all, with the water and sugar in a large, heavy-bottomed non-reactive saucepan. Stir to combine and bring to a boil over medium-high heat.
4. Boil uncovered, stirring often, until mixture reaches the jellying point. You can test for doneness with a thermometer — you want 220 degrees — or check for visual cues. If you're going the visual route, begin checking after 20 minutes by placing a teaspoon of the marmalade on the chilled plate. Hold the plate vertically and see if the mixture "gels" and slowly moves down the plate in a jellied state. It should not be completely fluid and should not be so firm as to hold its shape. Err on the side of looser rather than firmer. You may need to boil the mixture for up to 40 minutes.
5. While the marmalade is boiling, bring the pot of water with the submerged towel to a boil.
6. Once the marmalade is done, stir in cranberries and cook for 2 minutes more. Remove from heat and ladle into sterilized jars, leaving ¼ inch of space. Wipe clean the tops of the jars with a clean towel and screw the metal tops on firmly but not too tightly.

7 Immerse the jars in the pot of boiling water using large tongs and boil for 10 minutes. The towel on the bottom will keep the jars from clanging. Remove the jars from the water with tongs and let cool to room temperature. The lids will begin to seal through the vacuum process that the heat has created. You might hear the lids pop as the small bump on the lids is sucked in. Leave at room temperature overnight, then check the seals; press very gently on the lids; they should be flat. If the bump remains, that jar did not seal. Simply refrigerate these and use within the month. The sealed jars are ready for gift giving and will remain shelf-stable for one year or until they're opened, after which the marmalade should be refrigerated.

Tip: *Use fresh cranberries for this recipe; the visual results are better. Frozen and defrosted cranberries work, but they bleed their red color into the golden marmalade. When you use fresh, you will have a truly stunning orange marmalade dotted with deep red cranberries.*

Optional Decorative Packaging

Special equipment: *Pinking shears*

18-inch-square piece of fabric

8 rubber bands

5⅓ yards ribbon cut into 24-inch lengths

8 decorative teaspoons

8 decorative self-adhesive labels (these usually come with the jelly jars)

Cut eight 6-inch-square pieces of fabric with pinking shears. Center the fabric over the jar top; pull sides down tightly and slip on a rubber band that fits under the lid. Tie a ribbon around the rubber band, tuck a spoon under the ribbon, and affix a label printed with the contents. You're ready to go.

Per serving: *Calories 36 (From Fat 0); Fat 0g (Saturated 0g); Cholesterol 0mg; Sodium 0mg; Carbohydrate 9g (Dietary Fiber 0g); Protein 0g.*

S'mores: More yummy when they're homemade

Sitting around a summer bonfire and eating s'mores (as in "Mom, I want some more") should be a rite of passage for every child. The ritual starts with hunting down the perfect slender, smooth, green stick to spear the marshmallows with and finding just the right place to sit around the fire so that the marshmallows get a chance to toast before you do. Then you hold the marshmallows just so over the fire, not too far away or your patience will wear out, but not too close so that the marshmallows become engulfed in flames. The aim is to gently toast the marshmallows to a golden brown so that their insides are soft and gooey, almost liquefied, while the outside develops a luscious crust to keep it all in. The next step is to nestle the marshmallow on top of a chocolate-topped graham cracker, top that with another graham cracker, and dive right in, leaning forward to avoid any dripping or crumbling pieces, but trying to get every last morsel in your mouth.

Not too many of us are making bonfires in the depths of December, and who says that a craving for s'mores is particular to the warmer months? Not only do you not have to wait for the calendar pages to flip by, you don't even need a bonfire. Set out a platter with graham crackers topped with pieces of chocolate. Spear marshmallows with a long-handled fork or a stick and toast the marshmallows over a fireplace, grill, or gas fire until they're golden brown. Place marshmallows on top of the chocolate, top with another graham cracker, and eat immediately. Repeat until you can't possibly eat any more.

Okay, suppose you have a s'more longing that you just cannot ignore; you need 'em and you need 'em now. Use the microwave. Place chocolate-topped graham crackers on a microwaveable plate and top with marshmallows. Heat on high for 15 seconds. Check — the chocolate and marshmallow should be softened, but not melted. Keep heating in short blasts if necessary. Obviously, the marshmallows have no chance of getting browned or toasted, but you will get your fix. This is really cheating and only for the desperate — but no one is looking, so go for it.

S'mores Graham Crackers

These are better than store-bought and easy to make. See the color section of this book for a photo.

Preparation time: *20 minutes*

Cooking time: *15 minutes*

Yield: *Forty 3-x-3-inch crackers*

½ cup (1 stick) unsalted butter at room temperature

1 cup lightly packed dark brown sugar

¼ cup honey

1 tablespoon vanilla extract

2½ cups all-purpose flour

1 teaspoon baking soda

½ teaspoon salt

¼ cup milk

2 tablespoons sugar

½ teaspoon cinnamon

1 Cream the butter with an electric mixer and flat paddle attachment on medium-high speed until soft. Add the sugar and beat until light and fluffy, about 2 minutes, scraping down the sides once or twice. Beat in the honey and vanilla extract. Stir together the dry ingredients and add alternately with the milk to the creamed mixture. Beat until the dough comes together.

2 Turn the dough out of bowl, flatten into a fat disk, and refrigerate for 2 hours or until it's firm enough to roll.

3 Preheat the oven to 375 degrees. Line three (if you have them) sheet pans with parchment paper.

4 Roll out the dough on a floured surface to ⅛-inch thickness, turning frequently to prevent sticking. Cut into 3 x 3-inch squares with a pizza wheel or knife. Transfer to sheet pans with a spatula, arranging them ½-inch apart.

5 Combine the sugar and cinnamon for the topping and sprinkle over the crackers.

6 Bake for about 12 minutes or until the crackers are light brown and firm to the touch, rotating the sheets front to back once during baking. They will continue to color and crisp up after you remove them from the oven, so don't overbake. Cool right on the pan set on a rack. Store in an airtight container for up to 3 weeks.

Per serving: *Calories 80 (From Fat 18); Fat 2g (Saturated 1g); Cholesterol 6mg; Sodium 64mg; Carbohydrate 14g (Dietary Fiber 0g); Protein 1g.*

Maybe you've never thought much about marshmallows — what they're made of or how they're made. Maybe you only think of marshmallows as those spongy nuggets with a shelf life of who-knows-how-long. Believe it or not, marshmallows are actually fairly easy to make and are made of readily available ingredients. If you make homemade marshmallows, you will not only have fun, but also impress the heck out of your kids and friends. I mean, this is a dealmaker. You will feel like you can do anything after your first batch. Just follow the directions. It's easy.

Marshmallows

A candy thermometer and a standing mixer help enormously here. As long as you have a candy thermometer and standing mixer, these marshmallows are so easy that you won't believe it.

Special equipment: *Stand mixer, candy (probe) thermometer, jelly roll pan, parchment paper, offset spatula*

Preparation time: *20 minutes*

Yield: *Twenty 2-x-2-inch marshmallows*

½ cup powdered sugar

¼ cup cornstarch

½ cup cold water

1 tablespoon unflavored gelatin

¾ cup + 2 tablespoons sugar

1 cup light corn syrup

2 egg whites

¼ teaspoon cream of tartar

1 tablespoon vanilla extract

1 Line a jelly roll pan with parchment paper. Combine the powdered sugar and cornstarch and sift half of it evenly over the parchment paper. Set the remaining mixture of powdered sugar and cornstarch aside for later.

2 Soften the gelatin in ¼ cup of cold water for 5 minutes. Meanwhile, combine the remaining ¼ cup of water in a small saucepan with ¾ cup sugar and the corn syrup. Stir to wet the sugar and then bring to a boil over medium-high heat without stirring. Brush down any sugar granules sticking to the sides of the pan with a pastry brush dipped in warm water. Place a thermometer in the pan. When the temperature reaches 220 degrees, begin to whip your egg whites.

3 Beat the egg whites until they're frothy with an electric mixer on medium speed. Add cream of tartar and beat on high speed until soft peaks form. Add 2 tablespoons sugar and continue to beat the mixture until stiff peaks form.

4 When the boiling mixture reaches 240 degrees, remove it from the heat and quickly stir in the softened gelatin. Turn the mixer to low-medium speed and pour the hot liquid slowly over the meringue, taking care to direct the liquid onto the meringue, not the beaters. Turn the speed to high and beat until stiff and glossy, about 5 minutes. The mixture will still be warm. Beat in the vanilla extract.

Immediately scrape the marshmallow mixture onto the prepared jelly roll pan and spread the mixture as evenly as possible, using an offset spatula. The surface will be uneven and sticky — that's okay. Sift the remaining powdered sugar and cornstarch mixture over the marshmallows and use flattened hands to press it out to a fairly uniform thickness of about ½ inch. Let the marshmallows sit at room temperature overnight to dry them out. Dust off any excess sugar or cornstarch and cut into desired shapes (2 x 2 inches is a good size for the 3-x-3-inch graham crackers) using a pizza wheel that you've dusted with sugar and cornstarch. You can use a knife, but the wheel is a lot easier. Store in an airtight container at room temperature for up to 3 weeks.

***Per serving:** Calories 100 (From Fat 0); Fat 0g (Saturated 0g); Cholesterol 0mg; Sodium 26mg; Carbohydrate 25g (Dietary Fiber 0g); Protein 1g.*

Make a s'mores care package to give as a gift. Just follow these steps:

1. **Buy or recycle a tin. Nestle the tin on top of its upside down cover and tape together. Fill the tin with tissue paper.**
2. **Place the homemade graham crackers and marshmallows in separate plastic bags and tie the bags with ribbon. Place the bags in the tin.**
3. **Add some candy bars to the tin.**
4. **Cut a large piece of cellophane. Place tin on center of cellophane. Bring edges up and over the top and tie in place with a ribbon.**

. . . And a few more ideas that didn't fit elsewhere

Where would you put a recipe for clay in a cookbook? The clay in this case is a food-based clay made from peanut butter that little kids can use to make figurines to give as presents. Pumpkin butter is like apple butter, a creamy, sweet spread that's great for toast and English muffins. The caramel sauce needs little introduction . . . read on and then head for the kitchen.

Edible Clay

Three ingredients have never added up to so much fun. Get the kids involved. They can mix the ingredients and then make figurines to give as gifts. Making edible clay is a perfect activity for the very young set, ages 3 to 5.

Preparation time: *5 minutes (not including the time it takes to create your shapes)*

1 cup smooth hydrogenated peanut butter (such as Skippy or Peter Pan)

1 cup nonfat dry milk

1 cup honey

Assorted candies (optional)

1 Combine all the ingredients in a bowl and mix together thoroughly with a wooden spoon, or combine the ingredients in a mixer and use the flat paddle attachment. If it is too stiff, add a bit more peanut butter; if it is too loose, add more dry milk.

2 Use the clay to make snowmen, Christmas trees, or anything else you can think of. Store the shapes at room temperature in an airtight container for up to a week. Use candies to decorate your shapes, if you like. Tiny redhots work well.

Tip: *If you want to color the clay, add a few drops of food coloring. Knead it in well so that the color is uniform, and then make your shapes as desired.*

Pumpkin Butter

This is a thick, rich spread for toast and quick breads. It's kind of like the insides of a pumpkin pie. It will keep refrigerated for up to a month, so you can make it early in the season and have some around for gift giving as occasions arise. See the color section of this book for a photo of a Pumpkin Butter gift.

Special equipment: *Four 8-ounce glass jelly jars with lids and screw bands (or any other glass containers with lids)*

Preparation time: *5 minutes*

Cooking time: *50 minutes*

Yield: *4 cups*

29-ounce can (3½ cups) pumpkin puree

3 cups lightly packed light brown sugar

2 tablespoons lemon juice

½ teaspoon cinnamon

½ teaspoon ground ginger

Wash and dry four 8-ounce glass containers with lids. Combine all the ingredients in the top of a double boiler and whisk together well. Cook over simmering water, stirring frequently until thick, about 50 minutes. Remove from the stove and cool to room temperature, stirring occasionally to release heat. Pack into containers, cover, and keep refrigerated until needed.

Going All Out: *See the Clementine-Cranberry Marmalade recipe earlier in this chapter for packaging ideas.*

Per serving: *Calories 43 (From Fat 0); Fat 0g (Saturated 0g); Cholesterol 0mg; Sodium 5mg; Carbohydrate 11g (Dietary Fiber 1g); Protein 0g.*

Caramel Sauce

Try this sauce over coffee ice cream with toasted walnuts on top. In this recipe, I recommend using jelly jars. Package with an instruction card that contains reheating and storage information and some serving ideas. See the Clementine-Cranberry Marmalade recipe for packaging ideas.

Special equipment: *Four 8-ounce glass jelly jars with lids and screw bands (or any other glass containers with lids)*

Preparation time: *10 to 20 minutes*

Cooking time: *15 minutes*

Yield: *4 cups*

3 cups heavy cream

3 cups granulated sugar

1½ cup water

1 tablespoon vanilla extract

1 Wash and dry four 8-ounce glass containers that have lids. Jelly jars are preferable.

2 Bring the cream to a boil in a small saucepan over medium heat; set aside.

3 Place the sugar and water in a large heavy-bottomed pot (the pot should hold at least 10 quarts). Stir to moisten the sugar and cook over medium-low heat, without stirring, until the syrup begins to color. Wash down the sides of the pot once or twice with a damp pastry brush if necessary.

4 Cook the syrup until it reaches a medium amber color. This might take 10 minutes or 20; just look for the color. Remove from the heat and carefully pour in the warm cream. The mixture may bubble up furiously. Whisk until smooth. If the cream is too cool, it will cause the caramel to seize. Just place the pot back over a low heat and stir until the sauce liquefies. Stir in the vanilla extract off the heat. If the sauce remains too thick, simply thin with a little warm cream.

5 Cool the mixture to room temperature. Pour it into the glass containers, filling them within ¼ inch from the top. (If you have any extra sauce, just pour it into any kind of airtight container). Screw on the lids and keep the sauce refrigerated until it's needed, up to one month. Reheat in a double boiler or microwave before using.

Caution: *The mixture reaches a very high temperature, so you must take care not to get burned. If you come in contact with the hot caramel, immediately flush the area with cold water, and then follow basic first-aid procedures.*

Going All Out: *For a grown-up version, add ¼ cup dark rum in Step 4 along with the vanilla extract. You can also try Grand Marnier, Kahlua, or Amaretto.*

Per serving: *Calories 75 (From Fat 36); Fat 4g (Saturated 3g); Cholesterol 15mg; Sodium 4mg; Carbohydrate 10g (Dietary Fiber 0g); Protein 0g.*

Packaging Food Gifts

One of the joys of Christmas is seeing all the elaborately packaged and wrapped presents waiting to be opened. The colors and patterns of the wrapping paper and the decorative bows and ribbons make the presents just beg to be opened. Perhaps you're the kind of person who carefully removes the tape first and then unwraps the paper (to be used later), or maybe you are the throw-caution-to-the-wind type who rips into those boxes, paper pieces flying, just to get at the present inside. Either way, you can appreciate a gift's packaging.

So you're not done after you've chosen or made a gift. You need to wrap it, and possibly, even before you wrap it, you need to package it. For instance, if you make the Hot Chocolate Mix, you first have to come up with a suitable container or jar and then you have to wrap that container. Or if you make the Super-Easy Fudge, the candy itself must first go into a tin or some sort of container, which will then be wrapped.

I provide some specific tips in the recipes, but here are some general ideas for clever containers and wrappings. The way you package and wrap a gift really is important. It makes a visual and tactile impact, which is part of the whole presentation. And you thought you were just wrapping up some food!

Containers:

- Recycled glass jars (that originally contained maple syrup, honey, jam, and so on)
- Antique jars — look for them at flea markets
- New and recycled tins, particularly candy and cookie tins
- Shoeboxes
- Small, strong cardboard boxes
- Baskets
- Small wooden crates (clementine crates are perfect)
- Small metal boxes

Wrapping and decoration:

- Scraps of fabric
- Cellophane
- Raffia ribbon (a stiff, easy-to-tie ribbon)

- Yarn
- Recycled ribbon
- Dried or silk flowers
- Colored, metallic, or white tissue paper

One type of container that's particularly handy is the *jelly jar.* These jars are sold for canning and come in a variety of sizes and shapes. You can find them at supermarkets or hardware stores.

Part VI
The Part of Tens

"Let's see, what've we got here? Eel, squid, octopus... I knew they made nice stocking-stuffers, but I never thought of cooking with them."

In this part . . .

Every book *For Dummies* has a Part of Tens, a sort of handy quick reference on topics suggested by the front chapters. So, this is where you can find my ten best tips on holiday cooking and entertaining, in Chapter 16; and my top ten list of mail-order sources for cooking tools and ingredients, in Chapter 17. Use these chapters as resources throughout the holiday season.

Chapter 16

Ten Best Holiday Cooking and Entertaining Tips

In This Chapter

- Tips galore
- Easy-to-read-and-use list

Christmas is a busy season, and we need all the planning help we can get. In this chapter, you find a compact list of cooking and entertaining tips.

Plan as Far Ahead as Possible

The importance of planning ahead may seem obvious, but people don't take this advice. You should! If you want to hold the Christmas day meal or the Christmas Eve dinner at your house, stake out your claim as early as possible. Other family members may be thinking the same thing, and the early bird gets the worm. The key word here is *plan,* and the key concept is *ahead.* If you know that you're going to need a new tree stand this year and you plan early enough, you'll be ready to pounce when you see a sale. If you know that you're going to need an extra dining room table, you can call rental companies or ask neighbors about borrowing one ahead of time so that you don't have to worry about tables and whatnot come December 21.

Your first step in planning should be to write down a general idea of what you want to accomplish. Include any specifics that you know at the time. Doing so gives you a place to start.

Decide What You Want from the Holiday

If your priority is a small get-together with immediate family members, keep that first and foremost in your mind. All your planning should work toward helping you attain this goal. If someone proposes bringing home friends from college to share the meal, simply suggest that this might not be the year. If someone mentions turning the get-together into a buffet, you can decline and mention that you really hoped to have all the family members together at the dinner table.

Make Lists

I love lists. They help you keep all your tasks organized, and you can cross items off as you accomplish them — what a freeing feeling! Make lists of people you want to invite to gatherings, lists of ingredients to buy, lists of recipe steps to do ahead, lists of serving platters or glassware that you may need. Get a pad and use it!

Read the Instructions All the Way Through

I can't stress enough how important it is to read directions, and I mean from start to finish. You don't want surprises halfway through a recipe. You don't want to find out that you don't have the right pot or pan or special ingredient. By reading through the recipe, you also acquaint yourself with the techniques that you need to be familiar with.

Use at Least Some Familiar Recipes

When you're planning your menus, include some recipes that you've made before and know that you like; maybe those recipes are even your signature dishes. All the recipes in this book have been tested and retested so that they'll work the first time, but it's nice to have some recipes in your repertoire that you're comfortable with and that your family enjoys.

Make Recipes and Projects Ahead

One very important thing that I've learned from observing home cooks and professional kitchens is that the pros know how to prepare foods ahead of time in order to maximize their efficiency. Most of us walk into the kitchen, begin a recipe, and work through it beginning to end. That's fine if there are no time constraints — but show me one person who isn't working under the gun during the Christmas season!

There are two ways to approach a recipe to see whether you can make it ahead of time:

- Read through the recipe and see how many days, if any, you can make it ahead and either freeze it, refrigerate it, or store it at room temperature. I always err on the side of caution, so if a recipe in this book says that you can make it a week ahead, you can definitely do so.
- See what individual tasks you can take care of ahead of time. To do so, take a thorough look at each recipe that you're thinking of making. Say that you're making two recipes that call for chopped onions. You can chop enough onions for both recipes the day before and store them overnight in a plastic bag. This way, the onions will be ready to go when you need them, and you save time by combining prep work from two recipes.

Label anything you prepare ahead of time. You may think on Tuesday that on Saturday you'll remember what that 1 cup of sugar combined with 1 cup of brown sugar is for, but Murphy's Law says that you probably won't.

Here are some ingredients that can be prepped ahead of time:

- **Vegetables:** Onions, bell peppers, celery, broccoli, carrots — almost any veggie. Cut to the desired size a day ahead and store it refrigerated in a covered container or resealable plastic bag.
- **Dry ingredients:** Sugar, flour, baking powder and soda, cocoa, chocolate, nuts, dried fruit, and so on. Measure the proper amounts up to a month ahead and store at room temperature in a covered container or resealable plastic bag.
- **Wet ingredients:** Liqueurs, milk, cream, water, juices, sour cream, corn syrup, chicken stock, and so on. These vary in their ability to be stored; use your judgment. But all of them can be measured at least two days ahead. Store them in covered containers and either refrigerate or leave at room temperature, depending on the ingredient.

To make using the recipes in this book as convenient as possible, here is a list of the recipes broken down into how far in advance they can be prepared. Refer to individual recipes for specific instructions. You may not be able to complete the entire recipe ahead of time, but you will be able to complete most of it.

Can be made one month ahead:

- Spiced Cashews (Chapter 5)
- Shortcut Cassoulet (Chapter 8)
- Five-Cheese Spinach Lasagne (Chapter 8)
- Bittersweet Chocolate Sauce (Chapter 10)
- Classic Sugar Cookies (Chapter 11)
- Gingerbread People (Chapter 11)

- Chocolate Shortbread (Chapter 11)
- Meringue Wreath Cookies (Chapter 11)
- Snowdrop Cookies (Chapter 11)
- Basic Pie Crust (Chapter 12)
- Sweet Tart Crust (Chapter 12)
- Bittersweet Chocolate Truffles (Chapter 11)
- Stollen with Marzipan (Chapter 13)

Can be made one week ahead:

- Balsamic Vinaigrette (Chapter 6)
- Marmalade Butter (Chapter 7)
- Cranberry Sauce (Chapter 10)
- Spiced Cranberry Relish (Chapter 10)
- Horseradish Sauce (Chapter 10)
- Roasted Apples (Chapter 10)
- Gingered Pear Sauce (Chapter 10)
- Raspberry Apricot Sauce (Chapter 10)
- Royal Icing (Chapter 11)
- Mocha Baked Alaska (Chapter 11)

Can be made four to five days ahead:

- Cheddar, Port, and Blue Cheese Ball (Chapter 5)
- White Bean Soup with Kale and Parmesan (Chapter 6)
- Roasted Squash Soup (Chapter 6)
- Creamy Cheddar Potato Soup (Chapter 6)
- Cherry Orange Florentines (Chapter 11)

Can be made two to three days ahead:

- Christmas Salsa (Chapter 10)
- Herbed Asiago Crisps (Chapter 5)
- Caramelized Onion Dip (Chapter 5)
- Easy Homemade Gravlax (Chapter 5)
- Basic Green Salad (Chapter 6)
- Green Goddess Dressing (Chapter 6)
- Corn Chowder (Chapter 6)

- Maple-Orange Syrup (Chapter 7)
- Blueberry Sauce (Chapter 7)
- Goose with Apples and Cognac (Chapter 8)
- Wild Rice Dressing with Golden Raisins and Pecans (Chapter 9)
- Bread Stuffing with Sausage, Apples, and Cognac (Chapter 9)
- Cranberry Cider Sorbet (Chapter 11)
- Eggnog Ice Cream (Chapter 11)

Can be made one day ahead:

- Kid-Friendly Eggnog (Chapter 4)
- Warm White Truffle Bean Dip (Chapter 5)
- Citrus Breakfast Fruit Salad with Yogurt and Granola (Chapter 7)
- Breakfast Baked Apple (Chapter 7)
- Overnight French Toast (Chapter 7)
- Classic Mashed Potatoes (Chapter 9)
- Mashed Sweet Potatoes with Bourbon and Brown Sugar (Chapter 9)
- Sautéed Broccoli Raab (Chapter 9)
- Brussels Sprouts and Chestnuts (Chapter 9)
- Roasted Carrots (Chapter 9)
- Creamed Onions and Mushrooms (Chapter 9)
- Apple Pie (Chapter 12)
- Pumpkin Pie (Chapter 12)
- Chocolate Pecan Pie (Chapter 12)
- Chocolate Truffle Tart (Chapter 12)
- White Chocolate Bûche de Noël (Chapter 12)
- Pumpkin Toffee Cheesecake (Chapter 12)
- Christmas Pudding with Rum Cream (Chapter 12)
- Pear Almond Trifle (Chapter 12)
- Cranberry Orange Quick Bread (Chapter 13)

Ask for Help

If you're like me, you like to do it all yourself. Sometimes, I even dupe myself into believing that I can always do it best, whatever "it" is. Well, I'll step down from my pulpit and gently bring you down with me. Asking for help is important for a couple of reasons:

- There's so much to do that spreading the responsibilities around just makes sense from a logistical point of view. Children can help cook and set tables. Almost any family member can vacuum and clean bathrooms, readying the house for your party. You do not — I repeat, do not — have to do it all yourself.
- This is a family holiday. The family members should be involved. Sure, some of the things that have to be done are chores, such as cleaning the bathrooms, but how about decorating the tree, stringing lights, and making ornaments and gifts together? These projects bring families together and make memories (although if my mom had asked me to clean the toilet on Christmas morning, I would remember that, too).

  Family members who don't live with you count, too. Ask visiting family to bring food. Ask an in-law to bring a salad to round out the meal or a cousin to bring a pie for dessert. If family members don't cook, they can always bring cheeses for the cocktail hour or a bottle of wine or gallon of cider.

Be Prepared for Surprises and Take Them in Stride

Even with all your planning, there will be glitches. The turkey may take longer to cook, or the first half of your guests who go through the buffet line may wipe out your entire sweet potato supply. But you know what? It's okay. Christmas is not about getting one's fill of tubers.

Don't Worry, Be Happy

Yeah, I know, I didn't make that up, but the sentiments are tailor-made for this holiday. Whether you're throwing a formal dinner with white tablecloths and silver or a casual open house with finger foods and paper plates, relax enough to enjoy your event. You've done the planning and prepared the food — now it's time to be a guest at your own party.

Breathe

Breathe in, breathe out. Repeat. When you breathe, life flows. Breathing enables you to accept help, accept presents, and take in the spirit of the holiday.

Chapter 17

Ten Great Mail-Order Sources for Ingredients and Tools

In This Chapter

- Mail-order sources for ingredients and tools
- Web sites where you can purchase the stuff you need

Shopping locally is a way of supporting your local economy. But you may not be able to find what you need at a nearby store. If that's the case, don't fret. Specialty ingredients and tools are as near as a phone or a computer with an Internet connection.

Bridge Kitchenware

214 East 52nd Street (between 2nd and 3rd Avenues)
New York, NY 10022
Phone: 800-274-3435 or 212-688-4220
Fax: 212-758-4387
`www.bridgekitchenware.com`

This New York institution has everything you need to outfit your kitchen — pots, pans, cake-decorating equipment, steamed pudding molds, knives, spatulas, tart pans, popover pans, and more. A catalog is available.

Citarella

2135 Broadway
New York, NY 10023
Phone: 212-874-0383
Fax: 212-595-3738
`www.citarella.com`

This store, which has several outposts in the New York City area, has become an institution. It has all sorts of specialty ingredients, like sun-dried tomatoes, spices, and even shucked oysters. Perishable products are sent FedEx Priority Overnight within the continental United States.

Crate and Barrel

1860 West Jefferson
Naperville, IL 60540
Phone: 800-323-5461
www.crateandbarrel.com

This all-purpose housewares company puts out a Christmas catalog with gorgeous linens, candles, candleholders, bowls, serving pieces, dinner plates, and more, all with a Christmas theme. Their regular catalog is worth taking a look at, too.

D'Artagnan

280 Wilson Avenue
Newark, NJ 07105
Phone: 800-327-8246
Fax: 973-465-1870
www.dartagnan.com

This is the source for fresh game, mushrooms, and truffles of the fungal variety — foie gras, too, if you're so inclined. Some items, like goose, are available but should be ordered at least one week ahead. A catalog is available.

Dean & Deluca

Catalog Center
8200 East 34th Street Circle North, Building 2000
Wichita, KS 67226
Phone: 800-221-7714
www.deandeluca.com

This New York City culinary mainstay has a catalog and a Web site for those people who can't make it into the Soho store. From the comfort of your own home you can order fine cheeses, like mascarpone and pâtés, olives and olive oils, balsamic vinegar, white truffle oil, linen cocktail napkins, fine-quality chocolate, vanilla extract, amaretti cookies, teas, coffee, carving knives and forks, herbs and spices, and even handmade candy canes. Definitely order the catalog or peruse the Web site.

King Arthur Flour Baker's Catalog

P.O. Box 876
Norwich, VT 05055
Phone: 800-827-6836
Fax: 802-649-5359
www.kingarthurflour.com

This constantly updated catalog has flours of all descriptions, vanilla extracts, chocolates, including couverture chocolates; high-quality dried fruit, candied fruit rinds, scales, all kinds of thermometers, high-quality measuring cups and spoons, and more. A catalog is available.

New York Cake and Baking Distributors

56 West 22nd Street
New York, NY 10010
Phone: 212-675-CAKE or 800-94-CAKE-9
Fax: 212-675-7099
www.nycakesupplies.com

Here you'll find chocolates, including couverture chocolate; decorating tips and bags, baking sheets, parchment paper, egg white (meringue) powder, food coloring, and more. Visiting the store is a must when you're in Manhattan. A catalog is available.

Penzey's Spices

P.O. Box 933
Muskego, WI 53150
Phone: 800-741-7787
www.penzeys.com

Penzey's is possibly the best source for high-quality herbs and spices. Supermarket spices don't hold a candle to these. A catalog is available.

Sur La Table

Pike Place Farmers Market
84 Pine Street
Seattle, WA 98101
Phone: 206-448-2244 or 800-243-0852
www.surlatable.com

Sur La Table has a general catalog and a catalog devoted to baking. You can find pans, tips, rolling pins, sheet pans, offset spatulas, ice cream makers, and more. Sur La Table also offers cooking classes through some of its stores around the country. Call the 800 number for locations.

Williams-Sonoma

P.O. Box 7456
San Francisco, CA 94120
Phone: 415-421-4242 or 800-541-2233
Fax: 415-421-5253
www.williams-sonoma.com

Famous for its mail-order catalog, Williams-Sonoma also has stores nationwide. You can find great pots, pans, cookie sheets, measuring tools, a heavy-duty apple peeler, some chocolate and cocoa, colored sugars for cookies, cookie cutters, and other cooking and baking equipment. During the Christmas season, Williams-Sonoma has seasonal products as well, such as handmade candy canes, wreaths of all sorts, and some ornaments. A catalog is available.

Three bonus resources

Here are three bonus resources with Christmas themes:

- **Christmas.com (www.christmas.com):** This Web site is all about the holidays. You can find information about music selections, party-planning tips, ideas on creating themes for your party and tree, and party etiquette. The site also has a whole section on the spirit of Christmas.
- **Christmas Depot.com (www.christmasdepot.com):** This huge site bills itself as the largest Christmas retail store on the Net. You can buy trees, tree stands, wreaths, ornaments of all kinds (from glass to plastic), garlands, and even outdoor decorations. Call 888-419-1693 for customer service, call 877-ELF-LAND for phone orders, or fax inquiries to 201-437-3218.
- **HowStuffWorks (www.howstuffworks.com/Christmas):** This site has all sorts of background information about the holiday and answers to questions that you, or especially the kids, may have. It explains why Rudolph's nose is red, why we give presents, why kids sit on Santa's knee, and on and on. This is a fun site to peruse with the whole family.

Appendix

Metric Conversion Guide

N*ote:* The recipes in this cookbook were not developed or tested using metric measures. There may be some variation in quality when converting to metric units.

Common Abbreviations

Abbreviation(s)	*What It Stands For*
C, c	cup
g	gram
kg	kilogram
L, l	liter
lb	pound
ml	milliliter
oz	ounce
pt	pint
t, tsp	teaspoon
T, TB, Tbl, Tbsp	tablespoon

Volume		
U.S Units	***Canadian Metric***	***Australian Metric***
¼ teaspoon	1 mL	1 ml
½ teaspoon	2 mL	2 ml
1 teaspoon	5 mL	5 ml
1 tablespoon	15 mL	20 ml
¼ cup	50 mL	60 ml
⅓ cup	75 mL	80 ml
½ cup	125 mL	125 ml
⅔ cup	150 mL	170 ml
¾ cup	175 mL	190 ml
1 cup	250 mL	250 ml
1 quart	1 liter	1 liter
1½ quarts	1.5 liters	1.5 liters
2 quarts	2 liters	2 liters
2½ quarts	2.5 liters	2.5 liters
3 quarts	3 liters	3 liters
4 quarts	4 liters	4 liters

Weight

U.S. Units	Canadian Metric	Australian Metric
1 ounce	30 grams	30 grams
2 ounces	55 grams	60 grams
3 ounces	85 grams	90 grams
4 ounces (¼ pound)	115 grams	125 grams
8 ounces (½ pound)	225 grams	225 grams
16 ounces (1 pound)	455 grams	500 grams
1 pound	455 grams	1/2 kilogram

Measurements

Inches	Centimeters
½	1.5
1	2.5
2	5.0
3	7.5
4	10.0
5	12.5
6	15.0
7	17.5
8	20.5
9	23.0
10	25.5
11	28.0
12	30.5
13	33.0

Temperature (Degrees)	
Fahrenheit	*Celsius*
32	0
212	100
250	120
275	140
300	150
325	160
350	180
375	190
400	200
425	220
450	230
475	240
500	260

Index

• A •

• B •

• C •

• D •

• G •

• N •

• P •

• Q •

• R •

• T •

• U •

• W •

FOR DUMMIES BOOK REGISTRATION

We want to hear from you!

Visit **dummies.com** to register this book and tell us how you liked it!

- Get entered in our monthly prize giveaway.
- Give us feedback about this book — tell us what you like best, what you like least, or maybe what you'd like to ask the author and us to change!
- Let us know any other *For Dummies* topics that interest you.

Your feedback helps us determine what books to publish, tells us what coverage to add as we revise our books, and lets us know whether we're meeting your needs as a *For Dummies* reader. You're our most valuable resource, and what you have to say is important to us!

Not on the Web yet? It's easy to get started with *Dummies 101: The Internet For Windows 98* or *The Internet For Dummies* at local retailers everywhere.

Or let us know what you think by sending us a letter at the following address:

For Dummies Book Registration
Dummies Press
10475 Crosspoint Blvd.
Indianapolis, IN 46256

CPSIA information can be obtained at www.ICGtesting.com
Printed in the USA
BVOW061222281211
279316BV00004B/2/A